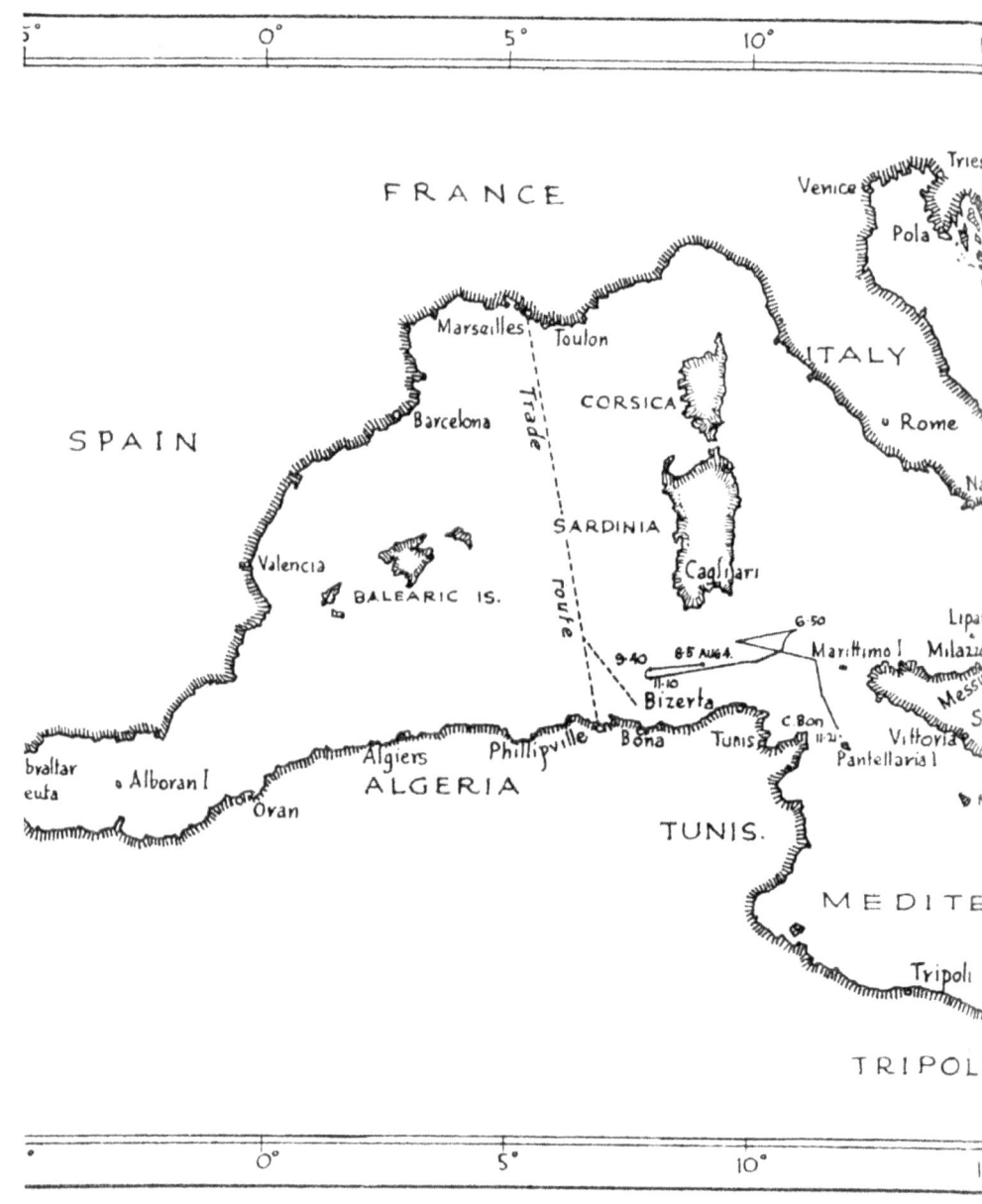

THE MEDITERRANEA
August 1914–
The movements of the two British battle-cruisers from 8.5 a.m. of August 4 till 11.21 a.m. of the next day are show
The position of Rear-Admiral Troubridge's squadron below Corfu is marked b

N THEATRE OF WAR
January 1916.

vn by a thick line. The course of *Goeben* and *Breslau* from Messina to Constantinople is indicated by a dotted line.
y an X. For details of the Dardanelles Straits, see other maps in this volume.

DARDANELLES DILEMMA

BOOKS ON THE SEA
BY
E. KEBLE CHATTERTON

SAILING SHIPS AND THEIR STORY
SHIPS AND WAYS OF OTHER DAYS
FORE AND AFT: THE STORY OF THE FORE AND AFT RIG
THE STORY OF THE BRITISH NAVY
KING'S CUTTERS AND SMUGGLERS
STEAMSHIPS AND THEIR STORY
THE ROMANCE OF THE SHIP
THE ROMANCE OF PIRACY
THE OLD EAST INDIAMEN
Q-SHIPS AND THEIR STORY
THE ROMANCE OF SEA ROVERS
THE MERCANTILE MARINE
THE AUXILIARY PATROL
WHALERS AND WHALING
CHATS ON NAVAL PRINTS
THE SHIP UNDER SAIL
BATTLES BY SEA
SHIP MODELS
STEAMSHIP MODELS
SEAMEN ALL
WINDJAMMERS AND SHELLBACKS
THE BROTHERHOOD OF THE SEA
CAPTAIN JOHN SMITH
OLD SHIP PRINTS
VENTURES AND VOYAGES
OLD SEA PAINTINGS
ON THE HIGH SEAS
ENGLISH SEAMEN AND THE COLONISATION OF AMERICA
THE SEA RAIDERS
THE BIG BLOCKADE
GALLANT GENTLEMEN
THE *KÖNIGSBERG* ADVENTURE
SAILING MODELS
DANGER ZONE
AMAZING ADVENTURE

CRUISES

DOWN CHANNEL IN THE *VIVETTE*
THROUGH HOLLAND IN THE *VIVETTE*
THE YACHTSMAN'S PILOT
THROUGH BRITTANY IN *CHARMINA*
TO THE MEDITERRANEAN IN *CHARMINA*

ADMIRAL SIR JOHN DE ROBECK, K.C.B.
Who commanded the Dardanelles Naval Operations.

DARDANELLES DILEMMA

THE STORY OF
THE NAVAL OPERATIONS

By

E. KEBLE CHATTERTON

Author of
"Danger Zone," "The Sea Raiders," etc.

With 69 *illustrations*
and 10 *maps or plans*

The Naval & Military Press Ltd

Published by

The Naval & Military Press Ltd
Unit 5 Riverside, Brambleside
Bellbrook Industrial Estate
Uckfield, East Sussex
TN22 1QQ England

Tel: +44 (0)1825 749494

www.naval-military-press.com
www.nmarchive.com

In reprinting in facsimile from the original, any imperfections are inevitably reproduced and the quality may fall short of modern type and cartographic standards.

TO
W. E. HALL

PREFACE

THIS is an independent history of the Dardanelles Naval Operations, beginning with the events which led up to the entrance of *Goeben* and *Breslau* into the Straits, and ending at the date when the Navy transported the last soldier during the final evacuation of the Gallipoli Peninsula.

It is not the story of the Military Operations ashore, but an endeavour to afford a clear and full account of the problems and work which faced the Allies afloat. I have relied, for the most part, on original documents very courteously placed at my disposal by officers who were present and played important parts in this great drama. The value of their narratives cannot be over-estimated. This material comprises personal diaries written from day to day, private letters sent home shortly after big events, impressions set down at the time, accounts specially contributed for this volume, correspondence and conversations with the author, sketches and photographs made during the hour of battle. It would be difficult to find data of greater authenticity, and I am very conscious of the debt which is owed to these officers. In years to come, when lives shall have passed away and manuscripts have become lost or faded, such first-hand information will still be preserved for future generations.

Some officers have preferred to remain anonymous. To them, as well as the following, I desire to return every thanks for their very great courtesy and assistance both in regard to facts and in allowing me to reproduce illustrations:

Admiral Sir Richard F. Phillimore, G.C.B., K.C.M.G., M.V.O.; Admiral Sir Frank Larken, K.C.B., C.M.G.; Admiral A. V. Campbell, C.B., D.S.O., M.V.O.; Admiral P. H. Hall-Thompson, C.B., C.M.G.; Vice-Admiral H. R. Godfrey, C.B., D.S.O.; Captain Hughes C. Lockyer, C.B., R.N.; Captain Bertram H. Smith, C.B.E., R.N.; Captain Kenneth M. Bruce, D.S.O., R.N.; Captain Michael Barne, D.S.O., R.N.; Captain Wilfrid W. Hunt, D.S.O., R.N.

E. KEBLE CHATTERTON.

CONTENTS

CHAP.		PAGE
I.	Introduction	1
II.	Germany and Turkey	6
III.	Mediterranean Suspense	15
IV.	The Escape	28
V.	The Turkish Scene	39
VI.	The First Dilemma	49
VII.	Cruiser Adventures	57
VIII.	The Russian Problem	62
IX.	Dardanelles Diversion	73
X.	Bombarding the Outer Forts	83
XI.	Demolition Gallantry	95
XII.	The Second Dilemma	105
XIII.	Mines and Shells	114
XIV.	The Great Attack	130
XV.	Smyrna Interlude	149
XVI.	Reaction and Preparation	159
XVII.	Change of Principle	169
XVIII.	Night of Nights	182
XIX.	Landing the Army	199
XX.	Through the Straits	219
XXI.	The Story of "Goliath"	231
XXII.	The Submarine Phase Begins	245
XXIII.	Dardanelles Deadlock	264
XXIV.	The Suvla Dilemma	273
XXV.	Evacuation	299
	Appendix	308
	Index	311

LIST OF ILLUSTRATIONS

	FACING PAGE
The Mediterranean Theatre of War	*End paper*
Admiral Sir John De Robeck, K.C.B.	*Frontispiece*
The Russian Cruiser *Askold*	58
H.M.S. *Doris*	58
Turkish Prisoners at Mudros	66
Kephalos Bay	66
The " Cow-Catcher " Mine-Raker	70
A 6-Inch Howitzer	70
The *Ark Royal*	72
British Naval Seaplane	72
Beginning of the Dardanelles Campaign	76
The First Shot Fired	76
Bombardment of Outer Forts, February 19, 1915	78
Sedd-el-Bahr Fort	91
Naval Route March	91
The Dardanelles Straits	94
Landing at Kum Kale, February 26, 1915	96
One of the *Majestic* Class	116
12-Pounder Anti-Aircraft Gun	116
A Big Shell	118
H.M.S. *Queen Elizabeth*	118
Principal Forts and Batteries	120
The Narrows as seen from the Entrance to Dardanelles	130
Trawlers off the Entrance to the Dardanelles Straits, off Cape Tekke	132
H.M.S. *Prince George* in Action	132
H.M.S. *Lord Nelson*	134
The Dardanelles Straits	136
Sinking of the French Battleship *Bouvet*	140
Caught in the Searchlight	146
Crow's Nest	146
Officers of H.M.S. *Prince George*	148
Ward-Room Wrecked	162
Hole in Her Side	162
French Battleship *Henri IV*	168
Boat Deck of H.M.S. *Prince George*	168
British Destroyer *Louis*	168

	FACING PAGE
Hoisting Out Picket-Boat	186
The Admiral Comes Aboard	186
Troops on Board H.M.S. *Beagle*	204
Beach Party Aboard H.M.S. *Prince George*	204
X Beach from the Sea	206
Plan of X Beach	208
Diagram to Illustrate the Approach of H.M.S. *Implacable*	210
Landing at X Beach	212
Anzac Beach	214
The Famous *River Clyde*	214
Minesweeping under Fire	236
Net Protection	236
H.M.S. *Beagle* at Malta	238
In Harbour	260
The Wreck of H.M.S. *Majestic*	260
Monitors at the Dardanelles	266
The Cunarder *Mauretania*	268
The Protected *Edgar* Class	268
Loss of the S.S. *Carthage*	270
Plan to Illustrate the Landing at Suvla Bay, August 7, 1915	272
Landing the Australians at Suvla Bay	274
At Suvla Bay	276
The Transport *Southland*	278
E-Class Submarine in Harbour	284
Return of the Victor	284
H.M. Submarine *E* 14	284
Captain K. M. Bruce, D.S.O., R.N.	290
Plan to Illustrate the Evacuation from Helles, January, 1916	300
Plan of W Beach	302
Plan of V Beach	302

CHAPTER I

INTRODUCTION

WHETHER we approach the Dardanelles campaign as a grand drama or a gorgeous gamble, a brilliant failure or a wild adventure, that effort of brave men at their bravest will remain for all time one of the most spectacular and thrilling periods of our naval annals.

The array of battle-cruisers, battleships, light cruisers, destroyers, submarines, depôt-ships, transports, trawlers, and other units, gathered together and employed with unprecedented disregard for the value of men or money, presents a panoramic grandeur so vast that one's imagination is at first unable to take in the entire picture. All the wonders of modern invention—of turbines and wireless, of aerial and under-water craft—are there side by side with human nobility of courage which time and progress have not been able to kill. And the setting for this immense contest was that Ægean area already rich in maritime history. For it is geography which so often causes history to repeat itself: ships and men are confined to ancient seas and channels of effort because rocks and cliffs are less yielding to time's rude hand and unaffected by outside influences.

Just as the sensitive mind instantly reacts to certain environments with the definite feeling that something out of the ordinary ought therein to happen, so that part of our planet accustomed to the coming and going of mortal beings contains straits, headlands, coasts, which throughout the ages have repeatedly suggested the perfect background. If the Dover defile was destined to be not less attractive for the galleys of Cæsar, the flat-bottomed boats of Napoleon, and the submarines of Germany; if Cape St. Vincent, by reason of its situation, occupied in the strategical mentality of Drake, Nelson, and U-boat captains a very special value for opportunity; so the straits of Gallipoli, the Hellespont or Dardanelles separating Europe from all Asia, could not help becoming the scene of notable endeavours irrespective of century.

The narrowest part of that waterway lies between the ancient Sestos and Abydos, where Xerxes made a bridge of boats (in 480 B.C.) for his army bound from Asia towards Greece, and only a century and a half later Alexander the Great crossed at the same spot. This, too, was the scene of Leander's classic swimming, as of Byron's, many centuries afterwards. Now, Abydos is only slightly north of Chanak, and the maritime key to Byzantium lay in those self-same Narrows which Admiral Duckworth in 1807 forced on his way to Constantinople, and Admiral de Robeck did not succeed in forcing during 1915.

Thus for thousands of years the Dardanelles, and the Chanak Narrows, have always attracted nautical events. Where the *Goeben* and *Breslau* temporarily anchored just above Chanak preparatory to creating one of the world's crises, the triremes of Xerxes assembled before starting out to invade Hellas and be present at the critical Battle of Salamis. And this exceptionally contracted passage, less than two miles wide, separating two great continents, dividing primitive orientalism from Western civilisation, will continue till the end to be the centre of effort. The locality clamours for the eternal clashing of wills expressed in terms of ships, forts, armies, and weapons; it awaits only the right political opportunity for inviting the bitterest struggle between defence and offence or, in other words, for displaying the warrior's furthest limit of enduring heroic trials.

It was because of the Gallipoli geography, the Chanak confine, that the Dardanelles operations in the great European War lost more sailors, soldiers, and tonnage in proportion to lasting success, yet witnessed more downright courage in just missing the prize of victory, than any combined naval and military campaign on record. During the last two decades official histories, political memoirs, and other volumes have appeared both in Germany and England. Sometimes the reader has found to his regret that accounts have been written too soon after the events, containing inadequate knowledge; or conceived in such a manner as to suggest the apologia rather than the impartial narrative. In justifying a certain line of action, in following a particular principle, too little space has seemed to remain for recording in detail the great deeds wrought by the men and their immediate officers. Amid much whitewashing and criticism, explaining this motive and rebutting that accusation, revealing the disputes and subterfuges of those in high places, the glorious achievements of ships have been too lightly noted.

Now that twenty years have elapsed, the time is neither too near nor too remote for attempting to give the Dardanelles story as a naval enterprise, and to illumine this account with every possible item of fact. Within the most recent months, published records have enabled some gaps to be filled in, explained many things not hitherto appreciated, and clarified a number of obscurities. Thus no longer there lies before us just an interesting patchwork, multi-coloured and confusing, but a bold pattern plainly presented, with the causes connected closely to results. The loose ends have disappeared, the correlation of events has been emphasised, and we realise why the unexpected happened.

But that is not enough to satisfy either present or future generations.

Of those British naval officers who at the Dardanelles either commanded His Majesty's ships, or at least were present and played their notable parts, witnessing and experiencing momentous episodes, some are happily still with us, living in retirement, their memories keen and mindful of the past. They have had time to reflect, to think out in quietness, to sift the essential from the casual. By personal conversation with these officers, or through correspondence, or most especially by means of the material which they have generously placed at my disposal, it has been possible to attempt this history before our generation passes away. Private diaries, letters written home immediately after big incidents, impressions from hour to hour recorded in rapid sketches, photographs snapped of ships about to sink: such are the documents of priceless historical import from which considerable information has been obtained.

Nor is that all.

These eye-witnesses in some cases have laid me under further obligation by their courtesy in contributing for this volume first-hand descriptions of this and that remarkable occurrence, as perceived from their own forebridge or shell-splintered deck. It would be scarcely possible to exaggerate the worth of these graphic recitals; indeed, as the years fade, such true stories will be appraised not less deservedly than by contemporaries. For most of us have long since learnt that official despatches by no means contain the whole truth and nothing but the truth. Not infrequently, for reasons of expediency, the most illuminating paragraphs have had to be omitted at the time of compilation and release to the public, with no possibility of a revised edition. For example, one very commendable action at the Dardanelles had to be mentioned in print only with caution and sharp abbreviation. Why? Not for any other reason than its naval excellence! The public critics in Press or Parliament would have asked awkward questions. "Could there not be one all-round, universal, standard of perfection?"

Other events, golden with gallantry, could not be told at the time because it would have meant revealing our heavy losses, both to the enemy and to the British nation already depressed with anxieties. Years passed; the big tomes of small print had such a concern for policy and strategy, for results and consequences, instead of the daring methods which brought about this brilliancy of achievement, that many of the most heroic moments were squeezed out. But the machine will never possess the fascination peculiar to persons; the sailor of any rank or rating doing his dangerous job in the presence of the enemy provides us with the most gripping of all dramas. And it is with the intention of obtaining a detailed picture, remarkable for its dark-hulled ships no less than its variety of types, that every scrap of available data has been here gathered. Could ever a more noble sea subject be contemplated?

For almost we forget the painful tragedy of the undertaking; the mistakes and misconceptions; the errors of judgment, the lack of vision, on the part of honourable though badly calculating directors. In those days we could, so to say, never see " the other side of the wall "; we were unable to know all that was going on round the corner above the Narrows. To-day, however, we can view the whole theatre of naval endeavour as if we were poised aloft. And we get the proper unity of Atlantic, Mediterranean, Ægean, Sea of Marmora, Black Sea. It is like the procession of actors all bound for the producing of an Eastern pageant. We shall watch British and Germans bringing their vessels across the Bay of Biscay through all weathers; submarines of both nations dodging mines and traps; *Goeben* and *Breslau* at grips with the Russian Fleet; British bluejackets doing night landings to destroy railways; attack and counter-attack, surprise and sudden reverse; bluff and confidence; fears, and happy release at the last moment of endurance.

There is nothing dull about this colourful and variegated spectacle, which changes always both as to grouping and human interest. We can, if we wish, forget the while that these were living men in real ships; and consider this presentation as one magnificent legend wherein daring enterprise was fairly matched, and fate for several anxious years kept hopes in highest suspense. Under any consideration the Dardanelles adventure in its naval development gives us one of the most exciting and breathless struggles, planned on large scale, that the world is ever likely to experience.

Let us now see how one by one, and apparently by haphazard, the ships and seamen from even the remotest corners of the world come propelled towards the Gallipoli cliffs.

CHAPTER II

GERMANY AND TURKEY

The two years which immediately preceded the European War will ever be remembered as the brief and highly significant period during which Germany, by employing every intrigue known to diplomacy, contended fiercely to impress the Turkish mind. With all the ardour of a suitor seeking the fondest favours, with all the pushfulness of an enterprising business man bent on winning a highly profitable contract, Germany had sent to the Golden Horn her ablest expressions of Teutonic advancement and the shrewdest showmen for displaying her martial genius.

If Britain was still respected as the supreme Power in affairs of the sea, the Young Turks looked to Prussian reorganisation of an old-fashioned army as the only favourable road to reform. Gradually, however, the teacher became more of the tyrant than the trainer, and before Turkey could realise it she was less a friend than a vassal to the Kaiser. Exceedingly well did the latter select his representatives, sending only such as possessed unusually dominating personality and a striking presence. As Ambassador, for instance, he found in Baron von Wangenheim—bold, solid, big-bodied, self-reliant, ruthless and over six feet of stature—that sophisticated mediator who knows how far advance can be made by tact, but, when finally confronted with opposition, suffers neither precedent nor principle, difficulty nor danger, to impede his progress.

Wangenheim was the perfect instance of one who carries out orders, no matter how great are the obstacles or how serious the sequel. The bigger the task, the more seemingly impossible the duty, so proportionately did he succeed. By every method available, legitimate and otherwise, he was to subjugate the Turkish mind and to make the Turkish Army a ready instrument for Germany's use if, and whenever, the occasion should develop. Nor did this sphere of influence end on land.

Germany has never been notable for self-effacement,

modesty, humility: never inclined to under-statement. In the year 1912 she had just built a 22,640-tons battle-cruiser, mounting ten 11-inch, twelve 5·9-inch, and twelve 3·4-inch guns, which was possessed of such speed that nothing in the Mediterranean could surpass or equal her. That November, therefore, found this splendid and impressive vessel sent to Constantinople. Her name was the *Goeben*, and every opportunity was used for linking up her character with that of her country. If this was the fastest Mediterranean man-of-war, the ultimate picture of modern design and build, then Germany must be not less superior among nations. The local press spread the propaganda by extolling her tonnage, guns, armour, turbines. Lying in the Bosphorus opposite the German Embassy, the biggest ship visible, surpassing the two British light cruisers *Weymouth* and *Hampshire* which chanced to be present, she continued to be a unique advertisement for her country and the direct cause of that reasoning which ends up in coveting.

At night she was a blaze of publicity, when her Admiral Souchon did considerable entertaining. Up the lamp-clustered gangway came Djemal Pasha, Minister of Marine, and many other men of influence whose goodwill must most desirably be cultivated. Yes: she was a singularly fine war unit, and could become wonderfully useful to Turkey, whether against Greece or Russia. With such a battle-cruiser the integrity of the Dardanelles could be assured, the Russian Black Sea Fleet kept at bay, and the Greek Fleet sent to the bottom. Now, Admiral Souchon was another fine showman, and it was cautiously suggested that the Turks would be wise to negotiate purchase. Good-looking; with light eyes, strong open face, determined chin, big nose; clean shaven; Souchon might have passed for an English Admiral. Short, dapper, genial of manner, a good "mixer," alert and full of energy, he came of Huguenot stock. Like Wangenheim, he was faced time after time with apparently impossible tasks, yet by sheer force of will and effort he surmounted them all. As the reader will see for himself, there is much in Souchon's character which we can study with benefit, however we may criticise an enemy.

The sale, however, did not mature either that or the year following; yet in the meanwhile *Goeben* played a most notable political part.

Now, why was it that the Germans were so anxious to sell their brand-new acquisition? The answer is that actually she had not come up to expectations, and the Kaiser would be delighted if Turkey would, at a reasonable price, take her off the Imperial Navy's hands. In proof of this, let the following evidence be brought forward. An officer who up till the autumn of 1914 was one of the British Naval Mission tells me that the latter well knew, and Turkish officials spoke of, the *Goeben's* defects. "She was an unsatisfactory ship," states my informant, "from the day of her first commissioning." A British Admiral, who as Captain commanded one of our crack Mediterranean ships and was a friend of Captain (later Admiral) Underhill, sometime commanding officer of the above-mentioned *Weymouth*, informs me that the latter confirmed this statement about *Goeben's* imperfections. Captain Underhill and Admiral Souchon had known each other out in China, and one evening the German Admiral gave a dinner-party aboard the flagship. It was a friendly occasion—"only English spoken"—and, after the other guests had departed, Souchon confided in the *Weymouth's* Captain to this extent: he was hoping the Turks would buy *Goeben*, as she was drawing $1\frac{1}{2}$ feet more than her designed draught, with a consequent loss of $3\frac{1}{2}$ knots in speed.

Those who knew Admiral Underhill will remember that he was the last person who would make unwarranted statements; but we also know from one of *Goeben's* crew that she must have been too much down by the stern. For on a certain exciting day in May 1915, when she escaped from the Russian Black Sea Fleet only by using utmost speed, "the quarter-deck settled down into the water, sucked in until the after turrets were almost awash."[1]

[1] *Two Lone Ships*, by Georg Kopp, p. 224: London, 1913.

Now, in spite of Germany's influence at Constantinople, there existed right down till August 1914 a distinctly pro-British feeling both in Djemal Pasha and the Turkish Navy as a whole. Instead of finding funds to secure a second-hand "misfit" from Deutschland, the Turks collected money for building in England a 23,000-tons battleship that was to steam at 21 knots and mount ten 13·5-inch guns besides her secondary armament of sixteen 6-inch. She was actually launched in 1913 and named the *Reshadieh*. By July of the next year she was so nearly completed that a Turkish crew had come over to fetch her when, all of a sudden, the war-clouds gathered over Northern Europe, the British Government presently requisitioned her, changed her name to *Erin*, and sent her to join the Grand Fleet. A second "Dreadnought," also approaching readiness for delivery to Turkey though originally laid down for a South American republic, was likewise placed under the White Ensign, and henceforth became known as the *Agincourt*.

The last-minute transference of these two first-class ships was admittedly legitimate and inevitable. At the end of July, when our relations with Germany were about to break down, it would have been folly to have allowed *Erin* and *Agincourt* the chance of strengthening a neutral country: most especially, too, a nation already suspiciously friendly with Berlin. Nevertheless, this seizure was unfortunate, and destined to produce bitter consequences. In order to raise the money which should pay for the battleships, a good deal of spectacular patriotism had been beaten up, agents had gone from house to house collecting and extracting subscriptions, whilst Turkish women had even sold their hair.[1] The arrival of such powerful vessels, that would have given their nation an enviable predominance at sea over her immediate neighbours, had been awaited eagerly. But now, in the twinkling of an eye, Britain had broken their hearts, plunged them into grief and anger.

[1] *Secrets of the Bosphorus*, by Henry Morgenthau, formerly United States Ambassador at Constantinople. London, 1922.

Of this emotional situation Baron von Wangenheim did not fail to make the best for his Imperial Master's purpose. Violent anti-British attacks now swept through the capital, and never was come a luckier chance for German diplomacy to accentuate pressure. " There you are! Look how your perfidious English treat you! They accept your hard-earned savings, and refuse to deliver the ships. In future, why not put your trust in German ships, German firms, German character?"

That, in effect, was Wangenheim's powerful argument, and we shall do well at this stage to get the sequence of dates quite clear, that we may watch the working of international crises. Germany did not declare war on France until August 3, Britain did not enter into hostilities till midnight of the 4th, and for several weeks longer Turkey kept nominally at peace with everyone. Nevertheless on July 24 discussions began for an alliance between Turkey and Germany, on July 31 the British Government's veto was placed on the two battleships; and quickly afterwards, on August 2, the treaty between our two future enemies, Turkey and Germany, was finally signed, though the fact remained secret for a few days. Ever since January of that memorable 1914, Germany had in reality controlled the Turkish Army; and now, some hours before the Day of Days, she had made a triumph of the will and mind that gave her an unsuspected advantage. In the last resort, Constantinople could always be a home from home for Souchon's units. The *Goeben* had not been back to her fatherland since she first arrived from Kiel, but in May 1914 she had paid her second visit to the Bosphorus, and this gave the pro-German party a further chance for showing their sympathies. The battle-cruiser's officers were becoming familiar with the way up from the Dardanelles, no less than with the manner of a Turk's response to instruction.

By more than one treaty, dating from the mid-nineteenth century, foreign warships could pass through the Dardanelles only with Turkey's consent: a privilege seldom given. This must further be borne in mind when presently we come to place ourselves by imagination in Whitehall on August 6 and wonder whither Souchon was bound. It did not seem possible that he could be making for the north-east end of the Ægean: the Adriatic appeared probable, Egyptian waters possible, but certainly not the Gallipoli straits.

It is therefore necessary that we should first perceive more closely the condition of things immediately preceding the War: otherwise we shall fail to believe that it could be possible to unlock doors and remove barriers.

In the latter part of 1913, Wangenheim sent a request to Berlin asking for a suitable officer to be appointed as Chief of the German Military Mission for reforming the Turkish Army, and, in stressing the need of selecting the right type of man, the Ambassador remarked: "He should be a strong character who knows how to gain his point"; and this appointment " also would check British influence seeking to have British administration reformers called to Turkey."[1] Thus the diplomatic ruthlessness of Wangenheim was to be rivalled only by a Prussian soldier's forcefulness.

The choice of General Liman von Sanders exactly fulfilled the specified requirement, but the Kaiser warned him that he would find already in Constantinople Admiral Limpus, in charge of the British Naval Mission, with whom the General was to keep on good terms. Now, Sanders arrived in Turkey before the end of that December, and at once perceived the Turkish Army to be in a bad condition; men infested with vermin, cooking arrangements ultra-primitive, military buildings in a lamentable state, horses for mounted troops neglected—in fact most things wrong, with no sense of order or cleanliness.

Similarly, Admiral Limpus found the task of reforming the Turkish Navy not too easy. And one of the British naval officers of that Mission has given me the following impressions of the half-comic, half-pathetic environment which contrasted so brutally against the disciplined efficiency associated with service under the White Ensign. He found Djemal

[1] *Five Years in Turkey*, by General Liman von Sanders. Annapolis, 1927.

Pasha, the swarthy little black-bearded, dark-eyed Minister of Marine, anti-Enver, anti-German, and genuinely ambitious for the Turkish Navy: even if he did attire himself in the uniform of an infantry General. Reputed to be of gypsy birth, Djemal was neither popular nor generally trusted. Energetic, ferocious, able, cunning, he looked at you as if trying to pierce your very soul, whilst in the meantime his tongue was never still and his hand annoyingly fiddled with the pistol at his belt.

It was Djemal who had been at such pains to wring the purchase money out of the Turkish Treasury and people for the two " Dreadnoughts " that never came; but (says my informant) whilst Djemal and his friends believed that with these battleships Turkey would have become a naval Power to be reckoned with, " in practice the Turkish crews would probably have ruined the internal economy of the battleships in six months, if they didn't run them ashore." The system for entry into the sea service was curious: the Army took the best men and left the Navy to choose from the others. This led to strange results, as for instance when the Turkish naval official was confronted with a recruit who had been a camel-driver. For the reason that the latter had once driven something, they assigned him to the engine-room department!

The Turkish sailor was not over-paid, and his remuneration worked out at about tenpence a week. As to officers, owing to the uncertainty of promotion, the preference bestowed on favourites of the Palace or the politicians, and the disregard for professional ability, there existed little incentive for keen proficiency. Thus with crews taken straight from the plough, slow moving and inert of mind; native officers lacking in zeal; and the ships (excepting a few craft) hopelessly out of date; it would be a long, long time before the Ottoman Navy could become worthy of reckoning. Physically the recruits were a fine lot, and capable of being trained; yet, for the reason that it needs about as many years to make of a man a sailor as it requires months to drill him into a soldier, the task of General von Sanders was far easier than any facing Admiral Limpus. That results took shape so quickly in the Army, and just in time before peace ended, meant a very great deal both to Turkey and the trend of European history. She needed exactly that drive, vitality, organising ability, discipline, and military example, which the German officers could bring to the reforming task. Six or seven months of this stern drilling, marching, and general smartening up, before the fateful August 1914 could arrive, gave a new vigour at the right opportunity. Whatever might happen, Turkey was not to be defenceless on land.

Exactly the opposite may be said of her Navy, which would have needed not less than a generation of overhaul and development. For, consider its material strength that summer. Of battleships she had three only: the *Torgut Reis*, *Barbarossa*, and *Messudieh*. The first two were sister ships of 9874 tons, and completed in the year 1893. Twin-funnelled, mounting six 11-inch and eight 4·1-inch, as well as eight 3·4-inch guns, they were originally part of the German Navy, who sold them in the year 1910. The *Messudieh*, also two-funnelled, was of 9120 tons, and had been launched as far back as the year 1874, but reconstructed in 1902. Utterly obsolete, she mounted two 9·2-inch and twelve 6-inch guns. Not one of these three battleships could have steamed at more than 17 knots, so that, apart from the possibility of their being used as floating forts to defend the approaches to Constantinople, they were completely useless.

Turkey possessed a couple of light cruisers, fairly modern and moderately fast; that is to say, dating from 1904 and able to do 22 knots. The *Hamidieh* was of 3800 tons: the *Medjidieh* was of 3432 tons. Each carried a couple of 6-inch and eight 4·7-inch guns. These were likely to be quite useful if properly handled, but the small flotilla of gunboats can be dismissed as having no apparent value, and the same may be remarked of some ancient torpedo-boats fit only for the shipbreakers. On the other hand, she owned eight excellent destroyers, and several small torpedo-boats. For reasons which will be evident in subsequent chapters, we may well take notice that the former comprised two classes: four (of 305 tons) built on the Loire in 1907–8, and four (of 620 tons) built in Germany at the Schichau yard during 1910. The eight or nine torpedo-boats of varying tonnage and age included the 26-knot, 97-tons *Demir-Hissar*, which we shall observe enjoying her one bit of excitement, just as the destroyer *Muavenet-i-Millet* lived through a thrilling night. The Turks had no submarines, and that was perhaps fortunate. More to be desired than fine gold were under-water craft after a few short months: yet with native officers and crews they would have been a danger to themselves. Some months before the European War the Germans had built for Turkey at Kiel the *Nusrat*, a steamer of 380 tons, intended as a minelayer; and in due course we shall see what a magnificent result can be obtained from so small a ship.

In short, then, what the Turks really needed for the preservation of their independence and the resistance of invasion was not merely a couple of modern first-class warships, not merely a Naval Mission, but these vessels manned by expert north European crews under officers of the highest abilities; together with a surplus of junior officers, warrant officers, petty officers, and leading hands. These supplementaries could be apportioned to the eight destroyers and two light cruisers, with a view of stiffening the Turkish personnel, guiding and encouraging. By themselves, relying on their own material and unenterprising temperaments, they were merely lost sheep, when they might have become sea-wolves rivalling their mediæval ancestors.

And we shall perceive presently that, precisely to fill these requirements, German naval effort came promptly on the scene.

CHAPTER III

MEDITERRANEAN SUSPENSE

In July 1914 the British Mediterranean Fleet consisted of the three battle-cruisers *Inflexible*, *Indefatigable*, and *Indomitable*, each mounting eight 12-inch guns; the four armoured cruisers *Defence*, *Black Prince*, *Duke of Edinburgh*, and *Warrior*, all armed with 9·2-inch guns; the four light cruisers *Chatham*, *Dublin*, *Gloucester*, and *Weymouth*, having 6-inch guns. Based on Malta, they were under the Commander-in-Chief, Admiral Sir A. Berkeley Milne, Bt., whose second-in-command was Rear-Admiral E. C. T. Troubridge.

Besides the *Goeben*, Germany had in the Middle Sea only the armoured cruiser *Breslau*, 4478 tons, built in 1912 and armed with twelve 4·1-inch guns. It is thus very obvious that our superiority of sea power was immense: only a right employment of this strength could be necessary for making *Goeben* and *Breslau* for ever silent. But, in addition to this predominance, there were sixteen British destroyers, three submarines, as well as a few local torpedo-boats based on Malta and Gibraltar. Apart from the above numbers must be mentioned the French Mediterranean Fleet, which included twelve battleships, six armoured cruisers, four older units, destroyers and submarines. Those critics who prophesy success or failure by multitude of material things whilst omitting to weigh circumstance and human nature, would have risked the suggestion that on the first threat of war against Britain or France—and still more so if an Anglo-French alliance seemed likely—Germany's solitary pair would either seek refuge in a friendly Austrian port, attempt escape out through the Gibraltar Straits, or make some spectacular engagement and go down with colours flying. By no ordinary reasoning did *Goeben* and *Breslau* own a gambler's chance of remaining afloat, in active commission, after the first hours of hostilities.

It is only needful to remind the reader that *Breslau* continued very much alive until the year 1918; and *Goeben* is still in naval service to-day. The long story, which we shall now proceed to follow, pivots on these two men-of-war: their very movements and adventures were to be the road-signs of European history; their existence was for nearly four years one continuous source of anxiety to the Allies.

The narrative opens in June 1914, when *Goeben* very badly needed a refit. Not having been in dockyard hands since she left Kiel most of two years before, her engines and boilers were now in such a condition that whereas during her trials she had touched 27·9 knots, and for short spurts had been known to reach 29 knots, she could now steam at not over 20 knots for brief periods, though 14 knots represented her steady cruising rate. Now, at the end of June occurred the murder of Archduke Ferdinand, which caused Germany to think ahead: there might ensue international complications, so the battle-cruiser *Goeben* must immediately be made efficient. Austria being Germany's best friend, the ship was sent up the Adriatic to Pola, arriving at the dockyard on July 10.

The month was intensely hot, and she had twenty-four boilers, so the job could not be called trivial. By working day and night till July 28, the 4000 defective boiler tubes were replaced, so that she left on the 29th for Trieste (where she coaled), steamed down the Adriatic, called at Brindisi on August 1, and was now joined by *Breslau*, who had been to Durazzo. The latter could do her 28 knots, and slightly more at a pinch, but both consequently needed frequent bunkering; the *Goeben* requiring over 3000 tons to fill up, and the *Breslau* 1200 tons. On August 2 the political outlook was distinctly black, and that day Admiral Souchon brought his two ships into Messina so as to complete with fuel to the limit of capacity.

Be it noted that Italy was still neutral,[1] and determined to show herself impartial. She protested against German men-

---

[1] Italy did not declare war on Austria until May 23, 1915, nor on Turkey till August 21, 1915. But war against Germany she did not declare until August 28, 1916.

of-war refuelling in her Sicilian port, but (as usual) Germany had a very astute, wide-awake Ambassador at Rome, so the diplomatic hitch was smoothed over. The precious coal came alongside in lighters, and also from the German East African liner *General*. Now, here we have an example of Teutonic thoroughness. On the previous night, foreseeing the approach of war, Souchon had wirelessed warnings to several other of his nation's steamers in that part of the Mediterranean. It was thus the *General*, bound eastward via the Suez Canal, put back, and presently the harbour contained also the Hansa liner *Kettenturm*, besides the two Hamburg-Amerika liners *Umbria* and *Barcelona*. Thus, not merely had the Admiral saved these vessels from falling into other hands, but he had simultaneously requisitioned their coal. The quartette between them, and the lighters from the Hugo Stinnes Company's local depôt, would supply all his wants.

Every hour became more tense and, having received intimation that war with France was imminent, he got under way that night at 1 a.m., went out through the northern end of the Messina Straits, steamed at 17 knots with lights out, avoiding all shipping, and made to the westward. Why? In order to cut the Marseilles–Algeria route along which the French Army from North Africa would be likely to be transported at this time; and, if no transports were met with, at least he could bombard the African embarkation ports. There was the further intention that, having announced his presence so far to the westward, Souchon might succeed in suggesting that he was bound out past Gibraltar into the Atlantic.

It so happens that the French Mediterranean Fleet left Toulon at 4 a.m. of August 3—that is to say, three hours after *Goeben* and *Breslau* cleared out of Messina. Admiral Boué de Lapéyrère was bound south for the duty of watching Souchon and covering the passage of French Algerian troops. The rivals' courses were thus at right angles, and it is a thousand pities that no meeting and engagement occurred; for at

6 p.m. on the 3rd came the wireless news that war between Germany and France had broken out, and if only these two Teutonic units could have been sunk or crippled, thousands of lives, millions of pounds, to say nothing of wasted months, would have been saved.

About 6 a.m. of August 4 the *Goeben* was off Philippeville. She approached flying Russian colours; then, as she slowed down and got nearer still to the port, the false flag was lowered, up went the German ensign, and for ten minutes she bombarded the harbour-works. She next hurried off to the westward, but, when out of sight, swung round on an easterly course. Meanwhile the *Breslau* in the early morning had shelled Bona. Now, the nett result of these two visits was that in each case such buildings as barracks and warehouses, as well as the harbour-works, received much damage; the transports carrying the Algerian Army Corps being thus delayed for three days.

Souchon had wasted no time, and the subterfuge of false colours was legitimate because they were not flown when he attacked under the German flag. Presently he was joined again by *Breslau*, both ships intercepting French wireless announcing the bombardments. But much more important was that radiogram which at 2.35 a.m. on this memorable August 4 came to Souchon from the German wireless station of Nauen. It informed him that, Germany on August 2 having concluded an alliance with Turkey, the *Goeben* and *Breslau* were to make for the Dardanelles. As this meant steaming another 1500 miles, and these fast ships were so greedy for fuel, he must needs first make for Messina once more and coal. Let us then, for a while, leave the Germans at breakfast, and turn our attention to the three British battle-cruisers.

The first British battle-cruiser to be designed was the *Invincible*, launched in 1907, and to this class belonged the *Indomitable* as well as the *Inflexible*. The *Indefatigable* came a little later as an improved species of this modern fast type, and it was well realised that the *Goeben* was intended as the

German improvement on our *Invincible*.[1] As against the eight 12-inch guns of each British battle-cruiser were the ten 11-inch of the German battle-cruiser; and the twelve 4·1-inch guns of the *Breslau*, which could be relied upon to do her 27 knots without effort, and to approach 29 if pushed. Now, it will be seen that Souchon's flagship was superior to any one of our Mediterranean units, whether in regard to tonnage or speed, but in August 1914 the *Indefatigable* could not have maintained more than 27 knots, the *Inflexible* more than 25 knots, and the *Indomitable* much more than 22 knots. This I know from one of the commanding officers.

In a curious manner, the World War opened at a date not too convenient for Mediterranean battle-cruisers. We have seen that *Goeben* barely had time to complete a refit, and she still needed attention. The *Indomitable* on July 24 had gone to Malta for an overhaul that had been delayed: she had not been in dockyard hands since March 1913 before the trouble descended. On Sunday, August 2, at 2 p.m., this battle-cruiser was ordered to raise steam for full speed, recall everyone from leave; and seven hours later she left Malta with *Indefatigable* to search for the two Germans between Cape Bon (Tunis) and Cape Spartivento (South Sardinia).

It was easier commanded than executed. Just before starting, Admiral Troubridge had sent for the commanding officers and given them instructions. "After he had told us the orders," Captain (now Admiral) F. W. Kennedy of the *Indomitable* has informed me, " he had received from the Commander-in-Chief, Sir Berkeley Milne, he remarked, ' Now, does anyone want to ask anything?' I replied that though I had studied my duties as a cruiser captain, I still did not know how

[1] The following comparisons will speak for themselves :—

Name of Ship.	Tonnage.	When laid down.	Speed in Knots.
Invincible	17,250	1906	25 (designed); 28 (possible).
Inflexible	17,250	1906	25 (designed); 28 (possible).
Indomitable	17,250	1906	25 (designed); 28 (possible).
Indefatigable	18,750	1909	25 (designed); 29 (possible).
Goeben	22,640	1909	25½ (designed); over 29 (possible).

a 22-knot ship (mine) was to shadow a 27-knot *Goeben* if the latter did not want to be shadowed."

At this stage it was still firmly believed that the enemy would be found somewhere along the 860-mile transport route between Algiers and Marseilles; and the British Admiralty's first anxiety was for the French Algerian Army Corps' safe transit. On July 30 Admiral Milne had been informed that " your first task should be to aid the French " to that end. That was several days ago, and since then much had happened. First of all, the French Commander-in-Chief, Admiral de Lapéyrère, was considerably modifying the transport plans, and organising convoys; his covering force, also, so preponderated in strength that British assistance would have been superfluous. But, secondly, the sudden and dramatic alliance between Turkey and Germany made all previous strategy for the Latin Lake quite out of date. Unfortunately, such news had not yet reached either Malta or Whitehall.

Thus the position at 9 p.m. on the 3rd was that the *Indomitable* and *Indefatigable* were aware that Souchon had left Messina some hours ago, and that Sir Berkeley Milne had wirelessed the two British battle-cruisers ordering them to make for Gibraltar Straits and prevent the enemy from leaving the Mediterranean. So speed was increased to 22 knots, and away tore the fine-bowed ships with all lights out. The dark hours passed without incident, but at 9 a.m. on the 4th came the wireless news that Bona had been bombarded, which meant that the Germans between 6 and 7 a.m. could be only a hundred miles ahead, and nearer Gibraltar. What to do ? If the *Goeben* were bound home via the north of Scotland (it was roughly reckoned), she would just be able to arrive without coaling, provided she eased to 14 knots. In that case it might be the British battle-cruisers' duty to make direct at full speed for the Gibraltar Straits, and ignore the bombardment locality.

But, almost immediately, the question had its own answer. At 9.35 a.m. (G.M.T.), whilst still on their westerly course, there appeared, about two points on the *Indomitable's* starboard bow, the *Breslau*, heading about N.E. by E., and evidently coming along at high speed, for she was making a large bow wave. Then was seen, slightly more to the southward, the *Goeben*, which seemed to be steering about E. by N. Admiral Kennedy has told me that "almost as soon as the *Goeben* saw us, she altered course as if to cross ahead of us to the *Breslau*, but I altered to starboard, whereupon she apparently resumed her original course. We had sounded off 'Action Stations' directly *Breslau* was sighted."

The distance at this moment was about 10 miles: 18,000 yards. And a most delicate phase at once developed. Britain and Germany were still at peace, and not till after another $4\frac{1}{2}$ hours would the British Admiralty inform its ships far and wide—north, south, east or west—that the ultimatum would expire with midnight. Thus the international customs and courtesy of the sea still obtained, and if Admiral Souchon's flag was still flying, it must be saluted by the British guns. The two pairs of ships were approaching on opposite courses at an aggregate of about 42 knots. Was the *Goeben* flying an Admiral's flag? If not, then the salute need not be fired.

"Perhaps you will believe me," remarked the *Indomitable's* Captain to me when discussing this singular crisis, "when I tell you that every sort of telescope—binoculars, as well as range-finders—were focussed on the *Goeben*, but not a sign of a flag was seen by anyone on board *Indomitable* or *Indefatigable*."

They passed each other at a distance of about 9850 yards, and not a shot was fired. To-day we know that both sides were fully ready to open fire at each other; and that both kept their guns secured in the fore-and-aft position which would prevent any possible misunderstanding. "I had well considered the question," Admiral Kennedy has added, "and I believed that the salute was very likely to be the cause of the German replying by shot and shell."

We know something about the suspense which the Germans felt. Half a dozen books have since been published by our late enemies concerning the *Goeben* and *Breslau*, but we may content ourselves with the most recent, written by one of her crew;[1] and realise the thrill when the smoke of two warships showed up ahead. At first the bombarders of Algeria felt sure these must be the French; but when a nearer view established the true nationality, it was to make excitement still keener. Perhaps already Britain had entered hostilities without declaring war? Admiral Souchon had been warned that the former was likely to become inimical any moment. And now the first shells would hit German ships?

"But nothing happened," relates *Goeben's* narrator, Georg Kopp. "With the ships' companies on both sides at action stations, the ships glided past one another in uncanny silence . . . there was no salute." And no engagement. The meeting had been less casual than the result of two minds reasoning in a similar manner. Captain Kennedy thought it probable Souchon would be on a course well away from the land, and if possible from the steamship routes: having performed an act of offence to the French, the German would wish to avoid observation. That must be quite certain. But equally the British battle-cruisers desired their movements to remain unreported until either the French transport line had been reached or the enemy been located. Thus, the secret alliance having predestined that our future enemies should come eastward via Messina, this silent meeting of four notable sea warriors happened inevitably.

But now came the contest, the race, the struggle, the beginning of a great drama.

The great revelation—that Souchon was definitely bound east and not west—occurred about fifty miles north (and slightly east) of Bona; so Captain Kennedy wirelessed the tidings to Admiral Milne and proceeded to shadow these fast units. Alas! the *Breslau* had spurted off, so that by 11.30 a.m. she had vanished miles ahead, doing her duty as a good scout on her big sister's behalf. It was now just that hopeless, gruelling chase which Captain Kennedy had suggested

[1] *Two Lone Ships*, pp. 27–28.

during the interview with Admiral Troubridge: a battle between the engineers and stokers of one side and their opposite numbers deep down in steel hulls.

Steam! steam! Furnaces! Coal—shovel it in! Trim the bunkers! Keep the flagship hurrying along to Messina before the French or English make it too awkward, or the Italians join in with them! Every officer, every midshipman, every rating off duty, together with men that could be spared from the guns, went below to toil in the *Goeben's* bunkers or stokeholds. The clanging of shovels, the slamming of doors, the wild roaring of artificial draught; the half-naked bodies of men streaked with sweat and coal-dust; the fierce heat of a Mediterranean August and incandescent furnaces; trimmers collapsing in sheer exhaustion; harsh Teutonic shouts and tempers sorely tried: that was the rough environment for the swiftest race that even the Middle Sea in all its long history of ships had ever witnessed.

But our battle-cruisers were holding *Goeben* fairly well, though a haze kept settling down and obliterating that flagship altogether. Then the pursuit would again be normal until Souchon's vessel became so slow that Captain Kennedy must ease to 8 knots in order to keep his distance.[1] What had happened? It seemed quite a mystery then, but to-day we know that the enemy's boilers were still giving trouble; now and again the tubes would burst like soda-water bottles, pressure would fall, and speed drop. Like the *Indomitable*, she badly needed a scrub, and until noon (although the *Goeben's* engines were making revolutions for 24 knots) she was not doing more than 17 knots through the water, though for the next eight hours she was whacked up to $22\frac{1}{2}$ knots, and *Indomitable* (whose spare seamen were trimming coal most of the time) maintained 22 knots. Thus by 7 p.m. *Goeben* was just becoming invisible, and at 9 p.m. the thickening weather came as a separating curtain.

But anxiety became greater as August 4th passed towards

[1] It was accepted as a possibility that the Germans might either use torpedoes or drop mines.

its close and Souchon steamed ever nearer to Sicilian shores. Had Italy entered the war? And on which side?

It had been a long, very trying day; not more for the British shadowing battle-cruisers than for the Germans, who were about to proceed down the northern passage of Messina Straits, when some torpedo-boats were sighted ahead. For some minutes Souchon was extremely perturbed, since the conditions would have perfectly suited mosquito attack. Captain Kennedy, likewise, wished to avoid getting near the coast, lest *Goeben* should give away the battle-cruisers' position, and send forth these torpedo-boats to make a night assault.

So the two British ships were about to patrol throughout the dark hours north and south clear of territorial waters, and then at daylight sweep along the North Sicilian coast. As the Germans tried communicating with the Vittoria wireless station at the southern end of Sicily, Captain Kennedy's battle-cruisers were trying hard to jamb the messages. All was now set for an interesting morrow, when it was expected that Souchon would be found coaling not in Messina itself, but somewhere off the land, and before midnight the *Goeben's* wireless learned of Great Britain's entering hostilities. Thus far, then, the future was a little less obscure, and August 5 ought to afford one of two things: provided the Germans kept outside Italian regional limits, *Indomitable* and *Indefatigable* would hope and expect to sink the enemy before noon, but should Souchon tarry at Messina, he could either risk internment after the stipulated period, or find British men-of-war waiting off either end of the Straits.

Judge, then, of Captain Kennedy's painful surprise when, just before 7 p.m., Sir Berkeley Milne wirelessed that the two battle-cruisers were to steam west at slow speed; that is to say, away from where the shadowed ships were definitely known to be. A strange order indeed. But the Commander-in-Chief was still unaware of the secret Alliance, and still influenced by the belief that Souchon would turn westward in the direction of Gibraltar. It will always be a matter of regret that *Indomitable* and *Indefatigable* were not kept at the

Straits' northern end, just outside the Italian six-mile national range; and that to the southern exit Admiral Troubridge's cruisers were not forthwith despatched as a blockading force; or at least that the three submarines *B* 9, *B* 10, *B* 11 were not ordered thither from Malta, where they could have arrived in less than fifteen hours.

The French were certainly not obsessed with that fear of Souchon's returning westward, and on August 6 even offered to lend Admiral Milne four cruisers. Indeed, if ever we had a glorious chance of doing some simple and essential duty, that in the years to come would be acclaimed by posterity as an inevitable proceeding, that opportunity existed from the night of August 4 till the evening of August 6. For these are the facts.

Breslau had been sent on ahead to arrange about the coaling, and anchored off Messina at 5 a.m. on August 5. Just before 8 a.m. arrived *Goeben*, escorted by five Italian torpedo-boats. Now, at sunset on the 4th had arrived off the entrance the British S.S. *Wilster* with a cargo of Welsh coal in the ordinary way of business for the German-owned firm Hugo Stinnes Coal Company, who had a branch at Messina. The collier had been met by a tug, who told her to anchor in the roadstead, and the collier's master (Captain P. A. Eggers, of Sunderland) was just coming ashore in his boat at 8 a.m. when he saw the *Goeben* anchoring near the *Wilster*. That was the first knowledge which Eggers had that we were at war. Pressure was brought to bear on him, and a bribe even offered, that he might bring the *Wilster* alongside one of the German cruisers, but the master mariner strenuously refused to land his coal anywhere else except alongside the quay to which he now moored. He had been sent from Penarth, before the declaration of hostilities, to deliver his Welsh coal in a certain manner, and these orders he proceeded to carry out scrupulously. Consequently the Germans had to fall back on their own national steamers—*General, Kettenturm, Umbria,* and *Barcelona*.

Superfluous gear was placed aboard the *General*, so that

Goeben finally was stripped even to having but one boat aboard in davits. What with the heat and haste, and the lack of facilities, this final fuelling was a terrible business. The men were kept refreshed with iced lemonade, and cheered by the ships' bands playing encouraging melodies; but all day, and throughout the night, continued the black task which had been made no easier by the circumstance that the *General* must needs first discharge her general cargo before she could get at her reserve supply in the bottom of her holds.

It was a race against time, against the strength of Italian neutrality, against the lethargy which the sultry Sicilian summer inspired. Many of us know something about the worries which beset a commanding officer during his stay in port: everything seems planned to give him the maximum amount of obstruction and bother, so that he yearns ardently for the open sea, with any of its navigational problems, rather than suffer the snares of difficult landsmen with all their artificial regulations. But Admiral Souchon had to endure more than his full share; and only a clever, resourceful, determined character could have " got away with " the job.

His boilers and engines were still not perfect, the *Goeben* needed 1580 tons of coal, the *Breslau* 495 tons; the British Navy (he supposed) had some of its ships waiting outside, and the French might be sending some of theirs as reinforcements. He had asked the Austrian Admiral Haus to come down from Pola and escort him, but Austria was not yet at war against France or Britain, so Haus could not help. Aboard came a deputation of Italian naval officers to announce that Italy was strictly neutral, that the Germans were in neutral waters and must leave within twenty-four hours. It was now the evening, and Souchon had been in port already most of twelve hours. He ingeniously replied that he regarded this message as the formal announcement, and that the twenty-four hours would therefore be reckoned from now!

Nothing was going to stop him from every effort to carry out those original orders which directed him to the Dardanelles, but next came the hardest knock of all. Berlin telegraphed that, for political reasons, it would not for the present be practicable to reach Constantinople: he was thus without home or friends, saddled with the responsibility of two ships, to say nothing of their men's lives. Every unfavourable condition seemed to have conspired against him; every item that might have gone wrong had so decided. What, then, could Admiral Souchon choose amid this series of disappointments? Which was the one and only proper course of action?

Amid such contending factors a weak, vacillating man breaks down and yields to superior weight, but a strong personality rises to the occasion, gains a new courage and a clearer vision, selects the most perilous alternative, and with boldness resolves to succeed, despising all danger, looking forward only to triumph. That is the kind of leader who usually attains; because he deserves to win, because he refuses to accept defeat.

And to that category belonged Admiral Souchon.

CHAPTER IV

THE ESCAPE

ADMIRAL SOUCHON, like a Judge trying to see the plain issue out of many conflicting statements, sought the one decision which he owed to his country and service. Notwithstanding that last annoying telegram, he was still resolved to make for Turkish waters, hoping that he would be allowed to reach the Black Sea eventually and dominate the Russians. But such a design would be full of difficulties, and he must expect to succeed only by first fighting his way through British naval opposition. So his ships were cleared for action, and his men " cleaned " into fighting rig. At 5 p.m. on August 6 the *Goeben* left Messina, followed twenty minutes later by the *Breslau*. A speed of 17 knots was ordered. Two hours after his departure the S.S. *General* weighed and left likewise. She had painted her funnel black, obliterated her name, and was bound for a secret destination.

About 8 p.m. the daylight was ending, but already Souchon had been sighted an hour earlier by the *Gloucester* (Captain W. A. Howard Kelly), who had been watching at the southern end of Messina Straits, and it will always be a matter for regret that Malta's three submarines (*B* 9, *B* 10, *B* 11) had not also been sent to wait outside the Italian six-miles limit. As the reader will perceive in a later chapter, *B* 11 was mechanically so efficient and her commanding officer so daring that nothing but ill luck could have prevented this boat from torpedoing the *Goeben*. Admittedly the German battle-cruiser could have outranged and devastated the little *Gloucester*[1] in a straight fight; but the latter would have been slightly superior to the *Breslau*, and then, with the assistance of night, could have contributed her share in completing the destruction of a *Goeben* badly listing and robbed of speed. But this was not to be, though the obvious lesson can never be forgotten.

The immediate contest was one of wits, and not of explosives.

[1] 4820 tons, 25 to 27 knots. Armed with two 6-inch and ten 4-inch guns.

Admiral Souchon would have preferred a North Sea fog, or at least one of those dark nights with thick drizzle. In his mind was the one firm purpose of hurrying across the Adriatic mouth, round the Grecian peninsula, up the Ægean, through the fortified Dardanelles Straits to Constantinople, and not to be side-tracked by an engagement with British cruisers. As it turned out, this balmy summer's night was clear, moonlit, with fine weather; so that his only hope lay in pretence and speed, with a final reliance on his long-range 11-inch guns if the British attentions could not be shaken off. On the other hand, it was not less the *Gloucester's* task to avoid an engagement, but her essential duty was to keep the enemy in touch, so that Souchon's position could be wirelessed to Sir Berkeley Milne and to Rear-Admiral Troubridge. The latter was now lying with his four armoured cruisers *Defence, Warrior, Duke of Edinburgh, Black Prince,* and destroyers on the east side of the Otranto Straits below Corfu; since it was still believed that the Germans from Messina could be bound no whither than up the Adriatic to unite with the Austrian Fleet. The possibility of the Turco-Teutonic alliance, or of the desire to reach the Black Sea even now, had not been envisaged at Malta. And Souchon, with wise imagination, could guess what the British mind would be thinking.

So at first the German Admiral made a feint up the Adriatic: whilst the *Breslau* was allowed to drop astern and make towards *Gloucester*, the *Goeben* increased speed and stood off to the north-east, as if making for the Otranto Straits. At 10.21 p.m., however, she suddenly altered course, and not wishing to go farther out of her way than absolutely essential, swung to the south-east for the southern end of Greece. Captain Howard Kelly was not to be deceived, and could not be shaken off. In the most annoying manner he regulated his speed, so that first the *Goeben* and then the *Breslau* was made to turn back and threaten the *Gloucester* away. It was rather like the case of two men in a desperate haste to catch a train, yet compelled to stop every few minutes and throw stones at a growling dog that will not be appeased.

And whilst these delaying tactics were proceeding through the night, a sub-contest went on in the respective wireless offices.

"Every attempt of the *Gloucester* to use her wireless," writes one of the *Goeben's* operators,[1] "was skilfully frustrated by methods which had often been used with success. In exasperation she [*Gloucester*] jumped from one wave-length to another. But it was no use; at once our transmitter found the same wave-length and interrupted. This bitter, invisible struggle in the ether lasted for more than an hour." So the chase went on, and at 1.35 p.m. of August 7, being now off the Grecian coast, the *Gloucester* was distant about 13,000 yards from the *Breslau*, opening fire on the latter. We know from the above-quoted authority that the British cruiser's gunnery was so good at that range of nearly seven miles that one shell hit the German light cruiser on her water-line armour. The *Goeben* was compelled to turn back temporarily and open fire, thus again being delayed, which exactly coincided with Captain Kelly's intentions. Fifteen minutes were thus lost to the enemy in an all-important scurry. The pity of it—the pathetic tragedy—is that such excellent and solitary shadowing should have been unsupported. Where were the three British battle-cruisers? Why could they not have been waiting off Cape Matapan?

A few more of the *Gloucester's* 6-inch shells might have crippled *Breslau* so that the *Goeben* must either leave her to destruction, or else take her in tow and, with progress reduced to 6 or 7 knots, incur the most perilous delay.

But, alas! the old freedom of the seas, which belonged to sailing-ships, no longer obtains. The *Gloucester* had a fuel capacity of only 850 tons, and after all this fast steaming her bunkers were becoming empty. By 4.40 p.m. of the 7th, having watched her rivals up to the southern tip of Greece at Cape Matapan, she had to break off the chase, turn away, and lay a course for joining Admiral Troubridge. As she reported on her wireless, the operators in both German ships were busy jamming communication.

[1] *Two Lone Ships*, p. 48.

Now, this unexpected abandonment of pursuit gave great cheer to Souchon, who could at long last ease down and continue quietly; though not before this had become very necessary. For it was already a battle of boilers and engines against failure. Every spare officer and man in the *Goeben* had been sent below to help, the boiler tubes had collapsed under the strain, and four stokers had lost their lives. Her boiler brickwork had been badly burnt away, and altogether the flagship had been driven beyond breaking-point, yet even now she was not out of the danger region. That anxious night she proceeded furtively among the Ægean islands, with *Breslau* scouting ahead, half-expectant that at any moment the loom of a British destroyer might be the forerunner of a more powerful force. Avoiding traffic routes and lighthouses, they threaded their way, and finally sighted at noon something which had been much desired, yet might very likely have never taken shape.

Souchon, before quitting Messina, well recognised that if his ships should safely reach the Ægean, they would badly need fuel. For this reason, he had beforehand arranged that a German collier, disguised as a Greek coaster, should come out from the Piræus and meet him. In case this steamer should fail to make the rendezvous, he had also instructed the previously mentioned liner *General* to make for the island of Santorin, which is seventy miles north of Crete. Thus there would be two possible sources of coal supply, and his anxiety might be halved.

He had come up from Cerigo to the north-east, left Syra to starboard, Tenos to port, and at noon sighted the Piræus collier. This enabled him to send the *General* on to Smyrna, that principal seaport of Asia Minor, concerning which we shall have much to say in a subsequent chapter. It was for Souchon's purpose most convenient, as being in rail communication with Constantinople, and little more than 200 miles would be the distance for sending wireless messages to the Ottoman authorities. Souchon was in a critical position, and knew all too well that his safety must end in a few hours: he had been lucky to escape, fortunate to have had only one small cruiser pursuing him. But even now heavier units must be getting dangerously near, and German wireless must be reduced to a minimum. Thus, whilst the hour had arrived when he must talk with von Wangenheim and get a quick reply, it must be done by the merchant steamer much nearer the Golden Horn.

So the *General* got on with this important job, and the conversation was heard in the *Goeben's* wireless room. On August 5 Turkey had barred the Narrows to warships, and it would need all that even the forceful German Ambassador could persuade, if Souchon's two ships were permitted entrance. For, in spite of the new Alliance, a general anti-British feeling was as yet by no means rife in Constantinople. An officer of the British Naval Mission, whom I have already quoted, tells me that one of the most curious situations created by hostilities was within the Pera Club, where English, French, Italian, Russian, Austrian, German and American members met on neutral ground.

"What does one do when one is at war with one's fellow members of a club? What is club etiquette in such circumstances? Apparently much the same as in the average London club under normal conditions, since the human heart is incapable of cherishing deeper feelings of hatred than those of the member who sees another member get his favourite table for dinner, or occupy his favourite armchair. So perhaps it is unnecessary to record that there were no open hostilities in the Pera Club, with the exception of an altercation between a Frenchman and an Austrian, ending in the latter falling downstairs."

That first night of war with Germany, August 5, seated on the pleasant little verandah of the club, the British naval officer was talking to a fellow countryman, when a German Major came across and held out his hand. Over a drink and cigars the following conversation began:

"Well, Major, here's 'der Tag' at last?"

"So!" answered the German. "But what a pity!"

"Pity?" inquired the British naval officer.

"We are the two finest nations in the world. Why"—the German smote the table—"why do we not divide the world between us? You ally yourselves with the Fr-r-rench. Ach! Monkees! With the R-russians. Pfui! Savages!"

Weeks later, at the levée in the Dolma Bagtché Palace, General Liman von Sanders would be seen on pleasant terms with the British Admiral Limpus, "punctiliously exchanging commonplaces about the weather when they met in the anteroom." Indeed, not till after the arrival of *Goeben* and *Breslau* was the German domination of affairs complete. Nevertheless, Djemal, enraged because of the *Erin* and *Agincourt*, had begun to show a frosty coolness towards British officers. When, presently, there arrived from England the Turkish officers and men who had been sent to fetch home the two "Dreadnoughts," began simultaneously the first insults. Djemal had thrown in his lot with Talaat and Enver: the Germans controlled the Press, and represented every North European war incident to the disadvantage of Britain or France; so it next became quite obvious that Turkey could not much longer repulse Germany's help.

Now, the manner in which Admiral Souchon, aided by Baron von Wangenheim, forced his way through to Constantinople is just an example of what can be brought about by two strong men with clear intentions. Wangenheim had his private wireless station aboard the S.S. *Corcovado*, which lay in the Bosphorus. From her he had been able to communicate with the *Goeben* direct, and now, in this crucial hour, at the end of his three years' intrigues, plotting, diplomatic moves, and taking every advantage of events, he was able to arrange with the Turkish Cabinet for the passage of Souchon's ships through the Dardanelles. That the *General* could thus act as the connecting link, and thereby conceal the flagship from the British Mediterranean Fleet, was in keeping with Teutonic efficiency.[1]

[1] A further advantage lay in the fact that from Smyrna there existed a land telegraph line to Constantinople, along which a cleverly worded message was sent asking permission to pass into the Black Sea to attack the Turks' historic enemies, the Russians.

Temporarily made happy by the arrival of the Piræus collier, Souchon now retired to a nice secluded island. All he needed was a few hours without molestation, and the future would be all right. With the collier astern, he therefore proceeded to Denusa, which lies just east of Naxos and nearly 140 miles north-east of Cape Malea. He arrived at 5.30 a.m. on August 9, and found in a deep deserted bay, surrounded by high mountains as well as towering cliffs, just that privacy which was requisite. Denusa island was not quite unpopulated, but only a few ignorant fishermen lived there, and they would not know much difference between the German White Ensign and the British. It was no intention of Souchon that he should be taken by surprise, so he soon landed a signalling party, who went to establish themselves at the heights and maintain a good look-out for smoke on the horizon. Lest, however, the fishermen should suspect the truth, this party came ashore in plain clothes, with rucksacks and walking-sticks, before climbing the highest peak. And another bit of dissimulation must be mentioned.

Some weeks before the War, when the *Goeben* and certain British warships happened to find themselves in the same port, the sailors of both nations had fraternised. There had also been an exchange of cap-ribbons. The latter now came in very useful, when the steam pinnace's crew bringing the signalling party boldly displayed the name of a British man-of war. Certainly, for typical thoroughness, Souchon's people were remarkable. Meanwhile the collier was secured alongside, the coal-bags were hurriedly dumped and emptied, day vanished into another night, the signallers were relieved every four hours, and now dawned the early morning of August 10. Then something unpleasant happened.

There came into the *Goeben's* wireless room the unmistakable note of a British warship, and this radio was growing so loud, so near, that the " hiking " party had to be summoned back from the heights, all coaling stopped, the collier cast off. Both the *Goeben* and *Breslau* had kept steam ready to leave at half an hour's notice, so at 5.45 a.m., after just one day's halt, the two vessels weighed anchors, and were soon working up to full speed. As they rush up the Ægean, let us for the moment transfer our attentions to the pursuers.

We left the *Indomitable* and *Indefatigable* to the west of Sicily. Had these two battle-cruisers been immediately ordered from this position to chase Souchon, when *Gloucester* reported that the enemy had just left Messina Straits, there would have been a very different story to tell. The *Gloucester* was in a perfect position for leading the two bigger ships straight to the target, and then there would have been every probability of the *Breslau* being sunk at long range, followed by the fatal maiming or death of the *Goeben*. If this could not occur before reaching Cape Matapan, then it would certainly have happened before arriving off the Dardanelles. It is interesting to know that the *Indomitable's* Captain was convinced of this. To the latter's great surprise, however, *Indomitable* and *Indefatigable*, having been joined by Sir Berkeley Milne in the *Inflexible*, were steaming slowly to Malta to refuel. The *Indomitable* reached that base just before 2 p.m. on August 7, almost at the same time that the *Gloucester* was shelling the *Breslau* off Southern Greece.

The *Indomitable's* Captain tells me that he needed only 400 tons of coal and 120 tons of oil; that he could have done without either and gone in support of *Gloucester*. Sir Berkeley Milne was still of the opinion that the enemy did not seriously mean to continue in Eastern waters, but would double back into the Adriatic. However, at 12.30 a.m. on Saturday, August 8, the Commander-in-Chief set forth from Malta with *Inflexible*, *Indomitable*, *Indefatigable*, and the light cruiser *Weymouth* to seek the enemy. With ships darkened, and men at defence stations, they shaped a course for Cape Matapan at 15 knots. It was not the first time this flagship had been bound for the Ægean: only in July the *Inflexible*, during a cruise, had visited Constantinople, when the ship's company had been presented by the Sultan with a large gift of Turkish sweetmeats. But now, within a mere breath of time, the outlook had become entirely transformed.

Whilst Souchon was frantically coaling at Denusa, Milne's far superior squadron swept ever nearer. "At 4 a.m.," wrote the *Inflexible's* First and Gunnery Lieutenant,[1] "we rounded Cape Malea and spread fifteen miles, on a N.E. search line. At 10 a.m. we were startled by intercepting a wireless signal, force 12, *i.e.* maximum intensity, and evidently originating from a high-power installation close to us (? *Goeben*). Raised steam for full-speed and hoped for the best. Sent the *Weymouth* on to search the islands to the north and east of the Gulf of Athens."

Now, this was on Monday the 10th, and reveals a most interesting situation. Cape Malea is, of course, the southern extremity of Greece, just east of Cape Matapan. At the hour when Malea was being passed, the Germans were but seven hours' steaming distance away to the north-east, and it is scarcely surprising that the British wireless signals suddenly began to grow louder. Perhaps if our squadron had maintained silence a little longer, and the enemy been given time to complete coaling, there would have been even now a clash between the rivals. The preponderating superiority of three battle-cruisers and one light cruiser over one battle-cruiser and one light cruiser should have made the result of an engagement beyond all doubt. In the course of the day *Weymouth* might have been expected to sight the enemy, who in any case would not have delayed his departure from Denusa much longer. That the *Goeben's* wireless was heard so loudly only four hours after Souchon had quitted his hiding-place, indicated the smaller distance which now separated the last and glorious chance of bringing matters to a climax.

Unfortunately, the direction of these German signals could not be ascertained, and the difficulty of investigating the numerous Ægean islands demanded considerable time. To hunt among these isolated places, under the lee of which the Germans might almost anywhere find a convenient halt,

---

[1] See "Memoir of Commander R. H. C. Verner" in *The Battle Cruisers at the Action of the Falkland Islands*, p. 44. London, 1920. Edited by Colonel Willoughby Verner.

meant an anxious and perhaps profitless task; for at that date it still seemed a possibility Souchon might be making another feint before getting away south to Port Said or Alexandria, sinking every British ship in the latter, carrying on through the Suez Canal, and then harassing the trade routes to India as the *Emden* was to do.

But all doubt was set at rest when, at 10.30 a.m. of the 11th, Admiral Milne received the startling news that *Goeben* and *Breslau* had reached the Dardanelles the previous night at 9 p.m. At 3 p.m. came the further news that the *General* had also reached Constantinople. The *Weymouth* was sent on at full speed to investigate, who at 10 a.m. of the 12th reported that *Goeben* and *Breslau* passed through Chanak at 10 p.m. of the 11th; that they were now at Constantinople, sold to the Turks, and renamed.

The information seemed so utterly fantastic, that British naval officers could hardly give it credence. The two German Mediterranean warships selling themselves to a neutral Power within the first week of hostilities needed further confirmation from Whitehall to be accepted as truth. Aboard the *Inflexible* this amazing intelligence of such an unsatisfactory conclusion was received with dismay. "The Ward Room was rather a comic sight this morning," recorded Lieut.-Commander Verner.[1] "We had just finished our morning 'Action Stations' when the news arrived, and the sight of the 'Control' and 'Quarters' Officers sitting dejectedly about the room made one think of the Lions' House at feeding time and a butchers' strike just announced."

But the tidings were all too true. From the 12th till 3 a.m. of Thursday the 13th, Admiral Milne remained patrolling up and down between Lemnos and Sigri, and spoke to a French liner, "which told us that on Wednesday morning she was boarded at Chanak by an officer from the *Goeben*, who threatened to sink the ship if she did not dismantle her wireless." But

---

[1] See "Memoir of Commander R. H. C. Verner" in *The Battle Cruisers at the Action of the Falkland Islands*, p. 45, London, 1920. Edited by Colonel Willoughby Verner.

now the *Inflexible*, *Dublin*, and *Weymouth* left for Malta, whilst the *Indomitable*, *Indefatigable* and *Gloucester* (who had rejoined after having coaled) were kept at Besika Bay to maintain a watch on the Dardanelles. All four ships kept steam up, and whilst two were under way patrolling, the others were anchored within sight of the Dardanelles entrance, ready to slip at a moment's notice: all this during daylight hours. At night each of the four units was steaming about expectant. Finally, on the 18th, *Inflexible* left Malta for Plymouth, Sir Berkeley Milne was recalled, the French Admiral de Lapéyrère became Commander-in-Chief of the Allies' Mediterranean Fleet, whilst Rear-Admiral S. H. Carden, Admiral Superintendent of Malta Dockyard, became the senior British flag-officer in that sea, Rear-Admiral Troubridge being presently ordered home.

CHAPTER V

THE TURKISH SCENE

" His Majesty expects the *Goeben* and *Breslau* to succeed in breaking through."

That was the telegram which the Kaiser on August 4 had sent to await Admiral Souchon at Messina, and no one will deny that this order was obeyed literally; yet even to the very last there were difficulties and narrow escapes. Twelve hours after leaving Denusa in a hurry, the Germans were off the Dardanelles entrance with the knowledge that their pursuers were at no great distance astern. "Let us in—don't keep us waiting," the two grey ships seemed to demand; but the outer forts of Kum Kale and Sedd-el-Bahr, which guarded the gate, trained their guns on the strangers. In turn the two ships went to action stations.

But Wangenheim had done his persuasive work: between the time when Denusa was left astern and the forts came into view the requisite permission had been wrested from the Ottoman Government. Thus, when the *Goeben* hoisted the signal for a pilot, two Turkish torpedo-boats steamed out, whose leader signalled the Germans to follow astern. No further time was wasted, the *Goeben* and *Breslau* saved their daylight nicely through the Narrows, and came to anchor for the night just above the Nagara promontory, only about a couple of hours before the *Weymouth* arrived outside the Dardanelles approaches. Thus, Souchon had actually by the smallest fraction been able to break through. Had he run short of coal (through his collier failing to make a rendezvous); had his request for entry been not granted immediately; he must have fallen a victim to Admiral Milne's squadron, and Turkey would never have been forced into the War against us. If the Germans had succeeded only at the expense of the flagship's boilers, it was to be entirely worth while.

For three days the two warships lay at anchor near Nagara, with the Sea of Marmora ahead of them and the Narrows astern. On the 11th they had the satisfaction of seeing the

S.S. *General* come up. She had steamed round from Smyrna in response to Souchon's wireless instructions, and the rest was now only a matter of time. Very shortly the *General*, with her spacious passenger accommodation, would be found most useful at Constantinople, and now the *Goeben* with *Breslau* could finish their thrilling voyage by crossing the Sea of Marmora, turning to the eastward, and bringing up in the Gulf of Ismid at Constantinople's very threshold. Tension could be relaxed, steam let down, and no longer need Souchon have cause for anxiety. The hated English battle-cruisers might be only a few miles distant, but they would never hurt him.

Those remaining days of an Ottoman summer were to witness an extraordinary state of things entirely brought about by deficient British diplomacy, the unfortunate affair of the undelivered two "Dreadnoughts," and the sudden arrival of two German units. Every day the local Press, "per agence Wolff," kept informing the people of Constantinople of the numerous victories which the German Army was winning in the north of Europe. The capture of Paris and the annihilation of the British Army were foretold as imminent—and the prophecy was not questioned. Sexagenarian German colonels would be seen in the cafés celebrating such announcements with magnums of champagne, and up from Ismid would come the *Goeben's* officers to sit at tables and watch some troupe of dancing-girls whilst the crowd of Europeans, Asiatics, Africans, and vicious-looking young Turks formed the strange background.

For the British Naval Mission the position became increasingly delicate, and one English officer tells me how ludicrous was the appearance of those officers from the *Goeben*, who had been ordered not to make themselves conspicuous whilst Turkey still continued nominally neutral. They used to land in plain clothes, pretending to be tourists from England! One, for instance, was noticed wearing " a sun-helmet with a puggaree hanging down behind (it was nearly midnight); riding-breeches, whose buttons meandered downwards towards the back of his calves to meet very much ready-made gaiters; and, for some reason best known to himself, carried a hunting-crop with a thong! It was odd seeing these people, knowing that one was at war with them, but there were no more conversations, or mutual exchanges of views upon the division of the world."

From now onwards the change speeded up. The arrival of Souchon with his impressive ships gripped the Governmental mind. Seeing was believing! These could become Turkey's own without the slightest difficulty, and the German-owned Press at once demonstrated that Germany's dilemma and Turkey's need coincided. Admiral Souchon was always coming ashore to interview Wangenheim and Ottoman officials; but the newspaper influence had already created the right atmosphere for the big deal that was to follow. "The very day that these vessels passed through the Dardanelles," wrote the United States Ambassador,[1] "the *Ikdam*, a Turkish newspaper published in Constantinople, had a triumphant account of this 'sale,' with big headlines, calling it a 'great success for the Imperial Government.'" By August 18 the transfer had taken place—at least outwardly. The German flag had been lowered and the Ottoman crescent hoisted instead. The *Goeben* became the *Yavuz Sultan Selim* and the *Breslau* was to be known henceforth as the *Midilli*. Fezes were dealt out to German officers and men, Turkish personnel joined for training, Souchon was appointed Commander-in-Chief of the Turkish Navy in lieu of Admiral Limpus, German ratings from the two ships became instructors both in the Turkish vessels and in signal stations; and the British naval officers were required to remain ashore, their places afloat being taken by Souchon's people. When finally the Mission was departing, the last words one of them heard were on the quay:

"Goo'-bye, Ingleezi. We fineesh with you."

But whilst the *Goeben* and *Breslau* might change their

[1] *Secrets of the Bosphorus*, p. 49.

names, and the German sailors change their hats, everyone in Constantinople knew that the sale was an utter sham: for the plain reason that Turkey hadn't the money. Nor did the German Government make any genuine effort to suggest that a bona fide purchase had been made. If we have admired the energy and enterprise of Souchon, we must remember that at the end he owed everything to Wangenheim. The pretext for getting the two ships into Turkish waters was nominally as a defence against the Russians; but this astute Ambassador well knew that henceforth they would always be based on Constantinople.

There was no immediate hurry for Turkey outwardly to enter hostilities, since she was quietly making detailed preparations that were not yet complete. As early as the latter part of August we find (on no less an authority than General Liman von Sanders)[1] that in Enver's office would be seen Souchon, Wangenheim, German Naval and Military Attachés, besides Turkish officials, already considering how the Suez Canal should be attacked if Turkey entered the War. "The representatives of the Navy warmly advocated such a step," adds Sanders. Nothing would have suited the ambitions of Enver so much as to make a conquest of Egypt. Meanwhile the Germans were improving and overhauling the Turkish shore batteries, repairing their coastworks, and energising Turkish crews. Wangenheim boasted at this time that there were 174 German gunners at the Dardanelles, and that the Straits could be closed within half an hour. Nominally Enver, Minister of War, was controller of the minefields, but it was Germany who controlled him. In the words of Djavid Bey, Minister of Finance, "The Germans have captured Turkey."

There is nothing like making oneself indispensable, if one seeks favours. The arrival of *Goeben* and *Breslau*, with their extremely efficient personnel, made the Constantinople sea force so potentially superior to the Russian Black Sea Fleet that the city felt a new sense of security. From that realisation it was certain that Turkey could neither let these

[1] *Five Years in Turkey*, p. 25.

two vessels leave her, nor that she could help throwing in her lot with the nation whose military officers had done so much during the last year reforming the army. Both parties were doubly happy that they could now keep Russia's corn from coming into the Mediterranean, though it was not till September 27 that Turkey finally closed the Narrows to shipping, and then defended the defile by laying rows of mines athwart the current.

With regard to this action, General Liman von Sanders[1] suggests that it was precipitated by one of our smaller craft that were watching the Dardanelles. "Colonel Djavid Bey, commanding the Dardanelles, told me later that the above defensive measure was caused by the unfriendly conversation of the commander of a British destroyer with the commander of a Turkish torpedo-boat which had gone outside the mouth of the Dardanelles." I well remember, however, a few weeks afterwards being aboard a North Sea destroyer and hearing of the British cargo steamer's Chief Officer, who happened to be coming out of the Dardanelles that day, and noted where the mines were being laid. This information reached the Admiralty.

But events were now being shaped towards an inevitable disrupture. From the day that the *Goeben* and *Breslau*[2] had been admitted within the Narrows, it was very obvious that either Turkey would be made to surrender this asylum, or else the Allies must use force. A further stage was reached when Britain demanded that the German naval personnel be dismissed, and Turkey was informed that the alleged purchase could not be regarded as real. At the same time, we were so anxious to prevent Turkey from becoming a belligerent on the side of the Germans, that the case was not pressed to its logical limit. The Turkish officials still persisted that these were no longer German men-of-war; nevertheless, the Ger-

---

[1] *Five Years in Turkey*, p. 33.
[2] Notwithstanding their change of flag and name, we shall continue throughout these chapters to speak of these ships by their original and German appellations.

man crews with their officers were very much on the spot. After Admiral Limpus' Naval Mission had been allowed to depart without even the most elementary courtesies, no fewer than 3800 Germans arrived from the Fatherland by train to be employed chiefly for manning the Turks' Navy and making ammunition. Having appropriated the Vickers Armstrong dock at Constantinople, they set to work repairing destroyers, riveting steel plates, hammering and working with such zest, night as well as day, that no one in that vicinity could get much sleep.

The penultimate stage began with the Turkish torpedo-boat's adventure just mentioned. She had passed out of the Straits, and was about to enter the Ægean, when the British destroyer stopped her. On being examined, she was found to have German seamen aboard, so the craft received prompt orders to go back. The destroyer acted legitimately, yet this snub could not be expected to make the Turks any more favourably disposed to us.[1] Then on October 27 a further complication occurred when a Russian minelayer, about to lay a danger area outside the Bosphorus, was discovered and chased by a Turkish torpedo-boat. On the next day out went the *Goeben* up the Bosphorus with the three-funnelled light cruiser *Hamidieh* and two destroyers into the Black Sea on revenge, whilst the *Breslau* was to expend her hate independently.

About 6.30 next morning the two Turkish destroyers bombarded Odessa and torpedoed a couple of Russian gunboats, sinking one. The *Goeben* exchanged fire with the Sebastopol batteries, and was hit in the after funnel, but presently to the southward encountered the Russian minelayer *Pruth*, which was supposed to have 700 mines and to be laying a trap across the *Goeben's* course. The latter signalled her to stop and abandon ship. According to one account she was abandoned and all left her except the Chaplain, and she

---

[1] This was at the time when (wrote the First Lord of the Admiralty to Sir Edward Grey) "We are daily trying to buy Turkish neutrality by promises and concessions." (See *The World Crisis* 1911-1915, p. 492.)

was then shelled and went down with him as the only man aboard. Another version is that she was sunk by the Russians themselves, her Captain refusing to leave the ship. Of the 200 people, only 72 were saved by the Turkish destroyers.

Meanwhile the *Hamidieh* had bombarded Theodosia, destroying barracks and harbour-works; whilst *Breslau* at Novorossisk had shot up the place so thoroughly as to sink all the steamers and wreck the petroleum tanks of this considerable oil port. Returning to Constantinople with the S.S. *Olga* as a prize, the squadron had done much more than destruction. Russia now declared war against Turkey; on November 1 the Allies' Ambassadors left Constantinople, and Admiral Carden, who on September 21 had been given command of the squadron off the Dardanelles, was ordered to commence hostilities against Turkey, and to bombard the outer Dardanelles forts at the first opportunity.

As for the *Goeben*, she now used as her berth an inlet known as Stenia Creek, which lies between the Black Sea and the Sea of Marmora, and just off the Bosphorus. Since she had brought back with her as prize the Russian S.S. *Olga*, this henceforth became a living ship for the German destroyer ratings when in harbour.

Thus, in more senses than one, Souchon's battle-cruiser and light cruiser were destined to commit Turkey to a long and elaborate struggle by the autumn; to involve the British and French Navies in a difficult and almost impossible task; and to lure our soldiers into a hopeless fight. We have seen by how small a margin Souchon had been allowed to reach the Dardanelles, yet is it not extraordinary that for two and a half months Turkey still remained neutral? It has been suggested from more than one source that had our diplomacy been the equivalent of Wangenheim's; had our favours offered to the Turks been on a more liberal scale; had the Russians been less independent and more co-operative with the Allies; the campaign which we are now about to follow need never have been undertaken.

But our own great weakness was to reveal itself: through

sheer lack of vision and failure to perceive what must inevitably follow a certain line of action, we soon found ourselves heading towards an awkward dilemma. From the first we had been overcome by surprise; which is the last thing a nation in war-time should wish to suffer. We had made plans, months ahead, for the Grand Fleet and the British Expeditionary Force in the event of Germany becoming our enemy; we had also (as already noted) arranged that the French African army should be ensured safe transport across the Mediterranean. But we had not taken such steps as would have enabled our sea and land forces instantly to be prepared for a Dardanelles campaign. And this blindness seems all the more strange when we recollect how in the final twelve months Germany was powerfully influencing Turkish tendencies. Thus by sheer want of imagination we had not suspected that a Turco-German alliance could be possible—not even with the Mittel-Europa idea well announced and the Berlin–Baghdad railway approaching reality; we had wilfully turned our backs on the clearest signs. It should never have been unexpected that Germany's weak Mediterranean force would make for the Sea of Marmora instead of the Adriatic. And, furthermore, we should have possessed detailed plans promptly to be enforced as the logical answer against this Eastern enmity.

The lessons of history, the conclusions derived from a study of strategy, all require time and peace for meditation and application. Sooner or later all important sea routes invite dispute in those neighbourhoods where the area begins to contract funnel-wise. The most perfect instances are such regions as the western approaches to the English Channel, or the Dover Straits at the opposite end, or the Straits of Gibraltar, or the restricted space between the north of Denmark and Southern Scandinavia, or the passage between Cape Bon and Sicily. These lanes mean so much politically and economically that they suggest both attack and defence: that is to say, the clashing of armed wills.

But the Dardanelles cannot be contemplated without thinking of some period when an angry contest will arise. Consider what it means that Turkey should be in the geographical position of denying all sea communication to Bulgaria, Roumania, and the whole of vast Russia whenever that country's northern ports are frozen. Reflect on the notable fact that the waters of the huge Black Sea can come out only through the Chanak Narrows and a bottle-neck not two miles wide; that therefore a few Turkish mines and forts can indefinitely separate Western Europe from Russian corn, oil, or sea communication. Surely, at the first signs of a general European war, the Dardanelles would be just one of those gateways which must be the scene of contention? After all the hints that the Balkans were the centre of future trouble, would it not have been plain precautionary sense to work out and pigeon-hole the necessary plans for the Dardanelles dilemma? Some day, as a sequel to increased steamer transportation, keener commercial rivalry, and German influence at Constantinople, it might be requisite to land on the Gallipoli peninsula and for the soldiers to capture those forts, for the sailors to sweep up the easily-laid mines, in order that freedom of movement might continue between West and East.

"Ships are unequally matched against forts. . . . A ship can no more stand up against a fort costing the same money than the fort could run a race with the ship." So summed up Admiral Mahan years ago in his well-known monograph on *Naval Strategy*; yet this very elementary principle, this basic idea, this inference from past history, this lesson learned from the mistakes of past centuries, was either forgotten or ignored by the autumn of 1914. There seems, from the outset, to have been no scientific, constructive scheme for conquering the Dardanelles, reaching the *Goeben*, and succouring our Russian ally; but an experimental, piecemeal method marked by impulsiveness and not reckoning in advance the cost.

Under such conditions a perfectly sound intention may be completely ruined and destined to collapse for lack of careful thought. A shipyard may produce the finest vessel with the most up-to-date engines; but if she is sent with the best of crews to find her way to Australia without compass, charts, or sextant, she may get wrecked on the voyage. Only a little more prevision and provision would have made disaster improbable. So it was with the Dardanelles adventure. We had all the material and the finest personnel, but they were not employed to the best purpose: yet arising out of this tremendous endeavour there emerged one of the grandest human dramas the world is ever likely to contemplate.

CHAPTER VI

THE FIRST DILEMMA

THE arrival of *Goeben* and *Breslau* in the Dardanelles almost synchronised with a further development, since it was on August 12 that Great Britain and France declared war on Austria, who was already at war with Russia. In accordance with a recent Franco-British arrangement, the supreme command of all British and French warships in the Mediterranean was from August 12 vested in the French Rear-Admiral Boué de Lapéyrère, with his base at Malta. This port, usually so full of ships flying the White Ensign, was to present the spectacle, for many a long day, of French warships with scarcely one British man-of-war within sight.

Admiral de Lapéyrère wasted no time, and within the first few days following the decision against Austria made a sweep up the Adriatic, encountered the small Austrian light cruiser *Zenta* (2264 tons) and destroyed her by shell-fire. Thereafter Austria's fleet, with the exception of a few rare occasions, remained throughout the War in port; the greater portion lying at Pola protected by minefields.

The end of August found Rear-Admiral Troubridge with his squadron watching the Dardanelles exit in case Souchon should emerge. The uncertainty of the Germans' intentions at that time created some anxiety with regard to the transports which were bringing troops through the Mediterranean to Marseilles and England, with a result that a powerful escort had to be provided. A further modification occurred on September 8, when Admiral Troubridge was recalled home to appear before a Court of Inquiry concerning the escape of Souchon's ships, but the Court eventually acquitted him.

Egypt, by reason of its canal as the lane along which transports and merchandise-carriers were coming northwards, was bound ere long to invite attack, though its distance from Constantinople and the temporary Turkish neutrality prevented immediate action. It is, however, to be borne in mind that the War's tendency had not sufficiently shown whether *Goeben* might make a sortie in the direction of Port Said and create havoc. On August 2 the German S.S. *Derfflinger* (9144 tons), of the Norddeutscher Lloyd, bound from Yokohama to Bremen, had arrived at Port Said, and next day her passengers with baggage had been put ashore. But if the voyage was suddenly ended, her Master, Captain F. W. Proesch, had not by any means finished. The *Derfflinger* began using her wireless to communicate with Souchon, and her coal would have been at the latter's disposal. Finally, however, this vessel was confiscated, as were nine other German and two Austrian vessels in Port Said, besides three German at Suez.

The British Naval Mission under Rear-Admiral Limpus had left Turkey on September 17, and at first there was some intention that he should succeed Rear-Admiral Troubridge in command of the Dardanelles squadron. A certain delicacy of feeling, even in time of war, vetoed this, and on September 21 Vice-Admiral Carden was appointed from Malta, Rear-Admiral Limpus taking his place at the last-mentioned base. But suspense still continued, since we were not yet at war with Turkey, though Admiral Carden was instructed that his sole duty was to sink the *Goeben* and *Breslau*, if they came out of the Dardanelles, no matter what flag they were flying. " You must deal at your discretion with any minor Turkish war vessel which may come out alone from the Dardanelles," he was instructed, " either ordering her back or allowing her to proceed as you may think fit."[1] Thus, when (as already noted) a Turkish torpedo-boat came out on September 26, only to be sent in again, wild indignation seized Constantinople, and next day the Dardanelles were closed.

On that date Admiral Carden had an overwhelming force capable of dealing with any sortie, even if Souchon should be accompanied by every Ottoman warship fit to be moved. Besides the two battle-cruisers *Indefatigable* (Flag) and *Indomitable*, the armoured cruisers *Warrior* and *Defence*, the light cruisers *Dublin* and *Gloucester*, the depot ship *Blenheim*

---

[1] *The World Crisis* 1911–1915, by the Rt. Hon. Winston S. Churchill, London, 1923, p. 491.

with her twelve destroyers, he had just been joined by Rear-Admiral Guépratte with the two French battleships *Vérité* and *Suffren*. The Germans were most thoroughly occluded, even if the door had been closed after they had been allowed to enter. A reminder of what might have happened off Messina was the arrival also of those three Malta submarines *B* 9 (Lieut. Geoffrey Warburton), *B* 10 (Lieut. S. M. G. Gravener), and *B* 11 (Lieut. Norman D. Holbrook). As proof of what could have been accomplished by such keen, daring young officers we shall in due course relate the manner in which the Victoria Cross was won. Based on Tenedos, with an old steamer as their mother ship, these three not very modern boats used to patrol the Dardanelles mouth that autumn from dawn to dark, waiting and hoping for the two targets which came not, till shortly before Christmas one of them gallantly went up against the current and found something to hit.

The Ottoman Empire, stretching east towards the Caucasus and Persia, south through Asia Minor and Syria to the Red Sea and Persian Gulf, comprising the entire littoral of the eastern Mediterranean, most of Arabia, and all Mesopotamia, was so vast that it provided in itself varieties enough for sea as well as land warfare, even if peace had reigned throughout Northern Europe. Thus, whilst the contest was centralised at the Dardanelles, the islands and indentations, the gulfs and bays immediately to the southward, could not remain wholly unaffected. Flanking the sea route through the Ægean, up which the Allied warships since August had been passing, and along which the transports would presently steam, were such significant inlets as the Gulfs of Alexandretta, Kos and Smyrna, out of which something interesting seemed sure to happen. The first two will come into the picture later, but actually on November 1, the initial day of war with Turkey, an Ottoman yacht about to lay mines was found lying alongside Vourlah jetty, Smyrna. It was two of our Dardanelles destroyers, *Wolverine* and *Scorpion*, who discovered them and compelled the minelayer to end her career by fire and shell. Of all the men-of-war types which, during the ensuing months, were to earn everlasting fame for never-ending toil and dangerous jobs, none was more conspicuous than the destroyer, as we shall eventually find; and it was a happy chance that to this class belonged the first honours of the campaign.

Then, two days later, followed that incident which has been so much criticised.

If the police are determined to capture two criminals, and know the latter are sheltering in the cottage of a third culprit, the most obvious and reasonable method is to creep up the garden unseen, surround the house, break in the door suddenly, and catch the wanted men asleep. The most foolish tactics would surely be to parade conspicuously in the road, make a great noise, smash the gate, go away, return after an interval, hurl stones through the windows, retreat yet again, and only *then* advance a third time for the purpose of trying to burst down the front door. Of course by this stage the men in the house would be in alarm, on the *qui vive*, with entrance barricaded and guns peeping through the windows. Now, that is, metaphorically, just what happened from November 3 onwards.

The "garden gate" was at the Dardanelles mouth, supported on the north side by the fort of Sedd-el-Bahr and on the south side by Kum Kale fort. The "windows" were the batteries further up the Straits.

Dropping all simile, let us plainly insist that the plan to seize and retain the Dardanelles should have been essentially one of surprise; that the Army and Navy should have arrived simultaneously and unexpectedly; that the troops should have been suddenly landed (as Admiral Mark Kerr has suggested) [1] at Kum Kale to take the forts in the rear and turn the guns on to Sedd-el-Bahr. Then, with soldiers on shore advancing from fort to fort, and the warships co-operating with their guns during the same progress, nothing could have stopped the minesweepers ahead from sweeping a safe passage for continued headway; and, having once passed the Narrows, it would have been a clear wide area across the sea of Marmora

[1] *The Navy in My Time*, p. 190.

to Constantinople itself. Astern would be the chain of forts held by our troops, guaranteeing a safe passage to colliers, ammunition ships, food ships, repair ships, and any other Fleet auxiliaries.

But, alas! before undertaking so important an effort at the Dardanelles those responsible for the task had not considered the subject in all its aspects. What was to be the cost? Could we afford it just now? If men and material were not yet available for doing the job properly, why not stay our hand, and not advertise our future intentions? In the meanwhile, let silent preparations be made not merely for collecting and training personnel, but also for working out detailed plans, so that our strength might be used to the best advantage. At least, before committing ourselves to certain acts, we should have calculated the likely sequels of such. If you begin by smashing up a nation's outer forts, the matter obviously cannot rest at that. Certain developments must inevitably follow. But of what nature?

If the enterprise were to stop at the bombardments, then this were little better than sabre-rattling. If, on the other hand, it was the first blow in a grand attempt to reach Souchon and open up means of communication with our Russian ally, the other blows should follow immediately. And were we ready to keep on striking? Furthermore, was this to be a naval operation entirely? Or a naval operation with some assistance from the Army? Or a military operation with some assistance from the Navy? If the first mentioned, was this decision in accordance with the lessons derived from history? Under modern conditions was it still true that no ships, however armed and armoured, could by themselves dominate land forts and not be themselves overcome?

One would have expected that the requisite information must have been known in Whitehall before November. Even at the beginning of June, the British Admiral who had been lent to the Greek Navy was aware that this must be a military operation—"a large military operation, with some naval assistance." "The British Fleet, backed by all the other

E

navies in the world, cannot force the passage of the Dardanelles."[1] Why? Because even at that date it was known that the Turks would lay seventeen rows of mines protected by batteries which could not all be destroyed by long-range bombardment from ships.

On November 3 Admiral Carden's squadron, in obedience to orders, took the first step towards that series of disasters which were to be the logical conclusion of false premises. The battle cruisers *Indefatigable* and *Indomitable*, with their 12-inch guns, attacked at long and safe range the six 11-inch and 10-inch guns of the ancient castle at Sedd-el-Bahr and the two 9·4-inch guns of the modern Cape Helles fort. These and the battery of 5-inch howitzers of Cape Tekke comprised the outer defences on the European side. Thanks to the battle-cruisers' superiority, this attempt was successful in putting most of the enemy's guns out of action, besides damaging the forts and causing many casualties. On the Asiatic side was Kum Kale, with nine guns of various calibres, from 11-inch to 6-inch, whilst to the south-west thereof, and on higher ground, was Orkanieh, with a couple of 9·4-inch. It was against Kum Kale and Orkanieh that the two French battleships *Suffren* and *Vérité* (each having four 12-inch guns as their primary armament) directed their fire, though with such less satisfactory results that on a later occasion we shall find afforded opportunity for one of the most gallant episodes in British naval annals.

This initial adventure has been much criticised as stupid and imprudent. Its outcome was certainly at the best inconclusive, since a free entrance to the Straits had to-day not been made certain. Mr. Winston Churchill, First Lord of the Admiralty at that period, has sought to justify the bombardment by saying it was essential " to know accurately the effective ranges of the Turkish guns and the conditions under which the entrance to the blockaded port could be approached."[2] On the other hand, the effect against the

---

[1] *The Navy in My Time*, pp. 182–184.
[2] *The World Crisis*, 1911–1915, p. 469.

Turks was exactly that which could have been expected. General Liman von Sanders, in his volume already quoted, says that whilst we did certainly silence Sedd-el-Bahr and Kum Kale, the bombardment threw the Turks into a state of apprehension. He sought to allay their fears, and when the attack was not renewed, and it became realised that it was a mere isolated incident, the enemy regained some of their previous complacency. Nevertheless, the German military officers at Constantinople well enough appreciated that, after we had smashed up half the Dardanelles' outer gate, it was time to take a hint, and no less a personage than Field-Marshal von der Goltz, who had been sometime Governor in Belgium, was sent south to become the Sultan's Adjutant-General, reaching Constantinople on December 12, 1914. The transference of such a high expert, and at such a time, is so significant as to require no further emphasis. So, also, this autumn came Admiral von Usedom from Germany to Constantinople as Inspector-General of coast artillery and mines.

Meanwhile the British Dardanelles squadron maintained its watch outside the Straits, and Souchon's squadron was able to go through the Bosphorus into the Black Sea, engaged in escorting Turkish troop transports along the coast to Samsun and Trebizond. On November 17 the *Goeben* and *Breslau* were in action with the Russian fleet, during which the *Goeben* received damage, as did the two Russian battleships *Evstafi* (12,733 tons), and the *Rostislav* (8880 tons), a vessel of questionable fighting value. A few weeks later, on December 10, the *Goeben* bombarded Batoum, and afterwards cut the telegraph cable in the Black Sea.

During this same month, however, the Turco-German naval forces were to receive a couple of pretty hard knocks. First of all they were given a very real surprise when the immunity of the Straits was violated by a small vessel of 314 tons: she was the old-fashioned British submarine *B* 11 (Lieut. Norman Douglas Holbrook), which on December 13 dived off Cape Helles, hugged the European shore, and slowly made up against the current. She got near the Narrows shortly before 10 a.m., and sighted the two-funnelled Turkish battleship *Messudieh*, which was guarding the mines, under five rows of which Lieut. Holbrook had bravely proceeded. This Turkish veteran was forty years old, and had been used till a few weeks before to fly the flag of Admiral Limpus of the British Mission. She would have been useless in the open sea, but her battery of twelve 6-inch and twenty-eight smaller quick-firers made it worth while for her to be anchored as a floating fortress, in case any of the Allies' destroyers, torpedo-boats, or submarines should dare to approach.

To attack her from a submarine of such weak power as *B* 11 possessed was no easy task; yet Holbrook succeeded in firing a torpedo, and the ship replied with a shower of shells that splashed all round. The last picture of her through the periscope was that she was sinking and settling down by the stern. Holbrook began to return home, but the current drove him ashore, whereupon all the guns within range assailed *B* 11 and made life full of excitement. Then, at length, she bumped off, and again she dived below the hidden dangers, till she reached the Dardanelles entrance soon after 2 p.m. and came to the surface. For this original and daring exploit Lieut. Holbrook won the first Victoria Cross given to a submarine, and his second-in-command, Lieut. S. T. Winn, received a D.S.O.; whilst everyone else aboard was awarded either a D.S.C. or the D.S.M. Later on the guns were salved, and the Turks down at Chanak preserved as a souvenir a piece of Holbrook's torpedo.

The second shock occurred about Christmas. On December 27 the *Goeben*, which had been out in the Black Sea having a brush with the Russian Fleet, was returning home when she found herself amidst a minefield which her enemies had laid about 700 yards short of the Bosphorus. That was the time when Field-Marshal Baron von der Goltz was aboard, and everyone got thoroughly shaken up by the explosion: yet this ship was to go through many perils, and in spite of the two large holes in her hull she floated back into Stenia Creek.

CHAPTER VII

CRUISER ADVENTURES

MEANWHILE a most interesting series of minor operations was taking place off the coasts of Syria and Asia Minor, which for blunt courage and hard-fisted enterprise carry one back to the juvenile fiction of boyhood's days. Those delightful yarns of night landings on an enemy's shore, of picket-boats and hairbreadth escapes, of occasional casualties but final victory, were now to become real: by a curious turn of war events, fiction had become fact.

These little episodes well demonstrate how much can be done by self-confidence united with courage, initiative, and determination. H.M.S. *Doris* was not a crack ship in 1914, but already sixteen years old and of 5600 tons. Nor was her speed anything to boast about, though in her palmiest days she could do her 20 knots. Her heaviest guns were eleven 6-inch, but her commanding officer, Captain (now Admiral Sir Frank) Larken, with Commander Kenneth Brounger, the other officers and crew, made up in keen efficiency for any weakness in *materiel*.

Our story begins in December 1914, when a certain amount of uneasiness was being felt in regard to Egypt. Were the Turks about to make an attack via Syria? And what preparations had the enemy so far arranged? For the settling of these queries two or three cruisers might be able to do some useful investigation; so Admiral Peirse, in charge of the Suez Canal defences, despatched the Russian cruiser *Askold* and H.M.S. *Doris* to reconnoitre the Syrian coast northwards for most of four hundred miles to Alexandretta; that is to say, along the flank of the enemy's advance. The very setting of this narrative suggests the primitive shipping of Biblical times: the mention of Jonah and Askelon, of Sidon and Antioch is made, however, in conjunction with modern rifles and railway locomotives. These cruisers set to work independently, and we will confine our attention to the *Doris*, which began her adventures off Askelon. Observing some

Turkish soldiers of the coast patrol, Captain Larken shelled the earthworks, and then steamed north, whilst scrutinising the shore for any other evidence. Passing *Askold*, who was bound south after capturing three steamers, *Doris* was some distance below Sidon when she sent off under Commander Brounger a landing party, who sawed through many a telegraph pole and cut the wires over a stretch covering several miles.

Having thus interrupted part of the Turkish communications, *Doris* next day spoke an Italian steamer, from whose Captain it was learned that Alexandretta was very active as a centre for troops and war stores. Here boats in sections (intended for crossing the Suez Canal) were being collected, and altogether the place was of considerable importance as a clearing town; for the Berlin–Baghdad railway at this date was not yet completed, nor was the tunnel under the Taurus Mountains constructed. Consequently the trains deposited their troops at Alexandretta, whence these soldiers travelled by road to join the line again at Aleppo before continuing south.[1] Obviously Alexandretta was deserving of Captain Larken's attention.

So, having entered the great bay of Alexandretta, and reached a position two miles north of Jonah's Pillar (erected to commemorate Jonah's memorable nautical experiences), a landing-party, with faces blackened and oars muffled, was sent ashore. The railway line and telegraph wires were successively cut, the party returned aboard, and at 2.30 a.m. through the darkness could be heard the rumbling of an approaching train. Thirty-five trucks, loaded with camels, were derailed and the line was blocked! Three and a half hours later a second train arrived and stopped, whereupon *Doris* shelled the engine, and then went north to shell a long bridge; thereby cutting off the locomotive's retreat.

To the Turkish Military Governor of Alexandretta, Captain Larken wrote a letter demanding surrender of all

---

[1] Acknowledgment is made to *Smoke on the Horizon*, by Vice-Admiral C. V. Usborne, C.B., C.M.G.

THE RUSSIAN CRUISER *ASKOLD*

H.M.S. *DORIS*

British and Allied subjects, all munitions of war, and any locomotives, under threat of bombardment. This letter was taken ashore in a cutter under a flag of truce, and a reply promised for next day; so at 8 a.m. the boat went in again. The answer however, was defiant, and stated that for every Turk killed, one or more Britons would be shot.

There came off, also, the United States of America's acting Vice-Consul, who said that 500 British subjects were imprisoned in Damascus, and that Alexandretta was also full of stores. So Captain Larken gave assurance that in the event of the threatened deaths occurring, the Turkish officer who should give such an order would be handed over for suitable treatment after the end of war. There now came another locomotive towards Jonah's Pillar to connect up the second train stopped by derailment and take it back northward; wherefore Commander Brounger with eighty men in a steamboat and two cutters were put ashore, protection being afforded by the steamboat's machine guns and the *Doris'* 6-inch.

This landing was received with opposition, for the Turks spattered rifle bullets, but the enemy were driven into flight by the bursting shells. That enabled the sailors to advance over a marshy plain to a long, low bridge which crossed a river. Now, the name of this place was Payas, about six miles north of Jonah's Pillar, the bridge being a mile inland from the coast. Not long was the demolition party setting to work with its gun-cotton, and up went the bridge, followed by the capture of the railway station, whence the telegraph instruments were removed and (at their own supplication) the Armenian station-master with his two officials, who were brought aboard.

The enemy's traffic arrangements between Constantinople and Alexandretta had thus been fairly disorganised, and now to the latter port proceeded *Doris*. A cutter was rowed ashore to fetch a letter from the Governor agreeing to destroy all the local rolling-stock. This consisted of two engines, which were eventually brought out of their shed and demolished. Nor was that all. Captain Larken's ship destroyed by shell-fire a road bridge near Jonah's Pillar on the main road, and visited the north side of Alexandretta Gulf and found the German S.S. *Odessa* had sunk herself to avoid capture. This steamer was now destroyed to prevent further use.

In short, the enemy's coast route had been stopped, and the Turks were compelled to make a long, tedious detour round the northern side of the Taurus Mountains to Aleppo, thereby causing both inconvenience and delay. *Doris* returned to Suez with the satisfaction of having rendered valuable direct aid by the simplest of methods.

This systematic worrying of road and rail routes was in January shared by another small cruiser, H.M.S. *Proserpine*, but in February H.M.S. *Philomel* was to suffer a serious reverse.

The latter was of 2575 tons, and the beginning of war found her in New Zealand waters, her commanding officer, Captain (now Admiral) P. H. Hall Thompson, being Naval Adviser to the New Zealand Government. " I had the one little ship only partly manned," he tells me, " and completed her manning entirely by volunteers of all sorts from the shore. So we went to sea, and placed ourselves at the disposal of the Admiralty. These men did not see New Zealand again for practically three years." After performing good service in the Red Sea, *Philomel* came into the Mediterranean. The appearance of Malta Harbour (whither she came for docking) was extraordinary. " It was full of men-of-war of every sort and description, but amongst them the *Philomel* was the only one flying the White Ensign, the whole of the remainder being French ships."

It was on February 8 (1915) that *Philomel* had sent off a landing party to examine a large number of pack-animals seen coming along the coastal road towards Alexandretta, the scene again being near that Pillar where Jonah is reputed to have been cast up by the whale. Before being landed, the party of two officers and fifteen men were covered by the *Philomel's* guns, which swept the place with shrapnel. Without opposition her people got ashore, but, unknown to them, some

300 Turkish regulars were behind the hills and coming through the adjoining thick trees. The enemy waited till our men were well away from the boats, and then opened a heavy musketry fire from several directions, which compelled a retirement along a dry river-bed, carrying all the wounded except one.

The boats could not be reached, as every man who showed himself was promptly shot, so they lay there till darkness fell, when they succeeded in embarking all, including three wounded and three dead; though one man was still missing. Everyone supposed the latter to have been killed, but the ship's searchlights that night discovered him on the beach, and a volunteer rescue party put off from the *Philomel*, the lights having first been turned off to prevent their presence being betrayed.

With muffled oars they gained the beach, groped about in the dark, moonless night, and alas! had to return without finding him.[1] Searchlights were again turned on, and again the man was descried moving. Once more the boat put off, and this time they fetched him on board. It was a plucky endeavour, for the enemy still remained about, and the search-party had been ashore altogether for some four hours. Unfortunately, the man was dangerously wounded, and he died two days later under the White Ensign. He had not come all the way from the Antipodes to be buried in Asia Minor.

[1] Admiral Hall Thompson has placed at my disposal an account written by him in *The War Effort of New Zealand*.

CHAPTER VIII

THE RUSSIAN PROBLEM

THE year 1915 opened with certain indications which were unsettling after the public had been lulled into excessive optimism by the speeches of our politicians and articles in the Press. Apart from anxieties on the Western Front, there was now to loom up a new complication in South-eastern Europe.

The mentality of Russians, with their extravagance in personal and public management of affairs, their inertia, their pessimism, their curious lack of efficiency, has always separated them from Western Europe farther than by so many geographical miles. Things were going badly now with Russia's armies; she had suffered immense losses of men, had become short of munitions, and it was quite within the sphere of possibility that she might throw in her hand altogether, make a separate peace with Germany, and thus (with so many thousand German troops released from the East) place an additional burden on the Allies that could not then be borne. In particular, she was being severely threatened in the Caucasus by the Turks, whose transportation had been assured by Souchon.

When, therefore, on January 2, Petrograd telegraphed the British Government asking for a demonstration to be made against the Dardanelles as a diversion, this appeal could not be denied. And, since at that early date Kitchener's Army was not yet ready and no British troops were available, it was decided that the Navy must be asked to tackle the effort of getting through the Dardanelles alone. Admiral Sturdee, who had but recently avenged the disaster of Coronel by his victory of the Falklands, was Lord Fisher's choice to force the Dardanelles Straits and Narrows, but the former wisely declined, having seen that such a project could not be practicable. Furthermore, since the Grand Fleet battleships could not be spared, the old-fashioned vessels from the Channel Fleet, such as the *Majestic*, must bear the new burden.

There was every reasonableness in the strategical idea of winning through to the Bosphorus. Even to-day German authorities are still convinced both of its wisdom and its practicability: there can be no possible doubt as to the soundness of this conception. I have been in conversation and correspondence with many of the British naval officers who played a leading part in that campaign, and there is a wonderful unanimity that we could, and ought to, have got through. Everything, however, depended on employing the right methods. It was because Russia was separated from her allies and unable to receive supplies of munitions, that ultimately she did collapse altogether. If only the Dardanelles could be freed, and Turkey kept quiet, all danger would be removed from Egypt, all threats against India swept aside, the wavering Balkan states would come in on behalf of the Allies, and the crafty Ferdinand of Bulgaria especially would perceive on which side it would be safer to show his sympathies. The Berlin–Baghdad railway running through his territory would in that case not be available in the near future for carrying German munitions for the Turkish forts. Besides Bulgaria and Roumania, Greece would have been with the Allies, Russia could have beaten Austria into peace, and Germany would have followed. Nothing, in truth, succeeds like success: nothing is worse than a vicious circle. All that the former demanded was a quick, sudden, competent surprise. Or, in plain terms, three army corps to capture Gallipoli peninsula, with the Navy assisting.

Such was the situation during the first two months of 1915. It would certainly have been a welcome convenience had we been able to send cargo steamers to fetch out Russian wheat and wood, and tankers to bring home Black Sea oil for our warships. Now the essential need was primarily strategical and political: our failure was destined to bring about not only Russia's defeat, but also the subsequent Revolution, the murders of the royal family, and to establish Communism as a world danger. History offers few clearer instances of what serious results may follow from mistakes created by persons in responsible positions.

Had the Russian temperament been different, much might

have been possible. With the British off the Dardanelles and our Allies pressing on from the Black Sea, the Turks should have been caught between pincers—armies advancing against Constantinople from both sides. That, alone, would have created a Governmental panic in the Ottoman capital. But Russia has never known how to use her fleets, either in the Japanese war or since. During 1914 and 1915, and even later still, the Russian Baltic Fleet was not allowed to pursue an active policy, but kept within harbour either at Helsingfors or Reval. Those in authority regarded it not as an independent force with its own war-like duties, but as a means for defending Petrograd and as an extension of the Army's right wing: in fact, the Commander-in-Chief, Admiral von Essen, was made subordinate to the General in command of the Army.

So, too, with the Russian Black Sea Fleet, whose material strength should certainly have stopped Turkish communication in and out of the Bosphorus. Here the basic defect was identical with that of the Baltic Fleet; for in the south the Grand Duke Nikolai Nikolaievich was Generalissimo by sea as well as land. He regarded squadrons as a mere adjunct to his army. But a secondary factor was that the Czar, mindful of the Tsushima disaster, was not eager to risk his ships. Now, of what did the Black Sea Fleet consist?

There were six battleships, two light cruisers, twenty-six destroyers, ten torpedo-boats, eleven submarines, besides minelayers and minesweepers. The battleships *Rotislav* and *Georgi Pobiedonosetz* were old and of inferior worth. The *Tri Sviatetelia* (13,318 tons), with four 12-inch guns, was built in 1896; the *Panteleimon* (12,480 tons), also with four 12-inch guns, dated from 1902; the *Ivan Zlatoust* and the *Evstafi* (12,733 tons), likewise with four 12-inch guns, dated from 1910 and 1911, respectively. But the best speed of any among this half-dozen was quite 9 knots slower than *Goeben* at her best, and the practical result of this we shall soon see.

The two light cruisers *Kagul* and *Pamiat Merkurya* (6645

tons), 24 knots speed, were only ten years old. Altogether, with sixteen 12-inch guns in four battleships, and an adequate destroyer force for screening by day and attack by night, one might have expected greater aggressive venture, instead of spending most of the time at the eastern end of the Black Sea. Three 23,000-tons super-" Dreadnoughts " were at this time being built at the Sebastopol and Nikolaieff dockyards, of which the first was due to be launched in 1916. With the commissioning of these, *Goeben's* life would have become precarious, and she realised it.

So, instead of any decisive action to settle command of the Black Sea, there was this winter just a series of detached incidents. From January 24 to February 18 (the day preceding the big Dardanelles effort) the Black Sea Fleet spent its time cruising about the eastern end to prevent an expected landing of Turkish troops, whilst the Russian Caucasus Army was being moved to different positions. As to the enemy, on January 27 the *Breslau* with *Hamidieh* made a reconnaissance into that quarter, when the former was chased for seven hours by the two cruisers *Kagul* and *Pamiat Merkurya*. The time soon came when Russian submarines also made it dangerous for Turkish transports to be risked, so that the *Breslau* had to do this work herself, and under cover of night.

Such, then, was the situation in the Black Sea, whence little help could be expected by way of co-operation. Instead of being an asset, our Russian ally was a serious liability, and was to force us into doing something for which we were far from being fully equipped. Time was wasted in Whitehall whilst the Departments made up their minds as to whether troops should be sent, days were spent in telegraphing between the Admiralty and Vice-Admiral Carden. This questioning and answering began on January 3, when Admiral Carden was asked if he considered the forcing of the Dardanelles by ships alone a practicable proposition. Two days later came the reply that the Admiral did not consider the Dardanelles could be rushed, but might be " forced by extended operations with a large number of ships."

That this was an unduly optimistic opinion—quite apart from its exaggerated belief in the superiority of ships contending against forts—was well proved when the Admiral's telegram arrived giving his scheme, which was divided into four sections :—

(1) Reducing the outer forts.
(2) Then overcoming the intermediate defences up to Kephez.
(3) Conquering the defences at the Chanak Narrows.
(4) Sweeping a channel through the minefield for the fleet to follow; reducing the forts above the Narrows, and then proceeding across the Sea of Marmora towards Constantinople.

The force he requested was twelve battleships, three battle-cruisers, three light cruisers, one flotilla-leader, sixteen destroyers, six submarines, twelve minesweepers; together with repairing ship, hospital ship, supply and ammunition ships, colliers, and four seaplanes.

On January 13 the War Council decided that the Admiralty should prepare for a naval expedition in February to bombard and take Gallipoli peninsula, with Constantinople as its objective, so preparations now began. Admiral Carden was informed that his plan had been approved, and that Rear-Admiral de Robeck would be his second-in-command; that battleships and cruisers, which had been employed in commerce protection and other duties in various parts of the world, would, together with twenty-one minesweeping trawlers, be sent to him.

In such circumstances was the resolve made to bombard an historical truth by 12-inch naval guns, and we are now to witness that the truth remained generally unbroken, even though guns wore themselves out, as men wore out their lives, in the valiant effort to achieve the impossible. If the attack on November 3 had been rather a private, departmental attempt lacking the Cabinet's authorisation, this fresh undertaking had certainly the War Council's backing, though none could have doubted that a great gamble was being staked.

TURKISH PRISONERS AT MUDROS

KEPHALOS BAY

There is something attractive in the tremendous preparations which were at once set going; in the summoning of this vessel and that from all the seas; in the fine organisation which could respond so promptly to Admiral Carden's wishes. Consider, first, the trawlers. A few short months ago these steam vessels, with their hearty fishermen crews, had been at work trawling out of Grimsby, Aberdeen, and elsewhere. Then they had been taken up by the Admiralty, one after another, and sent to sweep channels along the North Sea coast. Some of the men had been blown up on mines and gone down with their ship; others had been blown up more than once, and then gone out again in another ship. Now, at a sudden signal, thirteen of these trawlers with their men had been recalled to harbour, coaled, stored, provisioned, watered, sent down the English Channel, and on January 28 had left England for the winter voyage across the Bay of Biscay and round Gibraltar. It was quick work, for another eight soon followed, so that by February 21 the whole twenty-one had reached Malta, and then proceeded to the Ægean. Several of them actually arrived at the Dardanelles in time for the first sweeping operation of February 19.

The main Allied base was at Lemnos, opposite Tenedos (which had in ancient times been the base for the Greek fleet during the siege of Troy). Lemnos was inhabited mostly by Greeks, who, not wishing to be drawn into the War, withdrew, so that the harbour of Mudros, with its spacious area, virtually lost its nationality for some time. Situated some forty-five miles from the Dardanelles entrance, it was thus within easy steaming distance of the war theatre. But much nearer was the mountainous and wooded island of Imbros, only ten miles from Cape Helles, and twelve from Suvla. Here at the small bay of Kephalos was to be established another base. The entrance was wide, though the bay was exposed to easterly and northerly winds.

By a mere twist of fate some of these older ships which, but for the War, expected soon to be scrapped, were to see far more active service and firing than ever their Grand Fleet sisters. A large number of the officers and men had come back from retirement, after several years in civilian life, leaving their gardens, their houses and cottages, never daring to hope that they would once hear a gun bark in anger. When, towards the end of January, the sudden change of orders directed them through the Gibraltar Straits, it was to receive a welcome change from the boredom of patrolling. Calling at Malta, thence at that Ægean island of Skyros where Achilles was hidden by his mother to save him from the Trojan war, the far-flung ships converged singly on Tenedos.

The *Vengeance* (Captain Bertram H. Smith), which had been selected to fly Admiral de Robeck's flag, came up from Gibraltar to Tenedos, and arrived on February 8. Almost immediately Captain and Admiral went off in the destroyer *Mosquito* to inspect the Dardanelles entrance, and the coast up to the Gulf of Xeros. So, too, came the *Cornwallis* (Captain A. P. Davidson), and presently her officers with gun-layers were taken for a trip in one of the destroyers to see the kind of targets they were about to shell. All the way from China came the *Triumph*,[1] which had just gathered a considerable amount of valuable experience as to the effects of bombarding forts from the sea. One of her officers tells me that when she was employed in the siege of Tsing Tao " it was clearly demonstrated early in the operations that ships were almost entirely ineffective against modern land fortifications. It was impossible even to see the forts, which had no difficulty in hitting ships at considerable ranges, the accuracy of the forts' fire being most marked. At Tsing Tao there happened to be a blind arc of about 5 degrees in which the forts were unable to fire, and the *Triumph* did some valuable work bombarding redoubts whilst remaining inside this arc. On the only occasion when the ship inadvertently drifted outside the arc, the fort managed to land a 9-inch projectile which exploded in the main top, causing a number of casualties. A second round from this German fort missed the ship's

---

[1] This vessel in shelling Tsing Tao was the first British ship that, for a very long while, had engaged a fort.

stern by a few feet, and the whole occurrence lasted less than a minute, while the ship was being manœuvred back into the blind arc. I mention this as an example of the accuracy of land guns, the range being in the neighbourhood of 10,000 yards."

The oldest British battleship of all the assemblage getting ready for " The Day " was the *Majestic*, which had been launched twenty-one years previously, but she was about to play a most prominent part in the tragedy. During October 1914 she had been sent out into the Atlantic to escort the big Canadian convoy that was coming to England. Later, during that memorable New Year's early morning, she had been on her way down Channel, and had reached St. Catherine's Point, off the Isle of Wight, when news of the *Formidable's* sinking by the first German submarine to reach so far west sent the *Majestic* into Portsmouth, whence she proceeded to Portland. Then, on the last day of the month, it was obvious that something was bound to happen when the *Majestic* was ordered to embark four 6-inch howitzers. On the 1st of February she filled up with coal, and next day left Portland for Malta in company with the *Irresistible*. Both were bound eventually for the Dardanelles: neither of them ever came home again.

It was blowing a full gale in the Bay of Biscay, with green seas leaping over the *Majestic's* fore turret. At Malta, in the next dock, was found the French battleship *Jean Bart*, with an ugly wound that gaped as a warning of what might follow before long at the Dardanelles. On December 21 this very modern Dreadnought had been steaming slowly (9 knots) through the Otranto Straits, unescorted, when the Austrian submarine *XII* torpedoed her forward, and the *Jean Bart* was lucky that, instead of sinking, she managed to limp along to Malta.

It may seem strange that already the *Majestic*, too, should be dry-docked: but there happened to be a special reason. The Admiralty had decided that, in view of the mine menace which would have to be accepted up the Dardanelles, there should be not merely minesweeping vessels, but minerakers fitted to the bows of battleships, in the hope of thus sweeping the buoy-like danger aside; and in order to fit this weird, awkward, "cow-catcher" contraption, the ship had thus to be dried out. The accompanying photograph illustrates the clumsiness of this novelty, which was ever unpopular among officers and hated by the ship's company. Whilst excellent were the inspiration and purpose, it was an awkward affair to handle, with its great 60-feet beam, bits of iron, struts, tackles, wires and what not. When rigged, it had the effect of making the ship a beast to steer.

At Malta two howitzers per ship were mounted on the top of the turrets, as shown in the next picture, and this second innovation made it obvious that the old ships were intended to do their work at close range. "We heard that four ships were expected to be sunk during the coming operations, and that the *Majestic* was one of them. We resolved that should we meet with that fate," wrote an officer in his diary, "it should be with our tails up." Both prophecy and resolution were fulfilled to the letter. She arrived at Tenedos on February 25, a week late for the first big day, but her exciting rôle in the drama would begin during the next act.

On the same day steamed into Tenedos the battleship *Lord Nelson*, which likewise had begun the year with a thrill. In the middle watch, about 3 a.m., when it was still cold and dark, she was leading the line at the time *Formidable* went down. A horrible night, with a gale coming on and heavy sea, was made still more trying because the fleet had to make off at full speed, leaving the two small cruisers to do the rescue work. These presently came into Portland with their t'gallant masts carried away by the wind. Six weeks later the *Lord Nelson* ceased to be a flagship, and at night left for the Dardanelles, immediately encountering more heavy weather.

In time for the great occasion had anchored that fine battle-cruiser *Inflexible*. We last saw her leaving the Dardanelles and the Mediterranean for Plymouth. Since that date she had led a full, exciting, and historic life. Under her new

THE "COW-CATCHER" MINE-RAKER
Fitted at the battleship's bows.

A 6-INCH HOWITZER
Mounted on the turret in one of the *Majestic* class battleships.

commanding officer, Captain [1] Richard Phillimore, she had been at Scapa Flow serving with the Grand Fleet, patrolling the North Sea; then in November she had been sent with Admiral Sturdee, as his flagship, across the South Atlantic, and on December 8 had distinguished herself by her excellent gunnery when von Spee's squadron was defeated at the Battle of the Falklands. By the middle of January she was at Gibraltar, and on the 24th at Skyros, where the British battle-cruiser *Indefatigable* and the French men-of-war had also anchored. Thus, by a complete circle of events the *Inflexible* had come back to find the Dardanelles still sheltering the *Goeben*. As one of her officers now remarked, "We *ought* to have done" the job on August 12: both the right time and the right way of performing the essential feature had been missed. And the same opinion was held this February by many other officers. Want of thought, want of plan, want of adequate preparation seemed to foretell no happy result.

These immediately preceding days up the Ægean were marked by bad weather. On February 3, in fact, it was " blowing a hurricane (force of squalls 11–12), sleet, hail and snow. Coaling impossible, could not stand on deck owing to force of wind," recorded Commander Verner of the *Inflexible*. But presently she and other warships fuelled, and took aboard gravel in bags, which was to protect the feed-tanks. Altogether the *Inflexible* and *Goeben* were two of the most historic ships throughout the whole War, and the pity is that the two never had a chance of meeting in an engagement. So keen was the expectation, that a few days before Admiral Carden's inauguration of the February attack, the *Inflexible* was rehearsing her gunnery with a very realistic silhouette of *Goeben* for target.[2] Of the distinguished, and well-nigh fatal, part the *Inflexible* played in the Dardanelles we are about to become

[1] Now Admiral Sir Richard F. Phillimore, G.C.B., K.C.M.G., M.V.O. Her previous commanding officer, Captain A. H. Loxley, was appointed to the *Formidable*, and went down with her on New Year's morning, 1915.

[2] See Memoir of Commander Rudolf Verner, *The Battle Cruisers at the Action of the Falkland Islands*, p. 54.

acquainted: yet, even after her narrow escape, she went back to the North Sea, and was present at the Battle of Jutland. A wonderful record for one unit!

For Admiral Limpus it was a curious change-over that he, who a short while ago was assisting the Turkish Navy, now forsooth found his duty to be that of rendering every help against his late masters. Under this energetic organiser the British battleships calling at Malta were filled up with coal and beef, or whatever their wants. Before preparing for action, main and fore topmasts were taken down, and torpedoes transferred to a store-ship, lest there should be any sympathetic explosion when mines were hit. Pieces of cable were put over the upper-deck casemates in some ships, sacking and canvas protection around the conning-tower as well as signalling positions. If some of the vessels thus took on a more stumpy and less navy-like neatness, they were more inconspicuous, and ready for a fight.

On quarter-decks would be seen crews gathered to hear commanding officers address them as to what was about to be attempted, and loud cheers indicated the combatant enthusiasm. One Captain even had a blackboard erected, and on it drew sketchy pictures with the agility of a music-hall lightning caricaturist. The aeroplane-carrier *Ark Royal* reached Tenedos, and the Admiral went ashore to choose an aviation site, but the soft ploughy ground and stones made the problem a little complicated. In those early days of flying, aircraft were not the highly efficient weapons that carry heavy bombs over the enemy; but it was hoped that, by means of aerial spotting, the naval gunners would be guided reliably. On February 18 there was so much wind that aircraft could not have flown, but the 19th was a beautiful spring day, and now every battleship, battle-cruiser and destroyer selected for the Dardanelles Diversion steamed forth on her allotted occasion.

THE *ARK ROYAL*
Converted from a merchant ship to an aeroplane-carrier.

BRITISH NAVAL SEAPLANE
This craft, when over the Turkish lines, was forced by engine trouble to alight; but, in spite of enemy shell and rifle fire, was rescued and towed home by the British destroyer *Beagle*.

CHAPTER IX

DARDANELLES DIVERSION

On February 19, Vice-Admiral Carden, who asked for twelve battleships, already had under his command the following immense strength: the battle-cruiser *Inflexible* and battleship *Queen Elizabeth*; the immediately pre-"Dreadnought" battleship *Agamemnon*; the battleships *Triumph* and *Cornwallis*, which were then eleven years old; and the battleships *Irresistible*, *Albion* and *Vengeance*, which were two or three years older still. In addition to these British eight, were the French old battleships *Suffren*, *Bouvet*, *Gaulois*, and *Charlemagne*. Grand total, twelve. The *Queen Elizabeth*, with her eight 15-inch guns; the *Inflexible*, with her eight 12-inch; the *Agamemnon*, *Cornwallis*, *Irresistible*, *Albion* and *Vengeance*, each with 12-inch guns; the *Triumph*, however, carrying four 10-inch; as their primary batteries, represented forty heavy cannon—if only they could all be employed. In addition must be mentioned a much greater number of 3-inch, 6-inch, 7·5-inch, and 9·2-inch, which would be useful at least for dealing with the less formidable shore batteries and howitzers at closer range.[1]

It cannot be pretended that the assembling of these dozen units, with their prominent upper works, nor the coming and going of destroyers having a "look-see" up and down the coast, nor the arrival of attendant vessels, can have passed without notice. The element of surprise must be ruled out, and the condition of Turkish suspense emphasised. Ever since November they had been uneasy; Holbrook's submarine attack in December had created alarm, and now the reports, which watchers at the outer forts sent in to Constantinople, could not fail to exert the Turks for the best defence. At night the brilliant searchlights across the Straits were visible to our watchers, and vividly announced the enemy's alertness.

[1] The *Indefatigable*, having refitted at Malta, left the Mediterranean for the North Sea.

During these three months following the loud knocking at her gates, Turkey had removed modern guns from the Bosphorus to the Dardanelles, convinced that the real attack must come not from the Russians, but from the Anglo-French forces. The minefields, following the exploit of *B* 11, had likewise been strengthened. And how? Well, Turkey began the War with an inadequate supply of these floating perils, so she swept up those which the Russians had dropped at the northern end of the Bosphorus and relaid them in the Dardanelles. Of course it was a risky job, though not by any means impossible. Those of us who were in the North Sea during the War years remember fishing trawlers occasionally entering port with one of these ugly, horned, black globes hoisted over the stern. The Germans at Constantinople had technical experts who soon showed the Turks how to handle the mines without disaster.

On the eve of Admiral Carden's February diversion the enemy was in no comfortable mood, and of this we now have ample documentary evidence. " It was reported that the Allies had assembled a fleet of forty warships at the mouth of the Dardanelles," wrote the American Ambassador,[1] " and that they intended the forcing of the Strait." Both von Wangenheim and von der Goltz believed that by the sacrificing of ten ships it would succeed. (This forecast coincided remarkably with Lord Fisher's reckoning, who estimated our loss would ultimately be twelve.[2]) " The situation of Turkey, when these first rumours of an Allied bombardment reached us," continued Ambassador Morgenthau, " was fairly desperate. On all hands there were evidences of the fear and panic that had seized not only the populace, but the official classes."

Even Wangenheim had become nervous and apprehensive, and " asked me to store several cases of his valuables in the American Embassy. Evidently he was making preparations

---

[1] *Secrets of the Bosphorus*, p. 120.
[2] " I expressed the opinion at the War Council that the whole operation, if pressed to a conclusion, would entail a loss of twelve battleships." (Quoted on p. 342 of *The World Crisis*, 1915.)

for his own departure." And this diplomat, who had so long dominated everyone, and, more than any other, had been responsible for the subjugation of Turkey to German ideals, was now not the only person getting ready for a hasty departure. The leading Turks, convinced that the Dardanelles Fleet could reach the Sea of Marmora in ten hours, had made arrangements not to be there to witness this arrival. Two trains were kept in waiting, with steam at one hour's notice: one train would hurry the Sultan into Asia, the other would take Wangenheim northwards.

Talaat, the Grand Vizier, the Prime Minister, informed Mr. Morgenthau that the real reason for the attack on Egypt this February (between the 3rd and 11th) " was to divert England from making an attack on the Gallipoli Peninsula." One diversion, in fact, to thwart another diversion!

The able, cool-headed, far-sighted, extremely self-controlled General von Sanders, whilst refusing to be swayed into panic, could not altogether deny the seriousness. Warnings of the Allies' intentions had filtered in via Athens, and the details could be filled in by a military imagination. " A successful attempt of the Anglo-French Fleet to force its way to Constantinople was not considered an impossibility,"[1] though against its breaking through such precautions had been taken " as would at least have made its prolonged stay off Constantinople very difficult. From St. Stefano to the Sarail Point, on the Asiatic side, and on the Princes Islands, numerous batteries had been erected, whose fire crossed on the sea." And, too, there would have been *Goeben* and *Breslau* to reckon with, apart from a few efficient torpedo-boats for a night attack.

"Even in case the Allied Fleet forced a passage and won the naval battle in the Sea of Marmora, I judged that it would be in a nearly untenable position so long as the entire shores on the Dardanelles Strait were not held by strong allied forces. Should the Turkish troops succeed in holding the shores of the Strait, or in regaining them, the regular supply of food and coal would become impossible. . . . A decisive success could not be won by the enemy unless the landing

[1] *Five Years in Turkey*, p. 47.

of large forces in the Dardanelles was coincident with, or antecedent to, the passage of the fleet."

This final paragraph is exactly in accord with the theme which we have stressed already: Admiral Carden, all his ships with their guns and gallant men, were about to plunge into a hopeless effort, contrary to strategic sense. The only *certain* chance for the capture of Constantinople, sums up General von Sanders, was with the simultaneous co-operation of large Russian forces landing on one side of the Bosphorus. Otherwise it must be a sheer gamble. "Had the Allied Fleet once passed the defences at the Strait, the administration of the Young Turks would have come to a bloody end," Mr. Morgenthau has emphasised.[1] Enver, Minister of War, was the one Turkish authority who insisted that the fortifications were impregnable, but that did not prevent the Turkish women and children, together with gold from the banks, being sent away early in March.

The first impression of the American Ambassador's visit, about this time, to the Dardanelles fortifications was that he had come to Germany. Not the Turkish language, but the guttural German was generally heard. Practically all the officers were Teutonic, who were strengthening emplacements everywhere, though some of the inner guns were thirty years old, having been made by Krupps so far back as 1885. Against the range of these, the brand-new *Queen Elizabeth*, first of the 15-inch gun battleships, could be expected to do wonders. How this ship came to associate with such older-fashioned sisters is as follows.

One of the arguments in Whitehall supporting the theory of a naval diversion was that, in like manner as the German big guns had destroyed the emplacements of Liège and Namur, the new battleship's sheer weight of shell would settle the Dardanelles forts. She was ready to do her gunnery trials in the Mediterranean, so why not use them against the Turks? She had suffered recently some trouble with her turbines, and her speed came down to 15 knots in conse-

[1] *Secrets of the Bosphorus*, p. 128.

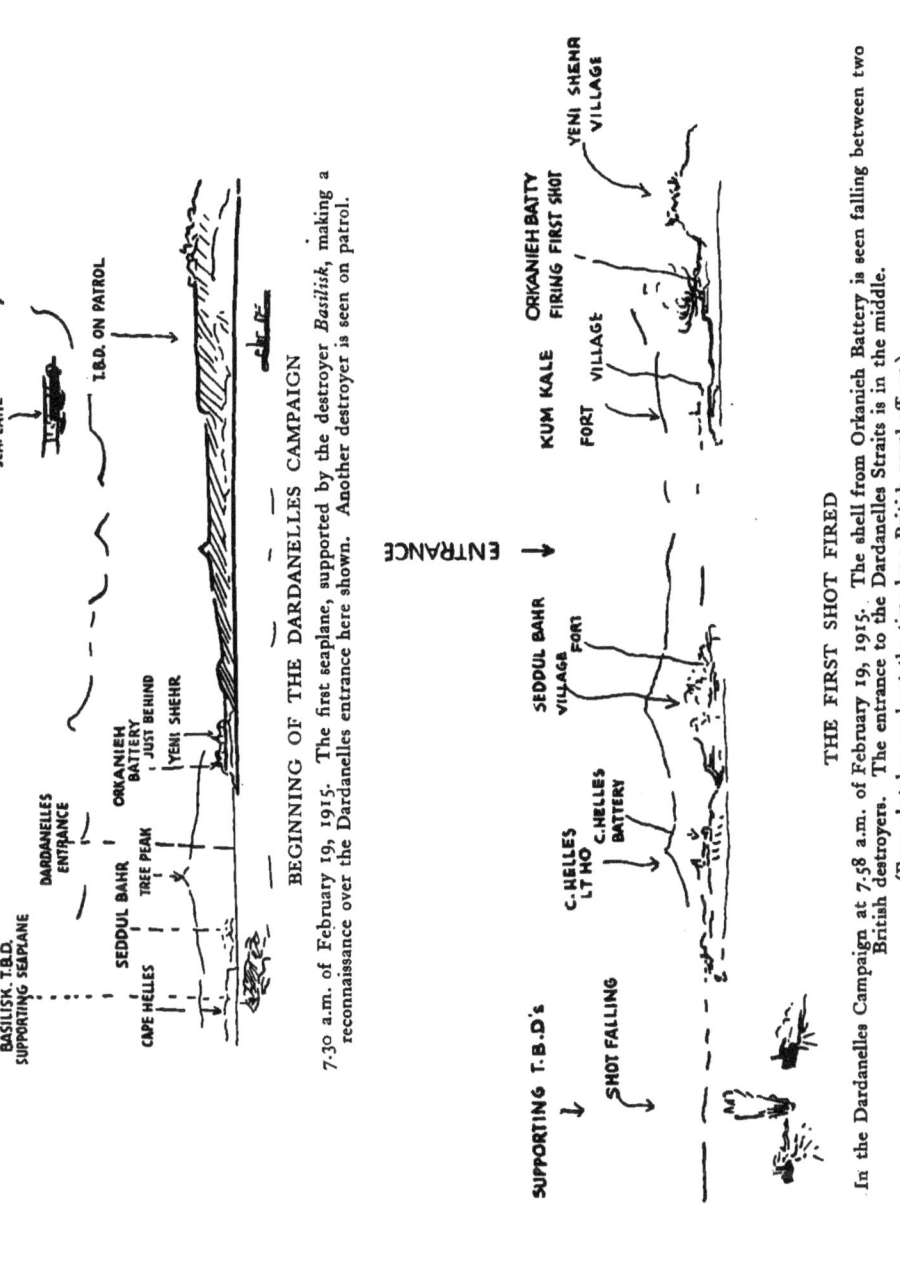

BEGINNING OF THE DARDANELLES CAMPAIGN

7.30 a.m. of February 19, 1915. The first seaplane, supported by the destroyer *Basilisk*, making a reconnaissance over the Dardanelles entrance here shown. Another destroyer is seen on patrol.

THE FIRST SHOT FIRED

In the Dardanelles Campaign at 7.58 a.m. of February 19, 1915. The shell from Orkanieh Battery is seen falling between two British destroyers. The entrance to the Dardanelles Straits is in the middle.
(From sketches made at the time by a British naval officer.)

quence; but this did not affect the range or power of her blows, and she remained out here three months, though Admiral Carden hoisted his flag in the *Inflexible*. What was to be the effect of these immense shells we shall presently understand. The *Queen Elizabeth's* range was 22,000 yards, whilst the *Inflexible's* was about 15,000, and that of the *Cornwallis'* 14,000. The older 12-inch battleships were effective up to roughly 12,000 yards. But it was one of the unfortunate conditions of this impetuously launched diversion that shells could be used only with economy: ammunition was as scarce as battalions.

The width of the Dardanelles mouth being only some 4000 yards, it was obvious that ships could not hope to enter and engage the intermediate defences until such time as the outer forts had been silenced beyond all doubt. Having in our mind, then, mounted at this gate Cape Tekke's 5-inch howitzers, and Cape Helles with its two modern 9·4-inch, all on the northern or European side; with Kum Kale's nine powerful 11-inch to 6-inch, plus Orkanieh's two 9·4-inch, on the southern or European side, we can picture the solemnity of this 19th of February. Would the first part of the plan—*i.e.* the silencing of these outer forts—to-day be completed, so that to-morrow the intermediate defences might fall, and next day the inner batteries?

It was indeed a momentous morning, as if men were standing tip-toe, eager to run the most dangerous gauntlet, or rush some impossible gorge thick with ambush. The opening move was when the first seaplane got off at 7.30 a.m.[1] to make her reconnaissance, followed by the supporting destroyer *Basilisk*. The accompanying sketch, drawn on the spot by a naval officer, will make this quite clear to the reader's eye. ' Soon afterwards two other destroyers, who were slowly steaming in the same direction, got within the line of fire from No. 4 (Orkanieh) battery, but fortunately the destroyers were

---

[1] These times were noted by orders of a commanding officer who has lent me the actual document. (East European Time, *i.e.* 2 hours earlier than G.M.T.)

at the enemy's extreme range (about 11,000 yards). The time was 7.58. This was actually the first shot of the newly started Dardanelles campaign. The shell fell between the two destroyers, followed by another " plop," as will be noticed in the next sketch. Edging out a little, both destroyers continued untouched.

By nine o'clock the bombarding squadron had advanced to their positions outside the mouth, the French battleship *Suffren*, supported by *Gaulois*, taking on Kum Kale from the south, with *Bouvet* to the north-west spotting for her about six miles from the target. The *Cornwallis* was to tackle Orkanieh from W.S.W., being well out of range, and making direct fire. The *Triumph* was to the north, attacking Fort Helles in reverse, whilst *Inflexible*, lying out of range to the westward, devoted herself to Sedd-el-Bahr. The *Vengeance* at first was rather to the north-west of *Cornwallis*.

The flagship hoisted at 9.51 the signal " Open fire," and one minute later the *Cornwallis* began shelling Orkanieh. Thus the first shot sent, and received by the Turks, was concerned with this No. 4 fort. Six minutes later *Triumph* began her work, opening fire at No. 1 fort (Helles), and eleven minutes later the *Suffren* was shelling No. 6 (Kum Kale). If the French battleship seemed somewhat slow in starting, the *Triumph* was not less deliberate, one shell falling over and the next short. Then she stopped. At this time— soon after 10.40—there came a modification of tactics. Having regard to the strict instructions from home that ammunition was to be used with economy, and this first ninety minutes having achieved so little, Admiral Carden ordered the bombarding ships to anchor and carry on their work from fixed positions, in the hope of attaining greater accuracy. The *Vengeance*, which had been lying to the north-west of *Cornwallis*, then took the latter's place, because *Cornwallis*' capstan happened to be defective. But wind and current were such as to place the head of the *Vengeance* on to the target, and thus prevent full use of her 12-inch guns, so Captain Bertram Smith performed the interesting seamanship

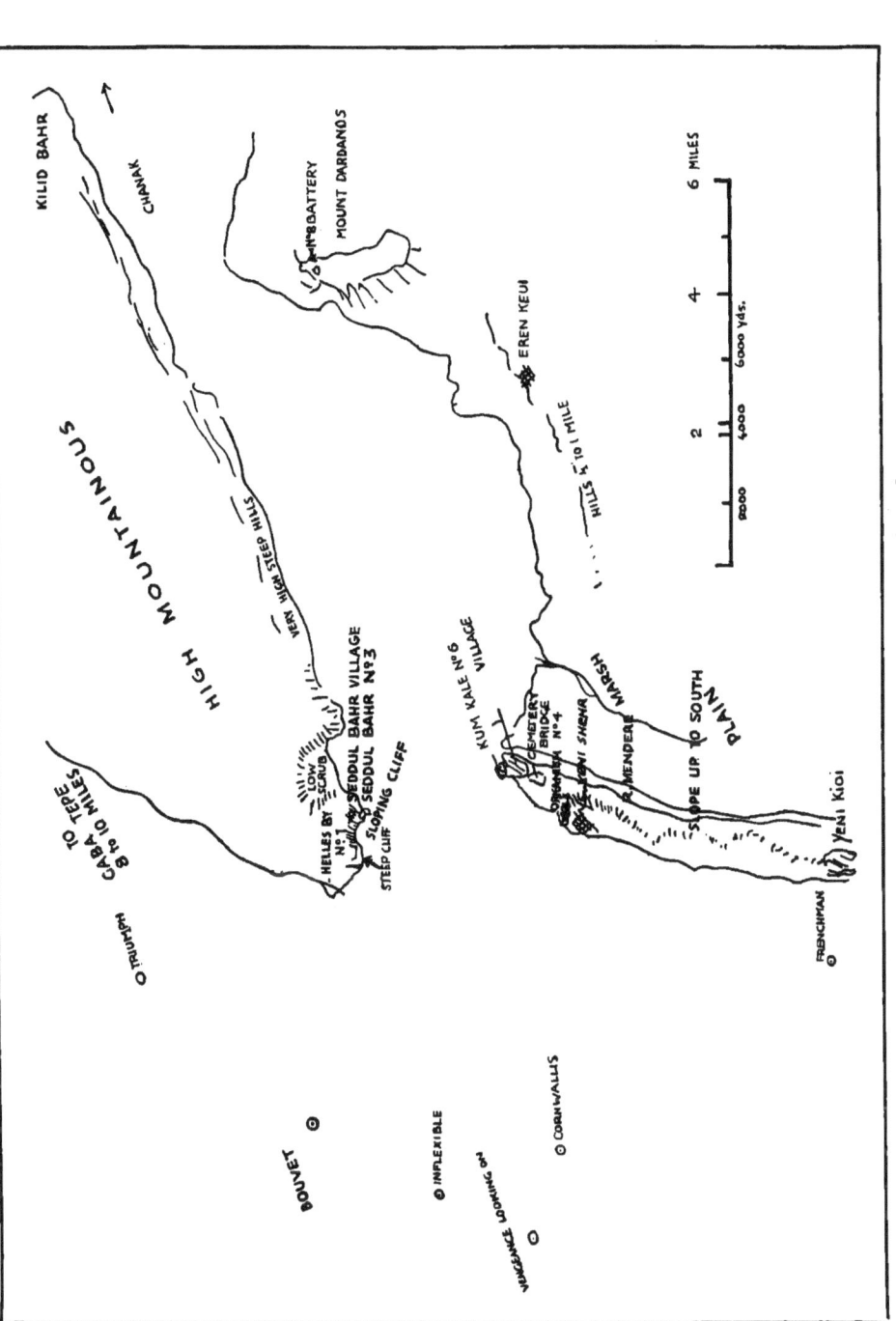

BOMBARDMENT OF OUTER FORTS, FEBRUARY 19, 1915
Showing respective positions of ships.

of bending on a "spring": that is to say, from the battleship's stern a wire was taken to the cable, and the stern hauled at right angles, enabling the full broadside to be fired.

Fire was then made by her on Orkanieh, three or four shots from each 12-inch, and at 12.38 one shot was seen to fall just behind the enemy's guns, causing a conflagration. No reply followed, and at 12.42 the shoot was stopped for lunch. Very significant was the fact of the forts having maintained silence up till then, and at 2.30 the Admiral considered that the time had come for his ships to draw nearer. Anchors were weighed, and at 2.32 the *Suffren* was again in action, followed by the *Vengeance* at 3.13, and the *Cornwallis* a minute later, directing her attention at Helles. Almost immediately the *Vengeance* secured a hit, which caused the Turks from Orkanieh to run "like blazes" (as one of the *Vengeance's* naval officers remarked at the time). The range had now been reduced to about 8000 yards, and the attack seemed to promise a more hopeful issue.

"We then got closer, and finally turned out and let go at Helles, which, after giving us a few rounds, stopped. However, we suddenly heard an almighty crash, and saw a splash just under our starboard quarter; then one just over us—short over—getting closer and closer. We thought it was from Helles. Then very close on our port bow—so close that the splash wetted us. We then slowed, to let Helles have it close with all guns, 6-inch included, the time being now 4.49. Then we found that it was not Helles, but Orkanieh, so remained."

It was a thrilling episode. The *Vengeance* was receiving most of the enemy's notice, and to onlookers it seemed certain that she must be hit. For most people on board this was the first occasion of being under fire. To their aid rushed *Cornwallis*, one of the French battleships, and the *Agamemnon*, which had arrived from Malta that afternoon. The roar of booming guns, the tremor which ran through each steel hull, the pyramids of splashes, the smoke and dust-clouds which rose every time a naval shell did its destruction ashore, were most impressive to senses already keyed up. And over to seaward in the background, just arrived from Malta likewise, but scarcely yet a participant, now appeared the latest thing in the world's battleships, the super-"Dreadnought" *Queen Elizabeth*, on the eve of her active service.

Very gallantly had the *Vengeance* closed nearer, yet nearer, so as to pour in the maximum amount of fire, and she led a charmed life. "Everyone had joined in to give us help, but Orkanieh was like a mad bull: he wouldn't look at anybody else." Sunset put an end to the day's excitement; at 5.10 the flagship hoisted the recall, and the squadron steamed off. Unhurt, unhit, the plucky *Vengeance* withdrew, having given Orkanieh a thorough shaking and incurred vengeance in return. Rear-Admiral de Robeck, whose flag was flying in her, begged permission to prolong the struggle, but the light was fast fading and the day's work had ended.

"There were splinters, from short bursts, everywhere aboard the *Vengeance*: through masts, boats, yards, and lying on the quarter-deck as well as outside the conning-tower. The sensation was strange: the little six-inch slit in the latter seemed six feet. The time from seeing an enemy gun fired, to the moment when the shot fell, was enormous. We used to wait till someone said: ' Orkanieh! (Or Helles!).' Then, after years, one of us would say casually, '*Now*, I think,' and we'd all slowly duck our heads, and either hear ' Crash! ' for a ' short ' (when we would wait to let splinters finish), or else ' Whooh—Whooh—Whooh—Whoooh ' over our heads, and then ' Crash! ' when we knew it had missed ' over.' The great thing was that we were *première danseuse*, and the men came out feeling they were everything."

Such was the legitimate pride of ship and performance after the first day, though there had certainly been difficulties. The *Triumph* had no easy task firing at Helles, since the fort was so well concealed that the target could not be descried.

DARDANELLES DIVERSION

Eventually *Inflexible* took her place. This battle-cruiser possessed a wonderful record for gunnery, and later in the day from a range of 12,000 yards fired twenty-one rounds into Helles. If this did not silence that fort, it certainly interfered with the enemy's accuracy. This battle-cruiser equally did good work at short notice when called upon to help *Vengeance* during the late afternoon; for nineteen of *Inflexible's* shells made excellent practice, and greatly annoyed the Orkanieh gunners.

The ships retired to Tenedos, and at 10.30 next forenoon Admiral Carden summoned his Captains on board for a conference.

Now, what had been the nett result of this February 19 ? The most that could be said was that it had proved, and attained, very little. Whatever future occasions might have in store, the day's adventure had been inconclusive. It had been well manifested that so far ships did not dominate forts; that ships under way could not—even with slow, deliberate firing—obtain accurate results; that the *Triumph's* firing over the land at Helles failed because indirect shooting was not to be relied upon. And, notwithstanding the deluge of shells on forts, the enemy was not permanently silenced: earthworks might be damaged, rubble and dust might be created, but nothing could avail except definite hits on the guns themselves. The enemy had not wasted his shots, but withheld his response until we had closed the range, and then surprised us after his silence.

True, we had driven the Turkish gunners temporarily away from their guns into shelter by our long-range bombardment, but most disappointing was the surprise to find all the guns of Helles and Orkanieh only biding their time and opportunity. Thus, from the very first, it was clear as day that the Navy unaided could not compete against forts; the old principle still obtained. And this was fast becoming apparent to Lord Kitchener, who had been opposed to sending troops. Finally, on February 24 it was decided to send General Birdwood, at that date commanding the Australasian Army Corps in Egypt, to visit Admiral Carden; but this military officer after reaching the Dardanelles did not share in Admiral Carden's optimism. For the sake of continuity we may anticipate by adding that on March 5 the General telegraphed to Lord Kitchener: " I am very doubtful if the Navy can force the passage unassisted," and next day confirmed this by: " I consider the Admiral's forecast is too sanguine." [1]

General Birdwood was dead right; and, unfortunately, Admiral Carden had from the 5th of January (when he telegraphed the First Lord of the Admiralty that the Dardanelles " might be forced by extended operations with a large number of ships ") based his hopes on a wrong foundation, which was bound to prove their insecurity. Doubtless he had been influenced by the desire to fall in with the Admiralty's wishes, to attempt even the most difficult problem, rather than say, " This is too much of an impossibility." He himself was at last to realise that troops, to the number of 10,000, were essential for holding the end of Gallipoli peninsula after the outer forts should have been destroyed. At home, Lord Kitchener in the War Office, with his profound understanding of the Asiatic mind, knew that it would be fatal for our prestige if we were not to succeed where we had attempted: so on March 16 it was decided to send out the XXIXth Division to the Dardanelles, and on this same day Admiral Carden, having had a most worrying experience during past weeks, went on the sick list. He took no further part in the campaign.

This resolve to despatch land forces marks an important change, and was the beginning of a still greater transformation. It must, however, be emphasised that the intention so far was only to supplement and complete the Navy's share: not to supplant it. Meanwhile the last of these bombardments had by no means ended, and much benefit would result if once the outer forts could be finished off. At any rate, this was the first of those obstacles barring the road to Constantinople.

[1] See *The World Crisis*, 1915, p. 188.

CHAPTER X

BOMBARDING THE OUTER FORTS

FEBRUARY 19 had been the first day when seven of those trawlers, so quickly sent out from the east coast of England, began their sweeping for mines off the peninsula. Under the protection of the battleship *Albion* and the light cruiser *Amethyst*, they had towed their wires close to the land north of Cape Tekke, with a view to ensuring a safe area from which the precious new *Queen Elizabeth* could begin her shooting. But no mines were found.

On Saturday (February 20) and the next two days a southerly gale had taken charge of the Dardanelles, and bad visibility prevented operations being immediately resumed. By day the Fleet was anchored at Tenedos coaling, and sometimes dragging their anchors owing to the wind. At night the big ships were under way off the Straits' mouth, in case *Goeben* and *Breslau* should come forth. On Tuesday the wind, after dropping in the morning, freshened, and again delayed a start. It was during these depressing hours that tidings reached the Fleet that 10,000 troops were coming from Egypt, who were to hold the peninsula up to Soghanli Dere (*i.e.* about half-way between Cape Helles and the Narrows) as soon as Admiral Carden had put the outer forts to silence. On Wednesday the weather was still bad, but on Thursday the 25th all was again in readiness, with a fine day. It was to be eventful.

" Things were a little different this time," records one of the Captains. " We found on the 19th that it was best to see the object. Indirect fire was wasteful. So the arrangement was for long-range bombardment on Orkanieh (4) by *Irresistible* (which had meanwhile arrived from Malta); on Helles (1) by the *Agamemnon*; on Sedd-el-Bahr (3) by *Queen Elizabeth*; on Kum Kale (6) by the *Gaulois*. Temporarily lying off were the *Vengeance, Cornwallis, Albion, Triumph, Inflexible*, besides the two French ships *Suffren* and *Charlemagne*."

In other words, there was to be a preliminary long-range

bombardment; and this was to be followed up by two pairs of battleships going in at close range to engage with their secondary armament. The idea was that, the enemy's gunners having been driven away from their cannon, the guns themselves could now be destroyed. So at 5 a.m. perceive the Fleet weighing from Tenedos and proceeding for the entrance, off which the long-range bombardment began at 10.14, when *Queen Elizabeth* opened fire at Sedd-el-Bahr, her shot falling short. Simultaneously the *Gaulois* commenced, and got a hit on Kum Kale, whereupon Helles started firing on *Agamemnon*, who immediately replied. At 10.28 *Irresistible* was attacking Orkanieh, and *Gaulois* was hitting Kum Kale again. But it became very evident that Helles would concentrate her wrath on *Agamemnon*, one shell at 10.31 falling just short, though four minutes later the *Agamemnon* received a hit; then pieces of shell were seen flying around her, and at 10.39 she was hit again. She therefore got under way, but seven minutes afterwards once more became a victim to the same fort, although the *Queen Elizabeth* now shelled Helles.

Nevertheless *Agamemnon*, having been hit seven times, losing three killed and eight severely wounded, registered two hits on her adversary; then one shell fell just over this ship, whilst a second fell just short. The *Queen Elizabeth*, who was to the north-west of her, both being to the south-west of the entrance, had got the range of Helles exactly, by 11 a.m. had made four hits on this fort, and another five by 12.2. Indeed, the shooting of this new ship, with her new guns, was superb. She enabled the *Gaulois* (who had been lying between the shore and *Agamemnon*, receiving dangerous attention from Helles also, including a hit at 11.10) to get under way and move further out. The light cruiser *Dublin*, who had been to the southward of *Gaulois*, though still nearer the Asiatic shore, where she was spotting for *Queen Elizabeth*, had at 10.50 also been compelled to move further seaward. Already she was being straddled.

The *Irresistible's* first shots at Orkanieh had fallen short, but at 11.25 she began hitting the target effectively, and actually struck both the 9·4-inch guns of that fort; which was very useful work. The *Queen Elizabeth*, during the attack on Sedd-el-Bahr and then at Helles, had distinguished herself by knocking out one gun and damaging a second. The *Gaulois'* bombardment of Kum Kale had not touched any armament.

So the sun rose to its zenith and noon passed.

But now came the second phase of the day's endeavours: the close-range attack. First the *Vengeance* and *Cornwallis*, who were lying about eight miles south-west of the Dardanelles entrance, were to get under way, make a run till they reached a position 4000 yards from Kum Kale, blaze at the entrance forts, turn round to port at that distance, and return whence they started. This being accomplished, Admiral Guépratte, with the *Suffren* and *Charlemagne*, was to perform a similar feat. It was a kind of cavalry charge with heavy, and not fast, ships: not the rush of light-hulled destroyers able to turn quickly, but of oldish vessels of 13,000 and 14,000 tons (as to the British units), each carrying a dozen 6-inch besides their ponderous 12-inch guns. And the most dangerous moment would be in their act of turning away to come home again: then, indeed, at such a tempting range, would the land forts have their unique chance.

"By 12.31," writes an officer in the *Vengeance*,[1] "the ships had reported ready, and we were told to start our show. It was like looking into a lion's den to see if he were there.

"No. 1 (Helles) had stopped, but no one knew if they'd open when we got close. By 12.45 we were on our course, and other ships began firing to support us. We went in at 12 knots, and at 12.54 *Vengeance* opened fire, slowly, with her starboard 6-inch at Orkanieh, and with her port 6-inch at Helles, beginning at 6500 yards. Five minutes later Sedd-el-Bahr opened fire on *Vengeance*, to which our port guns replied. The after turret also came into action. From 1.5 till 1.9 p.m. we were turning out to port, being distant about 2500 yards from Kum Kale (that is, about 1500 yards later than ordered), and in turning threw a few into Kum Kale as well as Sedd-el-

[1] In which Admiral de Robeck was still flying his flag.

Bahr. A good hit on Orkanieh was seen just as we finished turning out.

"Suddenly there was a bang! A shell from Sedd-el-Bahr fell short. Another! Then an 'over'—one from each gun in the seaward face. Apparently they had loaded, left them, and fired from elsewhere. However, we weren't touched, and slowly went out, so as to leave the Frenchmen their turn. At 1.37 we stopped engines. Stand easy."

It is noticeable that the enemy had been unresponsive until the turn to port was about to be made: doubtless the Turks were expecting an attempt to rush past, for which effort they were fully prepared, and everyone in *Vengeance* was surprised to have escaped scot free. The *Cornwallis* " fairly poured it in on Forts 4 and 1 in salvoes of 12- and 6-inch. All the time Fort 6 at Kum Kale fired at both ships. A shot from our fore-turret," relate two of her officers,[1] " capsized one gun in Fort 4, and later on we put a beauty on a gun in Number 1. The 6-inch salvoes fell in bunches all round the embrasures, and during the run, which lasted about twenty-five minutes, we fired one hundred and forty rounds of 12- and 6-inch. Two shots passed us very close. One just missed the bow, and the other, close to the foretop, fell over."

At 2.15 came along that splendid fighter Admiral Guépratte with his *Suffren* and *Charlemagne* on a fairly similar course to their predecessors. Thirteen minutes later the former opened fire on Sedd-el-Bahr, and at 2.37 began the turn to port, during which good hits were made on Kum Kale again and again, the *Suffren* not coming out for another seventeen minutes. One officer tells me that the French Admiral slowed down when opposite Sedd-el-Bahr and fairly " let the fort have it, bringing down masonry, and kicking up an awful mess. They made an enormous hole in the seaward left-hand tower." She was also seen to be hitting Kum Kale well; and at 2.48 *Charlemagne* began her share in the terrific shelling. As a result of all this rapid and accurate shooting, Sedd-el-Bahr

---

[1] *The Immortal Gamble*, p. 16, by Commander A. T. Stewart, R.N., and the Rev. C. J. E. Peshall, R.N. London, 1917.

was observed to be in flames, and to complete the operation there were now sent in the two British battleships *Albion* and *Triumph*. The former went in to the short distance of 2000 yards, being ordered to deal with the south side, whilst the *Triumph* was to finish off the northern forts. In order to cover and direct this final phase Admiral de Robeck in the *Vengeance* was also ordered up.

"Then," says an officer in that flagship, "it was fireworks. The enemy had an awful time. We saw one round of *Albion* hit a 9·4- or 8-inch gun in Kum Kale, which went flying up in the air in two bits. Sedd-el-Bahr started coming down by the run. Kum Kale was having explosions all over. We just fired a few rounds into the barracks to stir them out, in case they were hiding." The Turks had been given no respite, for a bare half-hour after *Suffren's* exit the *Albion* was punishing Kum Kale and Orkanieh, and *Triumph* was doing her work on Sedd-el-Bahr with thoroughness. Indeed, these entrance forts were being subjected to a series of explosive earthquakes. The *Vengeance* and *Cornwallis* had dealt some pretty hard knocks; the Frenchmen had steamed even nearer still, to a distance of about 2500 yards, but the *Albion* and *Triumph* were firing into the ruined forts at point-blank range. The last-mentioned ship (originally built for a South American republic) had fourteen 7·5-inch guns as her secondary battery, and one of her officers assures me that the *Triumph* was able, because of the quelled resistance, to stand in remarkably close. " I remember steaming slowly past the fort at the northern entrance, and with our 7·5's knocking each gun in turn out of its emplacement at a range of about 200 yards." The only reply—which was made just before dusk (save for a mild barking from one of Kum Kale's and a few light guns)—was from a hidden howitzer on the southern side; " but," reports yet another witness, " its fire was rotten, and we ignored it."

By 6.30 p.m. the position was thus: Sedd-el-Bahr a ruin; Kum Kale well smashed up; Helles and Orkanieh both out of action; the barracks and forts blazing with huge fires, making a raw red and yellow against the nocturnal background; for

Kum Kale village was not less aflame than Sedd-el-Bahr. Thus, not unlike a drama which begins quietly and develops its strength during progress, this Thursday's events ended in a grand and sudden climax, spectacular to the eyes, and a most impressive silence coinciding with the fall of darkness. Next, as a kind of epilogue, " before we knew where we were, the minesweepers were sweeping in to clear the channel to Kum Kale."

Bring up the North Sea trawlers!

The method of working the seven sweepers was under the orders of the leader. Keeping station on each other in pairs, *échelon* fashion, they were accustomed at the right moment to shoot the wooden " kite " and wire hawser into the water. Like a pair of oxen tethered to a plough, each two trawlers kept exact station, joined by the loop of wire being dragged astern; the triangular-shaped " kite " being employed for keeping the sweep wire down to the required depth. With three pairs thus spread out and advancing, it was possible to cover quite a wide enough channel to ensure safety for any following ships. The difficulty at the Dardanelles was, however, special and twofold. First of all it must be remembered that these little steamers were slow; when trawling for fish in peace-time, with the gear being pulled over the ground, speed was neither desirable nor possible. Thus, with a clean bottom, most trawlers in those days had an average of about 9 knots when proceeding to or from their grounds. But, secondly, they were unarmed and unarmoured. If, therefore, sent to sweep against the Dardanelles current, which in its lower portion runs at 2 or 3 knots, but becomes stronger still towards the Narrows, the trawlers would not be able to advance at more than 6 knots unimpeded. Having " passed wires " to each other and been still further slowed down, their ultimate progress would be somewhere about 3 or 4 knots. Under such conditions they would very obviously be easy targets for any fort, howitzer, or concealed light guns. How could fishermen, who had never till a few weeks before seen a gun go off, be expected to handle wires under shell-fire? And,

BOMBARDING THE OUTER FORTS

indeed, how could the little ships, with their thin steel hulls, be expected to endure five minutes of such assault ?

It cannot be denied that the sending of these slow, defenceless fishing vessels to operate opposed to the very efficient land fortifications at the Dardanelles showed a strange lack of imagination. It is yet another example of that impetuousness and incomplete planning which stigmatised this campaign. Arithmetical numbers of units on paper may look all very well. "Twenty-one minesweepers at once despatched to the Mediterranean." This seemed splendid. But the work was utterly different from the routine sweeping along the North Sea coast lanes, where no defiance from the shore could happen. In lieu of these virile slow steamers, there should have been sent out high-powered vessels to which a 3- or 4-knot current meant nothing. Armed with light guns for replying to the smaller batteries, and with some sort of protection at the bridge as well as the " gallows " aft (near which the wires and men working them are located), much more could have been expected. Actually, for such a job, the destroyer type, but slightly modified, would have sufficed.

But everything just then seemed inadequately considered, and makeshifts were introduced at the last minute which did not, and could not, compensate for the initial errors.

Thus, since rapid sweeping was out of the question and daylight attempts would render annihilation certain, the work must be done by night, under the protection of two battleships and six destroyers, with another battleship lying close off ready to succour. For this reason, on the night of February 25 there were assigned *Albion*, *Triumph*, and *Vengeance*, together with half a dozen of those restless destroyers whose work seemed to be continuous through the twenty-four hours. Some steel plating as protection against splinters and bullets was certainly added to the trawlers, though with what increased sense of security we shall see later. That night they swept the Dardanelles entrance, but with negative result. Why?

Just as on the 19th, the trawlers, after exploring to within 5000 yards of the north-western side of the peninsula, had discovered nothing, so it was at the entrance. The enemy made the best use of his few mines, and for the present at least the danger-area did not begin till abreast of Kephez Bay, where the Straits sensibly narrow. Thus on the morrow the battleships could enter between the headlands fearless of underwater traps. The outer forts having been thought to be conquered, the next step should be the attack on intermediate defences within the Straits.

But let us first be under no misapprehension. In narrating that which happened, we have tried to visualise events and results through the minds of eye-witnesses. But there lies a difference between narrative and history, so that before we enter the Straits we must now view the past in the light of the present. As contrasted with what we thought at the time, exactly how much had we really achieved before February 26?

Put briefly, the answer is that in Fort Helles we had certainly dismounted both of the long-range 9·4-inch guns; that in Sedd-el-Bahr, as well as across the water in Kum Kale, we had caused the garrison to abandon the forts, although we had not put more than one-third of their biggest guns permanently out of action. A mere handful of Turks had been killed, and the conflagrations noticed were the burning ammunition dumps. In Orkanieh we had destroyed one of the two 9·4-inch guns, besides seriously damaging the other. The valiant attack on the 25th by the three pairs of ships at close range, with secondary armament, had unquestionably injured the forts rather than the guns; and now came a stiffer, more perilous, and more stoutly opposed phase. The garden gate having been weakened, admission could be made up the pathway; but would there not be some fierce effort made to prevent this invasion getting near the house?

The 26th of February was a beautifully warm morning, and the conditions for inaugurating attack on the intermediate defences seemed favourable. The battleships chosen were three: *Albion*, who was to concentrate on Kum Kale; the *Triumph*, who was to aim at Sedd-el-Bahr, whilst the third unit was *Majestic*, who had but recently arrived from Malta. The

SEDD-EL-BAHR FORT
One of the guns damaged by the bombardment.

NAVAL ROUTE MARCH
After landing from one of H.M. ships at Mudros.

reader will remember that she had there mounted her two howitzers and been given a "cowcatcher" mine-bumper. To her was assigned the task of destroying by gunfire a certain bridge which spanned the Mendere river flowing out just east of Kum Kale, and it was this bridge which connected Kum Kale with the road up to Chanak. Immediately after crossing the bridge from east to west was a Mahommedan cemetery, from which the road divided, one portion running north to Kum Kale and the other going south-west, passing Achilles' Tomb (or Mound), then the Orkanieh Fort, and finally reaching Yeni Shehr, made conspicuous by its windmills. Between the cemetery and Achilles' Tumulus was a horsehoe hollow in the ground.

At first the *Vengeance* lay off the Asiatic side between Yeni Shehr and Kum Kale, Admiral de Robeck directing operations. Alongside presently came the destroyer *Grasshopper*, bringing Commodore Roger Keyes to see the Admiral. The Commodore, who had been at Harwich during the first six months of war, in charge of submarines, had now been appointed Chief of Staff to Admiral Carden. The *Irresistible* also lay ready to be called upon, and the trawlers were again needed: this time to precede the deep-draught battleships. Ubiquitous destroyers completed the lively picture.

Having arrived off the entrance, *Majestic* rigged her "cowcatcher" and then went to action stations; decks were flooded in case of fire, and all was in readiness for the first of her Dardanelles adventures. Two minutes after eight o'clock a mysterious big explosion in Kum Kale shook the shore, and at 8.40 the British attack opened with *Albion* as well as destroyers shelling that fort besides Sedd-el-Bahr. At 9.50 the *Majestic* with her starboard 6-inch guns was shelling the Mendere bridge, which seemed to be one of those wooden, trestle, affairs, and hard to hit; but within ten minutes it was well damaged, and some Turkish troops on their way up to Yeni Shehr "got it in the neck all right," as the ship's Commander joyously expressed it. Nor did the *Vengeance* fail to observe this interesting matter, or to improve the occasion.

"We found the Turks," noted one of that battleship's officers, "running up from the river and taking cover behind Achilles Mound, so we opened fire on that, and in five rounds got three hits, one blowing open the parapet and disclosing two antiaircraft guns. This again shifted them, and we next saw them retreating up a slope between Yeni Shehr and Yeni Koi. The *Dublin* then was sent to cut off their retreat, and opened fire with shrapnel."

The destroyers, protecting the minesweeping trawlers, then moved inside the Straits, and at first all appeared peaceful. Certainly it was an historic hour that at last warships should enter from the Ægean against the Turks' permission; but this defiance of an ancient independence must be only the preliminary to big achievements. In a curious manner the old mingled with the new, and the immediate purpose for which *Albion* together with *Majestic* were now entering was to tackle the modern battery of Dardanos, close by the classic ruins of Dardanus, famous for its connection with the world's history. If it had once been the site of a Greek city in the Troad, if also it had witnessed the conclusion of a great peace between Mithridates and the Roman general Sulla, some eighty years before the Christian era, it had likewise given its name to those Straits which were ever to be associated with the greatest gamble of the twentieth century.

Dardanos in the year 1915 consisted of at first two (and subsequently five) steel turrets having 6-inch guns. Perched on the top of a hill, they looked the easiest of targets, but the fact persisted that this facility was a mere illusion. We were now to begin wrestling with a defence that dominated the restricted passage abreast of Kephez, and this Dardanos Fort (otherwise known as No. 8) became one of those tough nuts which never were cracked during the whole campaign. To give some idea of the difficulty which this one battery created, to illustrate the uncanny character of its evasiveness, one may remark in advance that though about 4000 shells were aimed at it between now and March 16, not one of those five guns received damage, though eight men were killed and some forty wounded. When the American Ambassador paid Dardanos a visit on that day in March, he found the land for nearly half a mile around completely churned up; "it looked like photographs I had seen of the battlefields in France." " I naturally thought at first that such a failure indicated poor marksmanship, but my German guides said that was not the case. All this misfire merely illustrated once more the familiar fact that a rapidly manœuvring battleship is under great disadvantage in shooting at a fixed fortification."[1]

It was about high noon, whilst the *Triumph* was firing her lighter guns at a suspicious spot on the shore, under De Tott's battery, and *Vengeance* was using her 6-inch guns against snipers,[2] that *Majestic* and *Albion* introduced themselves to Dardanos with 12-inch shells. For the destroyers had excited the ancient site to speak with roused anger. One destroyer was retreating at full speed and being pursued by this fort's 6-inch gifts, so the *Albion* gave Dardanos hill full and undivided attention. The following graphic account, written by Commander (now Captain) Michael Barne, who was second-in-command of *Majestic*, has been copied from his diary:—

"We then turned our attention to Fort Dardanos, or No. 8 on the map. We went slowly up the straits, expecting every moment to get it good: and when within 11,000 yards of our target, started in with the fore turret. The *Albion* came up also, and, lying level with us, did the same. Having longer range guns, she was able to put her shells nicely on the top of the fort, whereas we could only pitch ours on to the embankment in front of it. Presently there was a puff of smoke from above Eren Keui, the village on the south side, and there came a whistling sound, followed by the faint bang of the first Turkish gun to fire on the old *Majestic*. The shell pitched wide, and everybody laughed at it. They fired a good few

[1] *Secrets of the Bosphorus.* See pp. 140 and 141.
[2] As it was difficult to indicate the snipers' position, Captain Bertram Smith himself fired one of *Vengeance's* 12-pdrs. to get the guns on.

more, with little better result, then ceased fire, and we went to lunch.

"After lunch we fired again at No. 8, and then commenced to turn round, which had to be done slowly and gingerly on account of our ungainly 'cow-catcher.' When we got halfway round, the Eren Keui batteries, which had been holding on until this chance came along, suddenly let us have it hot and strong. Our ship was surrounded by heavy splashes, and the air was full of a sound which reminded me of large flights of starlings flying over. I went down into a casemate to show them where to shoot. The shells were bursting all round and over us. Presently came a thump, which shook the whole ship: and we knew that she had been hit somewhere. I went round looking over the side for the hole. Nobody seemed to know where it was, until I met a man coming up from below with a scared face, saying that the after submerged flat was half full of water! On going down to see, I found that there was a little water leaking in: the port side had been bulged in by a big shell bursting in the water just outside, some of the frames were buckled and a few rivets started. I was glad to be able to tell the Captain that all was well.

"We were unable to turn, except very slowly, with our 'cow-catcher' down, and being within comfortable range of the enemy's howitzers and other guns on the Asiatic side, it was extraordinary how little damage was done. The ship was all wet with the splashes, but seemed to bear a charmed life. Our wireless aerial was shot away on both sides of the mainmast, and a spoke of the steam pinnace's wheel was shot off by a piece of shell flying over. We also found a good many shrapnel bullets about the deck. As we went down towards the entrance, so they followed us, and a battery behind the long, level, low grassy hill at Achillæum[1] (whose acquaintance we improved later) opened fire on us."

Now, during that afternoon there followed one of the bravest exploits in the whole War, to be remembered for all time as a wonderful inspiration.

[1] This was about five miles east of Kum Kale.

THE DARDANELLES STRAITS

Showing Outer, Inner, and Principal Intermediate Defences. The numbers refer to Forts and Batteries.

CHAPTER XI
DEMOLITION GALLANTRY

It has often enough been emphasised that no navy ever won a war by itself; but that, rather, organised warships are the shaft of the spear, whilst the army is the spear-head. To be precise, during the Great European War, whilst the Navy kept open the sea lanes for transporting the troops, supplying them with food, munitions, and stores—simultaneously maintaining such a blockade of Germany that she became starved for want of food and raw material—it was the Army which made the direct thrust. All that we have so far emphasised concerning the inability of ships *by themselves* overcoming forts is in line with this general principle.

We are now to watch a very gallant practical expression of how the Fleet co-operating with the Army, marines, or seamen employed as soldiers, can bring about the desired end. If the naval guns of mobile ships cannot alone, permanently, put forts out of action, they can temporarily overpower these batteries till parties are landed to complete the destruction and hold the positions against recovery. The ideal operation would be where a landing in force should immediately follow the bombardment, and that, under the protection of a creeping barrage from the Fleet, the Army should make its parallel advance along the shore. Thus, had the November attack on the outer forts been the precedent of khaki-laden boats nosing alongside piers and grinding their keels on to the beaches of Sedd-el-Bahr and Orkanieh, the conquest of the peninsula would have been easy. At that date, too, the enemy's guns still required to be replaced by modern weapons. Even in late February, after our repeated warnings had given them time to overhaul their defences, a combined naval and military effort could still have won through.

Late in time, however—that is to say on February 6—the Admiralty had sent from England two battalions of marines from Plymouth and Chatham, and before the month was out they were to be followed by the Portsmouth and Deal battalions, whilst ten other battalions before very long were to reach the Dardanelles likewise. But, it must be recollected, each battleship also had marines among her own complement.

We are still considering Friday, February 26. Lunch was over, *Vengeance* came steaming again into the Straits with *Cornwallis* astern. The *Irresistible* was already within. It was now the intention to land demolition parties on either side of the entrance and complete that destruction at the forts which the ships themselves had not attained. The *Vengeance* was to send her party to the Asiatic shore, and the *Irresistible* to the European. Let us now watch the first mentioned on their dangerous undertaking.

It was just 2 p.m. when the *Vengeance* closed Kum Kale to land the adventurers. These comprised: (*a*) A demolition party under Lieut.-Commander E. G. Robinson, R.N., the ship's expert in all such explosive matters as are generally considered under " torpedoes." As his aide-de-camp went Midshipman John B. Woolley. The orders for this party of officers and men were to destroy whatever guns remained in Kum Kale and Orkanieh besides any anti-aircraft guns, for which purpose sufficient charges of gun-cotton were brought. (*b*) A party of fifty marines under Major G. M. Heriot, D.S.O., who were to cover Robinson's contingent.

By 2.30 the two parties had been put ashore, and the *Vengeance* lay abreast of the cemetery already described, whilst the light cruiser *Dublin* lay off Yeni Shehr, and the destroyer *Basilisk* was ready to the eastward. With the accompanying sketches, made at the time by an officer watching from one of the ships, the reader will have no difficulty in visualising the parties' progress.

" We saw them go past the cemetery," writes the same witness, " up to the semi-circular hollow, and they then signalled that they were attacked : so *Dublin* fired a salvo at Yeni Shehr mills, which downed three mills and stopped the enemy's fire from there. We, also, gave Yeni Shehr a few rounds : however, the marines still remained in the hollow firing fairly

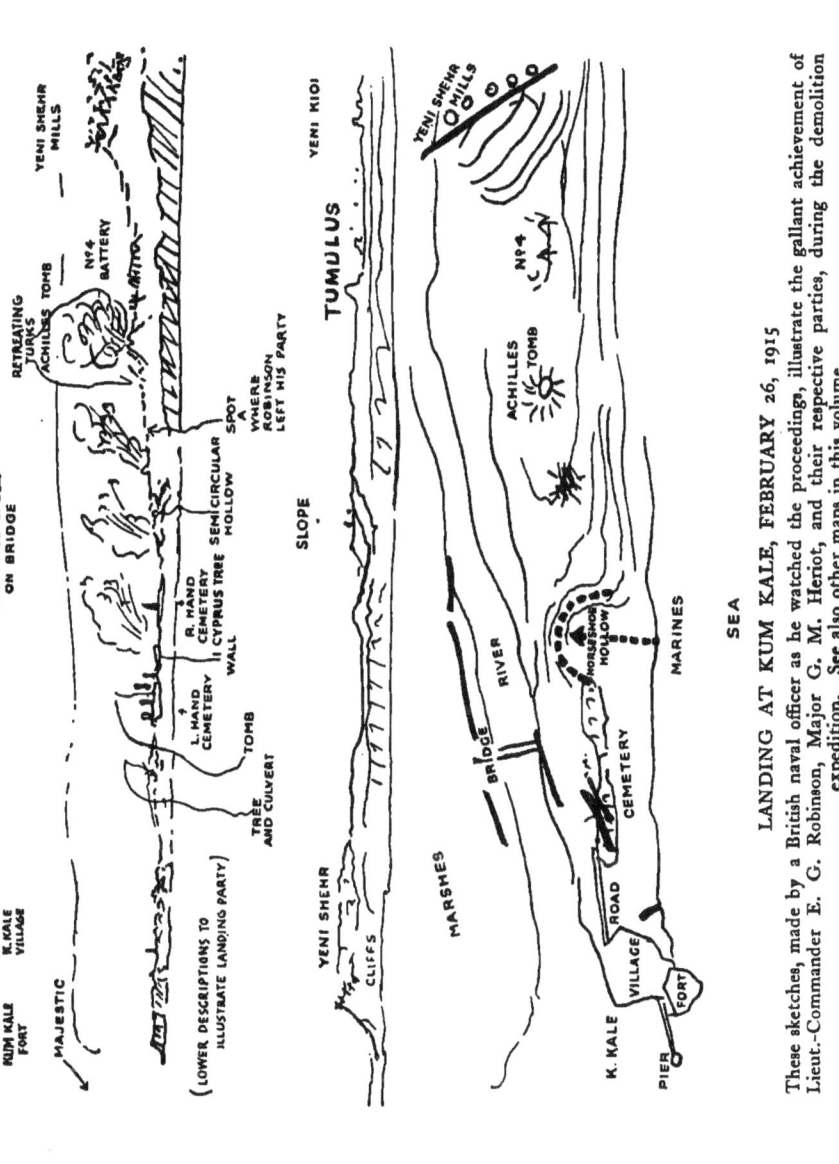

LANDING AT KUM KALE, FEBRUARY 26, 1915

These sketches, made by a British naval officer as he watched the proceedings, illustrate the gallant achievement of Lieut.-Commander E. G. Robinson, Major G. M. Heriot, and their respective parties, during the demolition expedition. See also other maps in this volume.

hard. It appears they were attacked from Mendere, on their left flank, and from hidden snipers in the left cemetery; also, till the guns stopped them, by a large force from Yeni Shehr. From the latter came very heavy rifle fire.

"When half-way up the slope (under fire all the time from Yeni Shehr direction) Robinson's party stopped and took cover, with the exception of one who went on up to Achilles Mound,[1] got inside the sort of crater at the top, walked calmly down again and, when he was just clear, we saw an explosion, and up went both anti-aircraft guns."

Now, this figure was Lieut.-Commander Robinson, who for the reason that the fire had become so heavy, and that he did not know whether the enemy might still be in Achilles Mound or in Orkanieh battery, considered it not fair to take his men forward: proceeding unaccompanied, he advanced with his charge of gun-cotton, placed it in the gun, the slow match allowed him just long enough to get away—and the brave deed had been accomplished. Merely for this splendid action he deserved, and was recommended for, the Victoria Cross; but during the next few weeks this officer qualified for that decoration several times over, as we shall perceive.

Meanwhile, to resume our story. After *Dublin's* salvo had put Yeni Shehr to silence, Robinson with some of his party were seen advancing some hundred and fifty yards towards the left-hand 9·4-inch, which still remained in Orkanieh. (The other one, as related in the previous chapter, had been capsized by the *Cornwallis* on the 25th.) If this surviving big gun could now be demolished, that fort might be crossed off the map altogether. Robinson, with unselfish devotion for his men, would again have gone alone, yet could not himself carry sufficient gun-cotton for this greater cannon, but the charge was rammed in as before, and once more success accrued. An extraordinarily fine effort, and affording valuable service to the Allied cause.

[1] It will be remembered that in the forenoon the *Vengeance's* shells had disclosed two Turkish anti-aircraft guns near Achilles Mound. (See previous chapter.)

It must not be expected that the Turks were to be passive during these operations, and now they had collected in strength to cut off the British party's retreat to the sea. Major Heriot signalled *Vengeance* that the enemy were in the cemetery at the left hand. From the ships this seemed to be two burial-grounds separated by a wall: actually it was continuous. At one end was Major Heriot, and at the other, among the white tombstones, lurked the enemy, athwart the escape down to the pier. Unfortunately, his left flanking party when going out had been ambushed, a sergeant of marines and two men being hit, so that for some while news could not reach the Major; who, having resolved that he would rescue his wounded, came not straight back, but for the achievement of his object saw he must fight his way through.

As these activities were being watched through binoculars aboard the ships, it was quite a problem to fire on the land without hitting our own men. So in the *Vengeance* the Captain temporarily left his forebridge and went down to let off the gun at the exact spot required. The shell burst among the Turks with such precision that the enemy bolted away. But now, when Major Heriot's wounded could be reached, it was to find that the Asiatics had brutally finished off their work by smashing in the sergeant's skull, jabbing him twice with bayonets, and adding two more bullet wounds. However, the marines found the leader of that enemy party hiding in the culvert which is shown on the accompanying sketch. Fired with indignation, our men had no time for mercy, and finished off this leader with promptness.

Thus, after avenging the death of Sergeant Turnbull, and having only two others seriously wounded, the whole party miraculously regained boats and ship. Of the above injured, one man lost an eye, whilst the other had been badly hit on the shoulder. A third man got off with only a scratch on the chin. Altogether the cost of this useful demolition had been remarkably slight: indeed, totally out of proportion to the risks and number of shells which must have been expended had battleships alone completed the required destruction. It was noted by the visitors that the enemy had been regularly living in the cemetery in a raised tomb. When our 6-inch lyddite reached this abode of the dead, a weird and gruesome jack-in-the-box effect was created of the previous year's corpses and limbs flying about the Asiatic air.

The corresponding assault on Sedd-el-Bahr was scarcely less enthralling, and the arrangements were not dissimilar: that is to say, Lieut. F. H. Sandford, the *Irresistible's* Torpedo Officer, was in charge of the demolition, whilst her Marine Officer, Captain H. B. N. Panton, commanded the covering party. Nor was this the final occasion on which Lieut. Sandford found himself engaged on a dangerous mission. Three years hence he was present during the St. George's Day attack against Zeebrugge, when the submarine *C 3* blew herself up beneath the viaduct connecting mole to shore, and his brother, Lieut. R. D. Sandford, her commanding officer, won the Victoria Cross.

The *Irresistible* at 2.53 p.m., just before sending in her demolition party, fired a few rounds into Sedd-el-Bahr. The covering party of forty-five marines got to the east of that village, whilst Sandford's contingent with their gun-cotton dashed in and very quickly demolished the guns. At first the marines, as might be expected, were met with some opposition, and against this the naval shells proved their worth as co-operators by driving away all resistance and allowing the invaders to do their job. It will not have been forgotten that in Sedd-el-Bahr the enemy had erected six great guns varying from 11-inch to 9·4-inch, and two had suffered during the bombardments. There now ensued four terrific explosions, such as had never been heard at the Dardanelles. The magazines, as well as guns, had been touched off, and an enormous smoke-cloud gave visible information that this fort had now lost its sting. Owing to the enemy's increasing opposition (as had occurred on the Asiatic shore), the whole party were recalled to their boats, and returned to *Irresistible* without any but the slightest casualties. By seven o'clock that night all ships' boats had been hoisted in and stations were being taken for the night patrol. Along came the minesweeping trawlers,[1] who explored to a distance of four miles from the entrance, but nothing was yet found.

The forenoon of the 27th was marked by bad weather, which deferred other endeavours to complete the good work so excellently begun. There still remained to be destroyed Helles, besides the guns at Kum Kale, and some modern Krupp howitzers near Sedd-el-Bahr. At present the gale, however brief, gave a short breathing-space and an opportunity to reflect. Nothing could be clearer than the evidence that the Dardanelles were still very far from being mastered—was indeed barely touched. Depression had not yet seized the mind, yet no one could disguise from himself that things were hardly progressing in accord with the original optimism. Not enough was it that bold battleships should come along making lots of noise and smoke, and loosing off ammunition at doubtful targets. Guns ashore had been carefully concealed, howitzers were being run about from this spot to that by bullocks, and neatly hidden among the hills; so that the target positions were being constantly varied. Then, again, thanks to German ingenuity, there would be made "powder puffs" or dummy explosions to mislead us; and the ensuing deluge of British shells would merely rouse mirth.

The enemy, being short of ammunition, but likewise being very shrewd, disciplined his hate till the opportunities were beyond doubt. The *Majestic*, for example, after closing in to within 5000 yards of Eren Keui, shelled it for a whole hour, without ever getting one single reply. "The Turks seem all to have gone to tea!" was the remark heard.

The weather on the afternoon of the 27th suddenly improved, which allowed *Irresistible* to land a second demolition party to the east of Sedd-el-Bahr. Once more went the gallant Lieut. Sandford, but this time they were covered by seventy-eight marines with a couple of machine-guns. Without opposition

---

[1] The final four trawlers sent out from England had left Malta on February 15, so that the entire flotilla of twenty-one had now joined Admiral Carden. More were presently to follow.

they gained the cliff-top, and the enemy's interference was frustrated by fire from *Irresistible's* 6-inch. This enabled four Krupp howitzers to be destroyed by gun-cotton, whilst Sandford (in the tradition of Lieut.-Commander Robinson), rather than risk his men, destroyed the other two mortars himself. Thanks again to the *Irresistible's* protective fire, the whole plan had been carried out, demolition party and marines got back to the ship, and there had been no casualty. Could anything be more satisfactory and significant? After a further day of bad weather, Sandford finally crowned his previous efforts by landing with his demolition party and fifty marines on the Asiatic side. There were nine guns in Kum Kale, the largest being of 11-inch, the medium 8-inch, and the smallest 6-inch. Entering the fort, Sandford's little band demolished the lot, and made their rapid escape to the water before the Turks could chase after them from Yeni Shehr village.

The strength of these outer defences had thus become considerably altered during the last three days. Sedd-el-Bahr, Kum Kale, Orkanieh, had all been robbed of their ferocity: the front teeth of the Dardanelles' jaws had been pulled out. We had learnt that ships could with difficulty bombard forts, unless anchored, and their fire spotted by other vessels; yet we had also learned, with pain, that in those circumstances the plunging fire of concealed howitzers could make a nasty mess of spotless quarter-decks and more casualties than had accrued to all the marines and demolition parties together. But the days for these heroic excursions into the enemy's forts were nearly finished, since the enemy now brought along sufficient force to prevent their recurrence, and on the top of all were to be reckoned the smaller batteries, as well as mobile howitzers; and whilst these became more numerous the farther one approached Chanak, there were further obstacles abreast of Kephez. With the powerful Messudieh (No. 7) battery on one side, confronted by Dardanos (No. 8), where the Straits narrow before widening out at Sari Siglar Bay, the same old problem of the once-active outer forts must present itself.

And with a greater intensiveness because of the minefields, and the minefield batteries, with their searchlight defences illumining the water by night. Farther up still were the exceedingly powerful defences at Chanak and its opposite shore, where the European coast bends elbow-shape. In short, reckoning from west to east along the north (or European) shore, and omitting everything till after Sedd-el-Bahr, there were not fewer than twenty-two howitzers and mortars, thirty-two intermediate guns, plus thirty-nine guns at the Narrows. Similarly on the south (or Asiatic) coast east of Kum Kale and Orkanieh, were not less than twenty-four howitzers and forty-seven guns up to Chanak, followed by another score above.

At the beginning of March, then, the Allied Fleet were still faced with the prodigious labour of having to reduce two lines of artillery that did not lend themselves to identification, and were well placed for denying a fleet's passage. The Narrows are only a dozen miles from the Dardanelles mouth, yet every yard would have to be contended, and then made secure for the entire naval procession. Whilst Dardanos would not cease to be rather more than a nuisance, the greatest trouble would come from Fort 16 (Hamidieh II), with its two long-range guns, and Fort 19 (Hamidieh I), with its nine big cannon. Thus the area for manœuvring battleships was considerably restricted.

Such was the prospect before us when, on March 4, there came the last of the intrepid landings, and on a more ambitious scale than hitherto. The previous day there had been seen arriving two transports, of which one was the *Braemar Castle*, with 2000 marines, which anchored at Imbros. The Dardanelles Fleet had by this date increased till it had added the *Lord Nelson, Ocean, Canopus, Swiftsure,* and *Prince George* to the battleships: there were now under Admiral Carden's flag no fewer than fourteen capital ships and four light cruisers, all flying the White Ensign, besides the four French battleships of Admiral Guépratte; destroyers, trawlers, aeroplane-carrier, and submarines (including *AE* 2, which had just arrived, all the way from Australia). Yes: what a collection of naval might! And now, with the beginning of ocean-going liners for transports, bringing marines from England as well as Australians from Egypt, this "diversion" on behalf of the Russians had already grown beyond all recognition: yet was not even now fully developed. In command of the Mudros base Rear-Admiral Rosslyn E. Wemyss had been appointed, and by the end of March this important harbour for every kind of Allied shipping had been protected with an anti-submarine boom. Actually, whilst this Lemnos port was the main anchorage, other islands were used, such as Tenedos and Imbros, which sometimes led to complication. "Another of the curses of the present complete lack of organisation," complained a naval officer at the time, "is that we have *six* bases! And no one knows where ships are. Consequently, 'Operation Orders' often arrive on board a ship *after* they should have been carried out." But fortunate it was that so near at hand was some haven where men-of-war could come in to clean boilers, repair their damaged hulls, overhaul machinery (long since due for the scrap-heap), and rest their men.

No other country in the world could have owned and maintained in commission two such great fleets simultaneously: the one in south-eastern Europe, the other among Scottish mists. In the older ships which made up the greater portion of this Dardanelles Armada, one-third of their complement, a Captain informs me, consisted of Royal Naval Reserve ratings, mostly from the west coast of Scotland. "We had thirty-two Macdonalds on board—which was nice for the Paymaster! My Midshipmen were all cadets straight from the Royal Naval College, Dartmouth. Their work was magnificent. As to the individual value of these older ships, their market price then was approximately only £40,000." (The *Queen Elizabeth*, on the other hand, cost several millions.) No wonder those in high places, who calculated in terms of money and material rather than in the lives of human men, talked freely of using these "old crocks" to lead the way when forcing the Dardanelles. Homogeneity did not exist in the Ægean, for whilst Admiral Carden's fleet comprised eighteen armoured vessels, they were composed of ten different classes. As if to make matters stranger still, there arrived during the first week of March two of those " Dummy Dreadnoughts ": that is, ex-merchant steamers which had been ingeniously altered externally to resemble battleships so closely as might deceive the enemy at a distance. Thus the S.S. *Oruba* (5971 tons) became H.M.S. *Orion*, complete with wooden "guns," and the S.S. *Michigan* (4935 tons) purported to be H.M.S. *St. Vincent*. The former finally concluded her career as block-ship at Kephalos Bay, and the latter at Mudros. Also were sent out the ex-S.S. *Manipur* (7654 tons) to represent the battle-cruiser *Indomitable* (that had long since quitted the Mediterranean), ex-S.S. *Patrician* (7474 tons), pretending to be the battle-cruiser *Invincible*, and the ex-S.S. *Merion* (11,621 tons), as the battle-cruiser *Tiger*.

The intention in sending these imitations to the Dardanelles was that they should be seen off the Straits' entrance, so as to mislead the Germans as to the margin of strength left in Home waters. They steamed out in great secrecy, avoided all shipping on the voyage, did not even call at Gibraltar, and on their arrival at Tenedos certainly misled some of our own people. "Two dummy warships arrived," wrote one naval officer in his private journal of March 6. "They are wonderfully good at a short distance, and deceived several people." The Turks were fooled, but the biggest joke of all happened on May 30, when the alleged *Tiger* was torpedoed in the Ægean by Germany's ablest submarine commander.

That story belongs to a later chapter, and we must now address ourselves to the remarkable affair of March 4.

CHAPTER XII

THE SECOND DILEMMA

IF the arrival of marines from England, and their immediate employment ashore for the very kind of work that they might be expected to tackle, seems quite in the natural order of things, it also denoted the change that was coming slowly but had long been foreshadowed. In Whitehall—and certainly on the eastern side thereof—an obstinate reluctance to send troops had been largely overcome only because the Fleet seemed faced with failure. But the Admiralty, in despatching part of the Royal Naval Division to reach the Dardanelles at such a stage in the campaign, were in effect suggesting the gradual transformation of a naval into a military campaign. Many events must precede such a complete turn round, yet the tendency to a new direction now existed. Not without interest will this be noted, whilst our main concern is with the actual striving against immense obstacles.

That which just now occupied Admiral Carden's mind was to make absolutely certain, beyond all possibility of doubt whatever, that Helles on the north, and Orkanieh on the south, really were toothless. With regard to the latter, as we know, Robinson with his demolition party had already done what was needed, and the *Queen Elizabeth's* 15-inch shells on the 25th had knocked out Helles. Perhaps it was natural enough that the Admiral should insist on perfect conviction, but the cost of " going to look inside " must be considerable now that the Turks were so wide-awake. Was the risk worth while ? In any case, the scheme has been greatly criticised by naval officers.

It was an ideal day, this first Thursday in March, with a calm sea and clear atmosphere. The *Lord Nelson* off Helles, the *Ocean* abreast of Sedd-el-Bahr, and the *Majestic* slightly farther east within Morto Bay, were to cover the northern shore; whilst the *Irresistible* and *Cornwallis* were off Kum Kale and the Mendere river; round the western corner being *Dublin* at her old position off Yeni Shehr, with *Agamemnon* near by. Five hundred of the Naval Division were to be fetched from the *Braemar Castle*: two hundred and fifty for landing at Kum Kale, and the other half at Sedd-el-Bahr. The demolition parties were supplied for the north side from the *Inflexible* and *Ocean* under the *Inflexible's* torpedo-specialist, Lieut.-Commander Frederic Giffard, and we may confine our attention to them first.

Long before 10 a.m. the sea was all activity. " Ships everywhere," wrote one officer at the time, " hoisting out boats and getting ready generally." The boats were being sent to disembark the marines, but destroyers were buzzing about conveying their quota. This is the lively picture as seen from on board the *Majestic*:

"At about 9.30 a.m. the marines and demolition parties, which had been brought in by destroyers from the transports and men-of-war, were put into ships' boats, launches, pinnaces, cutters, and towed ashore. It was sufficiently exciting to watch. We were so occupied with the Sedd-el-Bahr party that we did not see much of what was going on at Kum Kale. Just before the landing an aeroplane had flown over the cypress groves fronting Morto Bay, and had been heavily fired on by troops concealed among the trees. Their position having been given away, we searched the cypress and olive groves with shrapnel and common shell.

"As the boats, in tow of the picket-boats, approached the camber, the Turks, who were not in great force, opened fire among the houses just above; and the boats had a lively time. As soon as the latter were alongside, the covering party jumped ashore and took cover behind walls. We soon saw people being brought down on stretchers. Sniping was going on from the cottages and hovels of the village. The snipers, however, were answered by some fine rifle-shooting from the boats. The latter got hit a good deal by the enemy, yet only two of our men were grazed.

"Presently," continues this narrative, " we saw the heads of the Turkish troops appearing on the sky line, close to us, making for the old ruined fort above the village. We gave them plenty of 12-pounder shrapnel. Reinforcements being required, we got orders to land our detachment of marines. The announcement was greeted with delight by the detachment, numbering ninety-seven, who soon got into their gear, and were reported ready by our Captain of Marines. Meanwhile I witnessed a brave deed on shore. In front of the old fort ran a trench, to which access by the Turks was only to be obtained by coming over the top of the hill, and under our shrapnel fire. This, apparently, the Turkish troops were not inclined to do; and small blame to them. A German officer, as we could tell by his uniform, who was leading them, wishing to set them an example, walked slowly out in front of the old fort and stood there facing us, with his hands behind his back. Presently one of our 6-inch shells burst on the hillside just below him. It seemed almost at his feet. When the smoke had cleared away, he was still standing there. We took care not to fire at him again. Presently he strolled to the trench just behind the top of the hill, and reappeared dragging a Turk by the scruff of his neck with each hand. Pulling them in front of the fort, he threw them into the trench there. Then the rest followed. He had obtained his object."

It is a pleasure to mention this act of chivalry: this instance of courageous men immediately recognising the conspicuous bravery of a foe. The self-control and big-heartedness of sparing an enemy, as a reward for his good deed, deserve to be remembered amid all the battle and strife of those difficult days. Only a few weeks later the *Majestic* was destined to founder, by the action of a German torpedo. The battleship went down with many of her crew. Let it be part of the latter's memorial that, in the moment when passions ran high, this vessel had treated an enemy with courtesy, and spared his life.

"We were lying stemming the current," Commander

Barne proceeds, " and, as soon as we could, I got the detachment down into the boats, which were under the starboard quarter. Just as they were about to go down, there came the singing of a shell from Achillæum.[1] I was on the after-shelter deck at the time, and to my surprise there was a crash, with a few pieces of flying wood on the quarter-deck, and a heavy explosion down below, in the region of the after-deck. On opening up the starboard quarter-deck hatch, up came clouds of lyddite smoke, and on going down the ladder my feet trod on nothing, so down I went.

"The shell had passed through the covering board and exploded in the Paymaster's cabin, taking the whole of its contents (together with bunk, chest of drawers and bulkhead) out on to the after-deck, where it was on fire. The pieces of shell had gone through all the surrounding bulkheads and down through the main deck into the gun-room flat. Some of our people putting out the fire had been overcome by the fumes, and had been brought up to be restored.

"When all the marines were in the boat, the order to land them was countermanded by the Admiral, to their great disappointment, and they had to return on board. The guns at Sedd-el-Bahr fort having been successfully demolished by the demolition parties, the next thing was to get them all aboard again. To cover their embarkation, the battleships on our side were told to bombard the village, and in a few minutes there was in place of a village a smoking ruin.[2] Owing to this, the party got off without many casualties; the snipers having gone the same way as the bricks."

Summing up, the nett result of this northern expedition had not been commensurate with the risks. Major Harry Palmer, in charge of the marine party, having been held up by the Turks' opposition, signalled for another 200 men, and the battleships were preparing to send these when Admiral de

---

[1] On the Asiatic shore behind Eren Keui Bay.
[2] An officer who watched from the *Lord Nelson* writes: "The party had to come off eventually under a very heavy covering fire, which quite spoilt the pretty little village, including the minaret."

THE SECOND DILEMMA

Robeck (flying his flag in the *Irresistible*),[1] after consultation with General Trotman (in command of the Dardanelles marines), decided that the undertaking did not justify further jeopardising of men's lives. The episode ended with two enemy guns destroyed, three men killed, and three injured. Too many Turkish troops and German officers had prevented any but this slender success, and abandonment had been wiser than initiation.

Scarcely more happy had been the southern attempt. Here the demolition party was again under a Torpedo specialist, Lieut.-Commander William L. Dodgson, from the *Lord Nelson*, Lieut.-Colonel Godfrey E. Matthews being in charge of the marines. It is true that Kum Kale village was shelled, but it needed to have been shelled still more, before the parties leapt ashore. The plan was to destroy both forts, Kum Kale and Orkanieh. The trestle pier, which some time ago we saw being damaged by the *Majestic*, had not yet been entirely smashed up, and the houses at the back of the beach contained too many snipers, who poured an unpleasant fire on our men landing from the cutters and launches. In Orkanieh, too, were more enemy troops.

Opposed by superior numbers, it was never possible to get very far from the shore with any permanence: the snipers dominated the position, and the economy enforced by Whitehall in respect of shells (already too few on all our war fronts at that date) had made it impracticable for the covering ships to do their utmost. Many a plucky effort that long day was made by this precarious body of sailors and marines to achieve the impossible. Some of them sacrificed their lives quite early, even at the pier, and the resources for gaining a little protection were almost nil. Two of the men from *Lord Nelson* were seen actually taking cover behind a box full of detonators. Only the battleships' burst of fire enabled retirement to the beach without complete massacre; but, for the reason that these vessels could not always know where our parties had reached, and where the enemy were alone, it was not easy to direct the guns.

[1] Because the *Vengeance* was repairing her boilers at Mudros.

Let me present the picture as it looked from the *Majestic*. Her Commander has told me:

"The party were practically driven back to their boats. We saw one lot, who had advanced along the shore towards Orkanieh. They had got nearly to their objective, when they were cut off from the shoreward side by Turks concealed among the low sandhills which fronted the beach. It was a distressing sight to see them being shot down, and there was soon a row of them along the beach, some in and others out of the water. The Fleet fairly bombarded the shore above them, but did not succeed in stopping the sniping. I saw one wounded man crawl on all fours all the way along the beach, and was glad to see him reach the boats. That night Gunner Walter Thorogood took an armed whaler from the destroyer *Scorpion* twice to the beach, bringing away two officers and five men under heavy rifle fire. The day's casualties for this southern landing were nineteen killed, twenty-five wounded, and three missing."

The operation had completely failed to attain any result. Why? The answer is succinctly given by our former enemy General Liman von Sanders,[1] who says that our repeated attempts to land marines and take the forts by surprise "were unsuccessful because, in spite of the bombardment, small Turkish bodies had remained in places not reached by the artillery fire, and repulsed the landing." The same authority demonstrates that the Turks had ordered such erroneous preparations, between February 20 and March 1, to meet a likely successful passage of the Allied Fleet, that the latter were more favoured than they suspected.

"Had these orders been carried out, the course of the World War would have been given such a turn in the spring of 1915 that Germany and Austria would have had to continue the struggle without Turkey, because these orders exposed the Dardanelles to a hostile landing." This far-

[1] *Five Years in Turkey*, p. 53.

seeing General therefore protested so strenuously that the orders were cancelled. And from this same writer comes a further answer to a query that for many years had never been settled.

Human minds cannot tolerate suspense: curiosity demands to know the results following from certain causes. Conversely, it insists on knowing the causes of notable results. Thus, to leave a story unfinished, to come out of a theatre before the *dénouement*, to see the loose ends waving in the air untied, gives nothing but dissatisfaction. On the other hand, how pleasing is the occupation of observing the solution, and the settling of all that had been once uncertain! The puzzle has amused us till the pieces have been fitted exactly, and not till then can the box of tricks be laid aside.

But the actions and counteractions of mankind, which make up history, the variations and surprises, the doubts as to defined issues, the sustained eagerness of one rival to overcome the other, will never cease to provide the world's best stories. Quite half the fun of a fight belongs to the spectators, who witness both sides of the contest. And so, after two decades, we of our generation are permitted to take a universal view over the Dardanelles.

On March 1, 1915, the *Irresistible*, flying Admiral de Robeck's flag, the *Albion, Triumph, Ocean* and *Majestic*, were all concerned with the operation of reducing the guns along the south shore in the Achillæum, the howitzers and field guns in the neighbourhood of Eren Keui being especially included. The duty turned out to be somewhat annoying; for, having apparently silenced one position and gone on to the next, the first would begin again. Others would never even trouble to bark back; but then, all of a sudden, some concealed guns would challenge in the most menacing manner, which compelled these battleships, with their attendant destroyers, to cruise about in circles. I find in one of the private journals under that date: "We stirred up the Achillæum battery with a 6-inch shell," during the forenoon. "There was no reply until the afternoon, when they fired on us for half an hour."

Now, von Sanders accurately remarks that five British battleships with destroyers to-day entered the Dardanelles and engaged the Turkish howitzer batteries on Halil Eli (immediately behind the Achillæum) abreast of Eren Keui Bay. He says that the hostile ships directed their fire not only against genuine batteries, "but against dummy positions," specially constructed and frequently changed. Thus every day, and in many ways, the enemy, under German guidance, was luring us to waste the rare shells on perfectly futile purposes. The sparing use of marines during the abortive attempts against the empty forts on March 4 had once again shown the piecemeal, half-hearted methods which characterised our procedure. Big undertakings demand big risks, and big resources; but the craze for caution, during this phase at the Dardanelles, was extended so far as to defeat its own object. Sternly disciplined, trained, and led by German officers, the Turks were stationed so strongly at the most obvious posts, that we could never spring a surprise again. Only sheer superiority of numbers and bloody slaughter could in future ashore make up for lost opportunities.

Another disquieting development foretold a most serious dilemma, although its significance was not yet fully appreciated. The trawlers were still burdened with too much responsibility: on their backs, so to speak, the battleships must be carried beyond the Narrows. And if the backs broke, what then? On the night of March 1, six trawlers, and their guide—making seven in all—were sent to sweep an area that would enable the bombarding battleships to steam so far up as Kephez, and thereby reduce the inner defences. In order to be afforded protection, there were assigned to them the light cruiser *Amethyst* and four destroyers. Slowly they progressed against the strong current for several miles, and even got to within 3000 yards of Kephez Point. But it was full moon that night, and when off the Suandere river everything happened in a tick of time. Suddenly the enemy awoke, the first lines of searchlights on either shore flashed— to silhouette masts, funnel, wheelhouse, rigging and gallows.

Each dark-hulled trawler was now a white target. Several batteries on the European, and on the Asiatic, side concentrated their fire at point-blank range. The distance across the Dardanelles at this position is less than $2\frac{1}{4}$ miles, so that any pair of ships coming up the centre would be in range of barely a mile; and the enemy let fly at the fishermen so fiercely that the latter now slipped their wires and retired hurriedly downstream, whilst their escort shelled guns and searchlights too.

Another dilemma had indicated itself: for they had barely reached the fringe of the minefield. How would they fare when the Straits became less wide, the searchlights and protecting batteries more numerous?

If battleships could not wipe out defences till trawlers had cleared the mines, if trawlers could not sweep the mines till the defences had been demolished, then a deadlock was surely due. Nor were these mines imaginary, for on that self-same 1st of March a line of seventeen, stretching out from the Kephez coast, had been located by one of our seaplanes. During the night of March 2–3 the trawlers resumed their efforts, but could make no advance against the heavy fire, and subsequent attempts scarcely seemed promising.

CHAPTER XIII

MINES AND SHELLS

" I MUST, as an officer, declare it to be my decided opinion that, without the co-operation of a body of land forces, it would be a wanton sacrifice of the squadrons of both nations to attempt to force the passage."

This unequivocal statement was written by a British Admiral in the month of March concerning the Dardanelles. These words are the plain, straightforward utterance of a sailor who also asked for so many troops " as may be equal to land and destroy the batteries of the Dardanelles, and, by occupying the principal posts, to render our return secure." It is, however, of considerable interest to note that they were written by Admiral Sir John Duckworth, and the date was March 10, 1807. The geography was the same, the problem of forts *versus* ships was the same, there was even a *Canopus* in the British squadron; Russia was our ally, Tenedos our base, and the Turks our enemy. At the Narrows were no minefields, but the castles of Abydos and Sestos were heavily fortified. The strong current was much the same, and ships had to wait for a fair wind to sail up or down. In all the essential features the Dardanelles dilemma had not altered during 108 years: it was identically one problem, whether hulls were made of oak or steel, propelled by sail or steam. Thus, when, on March 5, 1915—the day following those two disastrous weak landings at the outer forts—General Birdwood telegraphed the War Office that he was doubtful if the Navy could force the passage unassisted, and on the 6th still further confirmed this opinion, one could hardly be surprised. That which makes one wonder is that Admiral Carden had not yet come to the General's verdict.

On March 3 the Dardanelles Fleet had been increased by the arrival of a strange vessel having five tall funnels. This was the fifteen-year-old Russian light cruiser *Askold* (5905 tons), and she now began her third campaign. Years ago she had served in the Japanese war, lost one of her funnels, but saved her life. She was part of the Russian Fleet which escaped on August 10, 1904, from Port Arthur; ten years later came the Great War, and she was still in the western Pacific. Hostilities had barely begun ere the German *Emden* sought to waylay her, in August 1914, but failed. In that same month the *Askold* joined up with the British Commander-in-Chief in China, Admiral Jerram; performed some useful work patrolling, escorting troop transports, and so on. (See photograph facing p. 58.)

After the fall of Tsing Tao in November 1914, she could well be spared in more western seas, and her twelve 6-inch guns, together with her speed (about 20 knots), might be found serviceable. Apart altogether from the work performed off the Syrian coast, she was most convenient off the Dardanelles as a means of communicating with the Russians in the Black Sea. The reader has noted how shut off from her Allies were Russia's forces at the very time when co-operation was deemed most requisite. So by means of the *Askold's* wireless, using the 1000-metre wave-length, she could now talk across Turkey to the cruiser *Kagul* in the Black Sea, who passed on messages to Sebastopol. The *Goeben*, of course, soon became aware of this, and did her best to jam such conversation.

Meanwhile, the Dardanelles bombardments went on against the inner forts. It was on March 5 that the *Queen Elizabeth*, whilst anchored 2½ miles to the south-west of Gaba Tepe, began indirect firing across the land at Fort 13. This was Rumili Medjidieh, situated at the Narrows on the European elbow. To have reduced this defence to impotence would have been greatly in our favour: its half a dozen big guns, including 11-inch and 9·4-inch, were too dominant and well placed against ships coming up the Straits. Only slightly farther up than Rumili Medjidieh was Fort 17 (Namazieh), which likewise had an 11-inch, a 10·2-inch, a couple of 9·4-inch, and two smaller. The *Queen Elizabeth's* project denoted an ambitious effort, since the distance across the peninsula was most of eight miles as the shell flies.

Anchored stem and stern, the area having been swept for

any mines, she had no easy task. It is true that whereas the *Inflexible's* range was about 15,000 yards, and *Queen Elizabeth's* actually 22,000 with her new 15-inch weapons, this big ship was to-day attempting nearly her extreme limit of effectiveness. In support of her, cruising about, were the *Inflexible* and *Prince George*. But there seems to have been at the Dardanelles, somehow, a condition which one critic on the spot referred to as " a screw loose." Letters written home at the time, or remarks jotted down from day to day, all kept expressing such remarks as " I don't think much of the way this Fleet is run "; or, again, touching some unfortunate operation, " Absolutely fatuous idea ! " " Folly and waste of time."

So the *Queen Elizabeth* did not receive her orders till 11 a.m., and then it needed about half an hour to get her into position, with a result that the best part of daylight had gone by the time she was firing. A field battery would not let her alone, and hit her twenty times, until the *Inflexible* silenced it with her two 4-inch anti-aircraft guns, whilst the *Prince George* in like manner " plastered " the Turks with thoroughness. But the principal difficulty was to know if these great 15-inch shells, after travelling ten miles, were really falling on the target. Therefore ships and aeroplanes were employed to do the spotting, and not too successfully. Those were the infantile days of aviation, yet it did not help matters when one aeroplane crashed, another had her pilot wounded, and a third did no good. A hot rifle-fire received the fliers with accuracy, and negatived the help which *Queen Elizabeth* had expected. Up the Straits had been sent the three ships *Irresistible*, *Canopus*, and *Cornwallis*, also to spot how the shells fell; and every few minutes whichever vessel chanced to be leading would wireless the result. It was for that date all wonderfully modern and interesting, yet a little complicated, and needing a good deal more experience. These last three ships were naturally attacked by howitzers and guns of various calibre; and the *Canopus* lost her main topmast, which saved her Commander the trouble of sending it down, as he had

ONE OF THE *MAJESTIC* CLASS
H.M.S. *Prince George* at Malta, with picket-boat alongside.

12-POUNDER ANTI-AIRCRAFT GUN
In H.M.S. *Prince George*.

intended, after the fashion of the *Vengeance* and others. The day's events may be summed up thus: Spotting only partially satisfactory, even from ships. Of the twenty-eight rounds which *Queen Elizabeth* fired on Fort 13, there had been eleven hits; and each of the five rounds on Fort 17 was a hit. But a hit on what?

To-day we know that though the forts were severely damaged, and the enemy's gun-crews badly shocked, yet not one gun was injured. That was the disappointing feature, and the one which essentially mattered, although some encouragement was found when a heavy explosion indicated that some of the Turks' shells had been blown up.

But our hammering did not cease, and next day *Queen Elizabeth* resumed her long-range blows. After all, much had been expected of her, and her very presence was based on the belief that she could apply the right weight. She did not begin till 12.30 p.m., and this time she was to aim at Fort 20—that is, Chemenlek—which lay on the Asiatic side of the Narrows just opposite the two defences that had been the previous day's objective. Chemenlek was well selected for its formidability, and a visible duel would have been worth watching, since it contained, besides four howitzers, an 8·2-inch and a 9·4-inch gun, but especially a couple of Krupps' 14-inch. Only two other forts possessed such a weapon; viz., the neighbouring Hamidieh I (just to the southward of Chanak), which had two, and Hamidieh II (on the European shore facing), which had one. To knock out any of these would be a very profitable achievement; but a very difficult and, indeed, impossible one.

Queen Elizabeth began from the same billet as previously, but she had fired only a single round when she was hit six or eight times, and had to move out 2000 yards. She was then hit again, and by the time she had reached her third position the indifferent light had failed. That was at 3.30 p.m. She had been compelled to edge off from the shore till she was at 21,000 yards from her target: or just 1000 yards short of her limit. When we consider that shells hurled from a distance of more than eleven miles must strike not merely the fortifications, but the Krupp guns themselves, and that these were invisible, we begin to understand the profitless expenditure of costly ammunition, the serious wear and tear of armament, the risk of the world's best ship—and the minute chance of the enemy's cause being weakened. The spotting had again been unsatisfactory, and apart from sending up smoke, earth, and dust, no material advantage had accrued. This long-range bombardment had proved a fiasco, but she herself had been hit no fewer than seventeen times that day, chiefly by concealed 6-inch howitzers.

Concerning the latter, a naval officer who was present gives me the following information:

"These were the beasts; you couldn't see where they were coming from. They were concealed in the hollows of the rolling European hills. At last I caught sight of some gun wheels, and after a lot of difficulty managed to show them to our guns. We then plastered the enemy with 6-inch. It was difficult to remember all the hidden places, but whenever we got opposite a certain ravine we usually heard the whistle, and then the wang as each shell dropped near us."

But a further development that day was a copy of our own methods. In an earlier chapter we observed that the Turkish Navy included an old battleship named the *Barbarossa*, which mounted six 11-inch guns. She would have experienced a very short life during any engagement in the open sea, for her best speed had never exceeded about 17 knots, and that was twenty-two years ago. Nevertheless, the Turks and their German leaders were becoming apprehensive of our persistency, and it was not pleasant that the British should drop explosives from outside the Straits nor receive the heaviest in return. For the weak feature of forts is the immobility of their cannon. So the *Barbarossa* was brought down to the Narrows with her 11-inch, and fired over Gallipoli peninsula, having placed observers at Gaba Tepe to report how the shoot-

A BIG SHELL
From the enemy falling short of H.M.S. *Queen Elizabeth*.

H.M.S. *QUEEN ELIZABETH*
At the Dardanelles.

ing fared. They were able to note that *Queen Elizabeth* was struck below her water-line thrice.

After the latter had ceased fire and " packed up," the four British battleships *Vengeance, Albion, Prince George,* and *Majestic,* assisted by the French *Suffren,* made four runs to above Eren Keui. At a range of 13,000 yards, Fort 13 (Rumili Medjidieh), on the European side of the Narrows, came under heavy fire, and Dardanos (No. 8) had been again assaulted. The latter (for the reasons mentioned already) was still very lively: notwithstanding hundreds of shells, Dardanos replied with energy. Rumili Medjidieh was both busy and accurate, as bits of his 9·4-inch shell fell aboard *Vengeance,* who received four hits that afternoon: three on her main armour (and so availed nothing), and one on her thin armour, which did little worse than creating a bulge and shifting a few rivets. The *Majestic* was struck on her port side aft with a lyddite shell, which made a hole in the deck, but no casualties occurred. Then the light faded, another Saturday evening had set in, and it was time for the big vessels to return. Out came the *Suffren* with true Gallic enthusiasm, crew cheering, the ship's band playing " Tipperary," and Admiral Guépratte an electrical figure on the bridge.

Now, that was but the conclusion of another scene; for at midnight along came the trawlers, whose work was dangerous enough by night and impossible by day. Guarded by the light cruiser *Amethyst* and destroyers, they renewed their efforts to reach the mines, but again the enemy with his searchlights and batteries was waiting, so the sweepers could not get beyond a line connecting Suandere with Kephez Bay. The deadlock was not less pronounced than hitherto.

Sunday (March 7) seemed just in accordance with the dull, unprogressive routine that in this period characterised the operations. We were getting into a hard, unimaginative, unprofitable procedure, and nothing but stalemate seemed ahead. Officers and men were beginning to feel the boredom; it was time something really happened, the opportunity seemed ripe for new measures and fresh ideas. It demanded a new leader—must we say as much?—with greater driving power and a more energetic direction. Hearts were not drooping, though interest was slightly wavering, and these daily bombardments availed nothing. But even a Nelson or a St. Vincent would have found himself equally at a dead end, and the fault lay in the beginning. With all those ships and courageous men, all these days and nights, we had been able to reach only a short distance inside the headlands. At this pace the naval guns would all be worn out, and the older boilers falling to bits, ere the Sea of Marmora came into sight.

So the *Agamemnon* and *Lord Nelson* came up to within 13,000 yards of Fort 13, but the light made it difficult to ascertain the latter's exact position, though Rumili Medjidieh and Hamidieh I could see the two battleships and answered them with hits. Then, after the *Suffren*, *Charlemagne*, *Gaulois*, and *Bouvet* had blazed at the annoying howitzers and field guns, the action was broken off at 3 p.m. Another day was crossed off the calendar.

During that night, however, something did happen, something that was to have dire results, something that could have been made possible only after noting our established routine. The results were not immediate, but they were severe; and their narration will fall into its proper sequence a little later. All that we need say now is that on this night of the 7th–8th the French minesweepers, covered by seven British destroyers, tried their efforts on the Kephez minefields, but received the same hot welcome that their brothers from Aberdeen, Grimsby, and Lowestoft were wont to expect from the shores. Now, the enemy must have waited till the trawlers had been driven down current again and out of the Straits, so at length the area in Eren Keui Bay was deserted.

From Chanak, under the dark cliffs, threading her way through the lines of mines, stole the Turkish naval steamer *Nusrat*. She was quite small—only 380 tons—and quite new, having been built in Germany the year before last.

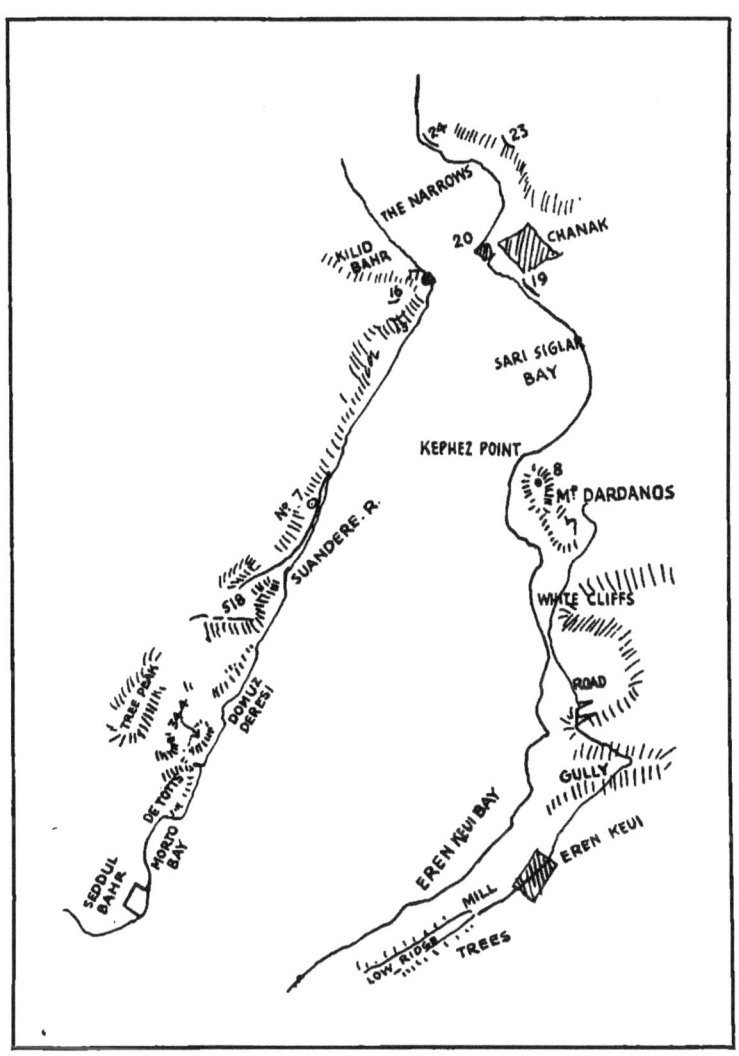

PRINCIPAL FORTS AND BATTERIES
This sketch by a British naval officer indicates the enemy's main defences beyond Kum Kale. See also map facing p. 136.

Aboard her were placed twenty mines, and accompanying her went Colonel Geehl, the Turks' mine expert. The enemy had become angry and wearied of our ships bombarding from Eren Keui Bay at distances varying between 12,000 and 14,000 yards: therefore the intention now was to lay a trap whilst our big draught vessels were spending Sunday night on patrol or in harbour.

The scheme was well conceived. If only two or three of these 12-inch gun carriers got holed, then that might have a deterring influence on the Admiral, who would be inclined to keep his units nearer the mouth, and therefore too far away for any more bombardment of the Narrows. The *Queen Elizabeth*, alone, would be able to have the longer range, but probably she might be considered too valuable to share the risk of hidden dangers. In all the forethought is a proof that the Turks and Germans had been shaken up badly by our squadrons, and that very little more accuracy would have knocked out the Krupp 14-inch, the 11-inch, the 10·2-inch, the 9·4-inch, and smaller defences. Perhaps with better spotting arrangements and superior aeroplanes this might have come, and if such steamers as the *Braemar Castle* were about to bring thousands of troops, then the minesweepers could go about their business with less interference, and the Fleet would indeed approach Constantinople.

Such a possibility must be stopped.

Colonel Geehl laid his twenty mines not athwart the current (as elsewhere) but fore-and-aft, up and downstream. Being laid not to catch any, but one, class of warships, they were set so that the keels of destroyers and trawlers would just escape: it would never do for one of these craft to blow up and reveal the lurking peril. That would certainly insure the others, and spoil the whole endeavour. The mines were set for a depth of not less than fifteen feet, which would be perfect ambush for a battleship. The ideal arrangement would have been to lay at least two lines across from shore to shore, running about north-west and south-east, the easternmost one being distant from Fort Hamidieh II about 11,000 yards, and the western one some 14,000. But we have seen that the Turks were short of mines, and the Straits' width was too great at those ranges. Colonel Geehl accordingly did the best with the score at his disposal. He placed them in the very area where deep-draught bombarders came daily; beginning his eastern end at about 11,000 yards from the above Fort, and the westernmost at 14,000. This provided a danger line that was very thin, but roughly 3000 yards long. And next, having dumped her cargo, the *Nusrat* scurried back home again. It might be only hours, or it might be a matter of a few days; but, with any ordinary luck, this Eren Keui trap ought to show results worth having. Let us leave it at that for the present.

Meanwhile, that night, and the next day, and the day after, the *Lord Nelson* was licking her wounds, what time the enemy rapidly sowed tares. The Sunday afternoon adventure in company of *Agamemnon* had been not without thrills. One of her officers tells me that they began their bombardment on Fort 13, the range varying between 12,000 and 14,000 yards, that it was difficult getting guns on the target, but then the firing became good and one magazine appeared to blow up.

" The fort replied quite well, with a slow accurate fire, and was putting shells round us. They misjudged our speed, however, and shells were falling chiefly astern. One burst on the water under the stern walk, and riddled it with holes. We silenced the fort after some time, and after a short burst on Fort 17 (Namazieh), turned our attention to No. 19 (Hamidieh I) on the Chanak side, the biggest of the lot, and certainly one of the best in action. Armed with two 14-inch and seven 9·4-inch old pattern Krupp guns, it had certain luxuries, such as range-finders, that the others did not appear to possess.

" No. 19 fired very well with alternative salvoes of five and four guns, but we gave it a good ' doing,' closing in eventually to 11,000 yards. At this range we appeared to be hitting the revetments repeatedly, and here also a magazine seemed to blow up. After this we had got rather close to Eren Keui on the south shore (about 4000 yards [1] or so) when a hidden howitzer let fly at us. I was looking over the side of the top, to see if a turret was trained, when a shell burst on the starboard side of the bridge, cutting the rigging; which made the top 'flick' across pretty sharply, smashed up the charthouse and cabins below thoroughly, also pitting the muzzles of some guns with fragments.

"We turned to the south-west and engaged with our port guns, having been hit several times; one below water on the armour-belt, which started a leak. We could see the howitzer shell coming, which was rather unpleasant. Another hit went through the port cutter. No casualties, but the 'Skipper,' Commander, and Chief Quartermaster were chipped by splinters in the conning-tower. The 'Snotties' behaved very well, though a bit white at first. We got back to Tenedos about 5 p.m. with a slight list to port, which became worse. Divers were sent down, and afterwards we went round to Mudros. Other ships were very surprised that we got off so lightly, as they said the shell appeared to be all round us."

It is fortunate that man is not omniscient, and that one combatant cannot at the time obtain a complete picture: otherwise human hope would never sustain the bitter disappointments and terrible anxieties. On Monday, March 8, although many officers had grave misgivings that all these bombardments amounted to very little advantage, we did not know definitely (as we to-day are well aware) that the positive results after ten days' attack within the Straits amounted to nil: that is to say, though forts had been hit, a few men killed, and more of them badly shaken up, yet not one gun had been struck, and the defences were not less powerful than before. Could anything be more disheartening?

Yes, it could. And only by a miracle was it avoided.

Suppose that wonder-ship *Queen Elizabeth* were to founder

[1] This was almost the distance from the shore in which *Nusrat* that night laid her mines.

on these newly-laid black " eggs " in Eren Keui Bay? What a loss to the Royal Navy! What a sensation at home! What joy in Constantinople! It is no good suggesting that the *Queen Elizabeth* always did her firing from outside, and never came within, the Straits; for on this March 8, the first day after the trap had been set, she did come inside for the first time. It makes one shudder to think what might have resulted. She arrived with the purpose of firing at Forts 13, 19, 16, 17, and 20: in other words, those at the Narrows. Again she began late, the light was bad, spotting almost out of the question, and she concentrated entirely on Fort 13 (Rumili Medjidieh), securing one hit, but not an effective one. No reply was made, and at 3.30 p.m. Admiral Carden (who was flying his flag aboard her) ordered a withdrawal.

Another useless occasion. But, likewise, a risky parade again.

This lovely ship was to have done marvellous things at the Dardanelles: that she failed to reach all expectations was not the fault of her guns or her personnel, but because the bad spotting from ships and seaplanes bereft her of eyesight. It was also wrongly inferred that we had silenced forts which (we now know) had not been reduced but stopped answer, as they were even shorter of ammunition than ourselves. Most fortunately, the *Queen Elizabeth* fired her eleven rounds—at ranges varying from 17,000 down to 12,000 yards—from an unpolluted area. She went in (one of the commanding officers tells me) " and took up a position in the middle, below Eren Keui." Thus did she escape the disaster that waited on the Asiatic side. The time was not quite due when Lord Fisher imposed restrictions on the use of this battleship, and for another two months she remained out from home: if the First Sea Lord could have learnt on March 8 that a death-trap so nearly engulfed her, this choleric old Admiral would have undoubtedly insisted on her immediate withdrawal.

She was supported this Monday by the *Vengeance*, *Cornwallis*, *Irresistible*, and *Canopus*, who were to keep down the howitzers from worrying the great ship. Luckily not one of these four touched the new ambush, though it seems quite certain the current must have released more than one mine; for the *Irresistible* sighted a couple and sent a picket-boat, who sank them.[1] Little was it realised whence these floated, and meanwhile the howitzers got busy. The following impression comes from an officer in the *Vengeance*:

" At last these howitzers got us. They whistled and fell all round—just missing—but finally one whumped on to the forecastle—a 6-inch. It did very little harm. We were watching, ducked as we heard it coming, and then, looking up as it hit, we ducked again, whilst chunks of wood flew up at the conning-tower. Two or three bits of shell hit the top, but only dented it. The big part went through the deck, making a few dents and cuts in the next deck. It smoked for a time. Later on we saw a flash of a gun to the right of Eren Keui village. Many others were firing, and being replied to; but this fellow no one seemed to notice. As it appeared to be worrying the *Queen Elizabeth*, we decided to have a try. Our guns just reached it, with not a yard to spare: it was a little to the right of a mill in a bunch of trees on a low ridge along which the road ran. Our first shot fell half-way between mill and trees, the next three-quarters of the way, but the third burst. Off went all the enemy, legging it like the devil, and their gun-teams also bolted on their own. I don't suppose we hit the gun, but it stopped them for the day."

Both this vessel and the *Cornwallis* noticed a big howitzer about half-way up Eren Keui village. By means of rails this gun could be moved about the village to new positions, and doubtless the German officer-in-charge hoped that ere long one of these supporting battleships would be shelled as she foundered on the minefield. But the occasion had not quite arrived, the *Vengeance* and *Cornwallis* got his range, treated him to some fine salvoes, and caused him to move farther along his rail-track.

That night, still ignorant of the Eren Keui mines, trawlers and picket-boats made a further effort to sweep the Kephez

[1] *The Immortal Gamble*, p. 34.

area, but were fired on as before. In regard to the daylight bombardments, fortunately a lull had set in. Admiral Carden realised that his advance was checked, that little more could be done till the Army took a share, and that for the present he was up against an impossibility. To that must be attributed the fact that *Nusrat's* mines still continued in suspense. On the Tuesday (March 9) the trio *Albion*, *Prince George*, and *Irresistible*, accompanied by destroyers, came a little way within the Straits, but only so far that they could destroy some Turkish boats in the Mendere river, complete destruction of the bridge over that stream, and shell some field-guns that had been sent to Sedd-el-Bahr. Otherwise the operations up the Straits were now confined to the minesweepers.

Three trawlers, and two picket-boats with explosive creeps, once more did their best off Kephez and once more failed. In spite of protection by the destroyer *Mosquito*, they were at once given attention by the searchlights and batteries, who promptly ended the adventure. Now, on the following night (10th–11th) an abler and more determined endeavour was undertaken. This time the seven trawlers, two picket-boats, and four escorting destroyers were supported by the battleship *Canopus* as well as the light cruiser *Amethyst*. Better tactics were employed so as to transform an adverse current into a friend.

The trawlers, instead of making slow progress with sweeps out against it, were first to get above Kephez, then connect to each other the sweep wires in pairs, and come down with the stream. Of course it is apparent that just as battleships when assaulting the outer forts had found the most dangerous minutes those when helm was put over and hull began swinging round, so it must be with the trawlers as they turned, veering their wires and kites.

Never did fishermen have a more nerve-trying experience. Here were the trawlers with their homely names—*Escallonia* of Grimsby, her sisters *Manx Hero*, *Syringa*, *Beatrice II*, *Soldier Prince*, *Avon*, *Gwenllian*—and their much-suffering crews. I remember one of these East Coast Skippers afterwards relating his adventures. He was wounded twice these nights without once reporting the fact, and merely treated his hurts with " Friar's balsam "—a good old North Sea remedy. This plucky old man, who was awarded a D.S.C., summed up these nocturnal operations in his own blunt manner: " Look 'ere, sir. If I had the choice of the Dardanelles and Hell to live in, I'd let the Dardanelles and live in Hell "; yet he was no coward. One of the first to go forth, he volunteered to remain out there even after his section had been relieved. His ship became disabled by the loss of her propeller from a shell striking it, but he got a new propeller and was back in time for the next job of work. Another Skipper, on being asked if ten years ago someone had prophesied he would be engaged steaming about in command of a warship, replied that he would have called such a person a " falsehood."

That night the first pair of trawlers had just got out their sweeps when they caught a couple of the Kephez mines in the dark waters. These exploded and blew up the *Manx Hero*, though her crew were luckily saved. The enemy took this for a signal, switched on the powerful searchlights, and now came a violent concentration of 6-inch and smaller guns. It was Hell right enough, and all the craft became targets. The *Canopus* dealt with the batteries, but she could not extinguish the brilliant lights; two trawlers were struck, and two men injured; but the fishermen of the second and third pair were now too agitated by the shells to carry out an effective clearance, and under cover of destroyers made their retirement.

During the night hours of the 11th–12th six more trawlers entered the searchlight beams, but could not tolerate the situation when the guns commenced firing. Turning right round for home, every trawler steamed off, and could not be persuaded to face the fire. Next night came the French sweepers' chance, but their slow speed prevented them from doing much against the current, and they too retired after some of their craft had been struck. With the fishermen's morale ruined in regard to mine-clearance, and the battleships' bombardment negatived, the Dardanelles outlook could not be called hopeful.

Certainly the brave picket-boats had gone higher up than had been previously reached, but on a fool mission. It was thought the enemy had laid observation mines about Kephez, connected to shore by a cable; and it was hoped that by towing a special kind of grapnel the little steamboats would be able to destroy them. But they had no luck, for the good reason that these were independent mines, moored singly.

What was to be done about it?

There could be only one answer, and that to try again—but with new crews. The fishermen had been asked to do the Navy's job, and had no more succeeded than if the Navy had been sent to catch fish off Iceland. So the Admiral called for volunteers, who were instantly forthcoming: officers and men alike. A final attempt against the Kephez area must be undertaken, as it was felt that the loss of men and small ships would be a fair price in return for obtaining a clear channel up to the Narrows. That was the crisis at which we had arrived, and the desperate adventure was now plunged into by men accustomed all their lives to naval discipline.

The superstitious may have thought that Saturday night, the 13th, was not to be the happiest of choices. Sunset came about six o'clock, and three hours later the cavalcade of trawlers and five picket-boats, headed by the light cruiser *Amethyst* with an escort of destroyers, steamed up on their doomed purpose. Officers from the Royal Navy and Royal Naval Reserve, and even young Midshipmen, with a stiffening of experienced service ratings, were going to complete the job or die.

Nor need we emphasise again the preliminary slow progress against the current, the passage through the illuminated area, before sweeps could be connected for the homeward trip. The enemy was awake, as ever, knew our methods exactly, and at the right time downpoured with his shells. Marvellous to relate, several mines were swept up in that terrible barrage, but only one pair of trawlers had time to get out their sweeps ere it was too late; since gallows, winches, and other essential gear were smashed under the destructive fire. In two trawlers the whole working personnel was wounded or killed:

four of the trawlers and one picket-boat being put out of action. It was a most gallant attempt to have got above Fort 7 (Messudieh), though it is also sad to relate that the two 9·2-inch guns of that new defence were those which had been salved from the battleship of the same name which Lieut. Holbrook in B 11 had torpedoed several months before. But the trawlers were not the only sufferers: the *Amethyst* in her martyrdom proved to the world that if ships persisted in trying to run the Dardanelles gauntlet, it was not the land defences which would come off worst. And I am indebted to a naval officer for giving the following mental picture of what it was like aboard that cruiser during those tense minutes.

"She had many casualties. A watch of stokers had been washing themselves in their bathroom at the time. A shell burst right among them, so that all the walls and roof were plastered with flesh and blood. The remains of the victims of that shell were put into sacks, but, on mustering, it was discovered that instead of twelve men having been in the room (as thought), there had been nineteen." Altogether that night's profitless daring had taken toll of twenty-seven killed and forty-three wounded; the *Amethyst* alone losing twenty-two dead and twenty-eight severely injured. The wonder is that she at last emerged, since her steering gear and engine-room telegraphs were disabled. "For twenty minutes she lay out of control in the glare of the searchlights, exposed to the fire of guns of all sizes,"[1] record others.

By now it was fully appreciated in Whitehall that naval operations at the Dardanelles might " at any moment become dependent on military assistance,"[2] and the opinion of a military expert on the spot was required. On the evening of that fatal March 13, General Sir Ian Hamilton was therefore sent by Lord Kitchener from London via Marseilles, where a light cruiser hurried him across the Mediterranean to the Dardanelles.

An entirely new phase, long foreseen as inevitable, must soon take visible shape.

[1] *The Immortal Gamble*, p. 41.
[2] *The World Crisis*, 1915, p. 209.

CHAPTER XIV
THE GREAT ATTACK

But the final expectations of forcing the Dardanelles without the Army's aid had not even now been quite reached: the heresy that forts could be destroyed by ships, alone, was a long while dying.

Always it will be a matter for regret that the false optimism was not at once dropped, and the unpleasant truth accepted that the original plan must be scrapped. To have gained such a recognition by March 17 would have been to save defeat and avoid the tragedy that awaited. Admiral Carden was convinced by the Saturday night *débâcle* that efficient sweeping must be done by daylight: he therefore set his Fleet from March 14 to prepare for a grand simultaneous attack to take place on the 18th against Kephez minefield and forts. During these intervening four days the trawlers, far from being put on one side, were very much in demand, employed clearing up the area within the Straits for the big bombarders that must have a guaranteed space wherein to manœuvre. First came the Frenchmen's turn, with nine trawlers and five picket-boats. Then we took over. During the night of the 17th–18th, whilst the trawlers were beginning to sweep south-east from Suandere Point, they once more came under heavy fire. After their first sweep they had their gear damaged, became scattered, and even got ashore. It was unfortunate they did not tow their sweeps across into Eren Keui Bay. Early on the morning of the 18th the commanding officer of the British minesweepers reported that no mines had been found between Kephez Bay and White Cliffs (about $1\frac{1}{2}$ miles below), whilst the French reported finding none below White Cliffs.

It is important to mention these two statements, though they do not affect the *Nusrat* line of traps, which lay to seaward and downstream of the area just mentioned. In any case, unless a very diligent sweeping was made of the Straits between Suandere Point and Eren Keui village (the width here being

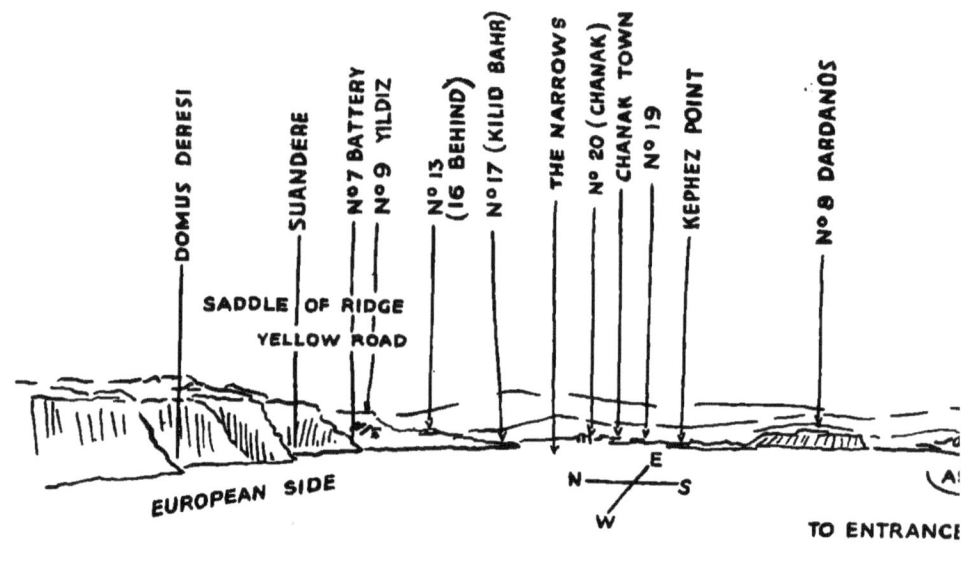

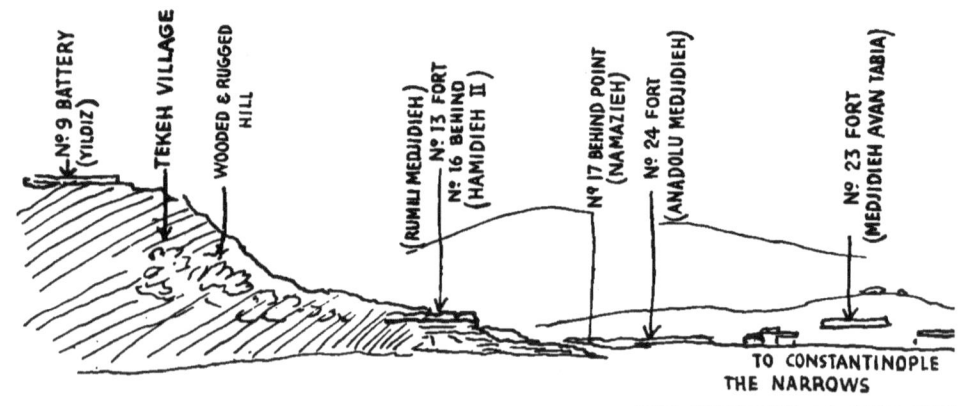

THE NARROWS AS SEEN FRO[M]

The above two sketches, made by a British naval officer, illustrate the features on both shores of the Dardane[lles]

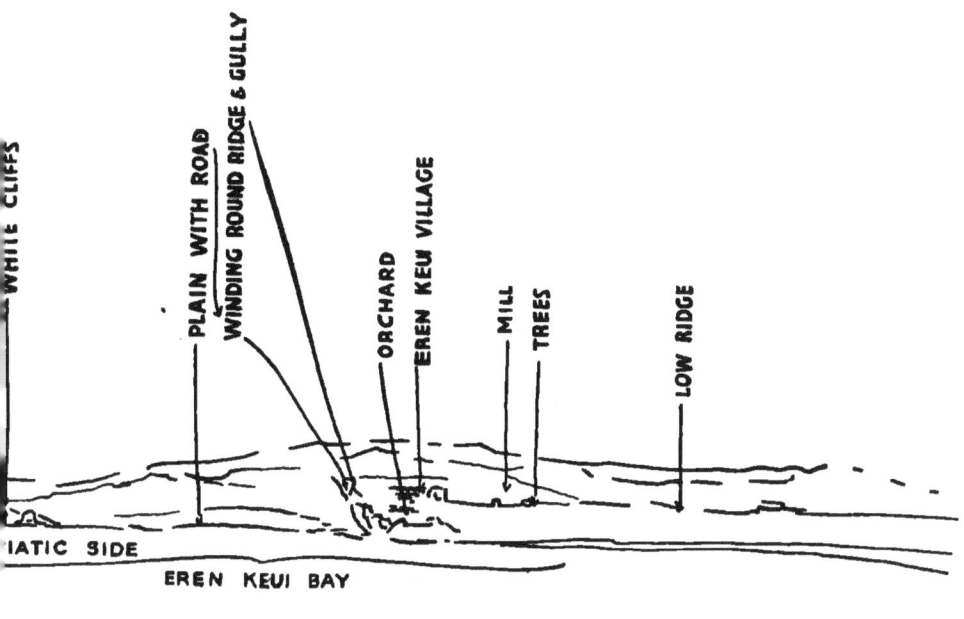

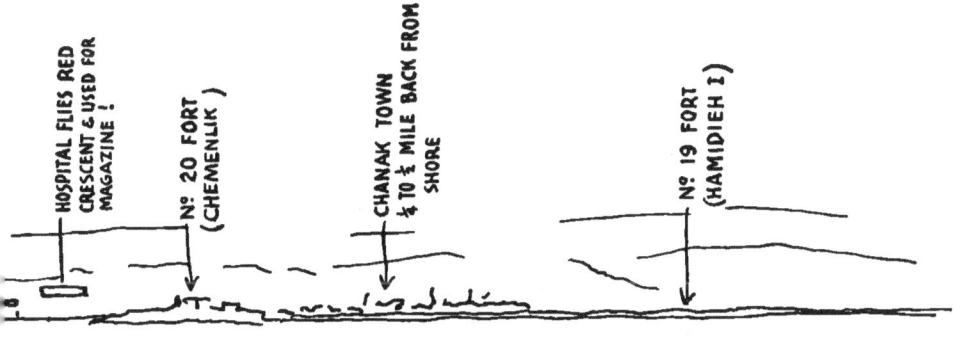

THE ENTRANCE TO DARDANELLES
Straits up to the Narrows. (Compare this with map facing p. 136.) The numbers refer to the Forts.

some 4½ miles) it would have been easy enough to have missed the *Nusrat* deposits.

That, then, was the position as to the hidden dangers on Thursday, March 18, the morning of the Great Attack. On Monday the Admiralty, with notable despatch, had arranged for plenty more minesweepers to be sent out. The naval officer in charge of Lowestoft was ordered to send thirty of his fastest trawlers to assemble at Falmouth *en route* for Lemnos, and they departed from their East Coast base on Wednesday. In like manner the French were providing some more, whilst eight Fleet sweepers [1] were being sent to Mudros by Admiral Jellicoe, and the Malta torpedo-boats then protecting the Suez Canal were summoned to the Dardanelles. Nor was this all. The splendid XXIXth Division of veteran troops was coming out to the Dardanelles, and much reliance was placed in their potentialities. General Sir Ian Hamilton, who was to command the military forces destined to support the Fleet, actually reached the Dardanelles on the morning of the 17th, and was to make his personal reconnaissance of the coast next day.

On the day of his arrival he was able to meet and discuss the situation with the British Admiral; but this was not Admiral Carden. The latter had finally succumbed to the heavy strain, the worries, the disappointments, and the uncertainties; so that on the 16th he had joined the sick list and yielded up his command. Next day he left for Malta, being succeeded by Rear-Admiral de Robeck, now promoted to acting Vice-Admiral. One can but sympathise with Admiral Carden at having been placed in a most difficult position from the first, yet the choice of appointing the Superintendent of Malta Dockyard has been severely criticised. Other names more suitable, men with greater gifts and deeper inspiration, might have been put forward in the autumn of 1914. But time was important, geographical distance had to be reckoned, and no one had foreseen that the mere blockading of the Dardanelles would quickly expand into the second most important theatre

[1] These comprised packet-steamers taken up from British Railway Companies.

of the War. For Admiral de Robeck the legacy of stalemate, and of the logical dilemma following on an erroneous conception, was no enviable inheritance; ten days sufficed before telegraphing to the Admiralty in the sense that the old idea had been conclusively proved wrong.

His predecessor had committed him to the forthcoming Great Attack; and with this tragic fulfilment, this day of wrath, we must now watch the final flickering of a forlorn notion that meant the loss of valuable lives, which had taken so long to train. Armament was being worn out, ships kept going in harbour to " shift over " guns that badly needed a " rest." On the 11th *Inflexible* left for Malta, went alongside the wall under a big crane, changed her two fore-turret guns, and was back at the Dardanelles by the 17th, just in time for the following day's big show. It had been planned for that day, but the weather was thick, and unsuitable for aeroplanes and gunnery; so postponement became necessary.

That evening her gunnery officer, Commander Verner, warned his brothers of the ward-room that they would have a " hot time " next day, mentioning that he was going to take up his position in the fore-control top the better to direct fire on the enemy's batteries, which would be firing from three sides. It was an extremely vulnerable spot, as the Battle of the Falklands had proved, and he was to be accompanied by Lieut. A. W. Blaker. Morning came with a light southerly wind, at 8.30 the Fleet left their base, and two hours later the first line of British ships, *Queen Elizabeth*, *Agamemnon*, *Lord Nelson*, and *Inflexible*, proceeded up the Straits, destroyers (fitted with light sweeps) going ahead of them at 9.10. Each battleship had with her afloat a picket-boat armed with a 3-pounder for the convenience of sinking any floating mines.

The sight of this squadron steaming away into the entrance made an impressive spectacle. One who watched it tells me: " It looked as if no human forces could withstand such an array of might and power." " We stopped in our positions across the Straits," writes one of the *Lord Nelson's* officers, " at about 15,000 yards from the Narrows, *Queen Elizabeth*

TRAWLERS OFF THE ENTRANCE
To the Dardanelles Straits, off Cape Tekke.

H.M.S. *PRINCE GEORGE* IN ACTION
This interesting photograph, taken aboard the French battleship *Gaulois*, shows the British battleship on March 18, 1915, under fire from Turkish 5·9-inch howitzers. A salvo of three has just been fired at her. (Notice picket-boat astern, looking out for mines.)

THE GREAT ATTACK

(flag), *Agamemnon*, *Lord Nelson*, *Inflexible*, reading from north to south, with *Prince George* guarding our north flank from field-guns, and *Triumph* guarding our south; whilst the four French battleships were ready to close the forts when we had silenced the enemy."

The *Suffren*, *Bouvet*, *Gaulois*, and *Charlemagne* were all under Admiral Guépratte as before, and it was intended that they should at the right stage approach to 10,000 yards from the Narrows. In neither line were the ships to anchor (because of the mobile howitzers), but to keep slow ahead against the current. It was hoped that the forts, by this massed amount of shell-fire, would be sufficiently silenced to prevent interference with minesweeping. Finally, the *Ocean*, *Irresistible*, *Albion* and *Vengeance*, supported by *Swiftsure* and *Majestic*, were to relieve the French line at a given signal, and thus bring a fresh wave of bombardment. If this series of terrific attacks would not drive the enemy's men away from their guns, whatever on sea could? The main forts having been temporarily dominated, and the light batteries controlled, three pairs of trawlers, supported by the two battleships *Cornwallis* and *Canopus*, were to sweep along the Asiatic shore to Sari Sighlar Bay. This would enable the Fleet to crash a murderous fire against the Narrows at very close range.

At 10.58 a.m.[1] the enemy's howitzers on the south shore opened fire, but the *Triumph* soon squashed that, whilst the *Prince George* did the same for the European side. The *Queen Elizabeth* had been told to deal with Fort 19 (the powerful Hamidieh I) and with Fort 20 (Chemenlek), both being on the Asiatic side of the Narrows. The *Agamemnon*, *Lord Nelson*, and *Inflexible* were to bombard Forts 9 (Yildiz), 13 (Rumili Medjidieh), 16 (Hamidieh II), and 17 (Namazieh), all on the European side of the Narrows. By 11.4 the *Lord Nelson* had opened fire and put a 9·2-inch into an enemy emplacement, but two minutes later a large projectile missed this ship's maintop by about three feet. "We all heard it,"

---

[1] These times are taken from a contemporary personal chronology of an officer in the maintop of the *Lord Nelson*.

K

says an officer in that top, "and saw it coming." At 11.22 another battery on the south shore barked, but the *Queen Elizabeth* with her 6-inch salvoes put that to silence.

Six minutes later the *Queen Elizabeth* with her 15-inch guns began her long-distance attack on Chemenlek, her first two shots falling into Chanak town. She then got on to the fort, and started a large fire, followed by an explosion, after which she shifted on to Hamidieh I. At 11.35 the other three ships just mentioned concentrated their fire on the European side of the Narrows, the *Lord Nelson* attacking Hamidieh II. The forts replied with slow determination, but the real trouble was the howitzers again—unseen yet most annoying—plus the field batteries. Although not always accurate, these two latter had a distracting unpleasantness, dozens of shells whizzing past the tops whence our fire was being controlled. "I had a lot of trouble," wrote one officer in charge at that height, "stopping the men ducking each time." Then a howitzer battery got so clever that she straddled the *Lord Nelson* with four shots, the time being 12.6 p.m. The *Prince George* and *Triumph* had been trying to reduce on the north-side Forts 7 (Messudieh) and 9 (Yildiz), as well as that elusive Fort 8 (Dardanos) on the south side.

More than an hour of this duel had passed when, at 12.15 (says one of the *Queen Elizabeth's* officers), the Admiral signalled the French ships to close in, the Turkish forts firing with vigour: whilst most of these shells passed over our ships, the enemy was not long in getting the range, so that *Queen Elizabeth* received three hits, and at 12.30 the *Gaulois* was so badly hit by a 14-inch shell from the Narrows that she was compelled to retire with a list and, running out of the Dardanelles, to beach herself on Rabbit Island. An 8-inch shell fell on board the *Queen Elizabeth*, wrecking the gun-room, but did not penetrate the armoured deck below. "The Admiral," says one of her officers, "ordered the First Lieutenant and others out of the foretop, which they obeyed with alacrity. Another shell smashed a derrick, penetrating the fore superstructure, whilst a third blew a hole in the fore funnel."

H.M.S. *LORD NELSON*
At the Dardanelles.

H.M.S. *LORD NELSON*
Right-hand 12-inch gun firing.

Things were now beginning to happen, and the enemy, at the sight of these ten Anglo-French battleships (with another four presently to come up), realised that the climax could not be far off: it was soon or never. The Fleet looked like breaking through and risking the loss of some units between Kephez and Chanak. Ah! Perhaps these four old French ships were being sent on ahead as mine-bumpers to cleave a channel for the British? So the defensive fire was resumed with the terrific intensity of men making a firm stand against invaders. If anything this afternoon should allow the Allies to get past Chanak, then Constantinople was doomed, Turkey finished, Austria and Germany defeated.

So the battle became fierce, what time the Turks watched their supplies of the biggest shells getting dangerously short.

Against the *Inflexible*, over on the Asiatic side, the enemy now especially poured his wrath; and the Eren Keui howitzers had evidently been ordered to give her no respite. The reason is now pretty obvious: if the Turks and their German leaders could by any means cause the *Inflexible* to move just a little farther, she would hit one of the *Nusrat* mines. And if every Briton and Frenchman was blithely ignorant of the watery ambush, it must have been extremely thrilling for those of our enemies " in the know " as they watched the fatal area being approached. The sight of a battleship sinking is not an everyday occurrence, and supremely rare in history is such a spectacle to be witnessed inside two arms of land: never was drama raised to such heights, never was suspense so tremendous. The fate of European development, the future of Turkey, Germany, Austria-Hungary, Roumania, Bulgaria, Serbia, Russia; lay hanging just then on one single line of twenty mines. Would they do what was intended? Would they go off as soon as hulls drawing 30 feet smote the soft-nosed horns? Certainly this period immediately following the noon of March 18 was one of the most decisive in the annals of civilisation, and if we failed in our enterprise to-day, then the Dardanelles dilemma had defeated the Navy.

Seeing how sore pressed was the battle-cruiser, *Lord Nelson*, with her starboard 9·2-inch guns, tackled the dangerous howitzer battery west of Eren Keui. This was at 12.30, but ten minutes previously a shell had struck the *Inflexible's* centre tripod of the foremast, setting fire to the forebridge and deckhouse below. Three minutes later one of the turrets was hit, and almost immediately the ship received three more hits. At 12.27 the foretop was reported out of action: that is to say, most of the communications (telephones and instruments) with the guns below had been disabled; but was this all that chanced to be wrong up aloft? At 12.37 the *Inflexible's* picket-boat, which was close on her starboard beam looking out to sink any mines, was struck and foundered, though the crew just managed to scramble out in time. Of course the Turks had reason to know what these pickets were doing, and the least desirable thing must be that the little boats should destroy any of *Nusrat's* cargo which might bob up to the surface.

Twice more did *Inflexible* receive wounds, and just then a shell came hurtling along, aimed evidently aloft against her fire-control, as so often had been the enemy's wont. This shell struck the fore signal-yard, only a few feet above the fore-control station, and, in exploding, poured downwards its fragments like a bursting rocket, penetrating the control's roof and sides, bringing with it disaster. For Commander Verner was up there spotting the effects of his ship's gunnery. His hands were grasping his binoculars, both his arms raised up. Suddenly his right arm was pulped, most of that hand blown away, his left arm and leg wounded in many places, and his skull fractured. His assistant, Lieut. Blaker, was hit in one arm and his left leg broken. Of the eight men who were with these two officers three were killed on the spot, and four struck down, whilst only one young A.B., named Arthur Robinson, remained unhurt.[1]

Isolated from the rest of their shipmates, poised between sea and sky, this fore-control party was for some minutes

[1] For some of the details concerning the *Inflexible* I am indebted to the "Memoir" of Commander Verner, previously cited.

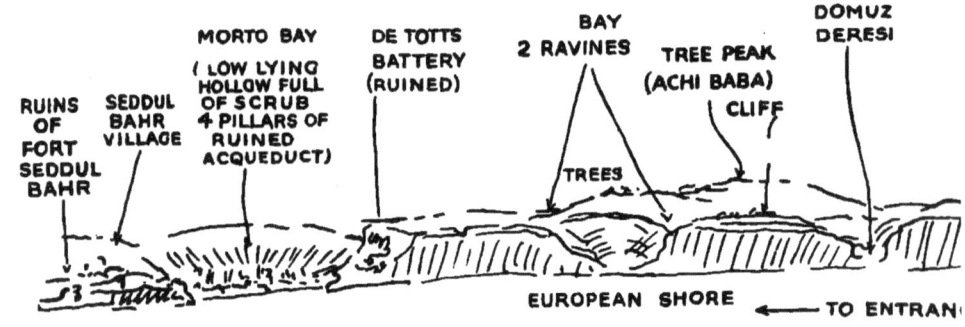

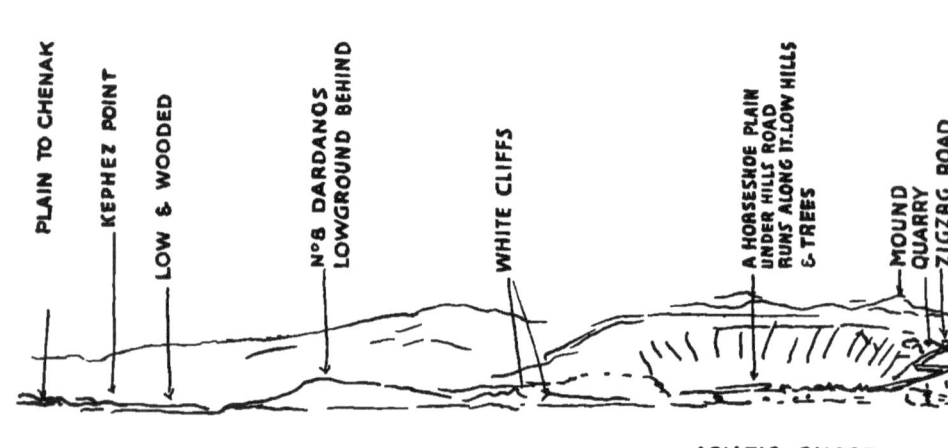

THE DARDAN

These sketches were made on the spot by a British naval officer, and

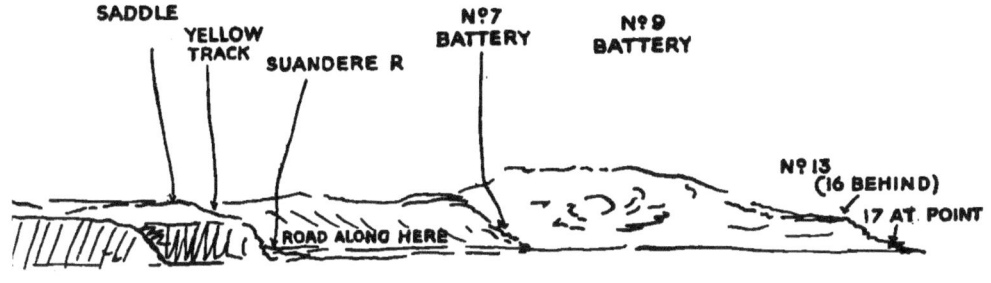

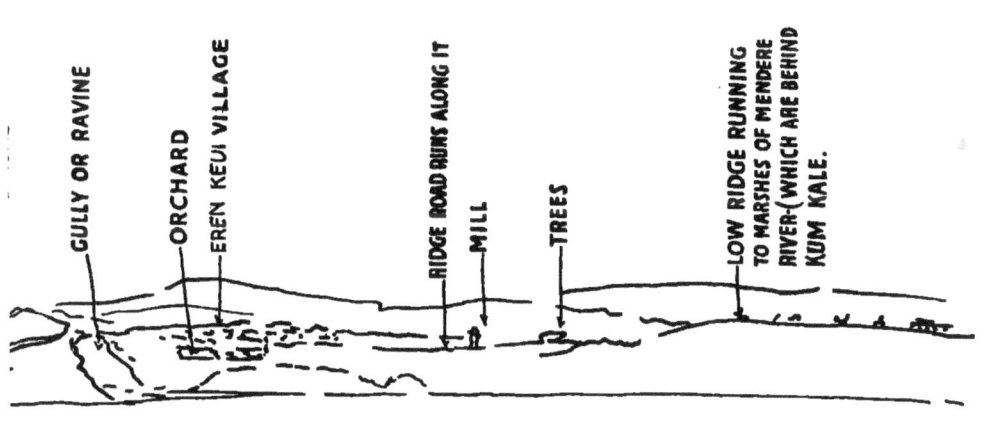

TRANCE
ELLES STRAITS
vividly show the features along both the European and Asiatic shores.

knocked senseless where death had left any life. Below it was not immediately possible to realise exactly all that had happened above, since the Turks' fire waged hotter than ever, and the cabins of the forebridge were now in flames. Meanwhile some genuine heroism, and sailor-like unselfishness, were being enacted. Notwithstanding his terrible injuries, Commander Verner was still in command of himself and of his job, giving orders, and bearing excruciating pain with amazing manliness. Robinson, assisted by his wounded mates, managed to get Commander Verner on to some "gym" mats and make him as comfortable as the circumstances permitted. "Thank you, old chap," came the thanks of one hovering between death and life.

Then, with an effort of will, remembering that he was still an officer in charge, he succeeded in raising himself from the mats to the level of a voice-pipe which connected with another officer, Lieut. Leicester Curzon-Howe, in the fore transmitting station. "Report to the Captain fore-control out of action," he ordered; "we are all dead or dying up here. Send up some morphia." And the words were uttered so clearly, so calmly, that it could not be suspected how much the speaker was suffering. The latter part of this message was passed to the Fleet-Surgeon, who was in the lower conning-tower, and at once went on deck. He tried to make his way aloft, but the bridge was in flames and the iron ladder too hot.

Next came Verner's pathetic message to Lieut. Curzon-Howe: "For God's sake put out the fire, or we shall all be roasted."

Efforts were made to comply, but already a fire-party had been summoned, of which one man had been killed and four wounded. Some of the men with Commander Verner managed to get down, and by one he sent a message asking the Captain to go astern, so as to get clear of the smoke and fire; for the breeze was now blowing strongly. A sailor returned aloft, and the ship's second-in-command, Commander Ernest Wigram, pluckily went up. Burning his hands severely on the iron ladder, he gained the top, found Verner standing up against the side, looking out, talking quite sensibly, and remarkably brave. The matting was already smouldering, and the crews who would have been fighting with their 4-inch guns against the Turks were now fighting to put out the conflagration on the forebridge.

Verner was given first aid after being brought down in a bamboo stretcher. It had been no easy job lowering him from that awkward eminence, and whilst this was being done, Captain Phillimore, because of the conflagration, had dropped back about a mile from the line, and then took his ship into action once more. Placed below armour, with the other wounded, the gunnery expert kept inquiring after his companions, how the action was going, and what damage we were doing to the enemy. Everything in the true Nelson tradition: all in keeping with the Navy's glorious story through generations and centuries; all the fine examples from the age of sail re-enacted aboard a modern battle-cruiser!

It was at 1.25 that the *Inflexible* had temporarily withdrawn for the extinguishing of the flames and clearing the fore-top of her wounded. An hour later all this had been done, and at 2.36 she reopened fire with her guns, becoming as heavily engaged as ever. Now, in the meanwhile other events had been accumulating. Just before one o'clock the *Agamemnon* had been hit by three shells all at once, her after-funnel being so struck that it opened out (as one eye-witness tells me) " like a lotus." We had been able to drive away the gun-crews from both Chemenlek and the difficult Dardanos; the French had done good work against the Suandere defences (Fort 7a), as well as Rumili Medjidieh, and Hamidieh II. Although *Agamemnon* had been hit a dozen times below the armour, five times on the armour, and seven times above, by two o'clock the enemy's fire seemed to have been dominated; wherefore Admiral de Robeck now called up his six minesweepers, but there burst over them a fierce attack from howitzers and field batteries, so that it was impossible to reach Kephez Point.

THE GREAT ATTACK

So all hope of clearing a channel was yet again demonstrated out of the question. The most they did was to drag up several mines: that is to say, only the fringe of this upper area had been touched. And the longer these trawlers remained on such an important, such a vital zone, the more ferociously would the enemy shell them. Not one trawler would have been afloat for long.

It was at two o'clock, also, that the *Ocean, Irresistible, Albion, Vengeance, Swiftsure,* and *Majestic* were ordered in to relieve the French squadron, who now began to pass too far in towards the southern shore during their exit. There had been a temporary lull on the part of the enemy, but, just as the latter had freshened to sudden vigour when our Allies came steaming in through the first line, so it was when this last line of the older British battleships went forward. The Turks, so to speak, roused themselves to withstand the final wave that threatened to swamp them into submission, and the *Queen Elizabeth* seemed to be receiving more than her full share, yet not to be much damaged.

In order to describe the advance of these six ships, I cannot do better than avail myself of Commander Barne's impression as obtained from the *Majestic*.

"We had to pass the *Queen Elizabeth* on the north side," he tells me, "and came in for plenty of her 'overs,' but were not hit then. The row was prodigious. We steamed slowly up until we could see the buoys marking the enemy's minefields just ahead: so we went no farther. There was a battery high up on the Asiatic side, just to the north-east of Eren Keui, that was making extraordinarily good shooting at us, but which did not hit us. Every now and then the big fort at Chanak would fire a heavy one right alongside us, sending up huge columns of water to a great height.

"Now began the tragic part of the day's work. I remember I was on the boat deck, giving orders about flooding the deck to a greater extent, when Ryder, one of our chief yeomen of signals, remarked to me 'they' had got one of the Frenchmen. Sure enough, there was the leading ship of their line (which was coming out of action) literally bottom up in a cloud of smoke, and still with headway on. We could hardly believe our eyes. We got a gun's crew up and commenced turning out our port cutter, but we saw two picket-boats making for her, and these, whilst rescuing survivors, were being heavily fired on by shrapnel. In almost less time than it takes to write it, she had disappeared, and from where we were we could not see the sign of a survivor, though we heard later that some were saved."

So the *Nusrat's* mines had begun to act; for, whilst turning towards the Asiatic shore when coming out, the *Bouvet* struck right on to the hidden danger line, capsized and sank—all in two minutes and thirty-five seconds. " It was a perfectly horrible sight," says one of the *Lord Nelson's* officers, " and only very few were saved. One man got out of the hole in the bottom of a turret, when it turned upside down, and was picked up. The others that were saved ran down her side and across her bottom as she went over, like squirrels in a wheel. Picket-boats and destroyers did all they could to save life."

" A cloud of whitish smoke was seen over the forecastle of the *Bouvet*, heeling over to about 15 degrees to starboard, and listing rapidly to 30 degrees," confirms one of the *Queen Elizabeth's* officers. " Men could be seen running up over her bottom. She turned turtle, went down stern first, her bow remaining for a few seconds upright, and then she was completely gone. Of her total complement (between 600 and 700) only 5 officers, 10 petty officers, and 51 men were saved."

The *Triumph*, which had been stationed over on that side and had just been relieved by *Swiftsure*, had a narrow escape. " The *Bouvet* was steaming a short distance ahead of us," says one of the *Triumph's* officers, " but fortunately we got safely out, although we must have passed within a few yards of the mines." Naturally enough, the *Bouvet* in her death agony had released several mines from their moorings, and one from the *Nusrat* group, or from some other spot, was

SINKING OF THE FRENC
This unique photograph, taken (at 600 yards distance) aboard H.M.S. *Prince George*, covers a peri
The Asiatic shore is se

:H BATTLESHIP *BOUVET*

od of 2 minutes 35 seconds. During that time *Bouvet* struck a mine, capsized and began sinking.
:en in the background.

sighted floating down with the current past the *Lord Nelson*, which "just missed our bows."

Now, at 2.30 the *Vengeance*, *Albion*, *Irresistible* and *Ocean* had begun to engage the forts at a range varying from 13,000 to 11,500 yards; *Swiftsure* and *Majestic* supporting. Most of the forts then became quiet and economised with their shells, though the effect made on Fort 19 (Hamidieh I) had by no means been conclusive. The *Majestic* was having a busy time with the intermediate defences, as her Commander describes:

"We had drawn up abreast a valley on our northern flank, in which was a little house; and, seeing some horses tied up outside it, we took it to be an observation base. We put a 6-inch alongside it, and were proceeding to search the valley, which was full of fir trees from amongst which smoke was rising, when just above our heads came a heavy double explosion. Two shells had burst almost simultaneously in the fore lower top. I thought the foremast had come down and, on going outside the conning-tower, saw that half of the lower top was blown away. I wasted no time in getting back into the conning-tower.[1] They had pounced on us from some battery at the top of this valley.

"Our engines were put full astern, to place the bluff on the west side of the valley between the battery and ourselves, but before we had gathered sternway, came another salvo, probably from the same pair of guns. Their shooting, though at close range, was excellent. There came a loud crash, a cloud of black smoke and showers of splinters, some of which hit the conning-tower, while some flew and hit the inside of the top, though none of us was touched. I could hear cries from below the fore shelter deck, and on going there found several men lying about in a large pool of blood.

---

[1] A ship's conning-tower is just a small steel house with a slit (about six inches deep) between wall and roof. The control station in the foretop is a small oblong chamber of thin steel with a thin steel roof. Here were voice-pipes, telephones, for communicating with conning-tower, engine-room, batteries, and transmitting room; also up here was the *Inflexible's* range-finder.

"The stretcher party were quickly on the spot, and took them down to the fire distributing station. This last salvo had struck us on the port side, just abreast the fore turret, one going down through the deck, and the other in through the side."

But the danger from mines was not less real than that from the guns. At one time it was thought that the enemy this afternoon purposely released a number of mines from the Narrows to come down and do their work among the Fleet. We have seen that the *Lord Nelson* just missed one floating mine, which was before four o'clock, and an officer in the *Vengeance* says that mines were sighted off the port bow at five minutes past three, so that to clear them the ship had to reverse her engines. It is not quite certain whence these floating dangers originated. That which the *Lord Nelson* observed may have been released from its moorings by the sinking *Bouvet*, and diverted in its course by one of the many Dardanelles eddies;[1] but those which were sighted by *Vengeance* seem to have been so far under the European shore that we must look for some other cause. If it be doubted whether the enemy did let loose from up-current a number of these objects, then we have to remember that the previously mentioned minesweepers claim to have exploded three mines in their sweeps, and quite likely may have plucked others from their moorings.

At 3.32 the *Irresistible* either struck a mine or was hit by a shell, for she was noticed by the *Majestic* and *Vengeance* to have a list, but about half an hour afterwards the much-battered *Inflexible* again suffered misfortune. About 3.45 she felt a very violent concussion externally, which may have been another mine, or again it may have been a shell bursting. In any case, it upset those wounded who had been brought below from the fore-top. Whilst the hull was not penetrated, the tremendous shock threw Commander Verner against the steel

---

[1] As evidence of these swirls and eddies see Chapter XVIII and the incident which occurred to *U* 21 mentioned on p. 262.

side, further injured his head, and caused his and Blaker's wounds to start bleeding once more. But it was just after 4 p.m. that to this long list of hard knocks must be added another: she struck a mine on the starboard bow.

Her Captain (now Admiral Sir Richard Phillimore) has very kindly given me some details of this sad incident.

"According to the Engine Room reports," he says, "the ship appeared to be lifted bodily, and to quiver fore and aft, after which she slowly listed over to starboard. The noise of the explosion was very loud: the sudden silence and pitch darkness which followed, seemed intense by contrast. All lights were extinguished, but when the oil lamps were re-lighted, it was found that the engines were still running smoothly, which spoke well for the nerves of the boiler-room personnel. The ventilation had stopped, and the fire main was used to flush the floor-plates and to cool the men themselves. The behaviour of the engine-room petty officers and men was superb: they all wished to stay below and steam the ship."

But the *Inflexible* was in a bad way and settling down by the head, and thirty-nine of her men who were below in her submerged torpedo flat were drowned by the inrush of water. "Clear lower deck," came the order, which caused all the unfortunate wounded to be hurriedly shifted. The vessel had now some 2000 tons of water in her, and had to quit the line, though it was extremely doubtful if she would ever keep afloat. Slowly she steamed out of the Straits, and meanwhile three shells missed her by only fifty yards. It was now 5 p.m., so that she had been in action for six exciting hours, during which all her boats had been rendered unserviceable with the exception of one. The latter was now slung out, and the wounded were placed therein, so that if the ship should sink, Verner and his fellow sufferers would have some chance. Whilst the boat was being prepared and the wounded were temporarily laid on deck, Commander Verner, remembering his prophecy made in the ward-room the previous night, now said to some of his brother officers standing around: "You see, I was right about our having a hot time of it."

Thanks to the dogged gallantry of her Captain and ship's company, this smart battle-cruiser, that had fought so splendidly at the Falklands, and that day won a new glory, alike by the excellence of her gunnery and the persistent manner in which she went in to her duty however violently assaulted, at last reached Tenedos, where she anchored at 6 p.m. It was a magnificent achievement to have nursed her afloat in spite of shells and conflagrations and mines.

"After anchoring safely at Tenedos," says Sir Richard Phillimore, "it was found that though the hole was only 30 feet by 26 feet, no less than twenty compartments (large and small) had been completely or partially flooded, including all the forward magazines. Water had also obtained access to the foremost boiler-room."

The marvel is that the bulkheads did not collapse under the strain; but human nature presently succumbed. For, though the wounded were at once sent off in the cutter after reaching Tenedos, and were aboard the hospital ship *Soudan* half an hour after anchoring, Commander Verner died that night and Lieut. Blaker next morning. A few hours later, the bodies of these two fine officers, as also of six seamen, all sewn up in canvas and weighted according to the custom of the sea, were taken five miles out and given sailors' burial in thirty fathoms. It was not till some time later, and after the flooded flat had been pumped out, that the other bodies could be recovered.

Never was a brave and distinguished Captain better served by his officers. His second-in-command, Commander Ernest Wigram, had the difficult duty of putting out two serious and awkward fires. Lieut.-Commander the Hon. Patrick Acheson, officer of the fore-turret, who led his men down below to close all the doors in the fore magazine and shell-room, had a race against the rising water, but won: he was the last to leave the shell-room. Both these officers were awarded the D.S.O., as also was the senior Engineer-Lieutenant, whilst the Engineer-Commander was made a C.B., the Fleet Surgeon was given the C.M.G.; a number of other decorations and some well-won promotions being also made.

But, to resume our narrative, the *Inflexible's* mine was one of the *Nusrat* score: mere luck had placed this battle-cruiser, rather than the *Queen Elizabeth*, in the vicinity of Eren Keui Bay, and about a quarter of an hour after *Inflexible* had been holed, there came an even worse event. This time it was the *Irresistible's* turn. She had advanced, as we have seen, in company of her sisters, at two o'clock to relieve the French, and one and a half hours later was seen to develop a list. She had got to about 10,000 yards range from Rumili Medjidieh, and had turned round towards the Asiatic shore, being about to lengthen the range. At 4.15, whilst drifting with engines stopped off Eren Keui Bay, she struck the northernmost end of the *Nusrat* mine line and was holed underneath her starboard engine-room.

This battleship had been severely hurt by Fort 19 (Hamidieh I), but her drifting on to the ambush, which had in the last two hours waylaid both *Bouvet* and *Inflexible*, was a piece of rare bad luck. At the time it could not be ascertained whether the cause of trouble was mine or torpedo, though the watching Turks and Germans well enough knew, as to-day we also share that information. *Irresistible's* port engine-room also became flooded, with the loss of some lives, and she was as doomed as *Bouvet*; preparations were rapidly made for abandoning her, and the other ships could see " all hands on deck throwing all woodwork overboard " as something to which to cling. " She was evidently sinking, and the enemy, having got her range, were pouring shell into her." Thus the *Nusrat* scheme had worked out exactly as intended. Under this galling fire ten men were killed, three were missing, and sixteen were wounded. To the rescue steamed alongside the destroyer *Wear*, who took off 28 officers and 582 men, which was performed by 5.50. There now remained on board her Commanding Officer, Captain D. L. Dent, the Commander, and a few volunteers who still hoped to save her.

To her assistance was sent the *Ocean*, who endeavoured, in spite of the heavy fire, to pass a wire and get her in tow. This soon proved impracticable, for the stricken ship was sinking without question. "Whilst the *Ocean*, who had been told to haul her out of action, was manœuvring to do so," an eye-witness informs me, "she also was damaged in the steering-gear and started turning round and round. Presently, to our horror, we saw her doing exactly as the *Irresistible* had done." For the *Ocean* (Captain A. Hayes-Sadler) had got on to the same *Nusrat* mine line about a quarter of the distance from the northernmost end, developed an ugly list, and was the target for renewed shelling. Once more everything had turned out as the enemy had planned.

As ever, the destroyers (states yet another spectator) were "marvellous"; the *Colne*, *Jed*, and *Chelmer* rushing in under a cross fire to take off the *Ocean's* people, though casualties were inevitable. "The *Chelmer* was hit in the boiler-room," says one of the *Lord Nelson* witnesses, "and came alongside us in a pretty shaky condition crowded with survivors. I believe a stoker sat in the hole, and saved her from sinking! We gave her our collision mat, and she got out of the Straits safely. All the survivors came aboard us."

By 7.20 it was too dark to carry on further efforts, the two battleships had been abandoned (though it was hoped later that by means of trawlers they would be towed out), and the Admiral withdrew the remnants of his fleet to Tenedos. It had been a most unhappy day with three of his sixteen capital ships lost, three put out of action and needing dockyard repairs, and other units more or less knocked about. *Cui bono ?*

The enemy, alone, had profited, and for them it had been the Day of Deliverance, whilst for us there had been, in addition to the French casualties, thirty-five of our officers and men killed, and twenty officers and men wounded. And the results ? Whilst we had unquestionably given the Turks a good hammering, had caused the explosion of a magazine in Chemenlek, and knocked out four of their big guns, we were still no nearer to Constantinople. The mines had the last word, and spelt it distinctly. "We left the forts and town of Chanak burning pretty well," one officer summed up his

CAUGHT IN THE SEARCHLIGHT

H.M.S. *Beagle's* anti-aircraft Maxim punctured by enemy shrapnel at night when inside the Dardanelles.

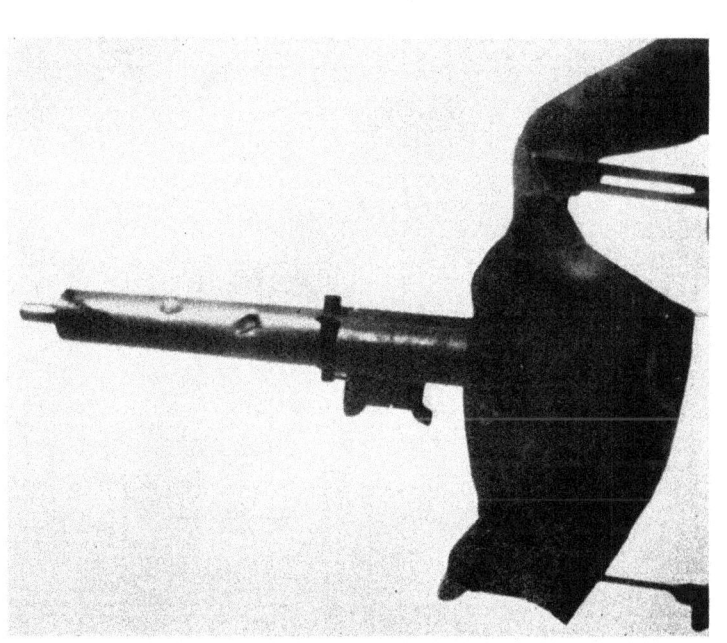

CROW'S NEST

In H.M.S. *Prince George*, to enable better observation for firing into Turkish positions. The "Frapping" seen in this and the photograph facing p. 116 was for the purpose of thwarting the enemy's gunnery by making the rigging appear less defined.

impressions as the Fleet left the scene to the darkness, " but one cannot estimate the real damage." " It was a depressing day's work," concluded another, " and wholly unsuccessful." That night the *Vengeance* waited off the Dardanelles entrance till 4.30 a.m., whilst destroyers and trawlers went in to search for the two abandoned battleships, but saw them not. Whirled about by the eddies, no longer controlled by human hand, mere deserted shells after years of flying the White Ensign; their guns untended, their engines immobile, cabins and wardrooms without inhabitants; the *Ocean* and *Irresistible* went for their final cruise uncontrolled between Europe and Asia.

There is something weird and pathetic in the two ghost ships—one displacing 13,000 tons, the other 15,000—careering about this way and that, occasionally coming under searchlights and shells, and finally disappearing below the black waters of the Straits, whilst their respective Captains sought them among the shadows in vain. It was the last act of a great tragedy. " Mines have quite spoiled naval warfare," remarked one of our gunnery officers at the end of this day; and many will agree with him.

" An air reconnaissance over the Straits was made next morning," wrote a Commander, " and it was reported that nothing could be seen of the *Ocean* and *Irresistible*. The *Inflexible* had been got into shoal water close to the northward of Tenedos, and arrangements were made for pumping her flooded compartments out. She had thirty-four other men drowned in her submerged flat, and it was a week before they could be got out." It was to be no easy job patching her up at this Ægean island, but the possibility of her foundering had been overcome after two days. Later on she was taken into Mudros, where they managed to cover the great hole in her bottom with a coffer-dam. On April 6 she left there with H.M.S. *Canopus* and *Talbot* for Malta, and nearly foundered during the voyage—the coffer-dam having worked loose. During the last six hours she was towed stern first by the former, but got in at last on the 10th. After further repairs at Malta, she proceeded to Gibraltar, where the Dockyard so completely overhauled her that exactly three months after the March 18 injuries she went to join Sir John Jellicoe in the Grand Fleet, and less than a year later " got her own back " at the Battle of Jutland, when her excellent gunnery carried damage to the Germans. Indeed, if you look through the biographies of ships who played distinguished parts in the Great War, I doubt if there are any who lived more exciting hours and were so consistently active as *Inflexible* on our side, and as *Goeben* on the enemy's.

Gaulois, which had saved herself from sinking by having beached herself on Rabbit Island (or, more accurately, on Drapand Island, which is one of the former group), was got afloat on March 23 and sent to Malta, whither likewise steamed *Suffren* for dockyard attention.

OFFICERS OF H.M.S. *PRINCE GEORGE*

CHAPTER XV
SMYRNA INTERLUDE

WE now pass to consider an interesting problem which, for its difficulties and the strategy employed—no less than the tactics—was indeed a Dardanelles in miniature. The vilayet of Smyrna is a vast area of more than 21,000 square miles. Nature has been very considerate as to her geographical gifts, with islands, islets, bays, coves, peninsulas, mountains, headlands, creeks, affording safe anchorage in many a fair spot.

As you come up the wide Gulf of Smyrna, leaving to starboard the peninsula of Kara Burnu and then Chustan (or Long) Island, the coastline begins to contract, so that shortly after passing Vourlah to the southward and then Pelican Point on the north, a ship must go through the very narrow channel of Sanjak Kalesi before the horse-shoe natural harbour of Smyrna widens out off Smyrna city. It is a densely populated capital of the vilayet, with all the characteristics of Asia Minor summed up, but with its own industries of carpet manufacturing, pottery, spinning, perfumery, besides its flour mills and iron foundries. Here come the tramp steamers from Northern Europe to load up with figs, raisins, tobacco, and the trade brings much wealth to the place. Steeped in ancient history, already tracing its ancestry back for some three thousand years, Smyrna has experienced all sorts of struggles, captures, sieges, destruction, at the hands of Greeks, Turks, and others. So that this twentieth-century European War came just in the long sequence of events. Expressed after another manner, Smyrna, by reason of its ideal situation, could not help becoming of first-rate importance and the stage of noteworthy happenings.

In an earlier chapter we first mentioned it as the convenient anchorage of the German S.S. *General* whilst the latter was acting the part of wireless-link between *Goeben* and Constantinople. From that day onwards Smyrna was always suspect: you never quite knew what might be sheltering up the Gulf, and the reader will remember the minelayer at

Vourlah being blown up in November. Briefly, so many were the nooks and hiding-places ideal for smaller and moderate-sized craft, that these inner waters seemed to conjure up torpedo-boats, destroyers, submarines: any special type commanded by some keen young officer who relished risks. As the War developed, and the Ægean became a busy highway for valuable liners transporting still more valuable troops to the Dardanelles, so the Smyrna area demanded and received deeper attention. Obviously it was ideally situated for any mosquito vessels to dash out, make a torpedo attack, and rush home again.

That was one aspect of the Smyrna matter.

Looking at it in a different manner, we can readily appreciate that, with all its wealth and importance as a maritime city, this capital was not less dear to Constantinople than is a daughter to her mother. A blow hurled at Smyrna would be felt on the Bosphorus, and the Turks could not afford to let this vilayet suffer. That is always the danger of an empire, or territory situated at a distance: the invitation to attack, and the need in turn for succour, combine to create an inevitable anxiety. It was the same with Germany, where any attack on Heligoland or Borkum would have brought out the High Sea Fleet at once.

At a time when our efforts against the Dardanelles were not progressing, and the Turks were filling both sides of the Straits with gunners as well as infantry, it seemed a favourable opportunity to smite Smyrna from the sea. This in itself would be something of a feint, and tend to cause the Turks uneasiness, so that they might be expected to withdraw some of their Dardanelles forces away from the main zone. But a further reason for the new operations was inspired by the terrible success which U-boats were enjoying off the British Isles. If submarines should come from Germany up the Ægean and torpedo our battleships, then a new and awkward dilemma would mark the Eastern Mediterranean campaign.

It is necessary to stress this point, for the possibility was very much in the mind of every naval officer and man out here. Only so recently as February 18, Germany had begun her

Submarine Blockade (without employing this description), and it was just a technical matter as to whether the distance from the North Sea would ever prevent under-water craft from coming south, making their base at Smyrna or some other nicely-tucked-in harbour. Thus on March 2 the Admiralty by telegraph instructed Rear-Admiral R. H. Peirse to bombard and destroy the Smyrna forts at the earliest moment, so that it might be blocked and prevented from becoming a base for submarines. He was to proceed from Egypt in his flagship the *Euryalus*, to take charge of operations, and would have at his disposal the two battleships *Triumph* and *Swiftsure*, which were being temporarily detached from the Dardanelles.

Admiral Peirse at the opening of war had been Commander-in-Chief of the East Indies, and it was characteristic of the centralisation in events that gradually he had been brought further away from the East. For some while he had been busy protecting that important lane between Bombay and Aden along which the north-bound transports must come. The Aden to Suez area passed by natural development under his command and, finally, his headquarters became not India, but Egypt, where his supervision in connection with the Suez Canal defences was of prime importance. From Egypt to Syria was another logical progression, and he had been responsible for that watchfulness over the Palestine coast which Captain Larken in the *Doris* so vigorously imposed.

Now, in February the responsibility for Syrian coast operations passed to the French under Admiral de Fourneau, which lessened Admiral Peirse's responsibilities somewhat. The Turkish attack on Egypt, begun on February 3, had been short-lived, so that eight days later the Canal was reopened for night traffic, though mines were next month found in the Red Sea. On March 3 the British Admiral was able to come north in *Euryalus* from Port Said, and the next day Admiral Carden sent towards him the two battleships that were to rendezvous south of Mitylene. Four minesweeping trawlers from the Dardanelles came likewise, together with the previously mentioned Russian light cruiser *Askold*, one destroyer, and the seaplane-carrier *Anne Rickmers*, which had once been a German merchant steamer.

The bombardment began on March 5 with deliberate firing by the *Triumph* and *Swiftsure*, at a range of 14,000 yards, against Fort Yeni-Kale, which controlled the narrow Sanjak Kalesi channel: indeed, unless that defence were captured or silenced, no surface vessel could possibly get through into Smyrna Harbour. It was, so to speak, another Kum Kale or Sedd-el-Bahr. This shooting went on during a whole hour under perfect conditions, and was very accurate; the fort receiving considerable damage, but no reply was made, for the excellent reason that its 9·4-inch guns could not hope to reach attackers at such a distance. The latter now closed to 10,000 yards and repeated the assault.

An excellent beginning!

Next day, under cover of the battleships, the trawlers set forth to sweep through the minefield, and the fun burst forth when the range suited the enemy. Instantly the batteries at, and around, Yeni-Kale gave tongue. Just as their brothers up the Dardanelles Straits never wasted ammunition, but waited only for the right moment, so did these Smyrna outer defences; and their fire was so accurate that the trawlers had to be withdrawn, whilst the big ships at 8000 yards hammered the batteries again for an hour, *Euryalus*, *Triumph*, and trawlers all receiving a certain amount of damage.

Operations were resumed on the 7th, when the squadron again shelled all batteries that could be located. To the south-west of Yeni-Kale, abreast of Pelican Point, where the Sanjak Kalesi channel had the mouth of its funnel-like passage, stood Chiflik, with a battery of field-guns and searchlights. During the latter part of that day *Triumph* succeeded in destroying these guns, and preventing the searchlights from being kept on. On the following day Yeni-Kale and Paleotabia battery (which lay between the former and Chiflik) were shelled, but in return *Triumph* was hit. *Askold* exchanged shots with Vourlah. Night fell, the *Triumph* and *Swiftsure* fired away at the searchlights, and practically kept them dimmed, so that the channel was actually swept by the trawlers to within

3000 yards of Yeni-Kale, though not without cost. The trawler *Okino* foundered on one of the mines, with the loss of ten men, only five being saved, viz., the Lieutenant in command, trawler Skipper, and three others.

On the 9th, totally different tactics were attempted. It was intended that Admiral Peirse, after having destroyed the forts, should get in touch with the Vali and negotiate with him the surrender of all small craft likely to be useful for landing troops at the Dardanelles or elsewhere. The Vali was to be informed that the fall of Constantinople could not be long delayed, and it was hoped that by a little tactful persuasion Smyrna could be brought under control, rather than under conquest; for the British Government had no intention of here becoming involved in military operations. Picture the scene this forenoon at 10 a.m., with the battleships flying a white flag and the signal " I wish to communicate," as they steamed towards the forts.

An exciting incident followed shortly after midday, which an officer in the *Triumph* has been good enough to describe for the reader thus :

" Arrangements had been made through diplomatic channels for the Vali of Smyrna to come with a view to discussing terms of surrender. To enable this to take place, an armistice was arranged which, so far as I remember, was to last from 10 a.m. to 6 p.m. The Vali was to come in a motor car along the shore road, where he was to be met by one of our boats that would bring him off to the ship. He was expected to arrive about noon. *Triumph* accordingly steamed in close to the shore, flying the International Code [just mentioned] accompanied by a ward-room table-cloth at the masthead in lieu of a white flag, with which H.M. ships are not supplied.

" At twelve o'clock the men were piped to dinner as usual when, suddenly, without any warning, a battery of 5-inch guns (which were hidden in the trees) opened fire, landing a salvo on board the ship at a range of three or four thousand yards. We had exchanged a good deal of fire with this same battery the previous day, and we knew pretty well where it was. As soon as their shells reached us, there was a rush to clear away the mess tables and man the guns. Almost instantaneously down came the ward-room table-cloth, and we opened fire with 7·5-inch broadside, which had the immediate effect of silencing the battery. A certain amount of damage had been done, and there were a few casualties. Fortunately most of their fire struck the armour plates and did no damage, but it was an unpleasant moment whilst it lasted, as so many of the crew were exposed on the mess decks. Later on—about four o'clock in the afternoon—an envoy from the Vali came along in his motor car and had a long talk with the Admiral aboard the *Euryalus*."

The Vali's representative apologised for the mistake on the part of the battery, and an armistice was agreed upon till 10 a.m. of the 11th; but in the meantime another unfortunate infringing of a contract ensued.

We mentioned just now that island, which is the biggest of all in Smyrna Gulf, and called Chustan, or Long, Island. More than once it will be necessary to observe happenings off this spot, and the reader is asked to bear in mind that the length was about five miles, with about two miles at the widest, its centre being crowned by a hill. Other officers who were destined to serve long weeks off Smyrna tell me that the largest anchorage of Long Island was at the north-west corner, where small ships could lie close to the shore. Another anchorage could be selected at the south-west end, with very small ones at the north-east and south-east extremities. The village of Nikola stood at the southern end, with a fine natural harbour that could shelter small vessels from most winds, but ashore were just a handful of semi-ruined houses. Hither that summer were brought refugees from the mainland: three thousand refugees of all nationalities to be sorted and examined before being sent on to Mitylene. Not surprisingly, some of them eventually turned out to be spies in the pay of the Turkish Government. But a good deal of the enemy's activity could be watched from Long Island, with Vourlah only six miles away and the Sanjak Kalesi channel thirteen miles: it was in many respects a most suitable observation outpost, but its defects will be considered dramatically on another occasion.

Meanwhile the *Triumph* was to find off this Long Island a most startling surprise. " We anchored that night," says one of her officers, " with a collier alongside, prepared to coal ship in the morning." And close by lay the seaplane-carrier *Anne Rickmers*. Let us see how chance and daring combine to create strange sequels.

On that memorable Sunday night, March 7–8, when the *Nusrat* sowed her fateful score of mines off Eren Keui Bay that sank three battleships and seriously wounded a battle-cruiser, all in one disastrous day, there also stole out of the Straits a Turkish torpedo-boat named the *Demir-Hissar*. She was somewhat old-fashioned, and of only 97 tons displacement, but this mattered little. Of low freeboard, with two funnels, lightly armed as to guns, she could be relied upon to do somewhere about 26 knots, and would be difficult to be seen under the land during the dark hours. Plenty of hiding-places along the ragged Asia Minor coast would conceal her when the sun was up, and, if chased, her speed would give her a fair chance to scuttle off. The essential feature is that she carried three torpedo-tubes.

It must have been apparent to any neutral, as doubtless it has more than once struck the reader, that, with the arrival of *Goeben* and *Breslau*, some of the junior German naval officers would be only too glad of any chance to quit big-ship routine and try some daring adventure. Turkey's handful of efficient torpedo-boats and destroyers afforded just such opportunities for a young ambitious officer desirous of an independent command. The Black Sea became their normal hunting area, but this Sunday night a more enterprising adventure was begun. Lieut.-Commander von Fircks, with a mixed crew of Germans and Turks, as he brought the *Demir-Hissar* out into the Ægean showed that he had tremendous courage, and the unbounded confidence of a young man; though many will accuse him of extraordinary rashness. Still, luck so often follows pluck, and he deserved what success came his way.

I have been at some pains to discover what was the weather that night, and it is not to be wondered that during the early hours of the 8th off Tenedos, at least, it was thick: ideal conditions for a blockade-runner. Von Fircks was bound for Tenedos, as more than one U-boat during the War made for Scapa Flow, with identical result. He hoped to torpedo one or more of the squadron which had been bombarding the Turkish batteries, but a patrol frightened him off. However, he certainly roused plenty of interest, and one of our naval officers humorously noted in his private journal:

"Der Tag at last! Destroyer panic last night, and out nets! But nothing in it."

The *Demir-Hissar* had failed in her objective, though the anchorage was far from anti-torpedo proof, and now she steamed away to the south, and eventually, after one nocturnal visit into Smyrna Gulf, followed by daylight hiding near Khios Island, she stole in again towards Long Island unseen, unsuspected, for there was no moon and the hour was 2 a.m., when human vigilance is not at its best. She loosed off a torpedo, which struck the *Anne Rickmers*, and then escaped speedily into Smyrna. She "appeared from nowhere, and was never seen by anybody," says one of the *Triumph's* officers. "We had to let go hastily of the collier, get under way, and beat an ignominious retreat to Mitylene, with our collier following."

Later the Vali denied any breach of the armistice, insisting that the torpedo-boat had acted on her own responsibility. For us the consoling fact remained that had von Fircks been slightly less dashing and a little more cautious, he might have bagged a battleship. A month later, when the *Demir-Hissar* crept out of Smyrna for another gamble, she still seemed to be handled impetuously rather than with care, as we shall perceive for ourselves. None the less, von Fircks proved, as history has always shown, that no blockade can ever be water-tight; and that by working such conditions as night or fog, a daring captain can often achieve his object. Equally we realise from such a raid the risks to which any blockading force is exposed with regard to small craft carrying torpedoes.

What, then, was the nett result of Admiral Peirse's visit to the Smyrna Gulf? The answer falls under two sections: diplomacy, naval offence. As to the first, when the Vali's envoy, accompanied by the American Consul-General, came off to the *Euryalus* on the afternoon following the white-flag incident, the Admiral handed the former a letter addressed to the Vali demanding unconditional surrender, destruction of all forts and batteries. An interval followed, and on the 13th the Vali declined to accept the terms. Further demonstration would have been useless, so next day we terminated the truce, the Admiral went back to Egypt, whilst *Swiftsure* and *Triumph* steamed north for the Dardanelles, where they arrived early enough to take part in the Great Day of March 18.

But Smyrna revealed precisely the same lessons that obtruded at the Dardanelles. It was learnt that the minefields would first have to be swept up if the squadron was to move about and assault batteries at short range; but that the trawlers could not sweep by day, owing to the batteries' accurate fire. Therefore sweeping had to be performed at night, which was not a success, although a certain advance did take place. In spite of the battleships' excellent gunnery, the only certain result after several days could be summed up thus: one heavy gun and four field-guns destroyed at the expense of one trawler plus one seaplane-carrier disabled, and the risk to a bigger battleship or cruiser which might have been at least holed. Nevertheless, by a curious twist of events, the primary object had been attained. So formidably had our guns threatened, so nearly had our sweepers approached the narrow entrance, that the Turks, in fright lest we should conquer Smyrna, sank several steamers at the narrows in Sanjak Kalesi channel, which was exactly what we desired.

On the other hand, the story could not end so suddenly, the fortunes of Smyrna would be influenced by those of the Dardanelles. The former's blocking up would need to be intensified, patrols inaugurated, Long Island occupied; all of which, in turn, would ultimately invite corresponding resistance, surprise, contest, and narrow escapes. But the pity is that continuity of purpose was still absent from our

Eastern Mediterranean strategy; we were so fond of beginning some new enterprise, dropping it, and then going on to something else. These occasional incursions to the Smyrna Gulf had the cumulative effect of putting the enemy on his guard, and strengthening his defences as time and opportunity allowed. It is very doubtful if anything short of occupying the city and port would have availed us, for experience shows that to block a river or harbour, tightly and effectively, against small craft is far more difficult than at first sight may appear. The attempts during the War in (1) the Rufiji river,[1] (2) Zeebrugge, (3) Ostende, proved that, notwithstanding every precaution, there is left a gap wide enough for emergence. Did not the Flanders submarines wriggle out of Zeebrugge after St. George's Day, till just before the Armistice? Did not the *Demir-Hissar* manage to wind her way out of Smyrna in April 1915, although five steamers had been sunk to bar the narrow channel? German submarines could have still been piloted in and out of Smyrna—had they so wished—as long as the place remained in Turkish hands.

Now, in the autumn of 1914 some tiny submarines of the early UB-type [2] were certainly laid down in the German shipyards and sent, by sections, on the railway to Pola, where they were pieced together. By the following April they were at work in the Adriatic. One of these was *UB* 3, which disappeared on her way to Constantinople, and the mystery has still to be cleared up. There is reason to suppose that she blew up on a mine off Smyrna, the date being April 9. This could not have been on a British minefield, since the first that we were to lay in the Smyrna Gulf began from the night of April 17. If *UB* 3 was trying to enter this port, it seems likely that she did so involuntarily, and perhaps owing to some temporary breakdown: had she set out from the Adriatic intending to use this port, she would have brought with her a chart of the safe channel or at least been met by a pilot.

[1] For details and photograph see my book *The Königsberg Adventure*.
[2] Measuring 90 ft. long, 10 ft. beam; 6¾ knots on surface, and 5 knots submerged.

CHAPTER XVI
REACTION AND PREPARATION

THE contemporary events of that terrible March 18, the reactions on Turks and Germans, together with the subsequent influence on the Dardanelles campaign are of exceptional interest.

It will not have been forgotten that on December 27, 1914, the *Goeben*, when approaching the Bosphorus on her return from a brush with the Black Sea Fleet, had the misfortune to strike one of the Russian mines. The shock caused results other than those strictly confined to mere steel. That so distinguished an officer as Field-Marshal Baron von der Goltz should have been on board was a coincidence, but the happening did not fail to have its effect. No one who has been once mined or torpedoed ever forgets, or can deny that his senses have been touched: however brave and light-hearted be the man, however many times he may come back, there is always behind his nerve and mind that sudden jolt which makes him somewhat less disposed to sustain sudden violence with equanimity. Even the most experienced soldier is so thoroughly out of his element afloat that a minefield quite upsets his balance. How often, indeed, when gallant British officers and men were crossing the sea during the Great War after achieving wonders on land, did the pluckiest feel a cold shudder as some horned black mine bobbed up into sight! A trawler-man would have been no more impressed than if a fish had leaped out of the water.

Von der Goltz on March 18 was still in the mood for receiving impressions; and this attack on the Dardanelles which failed to bring about its aim so deeply affected him that in a few days he was off by train to the north, and on March 31 had reached the German Army's G.H.Q. at Charleville. He would never have left his duties for this visit unless impelled by some special reason, and that reason is found in the thorough shake-up which our attack had caused upon mind⁴ and nerve already disturbed. The precise purpose of his mission will become clear later.

The damage to *Goeben* had been more than inconvenient. She had limped back into her customary berth at Stenia Creek with two holes each big enough for entry of a motor-car. But where could she be dry-docked? There was accommodation of this nature nowhere in Turkey, though ample facilities would have been available in Pola if only the incident had occurred up the Adriatic. Most annoying for the enemy was this lack of facilities at the Bosphorus, and the only alternative was to fit coffer-dams or caissons close to the hull. That, of course, meant a good deal of time and thought; the material and shipbuilding specialists had to be fetched from Germany, and her boilers were again in such a condition as to need re-tubing. By the irony of fate, there were dockyards as near as Sebastopol, but the Russian Black Sea Fleet would have to be defeated, or the Revolution arrive, ere assistance could be obtained in that area.

It so happened that when, at 10.45 a.m. of March 18, the Chanak wireless station flashed the message via the S.S. *General* announcing the Allied advance into the Straits and attack on the Narrows, the *Goeben* was found (so to say) with her boots off. All these dark grey battleships, destroyers, and others looked as if they were bent on forcing their way at all costs. Chanak was able to go on talking without interference from British jamming, and the news arrived hot enough. The *General* lay at the Golden Horn behind the Stamboul bridge, and in her Admiral Souchon had located his headquarters.

Continuing to maintain touch with the Admiral, Chanak that afternoon made the disquieting report that Hamidieh I (which was the Turks' strongest fort, with its two 14-inch and seven 9·4-inch) had already run very low in ammunition. Shortly the last shot would be fired, the Narrows could no longer be defended, and nothing would prevent the Allies from sweeping up the minefield. Heavens! The dreaded fleet would be off the Bosphorus within a few hours! The

Goeben must act as the final bulwark against such a dreaded possibility.

At this hour it chanced that she was putting on her " boots " —just fitting the newly finished coffer-dams, and one had actually been put in position. Ill-suited as she certainly must be regarded for action against preponderating superiority, she received orders to raise steam and go down towards the Narrows ready for action. Casting off the caisson, she got under way at 5 p.m., hurried across the Sea of Marmora as quickly as her two holes allowed, and seemed bound for the most desperate of all her adventures. The rush from Messina to the Ægean; the evasion of last August; now faded into dim memories compared with the real probability of facing the entire Anglo-French Fleet in a final martyrdom. Screened by destroyers, she was cleaving the calm waters of the inland sea as the minarets of a terror-struck capital got further away. Little hope had any of these Turco-German crews of seeing the city or Stenia Creek again.

But the days and hours were full of surprises and new developments, so that when Chanak station again wirelessed —this time that the Allies were withdrawing from the Straits —and it was now only 6 p.m., the *Goeben*, instead of turning back, readapted herself for subsequent complications. Carrying on towards the Narrows, she anchored that night just above Chanak, and lay there with torpedo-nets out prepared for the next move. The crisis passed, the danger disappeared— to the amazement and relief of everyone fighting under the Crescent, the Allies did not resume their attack next day; so during the afternoon of the 19th the *Goeben* stowed her nets back on their shelves, weighed her anchor, steamed off into Stenia Creek, and on the 20th got busy with the coffer-dams again. Forty-eight hours later that job was completed, and the ship ready for her next duty.

There is no sort of doubt that March 18 was the very climax, the pivot of all our Dardanelles hopes. Nor was there any exaggeration as to Fort Hamidieh's predicament. During the preceding duels we had caused this defence to reply against her will: the scanty supply of ammunition had dwindled till Hamidieh was left with only *four rounds*. And in regard to heavy shells the other forts were not much better off. So certain had it seemed this evening the Allies would open up the Narrows, and the Turkish collapse must follow, that a wave of uncontrolled joy swept over Constantinople in lieu of the worst depression it had suffered all these weeks. Henceforth this March anniversary was regarded as a day of honour, of pride, and happiness for having been granted relief and deliverance from the hands of invaders. Never again did the Fleet attempt the folly of trying to break through unaided.

Yes: the shell shortage was the one element in our favour, though at the time we knew it not, and were still staggering under the loss of our battleships. The limit of our progress had been to make the enemy waste ammunition, whilst, on the other hand, we had wasted infinitely more. General Liman von Sanders does not hesitate to show[1] that after all those hundreds of big and medium shells from the Allies' guns, the fighting efficiency of forts and batteries had been but slightly diminished, whilst the Turco-German losses in men had not reached two hundred. Against this figure weigh the Anglo-French naval casualties whilst so contending, and our original argument concerning unaided ships versus forts still stands unchallenged. When the *Bouvet* went down below the surface, more than thrice two hundred lives perished —not by gunfire, it is true—but the minefield could never have been laid except for the shore protecting guns. Nothing but the forts and batteries with their searchlights had prevented trawlers from ensuring a safe channel into the Marmora Sea.

Very significant was the heavy hammering which the Fleet received that day, apart from any damage by unseen mines. The *Agamemnon* had been hit below her armour a dozen times; the *Inflexible* had her control-top wrecked, her forebridge set on fire so that temporarily she retired; the *Bouvet's* fore-

[1] *Five Years in Turkey*, p. 55.

WARD-ROOM WRECKED

HOLE IN HER SIDE
H.M.S. *Agamemnon* after the battle.

turret had been silenced, and her hull knocked about; the *Suffren* was struck fourteen times, one 6-inch turret being damaged and its crews killed; the *Irresistible* had been seriously injured by Hamidieh I; and the *Gaulois* so maimed that she had to be beached to avoid foundering. Thus six out of the sixteen capital ships, in a fight against land defences, had come off second best by gunnery apart from disasters by mines. How many more actions of this kind could be undergone without every ship becoming a cripple?

Obviously this kind of warfare could not go on: the price could never be afforded. Among the seventeen 14-inch, 11-inch, 10·2-inch, and 9·4-inch heavy guns which defended the Narrows, only four had been put temporarily out of action. The fact of the forts themselves being damaged and barracks destroyed was of secondary, and not vital, consideration. In Fort Hamidieh I, which was the toughest nut to crack, and likewise the most formidable opponent, nearly all its officers were German; whilst 85 per cent. of its men were trained gunners from *Goeben* and *Breslau*, says Morgenthau, who just before this date made a personal visit. To the *Inflexible*, the crack gunnery ship which had done such good shooting in the Battle of the Falklands, belonged the distinction of having knocked out two of the Hamidieh 14-inch.

We know that our enemies did not fail to wonder at the accuracy of our fire, yet how disappointing had been the rewards! What could be done against the intermediate defences when they were situated (as, for instance, the Eren Keui battery) at the back of a hill never to be seen from ships, yet all the time most annoyingly active? How could we compete against howitzers, which the bullock-teams would haul to another concrete emplacement whenever a battleship found the range? A good joke on the enemy's part now to burn black powder smoke up some old sewer pipes in a spot different from that where howitzers actually fired, and all this deception might have continued till the country was drained dry of 6-inch ammunition. Only Bulgaria and Roumania during this period were making it impossible for such supplies to reach Turkey from Austria and Germany by land. At least we had command of the sea to stop any steamers arriving with explosives, but who could prophesy that these Balkan States would not be influenced on Turkey's side?

The feeling in Constantinople on March 19 may be summed up in a few words. Whilst undisguised relief from a heavy immediate anxiety had been granted, there were plenty of German officers and Turkish officials who realised that further efforts—if different in kind—would be resumed, and some firmly believed these attempts might succeed. Troops in the forts had been instructed to hold out till the last shell had been fired, and then to abandon each stronghold. Two men conspicuously believed that ultimately the Allies would break themselves against stubborn resistance: Enver was one, and von Sanders the other. This cool, self-possessed General, with the typical face of a military German, the hard eyes, big jaw, determined mouth, thick lips, moustache, and a ruthless personality, regarded the situation as by no means hopeless, but the opportunity for some drastic improvement.

Understand your opponent's psychology: get inside his mind, and read his intentions. Look at things from his angle.

That was what this able leader did; and he did not allow the time to be frittered away. Knowing something of our national characteristics, he reasoned that if we had failed by one method, we should not relinquish the prize before trying some other way. " It would not have been in keeping with British tenacity or energy " to have done otherwise, he has recorded in his reminiscences. " Hence a large landing had to be counted upon." Rumours now began to reach Constantinople from Athens, Sofia, and Bucharest concerning a large expeditionary force of British troops reputed to number somewhere between 50,000 and 80,000. The arrival of Sir Ian Hamilton and the French General d'Amade was duly mentioned. Spies and agents sent in such interesting items as the construction at Mudros of a landing pier, and that on March 17 four British officers visiting the Piræus had purchased for cash forty-two lighters together with five tugs. Clearly these signs collectively indicated nothing less than an invasion, this time by land. What was to be done to thwart such intention?

The answer must be to form a separate Army (designated the Vth) that would be employed for the Dardanelles defence and resist all Allied projects of marching to the capital. If any Anglo-French force were to get well on their way, then the Turkish populace would become panic-stricken, the Ottoman Government would totter, and a revolution break forth. On March 25, exactly a week after the Day of Wrath, it was decided by Enver, under the influence of Wangenheim and Souchon, that Sanders himself should be given command of this important Vth Army. Little enough time could be at his disposal, and he might even find it too short. All those transports arriving from over the sea, with their khaki-clad crowds of lean, sun-tanned warriors eager for a tussle, began to spell out a plain story; but Sanders was too consummate an organiser either to be flustered or to brook delay.

He could not foretell the very hour when the first landing would take place, though we know that Sanders had just one month to the day in which to make the Allies' new plans no more likely to succeed than had the bombardments; and during those four strenuous weeks the German General did wonders. Our own fatal mistake was that yet again we had banged loudly outside the enemy's house, and not *immediately* followed this up with violent assault. So circumstances were kind to this leader, and luck once again associated itself with a courageous resolve to overcome enormous difficulties. The lesson for all of us is too obvious for need of further stressing.

Four short weeks!

By constant marching and exercises, the troops of this new army were trained to become very mobile: this was necessary, since he had both sides of the Straits to consider, roads were few and mostly bad. He had no definite information as to where we were going to land, but he formed his conclusion thus: Opposite to Tenedos on the Asiatic side lies Besika Bay, just south of the Dardanelles, which had, indeed, been used by British forces during the Crimean War and again in 1878. He rather expected that this would be the selected spot. If the Allies should set their thoughts on the Gallipoli peninsula, he had in mind three probable places: (1) Sedd-el-Bahr, because the tract of country could be covered by our naval guns: (2) Gaba Tepe, off which the *Queen Elizabeth* had so often operated; (3) in the Gulf of Xeros at Bulair, where the peninsula contracts to a narrow neck.

For the present, and until developments gave some firm indication, he could make no further supposition; and in the meantime stationed two of his Divisions at (3), two more at the peninsula's southern end, with another couple on the Asiatic side. When the real objective declared itself, he could hope that mobility would enable him to concentrate as requisite. It might be that troops would need to be hurried from one side of the Straits to the other, for which reason he collected small craft in the harbours above Chanak. Roads were constructed from sea to sea, bodies of troops were sent under cover of night to dig trenches and conceal their occupation; along the coastline field fortifications were improved to greater efficiency, and that entanglement of barbed wire which was to be a horrible trap for so many of our soldiers was secretly laid under water just short of the beaches. With regard to this wire there is something at once ludicrous and resourceful.

The Turks had little, if any, of such material among their war supplies, yet the War in Flanders had shown its high value. So, too, for quite a different purpose had the Ottoman farmers and horticulturists made use of this modern manufacture, which was now plucked away from fields and peaceful gardens and sent westward.

These and many other preparations were rapidly made; by the end of March his Army had taken over the shattered forts of Sedd-el-Bahr and Kum Kale, and Sanders installed himself at the port of Gallipoli, which lies on the peninsula side of the Marmora Sea. All was now ready; the space of a month had just sufficed, the curtain could be rung up for the big act of this great Dardanelles drama; and by 5 a.m. of April 25 the first tidings were brought to him that landings of troops were about to begin.

* * * * *

We are now enabled to perceive the kind of reception that was to await our gallant soldiers who had been brought up by the Ægean and were to hurl themselves on beaches already turned into death-traps. Our immediate interest will be in watching the course of events which culminated in that April morning of bitterest memories. It came in the course of proceedings which had shown a remarkable disregard for the principles of strategy, and especially of surprise as a war principle. Half-heartedness, disjointed intention, failure to appreciate fully the task or the right methods, foredoomed whatever might be essayed. Heavy-footed, we had stumbled clumsily to a matter that should have been approached as comes a thief in the night, unsuspected and fully armed. Muddle-minded, not yet informed of the enemy's strength, unacquainted with the nature of his terrain, furnished with defective maps, lacking efficient intelligence as to so many essential details, we went plunging blindly and reckless of the cost.

On March 18 we ought to have had ready, and landed on Gallipoli peninsula, that military force which too late on April 25 came ashore. We had made a big gamble, relying on a vigorous naval attack of massed artillery, and had failed. Once again we were to under-estimate the Turks' opposition, and to lose more gradually but more thoroughly. The same unhappy inadequacy as to initial conception, preparation, and co-ordination ruined everything. Joint operations would have been the sure way to success, yet the strong military force assembled off the Dardanelles before the attack of March 18 was neither asked to take part nor was in the least ready.

The situation was as if the Navy had said: " This Dardanelles business is our own particular show, and we will see it through. The Army can stand by if it likes, and follow up our victory over the forts: but by the time we are off Constantinople there will be no fighting for the troops, who will merely hold what we have won." Sir Ian Hamilton has made this clear enough in his *Gallipoli Diary*, as also that the War Office Intelligence Department had practically no information concerning the Dardanelles and Bosphorus.

So all this vagueness, this independence, this unreadiness to use every opportunity and give the enemy no respite whilst the latter were still vulnerable, baulked a large Fleet and a powerful Army from sending every German back out of Turkey, rescuing Russia, and bringing the War to a close at least three years sooner. We never got the same chance after this March failure. General Hamilton had arrived just in time to witness the Day of Wrath, and his eyes told him the truth, so that he telegraphed to Lord Kitchener, " I am being most reluctantly driven to the conclusion that the Dardanelles are less likely to be forced by the battleships than at one time seemed probable, and that if the Army is to participate, its operations will not assume the subsidiary form anticipated." Its share would not be just landing parties for destruction of forts, " but rather a case of a deliberate and progressive military operation, carried out in order to make good the passage of the Navy."

But Admiral de Robeck, still in the tradition of Admiral Carden, had not yet reached that conclusion; and an immediate landing was not practicable on the 19th, or any subsequent March day, or till the middle of April; for the reasons that the details had to be worked out and rehearsed, complete landing-gear collected, and the XXIXth Division—the backbone of strength and reliability—had not yet arrived. To send an Expeditionary Force down to Alexandria for reorganisation, whilst the General sat down to work out his plans and the enemy made the peninsula impregnable, will always seem to posterity a strange manner of conducting warfare.

FRENCH BATTLESHIP *HENRI IV*

BOAT DECK OF H.M.S. *PRINCE GEORGE*
Protected against enemy shells. In the background H.M.S. *Inflexible*.

BRITISH DESTROYER *LOUIS*
Wrecked off the Gallipoli peninsula. In order to disguise her from enemy attentions, she was later painted to match the colour of the background.

CHAPTER XVII

CHANGE OF PRINCIPLE

At 9.30 a.m. of Friday, March 19, Admiral de Robeck had a conference with his Captains, and it was decided to persevere, notwithstanding the loss of so much tonnage. Six days before, two of the *Irresistible's* sisters, *Implacable* and *Queen* (15,000 tons, four 12-inch and twelve 6-inch guns apiece), had left England for the Dardanelles; and on the 20th *London*, together with the *Prince of Wales*, also of this battleship type, started for the same destination. To replace the *Bouvet*, France was sending immediately from Egypt the smaller battleship *Henri IV* (8807 tons).

Bad weather at first delayed resuming operations, except to make a reconnaissance in the Gulf of Xeros, but the Admiral was only biding his time for a day or two. He intended reorganising the minesweeping arrangements, and began by fitting eight *Beagle* class destroyers with sweeps; six of the *River* class destroyers and four torpedo-boats with light sweeps for locating mines; a flotilla of picket-boats with explosive creeps; training fifty British and a dozen French trawlers and other sweepers; the plan being to make a thorough clearance of the area in which ships would again try to dominate forts and batteries. To prevent the enemy sowing tares after the sweeping had taken place, nets were to be laid across the Straits during the night preceding the bombardment. Steel nets not having yet arrived of sufficient length, he was going to employ those strong tunny nets which Mediterranean fishermen are wont to use.

All this new arrangement and rehearsal would mean at least four days, and meanwhile such vessels as *Vengeance*, *Majestic*, and *Triumph* were making demonstrations up the coast for the purpose of drawing off the enemy's guns: proceedings which were criticised at the time by officers as quite useless, and we have since learnt that they did not cause von Sanders any disturbance from his purpose. A few shells were fired at houses, peasants, etc., in the Xeros Gulf, but no one was fooled by such mild activity.

On the 21st the Admiral still believed that the Narrows Forts, and the batteries guarding the minefields, could be dominated after a few days' bombardment, when the sweepers were to drag among the minefields, but by daylight only. Certainly his number of small vessels for this duty was prodigious, yet they would have been wiped out one after another by at least the 6-inch batteries, which had no shell shortage. It was just when this folly was about to be repeated that, on the 22nd, Admiral de Robeck completely changed his opinion, so that at length his judgment was in line with that of Admiral Sir John Duckworth of a previous century and the exponents of naval strategy.

Sir Ian Hamilton and General Birdwood had that day come aboard for a conference, and the former stated that the Army would not be ready to undertake its work until April 14. The Admiral now realised that the Fleet's communications, after it had succeeded in penetrating the Sea of Marmora, would be cut unless the guns guarding the Straits had all been destroyed. This could not be done by the Allies' naval bombardment. " The mine menace will continue until the Sea of Marmora is reached, being much greater than was anticipated." In plain language, the Gallipoli peninsula would have to be taken and held by General Hamilton's troops, before capital ships fit to deal with *Goeben* could be passed through.

This reversal from the original scheme is a most important feature of the Dardanelles' history. Such a decision was the final recognition that the Navy by itself could not get past the Narrows: the whole character of the campaign was to be transformed, and the direction to pass into the Army's hands. We had begun to tackle the job lightly as a blockade against the *Goeben* coming out. We had then made a noisy diversion and multiplied our floating gun-platforms. We had then discovered that real results could be attained only by landing parties to destroy the enemy's artillery, and from that we had been convinced against our will into admitting that we must have an army to conquer the shores, nor release this hold: otherwise the Anglo-French Fleet in the Sea of Marmora would be starved of coal, shells, food. The change over was not merely that there would be a joint naval and military expedition, but that the Navy would become ancillary to the Army.

It was as if the Sea Service had said: " We've done our best, but these Dardanelles defences have defeated us. Our job is fighting ships: yours is fighting on shore. We hand over the forts and batteries for you to settle, and we undertake in every way possible to help you across the water, bringing you supplies, covering you with our protection, and putting up a shell barrage whenever you say the word. We cannot silence forts or blow up the guns inside: that is for you to do. But we can render you assistance by first driving the enemy's gunners out of the area, and allowing your people to walk in."

Fortunate it had been that General Hamilton reached the Dardanelles just in time to witness from aboard *Queen Elizabeth* the supreme effort of March 18. He had admired the gallantry, but perceived that it could make no headway: so three days later the two leaders' minds were in tune with each other. And there could be no uncertainty on the part of the Admiral, who on the 27th telegraphed the Admiralty that the original plan for forcing the Dardanelles by ships was drawn up on the assumption that gunfire alone was capable of destroying forts. " This assumption," he now stated, " has been conclusively proved to be wrong . . . to obtain direct hits on each gun has been found impracticable, even at ranges of 700 to 800 yards. . . . The utmost that can be expected of ships is to dominate the forts to such an extent that gun crews cannot fight the guns. . . . To destroy forts, therefore, it is necessary to land demolishing parties. . . . The passage of supply ships for the Fleet through the Dardanelles with the forts still intact is a problem to which I can see no practical solution. In such a case it would be vital for the Army to occupy the Peninsula. . . . With Gallipoli Peninsula held by our Army, and Squadron through Dardanelles, our success would be assured." [1]

[1] Quoted from the long telegram given fully in *The World Crisis*, pp. 244–247. This clearly expressed reasoning, upsetting as it was at the time to some minds at home, deserves to be remembered always for its practical exposition of a strategical principle.

We can understand that to have changed his own mind, to have decided against his predecessor and the Admiralty in regard to a main consideration, demanded no little courage; yet those losses and injuries to ships cannot have affected him one whit less than they influenced General Hamilton. A day or two of quiet reflection, the opportunity for talking things over with a senior officer commanding the land forces, had resulted in a decision that will ever be accepted as inevitable. And from that nothing could shift the Admiral. So the General went off to Alexandria, whither also the Army proceeded to prepare itself for the landing that might gain possession of Gallipoli; whilst the Navy, among other tasks, busied itself with lighters, piers, and the entire organisation for transferring large bodies of soldiers from harbour to selected beaches.

Before the month of March went out came the news that our eastern Allies responsible for this "diversion" had captured Przemysl in their operations against Galicia. Activity in the Black Sea was indicated on the 28th, when a Turkish torpedo-boat patrolling outside the Bosphorus during the early morning sighted strong Russian forces approaching. This Fleet, at a distance which outranged the land fortresses, poured in a bombardment during a whole hour, and then went away. It was the first occasion that our Allies had taken such trouble, though, being an unconnected incident, it had little enough value.

Something more interesting followed on April 3, when the Russian Admiral Ebergard, with five battleships and seven destroyers, put to sea from Sebastopol. Aviators were sent to investigate smoke to the south-west, and reported that *Goeben* and *Breslau* were steaming north. When the light cruiser *Pamyat Merkurya* and destroyers approached, *Breslau* tried to cut them off, but was forced to resume her course, whilst the *Goeben* at long range drove the *Pamiat Merkurya* back to the Russian main squadron. The *Goeben* and *Breslau* turned off to the S.S.W. in an endeavour to lure away their

CHANGE OF PRINCIPLE

enemy, which succeeded; for the Black Sea Fleet at 16 knots followed on a parallel course till after midday. Keeping out of range, the Germans did not give battle, and presently sped off quickly towards the Bosphorus, being last seen towards sunset making for home. Russian destroyers were sent forward to make an attack about 100 miles short of the Bosphorus, but *Goeben's* searchlights picked them up and frustrated the effort: so Ebergard took his ships back into Sebastopol.

It was only then that the events became clarified. For the two Turkish light cruisers *Hamidieh* (3800 tons) and *Medjidieh* (3432 tons), with a couple of torpedo-boats, had come out with the purpose of destroying the Nikolaieff shipbuilding yards (hoping thereby to ruin work on the new Russian "Dreadnought" under construction). The two German ships had followed in support. Now, things did not work out quite as hoped for; the *Medjidieh* got into the Odessa minefield, and went down, though her crew were rescued by *Hamidieh* and the torpedo-boats. Thus crowded, these three latter were in no condition for an engagement, whereupon the two Germans drew away the Russians and enabled the smaller vessels to escape. Arrived back safely in Stenia Creek, the *Goeben* was able to carry on her work by jamming *Askold's* wireless, which was the only means of communication between Admiral Ebergard and Admiral de Robeck. Not that this really mattered very much; since the Russians never pulled their full weight with us against the Turks. They might have done so much with a diversion of their own on the forthcoming April 25, and relieved our troops from too heavy a burden; but whilst the Black Sea Fleet appeared off the Bosphorus at sunrise, shelling the batteries for a short spell, their co-operation ended at that. Merely were they repeating at one end of the water the same old mistake we had been making at the Dardanelles end. The nett advantage accruing was that the Turks had lost that one small cruiser, which amounted to little.

But outside the Dardanelles, in Mudros and at Tenedos, was the real scene of activity, in contrast with Russian lethargy. Admiral de Robeck had asked for better aeroplanes, and by the last week of March they had come, with Commander Samson—one of the pioneers of naval aviation—and his fearless troupe. He had already achieved good work at Dunkirk in the North European struggle, and had been sent hastening overland to the south-east. Here the battleships' companies, assisted by Greek labourers, helped to land his seven aircraft at Tenedos; tents as well as huts were erected, and a camp soon sprang up at this improvised aerodrome. Now, when a seaplane reconnaissance was made over the Straits just as the mouth ended, it was to justify the Admiral's decision regarding the future: from the air was revealed the truth that the forts had been surprisingly little damaged, and only one of the two guns destroyed in Hamidieh I (already mentioned as victims to the *Inflexible*) could be seen. To-day we have still further evidence that the Admiral's new change of plan was right. In theory not one stone in that fort should have remained standing on another; not one human being should have survived; yet we have German evidence, in Kopp's account, that in spite of our murderous onslaught, which made the area resemble huge craters, the damage was not too serious. Not less than 160 hits from our heaviest sea artillery were counted by the Turks and Germans, and forty shells dropped dangerously close, causing but few dead or wounded.

During the interval of March 19 to April 25, our enemy, if alert and energetic, could not fail to be nervous as to where and how we might spring the big attack. On Friday, March 26, one of their aeroplanes was sighted to the eastward of Tenedos, and on Sunday—just as the British men-of-war were about to have service—along flew an aeroplane which dropped bombs close to our aircraft-carrier *Ark Royal*, luckily causing no damage. The Germans had well directed their energies, since much would have depended in the past few weeks on reliable spotting, and much was now hoped for in regard to the future. We, too, were maintaining constant vigilance off the

Straits, with two battleships always patrolling each forty-eight hours, and a dummy " Dreadnought " visible in the distance to resemble the genuine *Inflexible*, which was about to leave for Malta. It was during her patrol that one morning the *Majestic*, standing in to have a look at Kum Kale, beheld the grim relics of that unlucky landing which had taken place on March 4. Three weeks had since passed, but lying on his face at the top of the fort was the body of a marine, with the corpse of a white-clad seaman stretched out on the sandhills towards Orkanieh battery. At one corner of the beach stood a $16\frac{1}{4}$-lb. tin of gun-cotton left by one of our demolition party— all tragic relics of a gallant failure.

But all this delay and waiting till the Army could be ready had to be endured by the Fleet with intense boredom. Steaming up to Xeros Bay, making a feint by a " dummy landing," occasionally shelling trenches and villages supposed to be training centres for Turkish troops; coaling ship; going for route marches in the hot sun when in port; loading ammunition; experimenting with nets out whilst under way; riding out gale after gale; watching Mudros harbour become crowded as Piccadilly Circus—all this seemed desperately dull. Even lending a hand to help patch up the *Suffren* lost its interest after a while. A shell from the Narrows on the 18th had holed her badly below water-line, so that after coming out of the Straits she had to be beached on Rabbit Island. Divers from H.M.S. *Triumph* went down and made temporary repairs, whereby she could steam round to Malta for dry-docking. To Malta also went *Vengeance* for a short refit, returning by the middle of April in readiness for the great landing. It was whilst the latter was still in dockyard that one Saturday produced the impressive sight of *Inflexible* arriving stern first, towed by *Canopus*. Each of these two latter had seen von Spee's squadron off the Falklands, yet infinitely more had been the risks within the landlocked Straits of the Dardanelles. Not all von Spee's shells together had been able to compete with the damage by underwater mines and shore artillery.

If our Gallipoli maps were not too accurate, the same must be said of the charts, but some valuable survey work concluded before the April 25 affair must have saved more than one grounding. We shall observe presently that 15,000-ton battleships had to nose their way close into shallows that would scare the life out of any Master Mariner, and would cause a naval Captain to be court-martialled had it been peace-time.

Mudros harbour was also re-surveyed about this date, and the new chart immortalised certain queer names which have puzzled many minds, but here is the explanation. It shows that by taking a long view of things and gathering information against the possibility of future eventualities, much valuable work can be done quietly and unobtrusively during peace-time. If we had before the War gathered as many details concerning the soundings and terrain of the Gallipoli coast, much profit would have subsequently resulted.

The story begins in 1892, when H.M.S. *Fearless* visited this Lemnos Island, which was then a Turkish possession. Her navigating officer was Hughes Campbell Lockyer, himself an expert in naval surveying, and he discovered that Mudros harbour was inaccurately shown on the chart: now was the time for remedying this defective marking of channels. During the merry 'nineties the British Fleet used to send a squadron here as a convenient place for its boat regattas. A light cruiser would drop a buoy in the entrance to mark a tricky spit, and in fact the native population were quite accustomed to seeing the White Ensign flying. Picnics, bathing parties, oared and sailing boats from the ships, became familiar sights. No awkward diplomatic questions could be asked by Turkey provided these sojourns were not too frequent or prolonged.

To have made a survey of Mudros harbour bluntly and openly would have certainly led to trouble: nevertheless, the navigator of the *Fearless* wanted to complete his job, so he carried it out whilst parties from the fleet were scattered all over the harbour, swimming and splashing about so naturally as to disguise the surveyor's actions. But the time came when the squadron must get under way again, and the chart still remained unfinished. The Captain of the *Fearless* called on the Commander-in-Chief, Vice-Admiral Sir George Tryon, who was flying his flag in the *Victoria*.[1] It was explained to the Admiral that a reliable chart was being made and could *Fearless* be allowed to remain till the job was finished?

The Commander-in-Chief was not pleased, sent for Lockyer, and gave him a good dressing-down for endangering international amity: serious complications might easily result from such desire for knowledge. In reply, the navigator produced his cartographical efforts for the Admiral's inspection, and these evidently had some effect. Next morning, as the squadron was about to leave, there came a signal from the flagship thus:—

"*Fearless* send boat for letters."

And at the end of a certain letter the Admiral had written:—

"You will remain here and continue search for the anchor lost by H.M.S. *Edinburgh* during recent exercises, but do not remain longer than one week. If necessary, you should show these orders to the Turkish authorities."

Anchor? There was no lost anchor: this was the first mention of the matter. However, the tactful manner of issuing instructions was understood, the navigator went on diligently with his searches for a week, finished his rough chart, told the Turks that the anchor could not be found, and away went the *Fearless*.

Several years intervened until this same surveyor found himself back at Mudros, but aboard H.M.S. *Hood*, and the date was 1899. Lockyer managed to continue his previous work, and to make some valuable additions, but it had to be done in spite of the Captain, who (says the former) "was not a

[1] It was in the following year—June 23, 1893—that the historic collision occurred between H.M.S. *Victoria* and H.M.S. *Camperdown*, with loss of the former, together with Admiral Tryon and over three hundred officers and men.

friend of mine. As a matter of fact, he did not know it was spy-work: otherwise he might have stopped the job." But the surveyor got to windward of his commanding officer without the latter ever suspecting it to the end: a quiet revenge for previous annoyances was perpetuated before the Captain's very eyes. For when Lockyer placed the new survey on the table, and all the hills now individualised with separate appellations, the Captain was moved in all innocence to remark:

"What peculiar names these Turks give their hills, Lockyer!"

The latter concealed a smile, and the Captain (whom, for the sake of argument, we will call Claver, though that was not his name) unconsciously read his own condemnation. The four hills were named " May," " Claver," " Be," " Damned "; but spelt backwards. No one ever suspected the joke, and two years later, when Lockyer was serving in the flagship H.M.S. *Bulwark*, the survey was at last completed, with these mysterious titles retained. At the end of March 1915 arrived in Mudros Bay H.M.S. *Implacable*, her commanding officer being Captain Hughes Campbell Lockyer, and when the re-survey was made preparatory to harbouring all aggregation of shipping, he was amused to find the comic names given an official immortality. This is a perfectly true story, related to me by Captain Lockyer himself, of whom further mention will be made presently.

Well may he have congratulated himself that more than twenty years previously he had begun defining two good channels instead of one bad entrance. To-day that base with its Armada of *Queen Elizabeth, Lord Nelson, Agamemnon, Swiftsure, Triumph, London, Prince of Wales, Cornwallis, Majestic, Goliath,* battleships; the cruisers, destroyers, trawlers, and tall transports, all protected by a recently completed anti-torpedo boom and representing a hundred varieties of vessels, seemed to be an epitome of steam navigation, its history and development. We were lucky to have had such a roomy harbour as Mudros geographically ready at the outbreak of hostilities, and that by a little diplomacy the Greek owners had placed no impediments in our way. But not less fortunate was the British Navy in having obtained full knowledge of the anchorage possibilities years before a war cloud came over the Eastern Mediterranean. Rear-Admiral Wemyss could now gaze through his monocle on to a bay that had never seen an assemblage of such shipping. Generations ago, when galleys could be quickly fashioned from the Ægean forests and launched into the blue sea, with rough oars ready to take their part in battle, these eastern ports were accustomed to number war craft by hundreds; but in 1915 the massed steel tonnage of fighting ships and merchantmen exceeded anything a poet could have contemplated. No artist's canvas would have been big enough to convey the idea of so gigantic a collection, wherein millions of pounds had been invested and so many high hopes were being transported.

And the very last thing that all this mixed fleet suggested was that their presence here had been the result of a diversion. Rather, one might have imagined, it foretold the advent of some Alexander, or a Napoleon, about to march eastward and sweep the whole of Asia into his hands. Might and power, majesty and dominion, wealth and unlimited resources, seemed to be expressed in these hulls. Was there anything in Turkey that could ever resist this displayed pre-eminence?

Aboard the flagship *Queen Elizabeth*, where Admiral de Robeck and Commodore Keyes, his Chief of Staff, were busy night and day, there was much coming and going, though the vessel herself had not moved or fired a gun for weeks. Admiral Peirse was sending from Egypt to Mudros all the barges and lighters he could collect, and they were to reach that port during the first week of April, and to spare any available warships; as a result of which the two cruisers *Bacchante* and *Euryalus* came up from Port Said, but before this the French had sent to the Dardanelles not merely the promised *Henri IV*, but also that old battleship *Jauréguiberry*, whose name was to be such a tongue-twister to our white-clad sailors and khaki "Tommies." The *Doris* had been selected to escort the torpedo-boats summoned from the Suez Canal.

During the first days of April, minesweeping trawlers were still being sent inside the Straits, but of course they had the same kind of reception as before. On the 3rd one trawler was struck by shrapnel, three of her crew being wounded, one man mortally. Next day another trawler was shot through the funnel, and there would soon have been some quite serious casualties if such operations had been continued. Rear-Admiral C. F. Thursby, who since March 29 had been entrusted with the minesweeping and went out himself to see what would happen, considered that the trawlers were lucky not to have been hit oftener, and that we should soon have considerable losses. As a result of this view, all minesweeping inside the Straits was stopped from April 7, as the achievements did not justify the heavy risks. Thus, in short, the volunteer crews of trawler men, Royal Naval Reserve, and Royal Navy, had been able to effect little more than the fishermen by themselves. This decision to give up the sweeping of essential obstacles to the Chanak approaches was certainly very serious: one may regard it as the final bolt which locked the door against entering Constantinople. No naval progress could possibly be made up the defile so long as these underwater dangers existed, and we now definitely delivered the Dardanelles' future into the Army's firm care.

Not that the Navy packed up and did nothing. They were to do many, and gallant, deeds, but rather in preparation or support of the soldiers. Early in April, for example, the *Prince of Wales* demolished Cape Helles lighthouse, which had been seen making signals; battleships, with aeroplanes spotting, shelled batteries within the Straits, and at night did the same to the villages of Kum Kale and Sedd-el-Bahr. On the Ægean side, and up to the Gulf of Xeros, British officers were making sketches from the sea of all possible landing-places. On the 12th Sir Ian Hamilton with other military officers inspected landing-places, both along the Gallipoli peninsula and at Besika Bay. Next day the Staff of the Anzac Corps made inspection of their destined beach, and in the meantime troops at Mudros were constantly, by day and night, practising the art of landing on a beach, so that the historic day was not far distant when Navy and Army would make a grand combined assault to begin the advance towards Constantinople at the point of land most distant from the ultimate objective. We were, in fact, to begin the months-old task afresh, employing a different strategy and new methods.

But immediately before the Army had a chance to start, naval forces found themselves engaged in a very desperate adventure.

CHAPTER XVIII

NIGHT OF NIGHTS

THERE reached Mudros from England on April 9 two of our "E" class submarines, whose arrival was to inaugurate a very special section of the Dardanelles story. What these little vessels were like in appearance the reader will be able to gather from accompanying illustrations: it will suffice if we add that they displaced 725 tons when on the surface, 810 tons when submerged; that they had twin propellers, which gave them a speed of 15 or 16 knots along the surface and 10 knots when below.

This "E" type was, of course, bigger, faster, and with greater radius of action than the "B" class, and it would mean much when we remember that the Dardanelles Straits are some 35 miles long, with a current that attains most of 5 knots in the Narrows. Although in theory an "E" submarine can remain submerged over a distance from 40 to 50 miles, her batteries would then be running pretty low, and she must come to the surface for re-charging. If, therefore, she were attacked by some fast-moving vessel (such as a destroyer) at the end of that long run, the submarine would be at her weakest: she would possess little enough reserve to get away unseen from any bombs that might follow. Also, it will be realised that where she met the strongest current she would be making good over the ground at only 5 knots.

These figures, allowing a slight margin for incidents that no one could see ahead, at once caused serious reckoning. Would the boats ever be able to penetrate into the Sea of Marmora, and reach there in a fighting condition? Apart from the question of power, was the journey practicable against the 400 mines, which were known to begin from abreast of Kephez Bay, and would be especially thick just below Chanak? The latter region would be the crux, not merely because here the current ran at its maximum velocity and the hidden black "eggs" would be thickest; but for the reason that if even so much as a periscope showed its tip, the shore batteries would rain death. Two other unpleasant obstructions could be expected along the route: a wire cable stretched from shore to shore, and steel netting. The former might do several things, such as fouling the hydroplanes, or damaging the periscope, or forcing the boat to the surface. The nets might entangle themselves around the propellers and entrap the visitor from going ahead or astern. Eventually the impotent submarine would consume all its air, and her crew would have a slow death.

The two most likely accidents would be, firstly, the fouling of a mine, or its mooring chains, and almost immediate explosion, when the hull would be holed and the admission of water, like some hydraulic ram, would compress the air till the act of breathing became painful: the boat would sink, and the last agony would be that of drowning. Secondly, there would be a very good chance of getting ashore. To navigate a submarine in the North Sea or wide Atlantic, with plenty of room and ability to keep rising and look-see through the periscope, is one thing; but to go blind through a twisting channel, where the space is circumscribed and the direction of the strong stream uncertain, is something quite different. If the Captain could rise to periscope depth every few minutes and snap a sight of the land on either side, he might see where he had reached and lay another course. Perhaps he might have made too much allowance for the current. Perhaps too little. There might be some eddy caused by the swirl out of a bay, completely upsetting his reckoning; yet the last thing he wished was to advertise his presence by the wake which his periscope would show when once hoisted in that rushing water.

Taking it by and large, the chances of an "E" boat getting through, reaching the Sea of Marmora, there escaping all the attentions of mosquito craft, running the Narrows gauntlet a second time, and emerging alive through the Dardanelles Straits, seemed hopeless. Considered naval opinion believed this was one of the things which would have to be let alone.

And for that reason, of course, it was attempted.

The first two arrivals were *E* 14 (Lieut.-Commander E. C. Boyle) and *E* 15 (Lieut.-Commander T. S. Brodie). Both were highly experienced officers of undaunted courage, as one would expect, and as events proved. For the present we will confine our attention to the latter boat, which had already performed good service in the Heligoland Bight. In order that they should learn the " hang of the land," and get some idea of the features, the newly come submarine officers were taken out on the 11th for a trip by destroyer. It was decided that *E* 15 should try her voyage on the 17th, so Brodie made a further preliminary inspection on the 12th by aeroplane, being taken up by Commander Samson at a fairly low altitude right along the Straits till above Kephez Point, thus affording a pretty thorough view of the geography and defences. Samson, who was himself fearless, and tougher than most people, a picturesque, short-bearded adventurer who might have stepped out of the Elizabethan age into the seaplane era as Air-Commodore, wrote [1] before he died, " I must say I preferred my job to his, and I rather felt as if it would be the last time I would see him." For, if five rows of mines had awaited Lieut. Holbrook when he brought *B* 11 during December through the same area, there now existed twice that number, leaving out the *Nusrat's* contribution off Eren Keui Bay.

With the intention of clearing a passage for *E* 15, a risky expedition was undertaken on the night of the 14th–15th. Picket-boats from the *Triumph* and *Majestic* with volunteer crews were to tackle the Kephez minefield, using explosive creeps. It was one more of those nocturnal adventures which (we might suppose) would be rewarded either by death or the Victoria Cross. I cannot do better than present the following account, for which I am indebted to Commander Michael Barne, the *Majestic's* second-in-command. The narrative is so modest and self-effacing that the reader should be reminded of a truth.

[1] *Fights and Flights*, by Air-Commodore C. R. Samson, C.M.G., D.S.O., A.F.C. London, 1930, p. 66.

Commander Barne as a young naval officer went out with Captain Scott on that leader's first expedition to the Antarctic. When the War came, Commander Barne had already been some years retired. A first-rate sailorman in the literal sense, he had continued his sailing up and down the Narrow Seas aboard his yacht. The summons of hostilities brought him back from retirement, nor had he been more than a short while in uniform than he dived overboard to rescue a man from drowning. It was a very plucky act under difficult conditions. Then one Monday, whilst lying in Portland, before starting for the Dardanelles, the *Majestic's* Captain had cleared lower deck and ordered "everybody aft." Prayers being ended, Captain Talbot stepped forward and began: "Before we go any farther, I have something to say." To the surprise and consternation of Commander Barne, the commanding officer proceeded to address the men, said some very nice things about his Commander, topping up by handing the latter the Royal Humane Society's medal and certificate for life-saving. " I was fairly scored off, and felt proportionately foolish."

But it was an excellent prelude to the perils which that ship's company and that battleship—she was the oldest man-of-war which fought at the Dardanelles—must soon experience before culminating in her final tragedy.

So we come to the night of April 14–15.

"Volunteers were called for minesweeping. All the officers (combatant) volunteered except five. I pleaded hard to be allowed to go," says Commander Barne, "but was told that the Commander could not be spared. Bayford (Sub-Lieut., R.N.R.) and Mr. Buckingham (Acting Bo's'n) were allowed. Bayford had got a D.S.C. for good work in picket-boats during earlier operations.[1] The *Triumph* and *Majestic* were each told off to send a picket-boat up the Straits to creep for the circuits connecting the Kephez minefield with the shore—if such circuits should exist. It was believed also that a wire jackstay had been laid across the bottom, below

[1] Already chronicled in an earlier chapter.

each line of mines, to prevent them from dragging down with the current.

"The *Triumph's* boat was to work the north shore, and the *Majestic's* the south, leaving their respective ships at 8 p.m., and they were to be supported by destroyers. I got permission from the Captain to go in charge of our boat, and heard later that Lieut.-Commander (T.) St. John of the *Triumph* was in the latter's boat. We went on patrol during the day in *Majestic* up the Straits and fired at Achillæum, who replied, but did not hit us. At 7.30 p.m., as it got dark, we stopped about three miles outside Cape Helles, and hoisted out the picket-boat. Dumsday, Petty Officer 1st class, volunteered to come as coxswain. Patterson, Engine-room Artificer R.N.V.R., who had volunteered for war service in any capacity, came in charge of the engines. I had met his brother, who was Secretary of the Bangor Sailing Club, when we had visited Belfast Lough in the Channel Fleet in 1899. He had been very good to me, and entertained me at his house near Belfast. Another excellent hand who, with several others, always volunteered for these picket-boat stunts, was Cox A.B. All these men were subsequently decorated for their repeated enterprises in our picket-boat.

"We got our creeps and gear into the boat, and at 8.10 p.m. left the ship, steaming in towards Cape Helles. We did not know whether the *Triumph's* boat was astern or ahead of us. By way of protection we had placed two sheets of $\frac{1}{4}$-inch steel-plate on either side of the cabin, and had boxed in the steering position with similar material. We did not use the forward steering position in the conning-tower. The Turks had established a searchlight of low power in the neighbourhood of the mouth of Mendere river, but we were far beyond its rays as we hugged the north shore.

"We went steadily up, keeping about $\frac{3}{4}$ mile from the north shore, and fortunately for us it was dark and inclined to be misty. When we got above Suan Dere valley, we were so much in the rays of the searchlights, that we knew it was only a matter of minutes before the first gun would bang off.

HOISTING OUT PICKET-BOAT

THE ADMIRAL COMES ABOARD
Admiral de Robeck received aboard H.M.S. *Prince George*, whilst still under way.

Presently Dumsday, who was steering, reported that he could see something white on our starboard bow. We approached it, and presently discovered that the white thing was the funnel and cabin top of the *Triumph's* picket-boat, just catching the lower edge of a searchlight's rays. She was stopped at the time and, we heard later, had got hold of something with her creep.

"Just as we got up to her, bang went a gun from the north shore, close to us, and a shell went whistling over her. We had, up till then, not been spotted, but very soon were; when they had lit up four more searchlights, these (with the one east of Mendere river) and one at Eren Keui, made nine in all. Then the excitement began, the shrapnel to whizz over us, and to bang quite close, tearing up the water around. I saw a big one pitch in the water right alongside the *Triumph's* boat, and a charge of shrapnel threw up the water on either side of her, looking as if it had gone clean through her. She turned round and cleared out at full speed, having, as we heard later, fired her creep, and cut the obstruction.

"I gave the order to stand-by with our creep, and made across to the north-east in order to reach our allotted pitch. Getting well over to that side, we lowered our creep and began to steam slowly down, just keeping steerage way. As we got farther down still, the firing eased, much to my gratification, as I confess I was in a mortal funk. Whenever the searchlight caught us, bang would go a gun or two, followed by that very unpleasant and rapidly increasing scream. The noise was deafening, and as the shell burst it seemed to light up the sea all round. When we had got down abreast of Eren Keui, and well below the minefield, we hauled our creep, turned round, and were just starting to go up and begin again, when a destroyer came to ask if we were all right, and what we were going to do. We replied that we were all right, and were on our way up for another tow down. (Later we heard that the *Triumph's* boat had reported we had either been hit or broken down, as we did not seem to be moving when last seen.)

"So we went up, but presently came the destroyer after us, which drew the Turkish fire upon both of us—to my annoyance. She hailed us with the order: 'Return to your ship.' I asked whom the order was from, and got the reply: 'From the *Wolverine.*'[1] Orders had to be obeyed, so we turned round, and found our ship beyond the Straits, getting alongside at 11.45 p.m. I was thankful to be back. On the following morning a general signal was made from the flagship saying what had been accomplished, and it wound up by saying that *Majestic's* boat on starting to go up again had been recalled by Admiral's orders, as the defences had all been aroused, and we should probably have been sunk."

There were no casualties, fortunately, but the nett result of this trying enterprise was just the severing of that one cable: a poor recompense for gallantry, and not likely to help E 15. But this was not the final picket-boat episode.

Two days still intervened before the submarine was due to make her trip. Wednesday night's excitement was followed by a daylight shoot in the neighbourhood of Gaba Tepe, where certain gun-positions were in course of preparation. Thither was sent the *Majestic*, with a seaplane to do the spotting, but the spotting was not a success. The enemy's positions, as usual, were hidden behind a low ridge, so the *Majestic* could not see her targets, and the 6-inch shells failed to find their billet. But while this was going on, a heavy shell came from somewhere and pitched a long way from the battleship. Then came another right over her quarter-deck, and burst in the sea beyond. Next came a salvo of two, quite close to *Majestic*, who now moved about to upset the range of this newly-made acquaintance. What had happened? Who was firing?

The answer could not be found until the seaplane reported that a Turkish battleship was firing from Kilia Liman, a bay in the Sea of Marmora across the Gallipoli peninsula, which is

---

[1] The *Wolverine* was a turbine destroyer of 914 tons, with one 4-inch and three 12-pdr. guns. Her captain, Commander O. J. Prentis, R.N., was killed a fortnight later, when a shell struck his bridge. He was succeeded by Lieut.-Commander A. St. V. Keyes, brother of Commodore Keyes.

here about five miles. The old *Barbarossa* with her 11-inch guns had on March 5 done a similar thing to the *Queen Elizabeth* when the latter was operating off Gaba Tepe also. The enemy had a convenient spotting station with telephones, and to-day the indirect firing had once more been very good, so the *Majestic* finally drew out of range.

Throughout Friday the *Majestic* was lying anchored at Tenedos off the aerodrome taking in coal, but during the forenoon of Saturday her picket-boat came off from the aerodrome with Lieut.-Commander Charles G. Brodie, twin-brother of Lieut.-Commander Theodore S. Brodie, also a submarine officer, but serving on the Admiral's Staff. The two were so alike that it was always difficult to distinguish one from the other. But the visitor was much agitated, and no wonder. He asked Commander Barne for the loan of the picket-boat to go and see the Admiral on a most pressing matter. This is the sad story.

At 2 a.m. that 17th of April *E* 15 had started off on the surface. She hoped to get through the Narrows and torpedo the *Barbarossa*, so hugged the north shore (as her predecessor *B* 11 and the picket-boats had done), and at 4 a.m., before it was daylight, submerged. She had thus not used any of her electricity until well up the Straits. In order to distract the enemy's attention, aeroplanes one after another followed and dropped bombs; and now flew Charles Brodie as an observer, that he might keep watch over his twin-brother.

To the former's horror, he saw *E* 15 run ashore in Kephez Bay, where she remained, and of course came under a withering fire from every Turkish gun that could bear. It was now 6.45 a.m., sunrise having been about an hour earlier. Her conning-tower was showing above water, and she was firmly stuck. Every one of Commander Samson's aeroplanes was aloft, and did their best to create a diversion, but soon realised that *E* 15 would not get free. The seriousness lay not merely in the possible loss of our first " E " boat to enter the Straits, but in the probability that the Turks would now obtain the free gift of a submarine which, with a German crew, might do untold damage against our Fleet. A second anxiety was that the confidential books would fall into the enemy's hands. Very promptly, therefore, did Admiral de Robeck take action. She must be destroyed forthwith.

We know now—though the news at that time was not possible—that under the terrible fire Theodore Brodie had tried to get his craft afloat by emptying her tanks and going full speed astern with his engines. He had just asked if the hull was badly hit, when a shell entered the conning-tower and killed him. Besides the crew there were also Lieut. Edward J. Price and Lieut. Fitzgerald, who destroyed charts and confidential documents whilst shells still battered and penetrated the boat. Six of the crew were asphyxiated, but the rest, after abandoning the boat, were picked up by the Turks and taken prisoners. Along came a Turkish destroyer, who tried towing her off, but Commander Samson's aeroplanes dropped bombs and stopped this.

First Admiral de Robeck sent up the old submarine *B* 6, who was to blow her up by torpedo, but she had difficulty in counteracting the rushing current, fired one torpedo, and was unable to see if it had been effective, though it apparently struck an enemy tug alongside, which now sank. Aeroplanes tried to drop bombs on *E* 15, but could not descend sufficiently low against the Turkish anti-aircraft guns. At night steamed up the two destroyers *Scorpion* and *Grampus* and got within half a mile of her, but could not see her for the searchlights, and were forced to retire. On the Sunday morning it was hoped that better fortune would be granted, for Lieut. Holbrook in *B* 11, wherein he had won his Victoria Cross, was sent to do the job! Alas! the fog was so thick that he could see nothing. At 1 o'clock that afternoon the *Triumph* and *Majestic* were ordered inside the Straits to destroy *E* 15 at long range, with an aeroplane spotting; but they were forbidden to go beyond the minesweapt area.

"At the appointed time," Commander Barne tells me, "we formed astern of the *Triumph* off Cape Helles, with several destroyers in attendance. What part these were to play, besides drawing the enemy's fire, we did not know. We went in at about 12 knots, and soon the shells began to fly, first from Achillæum, but later from Eren Keui. We saw a shell burst aboard the destroyer ahead of us, though it did very little harm. We could see very little sign of E 15, yet there was a small tug, or other steamboat, about where we thought she lay. This served as a mark, and on getting to within 12,000 yards of her we opened fire with our fore-turret. We did not know if we effected any good, as again the communications with the spotting aeroplane went wrong."

The two battleships then turned "in succession," being abreast of Eren Keui, engaged the shore batteries of Suan Dere as well as the Asiatic shore opposite with 6-inch guns; and on turning round fired at the supposed submarine conning-tower with the after-turret's 12-inch. It is scarcely surprising, the target being so small and indefinite, the distance nearly six miles, that E 15 received no hit; though the *Triumph* was struck for the twenty-third time by a howitzer.

Thus, to sum up, two days had been spent with no result, and it was now Sunday evening. The Admiral had tried aeroplanes with bombs, two submarines, two destroyers, two battleships. What else could he send? There can be no doubt that E 15 had either been caught in an eddy, and so carried on to the Kephez shore, or else the down-rushing current struck her on the port bow, and the Captain, not realising this, omitted to give her starboard helm. Almost blind as the navigation must be among those defences, and with no certainty as to where the mines stretched, Brodie had a very anxious job. Such currents were most tricky, and this 1914–1915 period was the first time since the world's creation that the variations began to be experienced. Why was that?

The answer is that until now no under-water navigation of the Dardanelles had ever been attempted. In the past ages rowing-boats had given way to sailing-ships, and the latter to steam; but always the passage had been made on the surface. That was not too complicated, since the current ran more or less from north-east to south-west. But there are different strata of water at different depths, and most of us have noticed when lying in a river that the flood tide will make up over the surface, whilst the river stream will still be running down at a few feet below. Even in the tideless Mediterranean I have observed a complication of currents caused by local conditions.

Now, picture to yourself the immensity of the Black Sea, with its 150,000 square miles of water expanse, and with depths reaching as much as 7000 feet. Filled by the long rivers of Russia and the swift Danube, this inland ocean has no outlet except via the Bosphorus through the Sea of Marmora and Dardanelles into the Ægean, where it meets the great opposition of the Mediterranean. Obviously something abnormal and powerful must happen where these two rivals meet near the Chanak Narrows. You would expect eddies, swirls, counter-currents, all still more complicated by the local insets to the little bays. During certain months of the year, following the winter, there is a thin stratum of warm water resting on a thin layer of cold, below which there is a uniform stratum of slightly warmer water; and only a submarine could have practical knowledge of all these problems.

In the course of writing this book I have had long conversations with one of the most successful British submarine commanding officers, who, in spite of narrow escapes, used to take his craft right through into the Sea of Marmora and back. When negotiating the Narrows, he generally submerged to a depth of about 80 feet, and I asked him how he managed to do so well against a 5-knot current. He told me that they found at that depth there was a reverse, and favourable, stream; whilst the Black Sea waters were pouring down over him on the surface, the pressure from the Ægean was sending up a contrary influence, and they could thus turn enemy into friend. Aviators in the same manner, by descending to a different atmospheric layer, can find a fair breeze instead of a head wind.

But these Dardanelles characteristics had all to be learned by our pioneers in submarines. There were inevitably trials and errors, surprises and more mistakes, narrow escapes and

"E" boats getting completely out of control,[1] and poor Brodie, by his voyage of discovery, gave his life in conveying a warning to his successors.

So we come now to the final effort for destroying his submarine, which the enemy could not haul afloat. Every hour was precious, every delay made it more likely that we should lose our chance. On Sunday evening the Admiral made the following signal:

> Two picket-boats from *Triumph* and *Majestic* are to attack E 15 to-night with torpedoes fitted to dropping-gear. Lieut.-Commander E. G. Robinson of *Vengeance* will be in charge of operations. Only volunteer crews to be sent.

This, of course, was that officer who, as an expert in all those general matters classed loosely under "Torpedoes," had so bravely distinguished himself landing at Kum Kale to achieve the demolition of enemy guns. For this intrepidity, as well as for some further brave work in mine-sweeping, he had been awarded the Victoria Cross: no one more deserved such a decoration. And now the *Vengeance* was lending him, by the Admiral's express orders, not solely because of Robinson's previous prowess, but for the reason that at the time when E 15 got ashore he happened to be on patrol and knew exactly the spot.

Naturally enough, Commander Barne longed to go out in the *Majestic's* boat with the party, and his disappointment was bitter that this was not possible.

"It was a still evening," he describes the preparation, "and we got the dropping-gear [2] into the boat a few miles outside Cape Helles. As bad luck would have it, one of our dropping-gear sets was a wrong one, and did not fit the boat, so we had to make a 'lash-up' of it, though it worked all right when the time came for using it. I had volunteered to go in our boat, but, as it was essentially a torpedo-man's job, and the officer of the boat had to be junior to that of the *Triumph's*,

---

[1] Compare the tragedy of *AE* 2 on a later page. Also the experience of *U* 21 on p. 262.

[2] This was an old and simple method of releasing the torpedo without the need for tubes.

the honour was given to Lieut. Claud H. Godwin,[1] and I know nobody could, or would, have done it better. We got the boat away at nine, after a terrible struggle, and she went alongside the *Triumph* for orders. I heard that, by way of commencing his exploit, Godwin fell overboard when alongside the latter. We closed in to the entrance after the boats had gone, and could hear heavy firing at them."

The Admiral's sudden order this quiet Sunday evening was something of an explosion in itself. To take these slim little steamboats right up under the enemy's guns into waters that would be brilliant with searchlights, meant a risk not unlike that of infants tottering headlong into motor traffic during a city's rush-hour. All the previous episodes of trawlers and picket-boats, of destroyers and cruisers, had shown that this maelstrom of shrieking shells signified sure death. The *Triumph's* Captain frankly told his own volunteers that they were under no obligation to go, and that he did not think there was much chance of any coming back. When it came to the point of deciding between two eager officers, and neither was willing to be omitted, they decided to throw the dice and leave the verdict to chance. So a miniature drama was enacted in the *Triumph* whilst these two young gallants stood by and shook the dice-box in turns: it was agreed that the best of three throws should win and entitle the lucky gambler to go in the boat.

Many a thrilling play, and a well-remembered novel, has had for its big scene just such a climax. Other members of the mess watched and waited; suspense developed to a high pitch when each competitor won a throw. Not till the fortunate adventurer threw four aces to beat his rival's four tens, was this detail settled.[2] As to the crew, many wanted to go, but the orders were that the fewest possible must be taken,

[1] Lieut. Godwin had recently qualified for torpedo duties.
[2] For the information presented in this chapter I have relied on personal conversation, private and original documents; together with an article in *Blackwood's Magazine* for October, 1915, entitled "A Dardanelles Exploit: by One Who Took Part in It," and the account given by Vice-Admiral C. V. Usborne in his *Smoke On The Horizon*.

and finally Lieut.-Commander Robinson had with him in *Triumph's* picket-boat: one other officer, Midshipman John B. Woolley, who came from the *Vengeance* as Robinson's aide-de-camp; one torpedo petty officer as coxswain, two seamen gunners for the Maxim mounted in the bows; four seamen torpedo-men (two for each side), and three stokers.

At 10 p.m., whilst it was still fine, these two 56-feet boats steamed off with a life-belt for each man, rifles and ammunition. It was a dark, moonless night, but rather too fine: the slight haze and threat of light rain, which would have been a help, had passed away. In order to diminish conspicuousness, everyone wore dark clothes, and faces had been painted black. Steaming at about 8 knots, with Robinson leading in the *Triumph's* boat and Godwin following some 800 yards astern in the *Majestic's*, they had about twelve miles to go from where they had left their homes off the entrance, but the last five would be the worst. Hugging the north shore, which had always been found the safer, and drawing only five feet (which ought to ensure safety among the mines), the boats, with lights out, eerily sped on up-stream, and then kept in more mid-channel to avoid being spotted by Suan Dere's searchlight. Alas! just as the boats were sheering across towards Kephez on the opposite side, the vigilant enemy got them within the rays and alarmed the other stations. So first came a focussed burst of brilliance, then a projectile flashed by, and the metallic sound of shrapnel cracked menacingly over their heads. Being the leading boat, Robinson's was given the hotter reception, but the two zigzagged about to throw the enemy gunners off their range.

To have looked down on this picture would have been better than any fireworks display, and more dramatic, more full of action, than any artist could have painted. For the Turks and Germans the sudden sight of a spark from the funnels, the loom of two lean hulls, the froth of water at the bows, galvanised watchers into apprehension. How many more of these night enterprises? Would the mad English never learn their lesson? Had they not yet received enough hints? A merry medley of din and illumination was let loose, terrifying to senses, with shells concentrating from half a dozen different directions and big splashes making pyramids of the leaden sea.

It is by the indulgence of nature that, after a while, human suffering has its limitations, and can receive no further impressions. The lights were blinding to the steersman's eyes, and the big bangs were deafening to the ears; but the current had now become very strong, and over in Kephez Bay it was like a whirlpool, making control difficult. For this reason there was some satisfaction, some respite, in switching off the mind from explosives to cautious navigation. A little too much helm this way, a turn of the wheel slightly in the wrong direction, and picket-boats would share the fate of submarine. To keep one's head, and boats' bows pointing in the right direction, amid an infernal environment of noise and dazzle was the supreme test of discipline.

Just then a dark mass showed up mysteriously. Was it poor Brodie's former pride of ownership? The searchlights were not lighting up this shapeless lump, but it might well be the night's objective, so one of the *Triumph's* two torpedoes was fired. . . . They waited . . . waited, but no explosion was heard. Back came this picket-boat to make a second shot, when she suddenly saw the *Majestics* in trouble and heard them calling for help. For several things had seemed to happen almost simultaneously. This second boat, coming up astern of her leader, had noticed a beam falling right on *E* 15, distant only 200 yards. Lieut. Godwin seized this momentary chance, fired a torpedo himself . . . and missed.

He then did a very brave thing: a precise and perfect expression of devotion to duty and obedience to orders. For his boat was now revealed in the lights, a shell had crashed through the wooden hull under her water-line aft, and she began sinking rapidly. None the less, he turned his boat again towards the stranded submarine, steamed in a little, fired his remaining torpedo, which struck *E* 15 just ahead of her conning-tower and caused a glorious volcano of noise and demolition.

Every minute, every second, was a separate story of itself, with its own changing suspense. His boat was already down by the stern and awash before this second shot; the enemy sought to complete the sinking by another shower of shells, so that the sea around Godwin and his shipmates was all of a jobble, some of the splashes rising twenty feet high. The *Majestics* would have to leap into the water, risk being drowned in the frightful current or swept into Turkish captivity: otherwise they would all be massacred before the boat fell from under them.

Through the eddying violence of the shrapnelled sea now steamed the *Triumph's* boat to go alongside her sinking sister. The handling was a test of seamanship, and made no easier when the Turks redoubled their fire. "How it was we were not hit, I cannot say," wrote an officer [1] in this boat. "One would imagine it was impossible to come out of such an inferno. All I can say is that God preserved us, and not a shot actually hit, though we were one and all wet with splashes. After some difficulty we got alongside the *Majestic's* boat, and they jumped on board."

The night's objective having been completed, and the rescue effected, off went the *Triumph's* boat to go home, when they saw a man creep out from the stern of the sinking wreck that had just been quitted. It was the *Majestic's* armourer, who had been badly wounded and overlooked as he lay there suffering great pain. What was to be done? To go back, and waste time manœuvring in the current trying to get alongside, would be to lose the lives of all; yet to forsake a fleet-mate under such conditions would be unpardonable. So back came the *Triumph's* boat; the man was told to get in the water and swim. This he did, but when picked up he had already become unconscious. Godwin looked after him, put him down in the forepeak, where it was found that the poor man's legs had been crushed by the explosion which wrecked his boat. He had been the only person aft at the time.

But now, with everyone on board, the surviving boat could

---

[1] *Blackwood's Magazine*, previously cited.

take advantage of the down-stream, retreating still under heavy fire, though, very considerately, with engines only at half speed, lest the wounded armourer should be shaken up too much by the vibration. Half-way down the Straits there awaited them a destroyer, who was able to wireless the Admiral that his orders had been carried out. The next stop was alongside the *Majestic*, whose Commander says:

"About 1 a.m. one picket-boat was discerned coming our way. She turned out to be the *Triumph's* boat. I had got a watch to work the main derrick for hoisting in ours, but this was now not necessary. We were all very proud of Godwin, who had so distinguished himself, and hoped his bravery would meet with due recognition. We buried the armourer at sea in the afternoon." For by the time the *Majestic* had been reached he had passed away. Soon after 3 a.m. the boat found her own ship patrolling with not a light showing, the derrick was worked, and another dark adventure had been added to the Navy's annals. A little later came a congratulatory signal from the well-pleased Admiral. The success had been "of the greatest value. The names of the crews have been telegraphed to the Admiralty." Lieut.-Commander Robinson, V.C., was specially promoted to Commander,[1] Lieut. Godwin was awarded a D.S.O., and Midshipman Woolley, a D.S.C.

Not content with all his exploits, Commander Robinson was conspicuously brave again when the time came for the landing at Suvla Bay, and received a wound which invalided him home. Later on he came out again in command of the monitor *M* 21, serving off the Palestine and Egyptian coasts; and rounded up this catena of adventures by commanding the Coastal Motor-Boat Flotilla on the Caspian Sea.

For such men-of-action as these one would imagine that the routine of peace must be dull beyond all endurance.

[1] He is now a Rear-Admiral on the retired list.

CHAPTER XIX

LANDING THE ARMY

WE last saw the Turkish torpedo-boat *Demir-Hissar* in the Smyrna Gulf, and here she concealed herself until the middle of April. The value of having such a base outside the Straits, and the necessity for the Allies to keep a watch, were soon manifested.

Up the Ægean came the procession of steamers bringing troops by thousands, and every kind of military stores, for the land campaign which was shortly to begin. Such a transport, sooner or later, must invite attack, though, curiously, neither German nor Austrian submarines had yet torpedoed in that sea.

But on April 16 the S.S. *Manitou* (6849 tons) was coming up, loaded with troops, when the *Demir-Hissar* dashed out upon her. One would have thought that with so big a target it would have been impossible for a torpedo-boat to fail in her aim. But there must have been something curiously inefficient regarding the command of this Turkish war vessel, or the Captain may have been too nervous for that combination of dash and coolness which torpedo-boat work demands of a man. At any rate, *Demir-Hissar* fired a torpedo, and missed. She then fired a second, and that likewise missed. A third time a silver missile went bubbling on its way, but that also missed.

The incident would be laughable, and just an example of inefficiency, waste of good opportunity, and unguided impetuousness, were there not also a tragic side. The average soldier hates the sea, and is entirely out of his element on board ship: a transport full of khaki units is anything but a fighting machine. These troops seem to have lost their heads in the presence of the small torpedo-boat, and were seized by a panic to get away in the boats. As usual when these are lowered in a hurry, something went wrong with the business—it is easy enough for landsmen to slack away ropes and let a crowded boat shoot its contents into the sea—and a number forfeited their lives as well as their senses.

But a couple of British destroyers came along, chased the enemy, and got her so tightly hemmed in that she ran herself ashore on a Greek island, where the crew were interned. The *Manitou* escaped, but the lesson she provided was that if transports were to reach their destination at the Dardanelles, they had better be escorted through the Ægean; and this was now done.

By April 20 the Navy had almost come to the end of its long wait for the Army. Unfortunate indeed was the delay which had intervened since the disastrous March 18, but, apart from other reasons, this had been caused by the unsystematic manner in which the transports had been loaded before leaving England and Egypt. The greater part of them had to be sent along to Alexandria for better stowage, in order that weapons, equipment, munitions, might be at the top, ready to hand.

On April 21 aboard the *Euryalus* Admiral Wemyss summoned a meeting of all the naval Captains detailed in connection with the landing of troops, which was to take place four days later. Already it had been decided that for carrying the Mediterranean Expeditionary Force some of the transport steamers were to leave Mudros two days before the 25th, and anchor on the north side of Tenedos; whilst others would go from Mudros early on the 24th at ten-minute intervals to certain rendezvous. Off Tenedos the former were each to load three lighters with a week's supply for the covering force and the beach equipment. There were to be eighteen picket-boats or steam pinnaces, each towing four pulling boats, thus forming eighteen tows. All officers and men intended for the landing were to assemble on board transports allotted to the respective beaches.

For direction of the landing there had been appointed a small number of selected officers as Beach Masters, Commodore Phillimore being given the highly responsible duty of Principal Beach Master. Having delivered his *Inflexible* safely at Malta Dockyard, he had thus come back to the Dardanelles in another capacity, bringing with him a party of picked volunteers comprising Lieut. R. B. Janvrin, a Midshipman, and twenty-six men. It is to be noted that the warships destined for covering the landing were to be in their allotted positions at dawn, and to bombard the beaches.

This last-mentioned instruction must be stressed. It appeared not only in a memorandum issued by Admiral Wemyss, but also in the orders issued by General Sir Ian Hamilton, and by the G.O.C. XXIXth Division. Nevertheless, there seems to have been some misunderstanding, since in actual results there was only one ship which shelled the beach before disembarkation took place, but we will return to this matter in due course.

Admiral Wemyss had closed the Captains' meeting with, " I know you will all do your best for the success of the operations," the outline of which was as follows. Sir Ian Hamilton's task consisted of starting from the extremity of Gallipoli peninsula, with the peak of Achi Baba as his Army's immediate objective. The general scheme embodied two main landings: one north of Gaba Tepe, and the second at the peninsula's southern side. A demonstration was to be carried out in the Gulf of Xeros, and a landing as a feint was to be made at Kum Kale on the Asiatic side.

Let us first follow the north landing. At 5 p.m. of the 23rd the transports began to leave Mudros, and the sight of these tall ships, each packed with troops, made a memorable spectacle to the most experienced mariners. The landing north of Gaba Tepe was to be carried out under Rear-Admiral C. F. Thursby, C.M.G. His squadron for this purpose included: the five battleships *Queen* (Flag), *London*, *Prince of Wales*, *Triumph*, *Majestic*; the cruiser *Bacchante*; the eight destroyers *Beagle*, *Bulldog*, *Foxhound*, *Scourge*, *Colne*, *Usk*, *Chelmer*, and *Ribble*; the balloon ship *Manica*, and fifteen trawlers.

To the *Queen*, *London*, and *Prince of Wales* was entrusted the actual landing of troops; to *Triumph*, *Majestic*, and *Bacchante* that of covering the landing by gunfire. Each destroyer carried 500 troops, the actual final transportation being done by means of boats towed by destroyers and the battleships' steamboats. In order to row the empty boats back, every destroyer provided three men. The following vivid narrative, written by Commander Barne of the *Majestic*, shows exactly how the plan was put into effect.

"We had orders to sail on the afternoon of Saturday the 24th, with the rest of the Fleet. I had all hands aft, and told them of what the main landing, and our own part, consisted. I had a most interested audience. We had plenty to do: according to programme, we were to send away the following morning both our picket-boats, launch and sailing pinnace, both cutters, and the two transport lifeboats that had been lent us for the purpose. Each of these boats was in charge of a coxswain, and in charge of each steamboat was an officer. Every boat had to be provisioned and watered, every man thoroughly *au fait* with his allotted work.

"On leaving our ship the boats were to go, without further orders, to the *London*, where they were to fill up with troops, and then a line of tows, each consisting of a steamboat with two cutters and lifeboats, was to form in line-abreast, but the flotilla was not to approach the shore before daylight. The launch and pinnace, towed by the other steamboat, were to stand by and bring off wounded.

"Early in the afternoon of Saturday, the last of the transports went to sea, and then came the men-of-war, headed by the *Queen Elizabeth*. It took a long time for this great fleet to get out through the narrow entrance of the boom defence, but our turn came at last, and we all went our respective ways. We were astern of the *London*, and could see a service being held on the quarter-deck for the soldiers. We were due off Gaba Tepe a little before dawn, and went at slow speed. It was a gloriously fine day, and everything seemed to augur well for the great movement so soon to be executed. We stood on all night, showing no lights, but keeping in sight of our next ahead.

"At midnight we called the hands, hammocks were lashed up, cocoa and biscuits served out. At 1 a.m. we passed the word 'Hands to General Quarters.' I had cautioned everybody that not a light was to be shown or a voice raised. The buglers had orders not to sound any calls, and the clappers of the bells were removed. At about 1.15 we all stopped, hoisted out and lowered all the boats except the launch, which we kept aboard. As we passed north of Imbros, the moon (which would not have showed but for the fact that the landing had been deferred a week) was setting astern of us. And I feared that the enemy would see us silhouetted against it. We could see the dark mass of the *London* on our starboard hand, and, in accordance with orders. our boats went over to her for the troops.

" We big ships kept creeping in, with the boats (formed up in tows, as already described) somewhere ahead. After a long time engines were stopped, the outline of high land to the north of Gaba Tepe appearing ahead of us. Our guns were ready for instant action. Presently dawn began to break, showing the outline of the land more distinctly. There was scarcely a breath of wind, and no swell. We saw the boats steal on ahead, and ere long they disappeared in the darkness and faint haze at the foot of the cliffs."

For, when three miles west of Gaba Tepe, 1500 officers and men of the Australians had got into the cutters, and made a landing at 4.20 a.m., 2500 more being landed from the lifeboats towed by the destroyers—these smaller warships anchoring as close to the beach as their 10-ft. or 11-ft. draught permitted. These 4000 had been landed in half an hour. Sunrise that morning was at 4.50, simultaneous with which the transports carrying the main body began to arrive, so that by 7.20 a.m. nearly 8000 troops had been put ashore. The first shot was fired at 4.53 a.m., a strong opposition by the enemy developing.

"We waited for the first shot, which seemed an age in coming," says the *Majestic's* Commander: " meanwhile it grew distressingly light. Presently came a single rifle shot, then another, then two more, and then a rattle of it: which continued thenceforward through days, weeks, and months. We could see the flashes of Turkish rifles from the lower portions of the cliffs, but there was a marked absence of rifle fire from the direction of our boats ; the reason for which was afterwards made plain. The Anzacs, thirsting for blood and mad to get at the Turks, leaping out of the boats—sometimes before the keels touched bottom—dashed ashore and, without waiting to form up on the narrow strip of beach, charged straight up the steep cliffs, taking the hillside and crest of the first ridge at the point of the bayonet. So eager were they to get ashore, that they had flung aside their impediment, such as hats and the like, in many cases jumping out of the boats and swimming ashore whilst the tow was being cast off. A special correspondent with the Australians afterwards wrote that the first Ottoman Turk to receive Anglo-Saxon steel since the last crusade was bayonetted at 5.5 a.m. (This was not strictly correct, for the bayonet had been used in the earlier naval landings at the Outer Forts.)

"When it got daylight, to our surprise and admiration we could see the figures of our troops far up on the sky-line of the first ridge: a sufficiently fine climbing achievement in the time, without the inconvenience of having to fight their way. Soon after this the charge up the hill commenced. The Turks opened fire on the boats, and on the destroyers which arrived packed with troops, which they discharged into boats close to the beach. Very soon we got a signal that three Krupp guns had been captured, but we were not allowed to fire until our troops' position had become definitely established."

Mercifully this landing had been effected not at the spot originally commanded, which was abreast of some low-lying ground immediately to the north of Gaba Tepe. Now, we saw in a previous chapter that General Liman von Sanders had already appreciated the possibility of our choosing Gaba Tepe, for which reason it had been put into a thorough state of defence, with wire entanglements not only along the whole beach, but also beneath the surface of the shallow water. The reason for our lucky error was that the ships, in approaching the land slowly, had not allowed enough for the current, which had set them slightly to the northward. The *Triumph* had been sent ahead of the other ships to anchor west of Gaba Tepe, and an

TROOPS ON BOARD H.M.S. *BEAGLE*
About to be landed, watching shells falling on peninsula.

BEACH PARTY ABOARD H.M.S. *PRINCE GEORGE*
Being addressed by Captain A. V. Campbell (commanding officer) before being landed at Suvla.

officer serving in her at the time tells me the landing had been intended "to take place on a sandy beach, but owing to a slight error of position the troops were landed a little farther north, opposite a steepish hill defended by a small force of entrenched Turks. Very severe fighting, however, took place, and we had a wonderful view through our glasses of the Australians carrying the Turkish defences at the point of the bayonet. All our boats were used to assist in the landing, and the casualties were heavy. It was a gruesome sight seeing the boats come back to the ship with their bottoms covered in blood, and some of the raw troops did not much like the look of it when it was their turn to get in and go ashore. They stuck it splendidly, and when once disembarked were truly magnificent."

During the forenoon a military station was established on the hillside, enabling communication to be made between ship and shore. It was then at last possible for our naval guns to get busy, firing as directed and in accordance with the squared charts. These covering ships did excellent service in keeping down the enemy's fire, to the great satisfaction of our troops. For the enemy, besides his rifles and machine-guns, had got the range of the beach with his field-guns, sending in a murderous shrapnel fire on the seized heights no less than the beach. Nevertheless, boat after boat kept bringing more and more men to the beach; so that by the afternoon, what with these men and their stores and establishments of many kinds springing up here or there, the shore resembled a busy town.

But, as the day waxed older, so the tragic aspect of all this gallantry showed itself more plainly. Even from early forenoon the sad procession had commenced of boats taking wounded off to the hospital ships, which soon became so full that empty transports had to be requisitioned. Floating about were water-logged, riddled, and capsized boats. At a spot now marked on the charts as "Hell Spit," just below that which will always be known as Anzac Cove, some boats, in attempting their landing, had come to a grievous end. One could be seen lying aground, the beach close by, but the boat packed with dead men. Opposite a fisherman's hut on a sandy conical mound (wherein the enemy concealed a machine-gun) was a piled heap of twenty more dead and wounded, some of them half in and half out of the water, exposed to the baking sun; nor could they be reached for three days.

By seven that first evening our casualties had so mounted up that 100 wounded were brought off to be accommodated aboard the *Majestic*. They were lying all of a heap in a sailing pinnace, just as they had been bundled from the beach. Hoisted in stretchers on to the battleship's deck, one by one, there was never a murmur or a groan. " We had them all put in the Captain's fore-cabin, and on the after-deck. The doctors commenced to dress their wounds, and we made them as comfortable as we could. They were indeed splendid specimens of men." And when, at 7.30 next morning, this ship closed the shore to shell the enemy at point-blank range off the fisherman's hut, all the wounded Anzacs who could crawl helped each other up the ladders to lie on deck watching the fun. Presently came a wireless message from General Hunter-Weston, down at Cape Helles, saying the attack on Achi Baba would be commenced that day. Alas! nine months later the British military forces were still contemplating Achi Baba from much the same position.

So much for the landing north of Gaba Tepe, where 18,000 troops had been put ashore during the first twenty-four hours, and 2000 of them taken off wounded.[1] By the second day guns and stores and still more troops had been poured in: at nightfall our position was secure within limits.

Let us now leave the Australians and New Zealanders to see what happened farther south. See map at p. 300.

This area comprised five beaches, named respectively Y, X, W, V, S, the last four being comparatively near to each other around the toes of Gallipoli peninsula. Rear-Admiral R. E. Wemyss, C.M.G., M.V.O., was in charge afloat, his squadron being: the seven battleships *Swiftsure, Implacable, Cornwallis,*

---

[1] Altogether 29,000 were landed on the six beaches of Gallipoli by the first nightfall.

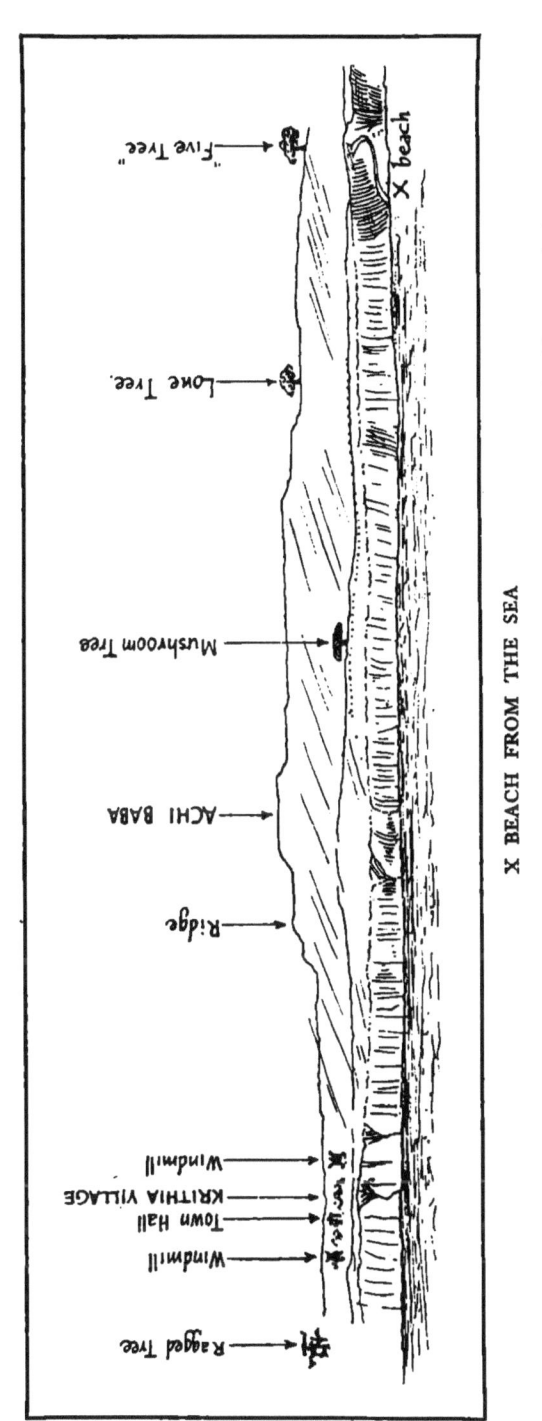

X BEACH FROM THE SEA

This sketch, made by one of H.M.S. *Implacable's* officers, shows the appearance of the land as the ship approached.

LANDING THE ARMY

Albion, Vengeance, Lord Nelson, Prince George; the four cruisers *Euryalus, Talbot, Minerva, Dublin*; six fleet-sweepers, and fourteen trawlers. At Y beach, which was some $2\frac{3}{4}$ miles north-east of Tekke Burnu (Cape Tekke), the King's Own Scottish Borderers and the Plymouth Marines of the Naval Divison were to land. They were brought in the two light cruisers *Amethyst* and *Sapphire*, and the two transports *Southland* and *Braemar Castle*, to within four miles of Tekke, when they were transferred to the trawlers and boats lowered from transports. At 4 a.m. of the 25th the trawlers in line abreast, with the boats alongside, covered on either flank by the two light cruisers, made towards Y beach, arriving there an hour later.

The method of landing was simple. For the trawlers (drawing about 11 feet) steamed on till their bows grounded, after which the boats full of troops shoved off and pulled ashore under the protection of H.M.S. *Goliath's* guns. Four trawlers carried the Scottish Borderers, and four brought the Marines. This beach happened not to have been considered by von Sanders as likely to be used: hence no immediate opposition occurred, although very heavy fighting followed later, so that on the 26th the troops were compelled to re-embark.

Now, X beach was situated less than a mile north-east of Tekke Burnu, and here (by general verdict) the landing was ideally performed, principally because the place was so thoroughly shelled. We have observed in earlier chapters that where the sailor can help the soldier is not by usurping the latter's work, but by preparing the opportunity for the soldier to walk right in. The perfect disembarkation on to a hostile beach is possible only if the man-of-war bombards the beaches and the approaches thoroughly; but immediately before the boats reach shallows. That moment when troops are about to leap ashore is the very time they most need a protecting barrage at the conclusion of a prolonged bombardment. Had there been possible a greater co-ordination, and a fuller realisation of this principle, other landings would have been effected more easily. To make a preliminary bombardment, and then allow most of an hour to elapse before boatloads leap ashore, is to give the enemy time to recover from the shock: his gunners will have come back and your efforts have been wasted.

The same basic strategical error which for so long prevailed when ships, unaided, tried to conquer forts up the Straits, was responsible for this lack of appreciation of great potentialities. It is true that X beach was not more suitable than any of the other beaches for the employment of naval artillery against it. Captain Hughes Lockyer, commanding officer of the *Implacable*, who had given much thought to this matter before the War, allows me to quote his statement that " at X beach the distance from sea to the steep cliff behind was only 25 yards. Ships could have approached the other beaches and shelled the whole of the area from water line to back slope with the greatest of ease " ; for these other beaches " had a gentle slope to the coast ridges up to a distance of 300 or 400 yards."

The *Implacable* had left Tenedos with the Fleet and transports [1] at 9.40 p.m. on the 24th, arriving off Cape Helles before daylight, with a calm sea, the weather bright and clear. She brought with her one battalion of the Royal Fusiliers and one battalion of the Lancashire Fusiliers. Having arrived at a spot about two miles from the landing-places, the troops were placed in the transport steamers' boats between 4 and 5.15 a.m. These boats were formed up in tow of four picket-boats, two on each side, and took station astern of *Implacable*, who now lowered her starboard anchor and veered her cable to $1\frac{1}{2}$ shackles. A " shackle " in the Merchant Service represents a length of 15 fathoms, or 90 feet. In the Royal Navy a " shackle " measures $12\frac{1}{2}$ fathoms.

Captain Lockyer was now making use of a time-honoured seamanship practice, which many an old shellback of sailing-ship days will recognise as akin to " club-hauling." To this day skippers of Arab dhows when approaching the East African coast go below and turn in for slumber, having first slacked away their anchor, well knowing that before the ship can hit the ground her anchor will pull her up. Much the same idea was employed by the *Implacable*. Her Captain wished to

[1] See Appendix.

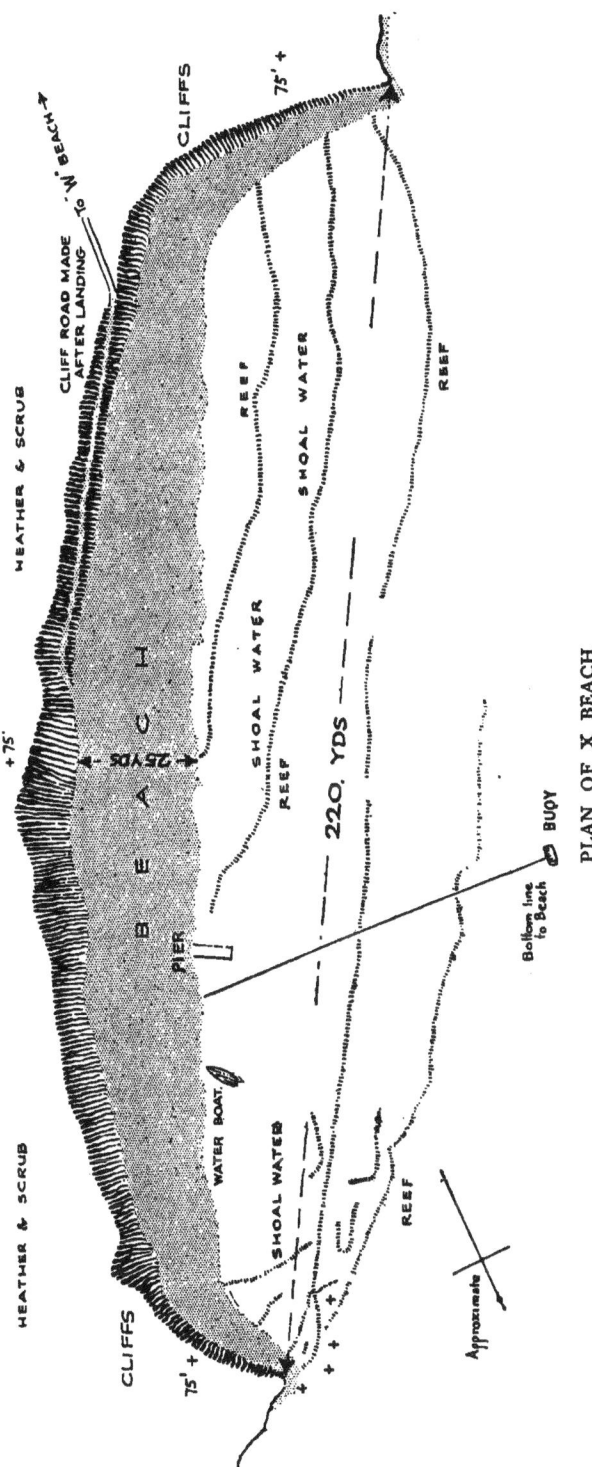

PLAN OF X BEACH

Made by an officer in H.M.S. *Implacable*. This indicates the distance between water and cliff as being only 25 yards.

stand in as near to the shore as possible without risking his ship, but the charts were inaccurate. Having therefore the inboard part of his cable stoppered to the riding-bitts with 3-inch rope lashings, and half a shackle ranged ready for running, the anchor might catch the sea bottom, carry away the lashing, and there would be warning enough to put the engines full speed astern before doing any damage.

At 5.30 the *Implacable* proceeded in with caution, and when 2500 yards from the shore reduced to 5 knots, finding the range with one of her 6-inch guns, then at 1800 yards stopped engines and opened fire with guns of this same calibre, the first rounds bursting over the beach about ten yards from the water-line. After this firing ended, the boats were sent in, followed by the ship using her quick-firers along the ridges until the troops had got out on to the beach. Finally *Implacable* was brought up by her anchor about 450 yards from the shore, with 6½ fathoms (= 39 feet) of water under stem.[1] By 7 a.m. all the troops for X beach had landed.

"When within about 1000 yards from the shore," Captain Lockyer has informed me, "heavy rifle fire was directed at the forebridge and fore lower top.[2] I did not notice it at first, as we were inside the sandbag redoubt erected on 'Monkey Island' (*i.e.* the Standard Compass platform) to protect that instrument from shrapnel fire. Suddenly the gunnery officer, Lieut.-Commander J. W. Scott, seized his nose, as if a wasp had stung him, and said: 'My goodness! What's that?' I'm afraid I laughed, and shouted, 'Down heads!', just realising what was happening.

"The redoubt consisted of a breastwork 2 feet thick, covered by a roof with oak beams, across which were laid all the condenser tubes lent by the Engineer-Commander, and over this were sandbags. Now, on my way down the English

---

[1] The official naval history here falls into error in saying that this ship "held on till close on the five-fathom line, and then anchored" (Vol. II. p. 326). Captain Lockyer tells me his ship was drawing about 29 feet, so that would leave only one foot under his hull!

[2] The same parts which the enemy had selected for their targets when attacking the *Inflexible*.

Channel I had been ordered to Spithead for twenty-four hours, so signalled in requesting the Dockyard staff to come out and cut the ends off my bridges; also asking for two truck-loads of sand, together with 800 sandbags. The reply came from the Commander-in-Chief (Sir Hedworth Meux), 'Bridge work approved. Sand, etc., not approved'; with a sort of witty remark such as 'Why take coals to Newcastle?' I replied asking permission to pay for the sand and bags, as 'I am the person who is going to be shot at.' I got my stuff—and a lucky thing, as it turned out."

The *Implacable* during this operation loosed off ten rounds of common shell from her 12-inch guns; 179 rounds from her 6-inch, and 154 of common and lyddite from her 12-pdrs. Then, having seen that the disembarkation was going on most satisfactorily, the ship went to her appointed anchorage off Tekke Burnu (Cape Tekke) between X and W beaches, shortly afterwards having the pleasure of witnessing the Fusiliers attack "Hill 114" (at the back of Cape Helles) with great success; the enemy surrendering in considerable numbers.

So the bombardment had been the greatest help to the landing troops, and a distinguished officer who was at W beach has been kind enough to send me the following interesting commentary: "A 'Sapper' Colonel of my acquaintance went to Hunter-Weston (commanding the Division that took the Southern Beaches) two or three days before the landing and said, 'I hope you won't attempt to land on a *beach*: of course the Turks will be ready. You have battleships with 12-inch guns supporting you, and a 12-inch shell fired into a cliff will make it climbable. Therefore land at the cliffs.' This is practically what happened at X beach. Lockyer came close in, and fired his fore-turret right into the cliff. There were no casualties in landing here."

But, by ill luck, shortly after *Implacable* had anchored off Tekke Burnu, her Medical Officer, Fleet-Surgeon A. A. Forrester, who had taken great trouble organising a scheme for the transportation of wounded from the shore, fell a victim.

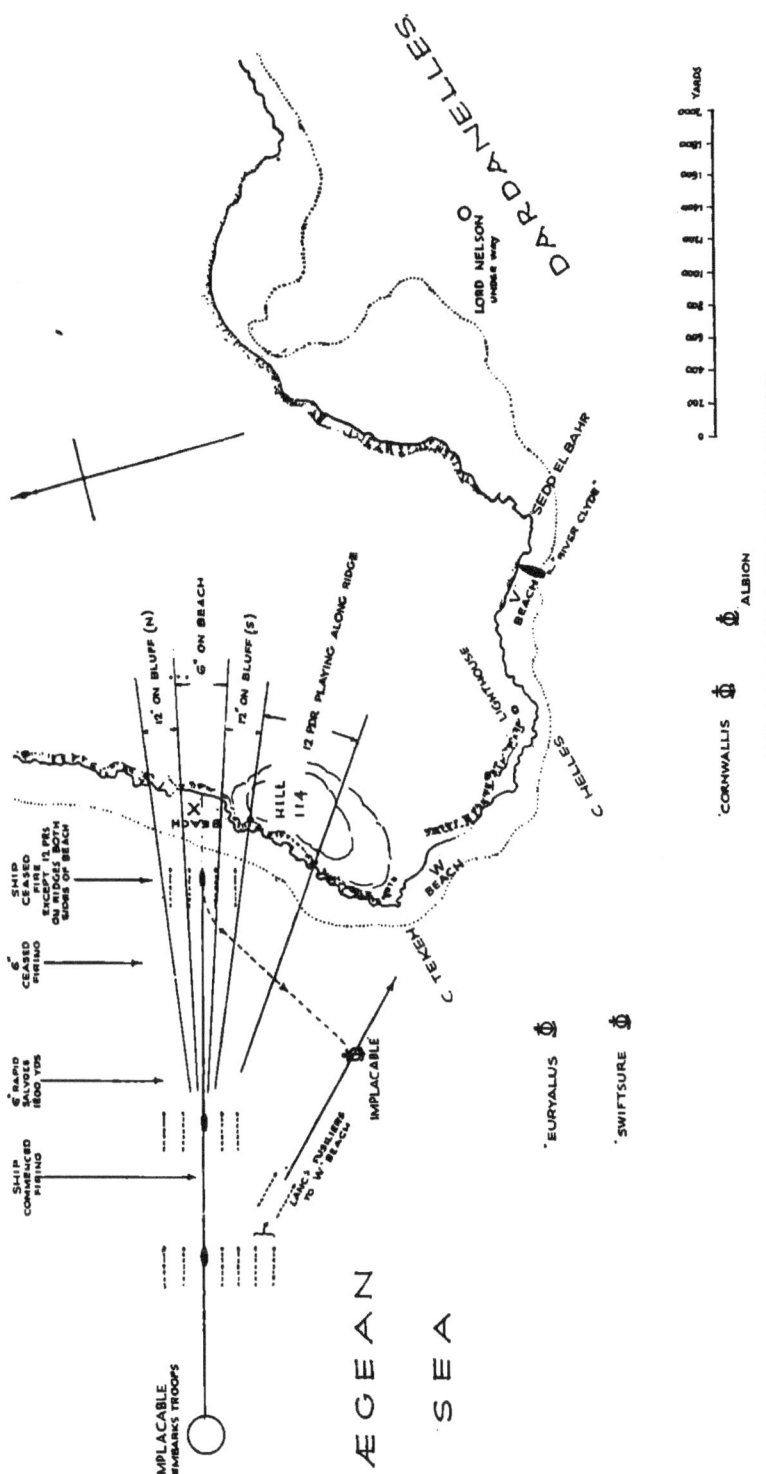

DIAGRAM TO ILLUSTRATE THE APPROACH OF H.M.S. *IMPLACABLE*
When landing troops at X and W beaches.

At noon, having just "shifted" out of naval uniform into khaki, he was standing on the quarter-deck talking to three of his shipmates in blue, when a sniper's bullet struck and killed him.

The Lancashire Fusiliers had been embarked in the *Euryalus* (in which Admiral Wemyss flew his flag) as well as *Implacable*, and made their landing on W beach from 6 a.m. to 7 a.m. The Principal Beach Master landed with the Principal Military Landing Officer (a Brigadier-General), after the second part of the covering force. Under the former, allotted to each beach, were a Captain R.N., Commander R.N., besides various ranks and ratings. These beach parties, not being required to storm the position, would have taken up valuable room in the first boats: they did not have rifles. Of course these separate landings were generally self-administrative, for it was impossible for the Principal Beach Master from W beach to exercise supervision over the others.

This W beach was covered with barbed wire, since the enemy had expected us, the cliffs on each side being lined with trenches at the top; and Maxims had been placed half-way up in sand caves. In spite of such defences the Lancashire Fusiliers made an attack which (remarks one witness) "will be their pride for ever." Leaving four officers and eighty-two men dead on the beach, they divided into two parties, right and left, climbed the hills and (all the while carrying a 60-lb. pack on their back together with 200 rounds of ammunition) by their bayonets drove the Turks out. A most gallant performance! Their achievement is perpetuated on maps and charts for the next generations where the two words "Lancashire Landing"—as "'Implacable' Beach" just above it—immortalise daring united with enterprise.

Meanwhile the naval beach parties were having a busy time when the main body arrived, hauling up boats, unloading them, getting out the horses and stores. When night came with the rain, these parties of sailors had not the campaigning kit which a soldier brings, and had to accustom themselves to new environment, well knowing, too, that not many yards off the Turks were trying to break through.

But there was an amusing side even to all this. Commodore Phillimore had brought ashore with him to W beach his faithful coxswain named Edwards, and his bow-man, named Angell. Now, Edwards was a diplomat. During the Battle of the Falklands, when the *Inflexible* came near the crew of the sunken *Gneisenau*, an indignant British petty officer on the *Inflexible's* forecastle had remarked to the Paymaster-Commander (who chanced to be standing near):

" Surely the Captain isn't going to pick up these men ? "

" I hope so," said the Paymaster.

" Well," insisted the petty officer, " I don't think that's right. They saved no one from the *Monmouth* at the Battle of Coronel."

The Paymaster related this story to his commanding officer (Captain Phillimore), who asked Edwards, " What do the ship's company think about rescuing the *Gneisenau's* men ? "

Now, Edwards was very much attached to his Captain, with whom he had served in no less than three ships. But, all the same, he had a difficult question to answer.

" Well, sir," he finally explained, " about half the ship's company think you were right, and about half think you were wrong."

But this miserable April night, having survived the shells and mines and conflagrations of March 18, he was bivouacking with his Captain on Turkish territory. When they landed, that morning, W beach was all-glorious with the spring colouring of virgin flowers, but within a few hours they had been trampled flat by fighting men, and the beach was just sand. Then darkness came, and the military Beach Officers could lie down for a spell, although no one was able to get much rest with that fusillade racketing all night.

To Captain Phillimore's surprise and delight, he found a water-proof sheet laid out for him under his bedding.

" Where did you get this from, Edwards ? " he demanded.

" Off a dead man, sir."

LANDING AT X BEACH

This photograph was taken at 6 a.m. on April 25, 1915, and shows H.M.S. *Implacable* in the background, with boats full of troops, and a minesweeper in the foreground. (Notice the latter's "gallows" at the stern.)

Next day the Captain had to borrow from his colleague, Brigadier-General Roper, a knife and fork with which to eat the " bully-beef "; but, before another meal came round, the Captain found himself provided for.

" Where did this knife and fork come from, Edwards ? "

" Angell took them off a dead man, sir."

As they were Army Service articles, and not private property, there could be no compunction in using them. Soon all the blue-jackets found themselves generally equipped, since there was, unfortunately, no lack of dead men's kits.

Now, further round the coast, and on the east side of Cape Helles, was V beach, where also the enemy had fully expected an attempt at invasion, against which they had made great preparations. Here lies that bay with the lighthouse on one side and Sedd-el-Bahr, its old castle and fort, at the other. The masonry that we had blown up during the bombardment of February 19, the village above, the cliffs, the ridges—how familiar they were to many of our crews who had been out there months! This indentation, situated at the peninsula's extreme southern end, seemed such an obvious place for disembarking that men wondered why it could possibly have been chosen.

The first troops to come ashore here arrived in cutters towed by the naval steamboats, but the rest of the covering force was landed by means of the collier *River Clyde*. So much has been written around this steamer, whose name has long since become legendary, that she needs only the fewest words of introduction. In the accompanying illustration she is well shown. At the inspiration of Commander E. Unwin, R.N., and under his own supervision, she had been specially prepared to act as a marine " Wooden Horse " on territory opposite ancient Troy. Large square ports had been cut in her sides, with wooden galleries to run out from either bow, so that her cargo of soldiers might dash ashore. A dozen little armoured houses built on her forecastle contained twelve Maxim guns.

On she came, towing heavy lighters, and the plan was that,

P

on grounding, the *River Clyde* would, of course, stop dead, whilst the lighters would carry on their way and reach the beach. The galleries or gangways would then be let down on to the lighters, and a ready-made bridge would exist.

In actuality what happened was that she grounded right enough, and the barges went on, but the latter failed to reach their proper stations, so that a gap existed between two of them, and only the tallest men could wade ashore. Picture the gallant Commander Unwin [1] up to his waist in water, a galling fire pouring down over him, assisted by Midshipman G. L. Drewry,[1] R.N.R., and Midshipman W. St. A. Malleson,[1] R.N., with two able seamen furiously striving to get the lighters into their required positions. The ships of war looked on, unable to do much, none of the entrenched Turks could be seen, yet from the sky our airmen gazed down with horror on an awful picture.

Eager to rush forth and close with the enemy, those soldiers who had emerged and got so far as the lighters were shot dead from rifles, Maxims, and small guns. Practically all who had landed from the cutters in the first trip were casualties, but the remarkable feature was that Commander Unwin and these two young Midshipmen, together with several others, managed somehow to live through one of the severest trials which human courage ever sustained. At a sudden summons every rank and rating, from Commander down to the most junior officer and seaman, leaped to heroism and self-sacrifice, winning the soldiers' unstinted admiration and affection, and gaining equally a glorious fame so long as the Gallipoli story shall be told. Swimming about with ropes after these recalcitrant barges, exposing themselves to hailstones of lead, struggling against the impossible, these modern seafarers showed that the old spirit of our ancestors who had fought under Drake, or Hawke, or Nelson, was still triumphantly alive. But all the good accomplished seemed of no avail. True, the *River Clyde* was fast ashore, and made a convenient

---

[1] These three officers, as also Able Seaman Samson, R.N.R., were all awarded the Victoria Cross, whilst Lieut. J. A. V. Morse was given a D.S.O.

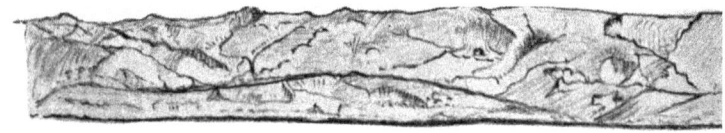

ANZ
As it looked from the sea. From a sketch

THE FAMOUS
As she appeared after having beached herse

AC BEACH
made at the time by a British naval officer.

RIVER CLYDE
lf at V beach. See also plan facing p. 302.

breakwater at the eastern end of this beach; yet it was useless to waste more men's lives by such a passage. Disembarkation of troops was therefore diverted to W beach; but, under cover of night, the *River Clyde* people dashed ashore and found shelter on the beach, though they could not get very far, as concealed Maxims were enfilading them from each flank.

During the night, however, the *Implacable* was able to render some valuable help. "By a piece of good luck," relates Captain Lockyer, "our anchorage off Cape Tekke was inside of the in-shore counter current running down the coast, and this kept our head north and south, broadside on to the shore, thus saving any necessity for using springs on the cable."[1] There came to *Implacable* about 1.30 a.m. a signal from General Marshall saying, "We are heavily engaged. Can you give us support?" The ship, as she was now lying, was parallel to the line which extended from W to V beaches, and for the next two hours fired 150 6-inch shells, being greatly helped by watching where the star-shells disappeared behind the ridge. "As General Marshall was wounded, I heard nothing about this interesting episode, but some time afterwards was told that the *Implacable's* guns on that night saved the situation. I wish to put it on record that, owing to the seamen ratings being away on transport duties, all the 6-inch guns were manned by marines and stokers under Captain L. Norcock, R.M.L.I."

Finally, at about 2 p.m. on this second day (that is, some thirty-two hours after the initial attempt to land), the slopes having first been heavily shelled by the ships, " a most wonderful attack," records an officer, " was made by the thousand-odd men who had sheltered in the *River Clyde* during the night; and the old fort at the top was stormed. The ships who saw it said it was a magnificent sight. Meanwhile from W beach the Worcesters and Essex were working round towards V beach, and about 6 p.m. the Turks retired, leaving us in possession of the end of the peninsula.... The XXIXth Division were simply magnificent. After losing fifty per cent.

[1] Reference to the use of "springs" has already been made on page 79.

of their men in the first twenty-four hours, they remained eighteen days in the trenches without relief."

Finally—to complete these historic landings of April 25—a half-company of the Royal Dublin Fusiliers had been able to disembark at Sedd-el-Bahr camber without opposition, since that restricted area was "blind" ground. In Morto Bay, just to the eastward, where on a previous occasion we have seen the *Majestic* bombarding, the 2nd South Wales Borderers came ashore from four trawlers, convoyed by the *Cornwallis* and covered by the *Lord Nelson*. This plain statement, however, does not indicate the difficulty or the anxieties of the undertaking which had been entrusted to Lieut. Janvrin and the twenty-four men who came from the *Inflexible*.

Morto Bay was another of those "obvious" places, and was looked upon as a forlorn hope: so dangerous was the attempt considered that it had been decided to make no effort to bring back the boats. The *Inflexible's* volunteer seamen, who had not been satiated by the Falklands battle or the Dardanelles excitements, were after reaching the shore to join up with these soldiers. Janvrin's four trawlers, each towing six boats, steamed in till they grounded; immediately after which the boats cast off and the soldiers pulled themselves the remaining distance of 400 yards to Eski Hissarlik Point (by De Tott's Battery). In each of the twenty-four was one *Inflexible* man as coxswain: otherwise every available bit of space was used for troop-carrying, transportation of heavy kits and provisions being made by two cutters from H.M.S. *Cornwallis*.

The current sets strongly past the Point, and soldiers are least at home under the conditions mentioned. But they got ashore about 7.30 a.m., and were shelled from trenches as well as from the Asiatic side. Morto Bay was veritably surrounded by trench-concealed hills, but thanks to the *Cornwallis*, which mothered these adventurers to the greatest possible extent, shelling both Asia and Europe, the landing succeeded, with only four killed and seventeen wounded. The seamen assisted the Borderers to storm the first trenches.

Two destroyers, *Basilisk* and *Grasshopper*, had been sent to support and to close in-shore. Captain A. P. Davidson, commanding the *Cornwallis*, himself landed with a party of his own seamen, leaving his ship at anchor. He was animated by the desire to help the soldiers all he could and ensure safe disembarkation. If it was an unusual precedent for a Captain to leave his ship, the occasion was exceptional. Unfortunately, amidst this fine endeavour came orders repeatedly for the *Cornwallis* to reach her station off V beach, where things had gone badly. He had therefore to leave the beach and to incur some delay, having been ignorant about the hold-up around the *River Clyde*. This delay was the cause of a certain displeasure at the hands of a higher authority, which seems regrettable. Captain Davidson, who is now dead, said to another commanding officer that he had been badly "scrubbed" for not returning at once. "He was infernally angry about it, as if the landing at S beach had not been successful it would not have been possible to land the French troops there a day or two afterwards."

As it turned out, the party that got ashore became isolated until (in the general advance of Tuesday afternoon) the French came up and relieved them. It had been a very worrying time, and on each of these two mornings those who were serving in the *Agamemnon* off this Point used to look and see if the little party were still on the cliff, where they hung on without guns and suffered continual attack.

To sum up, then, notwithstanding all the most detailed arrangements for putting thousands of troops on to Gallipoli; notwithstanding the thousands of shells fired to help them; and in spite of all the heroism, the battleships, the destroyers, the trawlers, the array of transports, the flotillas of oared boats and picket-boats, the day's objective of Achi Baba ("Archy Barber," as the sailors nicknamed it) was not attained—neither on April 25, the next week, nor the month after. And when eventually we quitted the peninsula, it still remained in Turkish possession.

Forasmuch as the Asiatic shore was not in our hands, and

the enemy therefrom might shell our transports lying off Cape Helles during the 25th, the French squadron, comprising *Jauréguiberry* (flag of Admiral Guépratte), *Henri IV*, *Jeanne d'Arc* and the Russian cruiser *Askold*, bombarded Kum Kale, after which a landing of French troops began there at 10 a.m. This diversion having been successful alike in preventing Turkish troops from coming over to the European side and in keeping down gunfire from Asia, the withdrawal of the French could take place next day. General d'Amade, who was in command of the French Divisions, had reached the Dardanelles about the same date in March as Sir Ian Hamilton. It had been from Bizerta, the French North African station, that these troops had begun to reach Mudros.

Nor was General d'Amade's the only feint that the Allies made for perplexing the Turks on this memorable April 25.

CHAPTER XX

THROUGH THE STRAITS

It was part of Admiral de Robeck's plan that a feint landing should be made in the Gulf of Xeros so as to keep the enemy in suspense till the last, and tie down at least some of his troops from the Gallipoli peninsula's southern end. For this purpose Captain Heathcoat S. Grant in the battleship *Canopus*, with the light cruisers *Dartmouth* and *Doris*, as well as two destroyers, was to make a parade. In order to add verisimilitude, and cause the Turks to believe that we really meant to land in the Bulair vicinity, three pairs of trawlers were to sweep for mines.

So at daylight on April 24 the *Doris* (Captain Frank Larken), having embarked a seaplane from the *Ark Royal*, left Mudros, accompanied by the six trawlers. The trawler-skippers having been on board and told what was expected of them, the *Doris* was prepared for battle, the expectation being that fire would come from heavy shore guns. Just after midnight the trawlers began sweeping, and four hours later the *Doris* met Captain Grant's other two ships.

By 5.40 a.m. of the 25th it was light enough to see, whereupon Captain Larken together with the *Dartmouth* (Captain Judge D'Arcy) opened fire on the Bulair Lines. Well out in the Gulf lay *Canopus* in company with some transports carrying men of the Royal Naval Division. To everyone's astonishment there came no reply from Forts Sultan and Napoleon: the seaplane was put in the water, but she came back from her reconnaissance without seeing any sign of the enemy. Next the *Doris* steamed close inshore, and noticed that intensive preparations had clearly been made against any infantry attack. She now fired on a redoubt, but still no reply was made.

Presently there came on board Colonel the Hon. E. Fiennes,[1] Intelligence Officer to the Royal Naval Division, having received instructions to watch the road running south from Adrianople; wherefore the *Doris* moved to the head of Xeros

[1] Now Col. the Hon. Sir E. Fiennes, Bt.

Gulf. On the upper bridge the Captain, the Colonel, and the ship's Chief Yeoman of Signals watched and scrutinised the land—the first two with their binoculars, the last with his long-distance telescope. Not an indication of life anywhere!

Then, suddenly, " I see horses in large numbers," remarked the Colonel.

The Yeoman of Signals readjusted his telescope, screwed up his eye, and spoke exactly as he thought.

" 'Orses ? ", he repeated, " 'orses ? "—closing his telescope with a snap—" 'orses with *'orns.*"

The man was right: these were some more of those bullock-teams which we saw being used up the Dardanelles for hauling the mobile howitzers.

" But," says Sir Frank Larken, " the Colonel was angry, and complained to me of the fellow's impudence. I reproved the Chief Yeoman, yet he was a privileged friend and, earlier in the day, when I expected the ship to be blown almost to pieces, and on many other occasions, he had been my faithful helper and adviser. Whenever I happened to be on the bridge, he was always by my side."

Now, this demonstration and suggestion of landing did not upset any of General von Sanders' dispositions, and soon after midnight came a wireless signal that the trawlers were to tow many of the transports' lifeboats down to Gaba Tepe, whither *Canopus* and *Dartmouth* hurried off also, *Doris* following. During the forenoon of the Army's second day's landing on the peninsula she was engaged, like other ships, in bombarding certain areas of the squared maps whose accuracy could not be relied upon. Notwithstanding all the shortage of shells at this time, and the insistence on economy, it must be admitted that considerable wastage went on ; for the ships could not tell whether they were doing any good. Occasionally could the Turks be seen, and they were also in khaki, difficult to distinguish from our own troops. Only the head-dress seemed different at a distance. Often enough, when one would have imagined that no living thing could have survived the naval bombardment, it was learned that the shells had fallen too far inland, beyond the Turkish trenches. Once, for instance, when the *Implacable*, on May 5, was shelling in support of the attack on Achi Baba, the ship's signalman suddenly reported that the sky-line between Gully Beach and Krithia was " moving about." This was actually a line of snipers, excellently disguised by lopped-off bushes, moving off to their appointed stations. Their trick was discovered, and the *Implacable* demonstrated this by treating them to a few rounds of 6-inch.

We have already emphasised that both land maps and sea charts were not dependable. It was whilst the *Doris*, this April 26th, was just about to let go anchor near the shore and begin her bombardment, that the *Bacchante* signalled her: " You are standing into danger." " I looked over the side," says Admiral Larken, " and could see the bottom! The leadsman at the same moment reported four fathoms—pretty nearly the ship's draught. I went full speed astern, but I think we touched."

All sorts of queer surprises kept happening. This same day a Turkish soldier came down to the beach and began waving. The spot was exactly where the Anzacs were originally to have made their landing, but (as we have noted) they missed this Gaba Tepe in the dark. " I thought it worth while getting this Turk on board," the *Doris'* Captain tells me, " so the cutter was lowered, armed, and sent inshore under cover of our guns, Midshipman Haldane in charge. The Turk ran to the boat as it touched the beach, was hauled in, and the cutter returned. He was the first prisoner to come afloat from Anzac, and I sent him to the flagship to be interviewed by the Intelligence department, who sent him on shore to be interrogated by the Army Intelligence Staff. We learned afterwards that this little headland was galleried for machine-guns, which at the time were manned, and could have killed the cutter's crew in five seconds—if the Turks hadn't wished to keep their presence unknown."

Whether the visitor was a spy, or a deserter, has not been made known.

The final remaining days of April found the Navy settled down in their new routine for covering the Army's further landing of troops and stores, whilst destroyers and French trawlers were sweeping for mines in Eren Keui Bay, that had once been such a death-trap to our Fleet. Of course, the usual result happened when the shore batteries resisted this intrusion—every vessel concerned being shelled, the destroyer *Wolverine* being hit on the bridge and her Captain (Commander O. J. Prentis) killed; after which sweeping was postponed until the Army should have made further progress. For the present there would be no request that the battleships should come along up the Straits spraying their barrage ahead of advancing troops.

Meanwhile the Turkish Navy was required to assist the Turkish Army. As the former dared not come out of the Straits, it must fire across the peninsula at the narrowest neck, which we saw to be from Kilia Liman to Gaba Tepe. This assistance was inaugurated at 4.15 a.m. on April 27, and began to be known to us as "the morning hate." It was just getting light when some 11-inch shells fell most unpleasantly around the *Majestic*, whose Commander tells me that the enemy made such excellent practice that half an hour later his ship had to weigh and move to another berth, with anchor ahead and kedge astern. The Turkish ship selected for this long-distance, indirect, fire was sometimes the *Barbarossa* and sometimes the *Torgut Reis*; those two sister-vessels which had once been purchased from Germany. No wonder they got so accurately on to their target, for near to Nebrunessi Point (which is the southernmost arm of Suvla Bay, distant from Gaba Tepe some half a dozen miles), and hidden behind an isolated hill known as Lala Baba, they had established a spotting station, connecting up by telephone over the five miles of land to the ship opposite Kilia Liman. The *Queen Elizabeth*, however, made a wonderfully effective reply by also firing indirectly across the peninsula and sinking a Turkish transport with her 15-inch.

Next morning the enemy battleship renewed her "hate,"

firing among our transports and colliers. One shell fell plump into a collier's after-hold, sending up such a vast cloud of smoke and dust as never was seen : yet, strange to relate, the coal did not catch alight, and the steamer was not sunk, but merely weighed anchor and shifted out of range. The seaplane-carrier *Ark Royal* was compelled to clear out also, but the *Barbarossa's* shells followed her, dropping just under the stern till the *Ark Royal* got beyond range. On the 29th, when day was dawning, again came the Turkish naval greeting, and all but got the *Majestic* with two salvoes, one shell falling right under the stern, covering the quarter-deck with splinters, the other almost hitting the port bow. A few hours later, after having once more moved away, the British battleship was yet again selected for this treatment, and had to depart. In addition, there was some quite nasty sniping from the shore every time several people were seen on deck together. One destroyer, anchored close in, lost seven of her company ; yet such is the phlegmatic Briton that our soldiers who came down to the sea for a bathe went on splashing about and thoroughly enjoying themselves whilst the showers of Turkish shrapnel bullets spattered above them.

All the same, something had to be done about this *Barbarossa* nuisance.

So that day (29th) the *Triumph*, with aerial aid, fired across the land. An officer serving in her gives me the following interesting comment :

" The signalling arrangements from the seaplane for spotting the fall of our shell were somewhat primitive ; ' O,' with the estimated number of yards, representing ' short.' ' O.K.' was reserved for a hit. One morning we got the signal, ' 300 over,' ' 100 over,' and then ' O.K.' As soon as ' O.K.' was received, we plastered broadsides, continually getting the signal ' O.K.' After five minutes of this, someone noticed the seaplane landing on the water, whilst the signals were still going on ; and our joy at the thought that we were sinking a Turkish battleship was turned into chagrin when it was discovered that the signals were being made by the enemy, who were just wasting our ammunition."

A more detailed plan had been arranged for outwitting the " morning hater " on the 30th. The *Queen, Albion, Canopus,* and *Majestic* were to have their turret guns loaded with half-charges by 5 a.m., and to elevate them " plum on " for Kilia Liman. " We then waited," narrates one who took part, " while a seaplane went up. Presently came a report that a Turkish battleship was in Kilia Liman. Just as this arrived there was a flash, lighting up the dark sky—a distant bang, and then came the song of three shells. They fell wide of us this time. We then got her exact position from the seaplane, and touched off. None of the sixteen (*i.e.* four 12-inch guns to each ship) hit her, but we heard that they fell all round her, and she was presently reported making off."

On this same day a separate effort was made also by the *Lord Nelson*, who was sent round to Gaba Tepe in the morning, the kite-balloon ship *Manica* being assigned to do the spotting. " As the balloon rose," says one of the *Lord Nelson's* officers, " it reported *Goeben* in the Narrows, and we touched off five rounds at her. We could not follow her right up, as we had not enough deflection on the sights. We then shelled Chanak pretty thoroughly, and started a huge fire." It was this same ship which, two mornings later, with the balloon spotting, bombarded Gallipoli town on the Sea of Marmora. Nevertheless, the enemy was determined to give our sea forces no rest, and this is proof enough in regard to the protection which the Navy was able to afford the Expeditionary Army. Almost every day would begin with the enemy's reveille of shells, so that it became known among the Fleet as the " Christians awake! salute." During the first week of May the time for *Goeben's* barking was altered to 8 a.m., and regularly would come the first three rounds. At the sound of No. 1, the British target would be seen to weigh anchor quickly, go full speed astern, and be just clear of the spot where No. 3 fell; for Nos. 1 and 2 always missed. But one day (May 8) the

Vengeance noticed there was no " morning hate " : the enemy had again upset routine. At noon the Captain of *Vengeance* was in his cabin engaged on official documents when *Goeben* suddenly sang her battle hymn. Along came the shells, which dropped each side, making an ugly bulge and burning the paint. The enemy was indeed very wide awake ! Two days later his Asiatic guns were aimed at the *River Clyde* (which had become a parent ship for boats), and hit her several times.

Now, whilst all this was going on, the Straits and the Narrows had actually been penetrated : the *Goeben* and the *Barbarossa*, or *Torgut Reis*, became seriously imperilled. One, or all, of these three ships might never have fired another shot. For there had reached the Dardanelles, all the way from Australia, the submarine *AE* 2, whose commanding officer, Lieut.-Commander H. H. G. D. Stoker, R.N., was anxious to be the first who should take his boat into the Sea of Marmora. Up till now there had been Lieut. Holbrook, who in *B* 11 went part of the way and torpedoed the *Messudieh* ; and Lieut.-Commander T. S. Brodie in *E* 15, who had failed, perishing in the attempt. No Allied submarine had succeeded in reaching the inland sea.

Admiral de Robeck was, indeed, convinced that such a feat was impracticable, whilst feeling very conscious that its achievement would be of immense value. Finally he yielded to the gallant desire of Lieut.-Commander Stoker, who was permitted to undertake the risk. It was well timed, so as to coincide with the Army's landing ; the hope being that our submarine might harass, interfere with, and partially prevent the transportation of Turkish troops on their way through the Sea of Marmora to the peninsula. Stoker [1] set off in the early dark hours of April 24, everything being in his favour : a lovely, clear, calm night, and the moon already set, as he entered the Straits on the surface so as to economise his electricity for long submergence.

---

[1] For certain details I am indebted to *Straws in the Wind*, by Commander H. H. G. D. Stoker, D.S.O., R.N. ; and *Dead Reckoning*, by " Klaxon."

Proceeding at 7 knots, keeping in the centre of the Straits, everything ready for immediate diving, he could see the searchlights that had once illumined $E\ 15$, now watchful as ever. When abreast of Suan Dere, AE 2 dived; but, by sheer bad fortune, she now broke the shaft of one of her two forward hydroplanes. This completely ruined the project, and back she must come.

She returned safely, several hours of strenuous work effected repairs, and at 3 a.m. of next day—the 25th, when thousands of troops were about to hurl themselves on the peninsula—AE 2 entered the Straits as before, but the searchlights picked her up, then the guns became active, so just short of Suan Dere she dived about 4.30, as the dawn was about to break. Going dead slow, first at 20 feet down, then at 70 feet from the surface, she was passing under the minefields. The sound coming from outside could be heard of the mines' moorings scraping against the boat's hull, and several times she fouled some net, or wire, or chain, which made an ominous noise for some considerable period, till the obstruction broke loose and scraped away aft free.

And the treacherous, swerving currents?

She avoided being set ashore, for her Captain twice rose high enough to observe through his periscope, and on the third occasion was surprised to find he had got through the mine area, being now 300 yards below the Narrows. Evidently the upflowing counter-current had helped his progress. Off Chanak he sighted one of the small Turkish gunboats, and torpedoed her; but the periscope had been observed in the all-too-calm water. Fire had been poured from both shores, and next a destroyer tried to ram the submarine, who dived. Now, one of the many things which, in these under-water craft, can go wrong is the gyroscopic compass, which incidentally was the reason why $E\ 13$ was lost in the following September on Saltholm, Denmark, whilst trying to reach the Baltic. Stoker's compass "wandered," and he got ashore a little way above Chanak, just under the guns of Fort 24 (Anadolu Medjidieh). AE 2's conning-tower, showed up all too conspicuously, and there came plenty of shells.

Of course, one would remark, here was the same situation in which Brodie had lost his life: Stoker and his shipmates must be doomed—finish! But, just as many months later, one of our M.L.'s, in the early hours of an April morning, escaped out of the Zeebrugge inferno simply because the Mole guns could not be depressed on her sufficiently, so even the smaller 5·9-inch guns of Anadolu Medjidieh could not be brought to bear on an object so close beneath. The submarine was not hit, and she got off, dived to 90 feet, ran ashore on the opposite side, bumped Gallipoli, did her hull some damage, but got off again after five minutes. The spot was evidently under another fort (No. 22), Derma Burnu, and the current thereabouts runs at its swiftest—roughly 5 knots, with numerous swirls and eddies.

Once more she had an exciting life as she bumped off and down to 70 feet, with the sound of propellers whirling above her, since all sorts of craft, from tugs to destroyers, were in pursuit. As *AE* 2 came on through a gradually widening channel, these chasers could still be heard, and terribly near; wherefore at 8.30 a.m. Stoker, having got so far as Nagara, with the Marmora Sea in front, completely fooled his enemies by sinking to the bottom, just above that Point, at 80 feet and remaining there till the fuss and stress had passed. Rising to the surface at 8.45 p.m., he charged his batteries, sent a wireless report to Admiral de Robeck, which arrived at the critical moment when a council of war aboard the *Queen Elizabeth* was discussing, at the end of this disappointing April 25, whether after all the troops should be withdrawn. The good news from Stoker—that he had been able to reach the inland sea—had the psychological effect of enlivening drooping spirits, shedding an illumination of hope, and giving the discussion a new turn. The council decided to hold on. Submarines might yet be the controlling influence.

At 4 a.m. on the 26th Stoker continued his pioneer voyage on the surface till dawn, when he dived, passed Gallipoli town, and near there unsuccessfully attacked two men-of-war. It is possible that one may have been the *Barbarossa*. Next day this submarine sighted a transport approaching escorted by two destroyers, and at 300 yards fired a torpedo; but the wretched missile rose to the surface, its engines refused to function, and the transport got away, whilst the submarine was pursued by destroyers. On the 28th Stoker arrived off the Bosphorus—a memorable hour, when one considers that though a fleet of battleships had been for months thwarted, an under-water boat had won through—and now made an inspection of Constantinople with the purpose of attacking on the morrow.

Next day (29th), being his fifth out from the base, Stoker sighted another submarine. It was *E* 14 (Lieut.-Commander E. C. Boyle), who had just arrived, and greetings were exchanged by megaphone. In parting, it was arranged that the two boats should rendezvous on the morrow at 10 a.m., but half an hour after that time, and when about to make an attack near Marmora Island, *AE* 2 suddenly behaved as if possessed of a mad devil. Her bow rose and broke surface a mile from a destroyer, who approached firing, as did a gunboat. The submarine refused to dive, and then took a steep plunge rapidly, till she was more than 100 feet down, which exceeded all safety limit of those days. After a hectic interval, she broke surface stern first, and was received with a shower of shells which holed her engine-room in three places. Finally all hands had to be ordered on deck, the boat was sunk, and everyone was taken prisoner by the destroyer *Sultan Hissar*. It was the difference in salinities, the variations of water strata (alluded to in an earlier chapter), that had made her uncontrollable. With dramatic crisis, this pioneer trip had ended sadly.

The rest of the story—the pain and grief of years in Turkish captivity, the attempt to escape—need not be recapitulated. Commander Stoker has long since retired, while to his career as an enterprising submarine officer he has added that of actor, playwright, and author.

E 14 had better fortune. At one time Boyle was chased by torpedo craft for most of three days and nights, but on April 29 sank one of two transports that were being escorted by three destroyers. Having no gun, he created havoc with his torpedoes and rifles at a most important stage of the War. On May Day, south of Sar Keui in the Sea of Marmora, he torpedoed a gunboat of the " Aintab " class (about 200 tons), the ship breaking in half and sinking in a minute, with no survivors. One transport he terrified back into Constantinople by the use of rifles; another he torpedoed, but the missile (though hitting) would not explode. Then on May 10 off Kalolimno Island he sank a big transport named the *Gul Djemal* (5000 tons), which has a special interest. Once she had been the British White Star liner *Germanic*, built in 1874, and was a popular trans-Atlantic passenger steamer. Later she changed her name to *Ottawa* and passed into Turkish ownership; but now carried six field-guns and 6000 troops, just as her famous sister the *Britannic* had been employed during the Boer War. In the darkness *Gul Djemal* was swallowed up by the waters, and von Sanders' army did not get these reinforcements: they never fought against our men on the peninsula. Months after the War the Prize Court finally awarded the large sum of £31,000 for this sinking. On May 15 Boyle frightened a small steamer so that she ran herself aground, and, in short, he had thoroughly disorganised the enemy's lines of communication.

Concerning this we have more than one statement from postwar writings: it will be enough to quote the following reference by a German writer [1] bewailing the work of our Marmora submarines:

> The depredations of these unwelcome visitors became more and more alarming. . . . Things came to such a pass that communication by water between Rodosto on the European and Panderma on the Asiatic side became impossible.

All movement of troops, munitions, food, stores, for the Gallipoli peninsula had thus for a time to be made by road.

[1] *Two Lone Ships*, p. 172.

This meant that instead of using a sea-route of 130 miles, everything must travel twice that distance, and with double handling: first 160 miles by rail, followed by 100 miles along indifferent roads. Lieut.-Commander Boyle had done magnificently,[1] sunk or damaged two gunboats, two transports, and after being away for three weeks was recalled by wireless, arriving safely back on May 18, to receive an ovation and in time to give some invaluable hints to Lieut.-Commander Nasmith, who was to start off next day in E 11.

Of the wonderful adventures performed by E 11 we shall read in a later chapter; it suffices now to add that between the setting forth of AE 2 and the return of E 14, two French submarines, anxious to share in such achievements, had tried and failed. Thus on April 29 the *Bernouilli* (390 tons) got as far as the vicinity of Nagara, but owing to the swift current and her batteries becoming exhausted, she was set downstream and had to return. A similar submarine named the *Joule* next tried, but on May 1 she struck one of the mines, and was lost with all hands.

---

[1] He was afterwards awarded the Victoria Cross for these exploits.

CHAPTER XXI

THE STORY OF "GOLIATH"

BEFORE we pass on to the next phase it will be interesting to see something of how all this activity of the last week in April affected the enemy.

That our troops had landed where they did surprised the German leaders only to the extent that so many places were used. Special detachments formed out of the *Goeben's* and *Breslau's* crew had been sent down towards the coast with twenty-four machine-guns, and did valuable work for the Turks; but that which filled our opponents with apprehension was this multiplicity of landings and the deluge of fire which came from the great semi-circle of warships lying off the coast.

General Liman von Sanders has put it on record [1] that whilst he had specially prepared for defence Sedd-el-Bahr, Morto Bay, Gaba Tepe, and Ari Burnu, he himself rode with his adjutants to remain for the present at the narrow ridge of Bulair, till matters developed. According to his opinion our own preparations " were excellent, their only defect being that they were based on reconnaissances that were old; and that they under-estimated the powers of resistance of the Turkish soldier. Hence they failed to bring, in the first few days, the decisive results which would have converted this grand operation into a decisive and swift achievement."

He considerably over-estimated our strength ashore as from 80,000 to 90,000, whilst it approximated roughly to that of Sanders' Vth Army, *i.e.* about 50,000. The superiority of our naval artillery he regarded as being " so immense as to defy estimation "; and our means of transportation " seemed almost unlimited." On April 25 he looked out with wonder along the coast, and counted nearly 200 warships and transports. To Germans and Turks alike this naval and mercantile review of a seafaring nation, already busily engaged with its far-flung trade routes in the oceans, and its central activity around the British Isles, made a highly impressive spectacle.

[1] *Five Years in Turkey*; see p. 63 and following pages.

Nor had the visit of the *Canopus, Dartmouth* and *Doris*, the destroyers, trawlers and transports into the Gulf of Xeros been altogether a failure: but only after these had been so suddenly withdrawn (as previously recorded) did he realise this had been merely a demonstration. Those " 'orses with 'orns " were but a slight indication of the concealed activity which would have awaited a landing, and the Turkish troops were ready to emerge from their hiding: but from 6 a.m. on the morning of the 26th, when the last trawler departed, the German General's anxiety vanished likewise. Furthermore, he was able to transfer these troops from Bulair to stiffen opposition at Sedd-el-Bahr. Thus, our little squadron under Captain Grant might have been more valuable had it remained in the Xeros Gulf to keep the enemy still in suspense. So, also, the feint by the French at Kum Kale had its ill effects: after several days of severe fighting, during which the Turks inflicted heavy losses, great was the joy to see the invaders go back into their boats. The Asiatic side being rid of visitors, the XIth Division was at once marched up to Chanak, whence it was transported across the Narrows by boats during the ensuing nights and brought round to strengthen the Sedd-el-Bahr defence still further.

And our submarines?

The same German authority makes it definite that their arrival in the Sea of Marmora caused the shipment of troops for Maidos (opposite Nagara) to be done by night. But that heavy shelling, which we saw at the end of April being put by our battleships across the peninsula from the neighbourhood of Gaba Tepe to the vicinity of Kilia Liman, as a reply to the two Turkish battleships, was not wasted even if it sank neither vessel: it demolished the port of Maidos so thoroughly that the place ceased to exist, and the shore-dwellers who survived had to betake themselves across to Asia. So, likewise, Ak Bashi Liman (the next port east of Kilia Liman), which was used for disembarking most of the food and supplies that came for the Army from Constantinople, suffered immensely from our indirect naval fire. It was this overland attack, together with the submarines, which really created alarm : if the ports did not exist for unloading the transports, and the latter dared not risk being sunk, then the peninsula campaign looked like collapsing. Admiral de Robeck should have been allowed at once every possible submarine that could be spared from Home waters. For, adds von Sanders, had these underwater craft succeeded altogether in closing the Sea of Marmora traffic, "the Vth Army would have died of hunger." And we shall find, later, that instead of entrusting all the cargoes to a few moderate-sized steamers, the Turks had to spread their risks over many small sailing craft which could hug the land.

It is to be noted that throughout the eight and a half months' campaign from April 25, neither the *Goeben* nor the *Breslau* came down below Kephez into the Dardanelles; but naval detachments under Admiral von Usedom remained in charge of the Dardanelles batteries. It was, however, not till the autumn of 1915 that the acute lack of ammunition for these could be remedied; so that, to make the infantry happy, the guns had sometimes to fire blanks! The Turkish artillery ammunition factories in Constantinople being inefficient, and that which was started by the German Navy being not much better—only one out of every twenty shells exploded—the defences must needs economise until Bulgaria should come in on the Turco-German side and enable a clear run of railway from Krupps works down to the Bosphorus.

Having regard to the fact that so many of our Dardanelles battleships were "old crocks" largely manned by reservists, it must be stressed that their pressure on the enemy had been powerful beyond all proportion. The acknowledgment which von Sanders makes of these ships is worthy to be quoted and remembered. They " protected the landed troops in the fullest sense of the word," and although the Turks made successful attacks after dark in an endeavour to drive our troops off the peninsula, " daybreak brought an overwhelming fire " from our vessels which compelled the Turks to retire, and kept them on the defensive. The chief difficulty for us was that both opponents were entrenched so near to each other by the Achi Baba ridge, separated sometimes by only a few paces, that we dared not use our guns to the fullest extent.

If, however, this bombarding fleet had been at their worst when attacking forts, they had "constituted a support of extraordinary power" for the troops ashore; one of the principal advantages of ship-fire being its ability to be moved about so that concentration could be made on the enemy's flank and rear, and yet simultaneously to withdraw from attack. But for these men-of-war arrayed off Ari Burnu, the Anzacs would have been swept from their slender hold into the Ægean. Never in all its ancient history had that sea contained such an expression of naval might, with the dense lines of grey hulls, the crowd of smoke-stacks, the thick forest of masts and signal yards, the flotillas of boats and small steamers. It suggested nothing so much as a great shipping port rather than an open anchorage; as if Southampton and Portsmouth had suddenly emptied their contents into the eastern Mediterranean.

But before the middle of May was reached, it had become painfully evident that our Army was confronted with too big a task. At 11 a.m. of the 6th a general attack was made on the Achi Baba position, when the wind happened to be so strong that aircraft were prevented from spotting. The ship's fire, controlled by the Army, nevertheless succeeded in keeping down the enemy's artillery. Next day the Army's advance was checked, and the first stage of this Gallipoli gamble ended on the evening of May 8 with the final effort against Krithia. Repulse, definite and undisguisable, had to be admitted; the Army had failed, as the Navy up the Straits had failed. Instead of one kind of deadlock, there would be henceforth a dual stoppage: Constantinople shut off from the land troops and the surface ships alike.

What next?

Should the Navy now try *forcing* the Narrows, without silencing the forts? That would mean a bigger gamble than ever. The Army had been checked by the trenches and machine-guns, but would not its position be worse if the sister Service left it to risk a death-ride into the Marmora Sea? The losses *en voyage* would be considerable, and in any case few ships could hope to reach Constantinople. But in what condition? Only a few days before (May 3) the *Prince George* had been hit by a shell below water-line, compelling her to make for Malta and undergo repairs. Supposing the Fleet were sunk, or seriously crippled, before getting clear of Nagara, would not the Army's very existence be jeopardised? Its food supplies and munitions stopped? Its very withdrawal to Mudros prevented? Then would come the *Goeben*, heading the two older 11-inch ships, and we should no longer have command of the sea. Already 20,000 men had been lost on Gallipoli by fighting. The rest would perish by starvation if the Fleet, which had supported them, were now reduced to one or two old battleships, some weak cruisers, and a few destroyers.

The moral effect following such a disastrous naval failure to reach Constantinople would be heard echoing all over the world. It would benefit no one except the enemy, and just now it might have the result of keeping Italy (who was about to come in with the Allies) from helping our side. No: the proposition could not be accepted for many reasons, and especially because we had now such a heavy commitment with the Army on shore.

Nevertheless Mr. Winston Churchill, the First Lord of the Admiralty, had more than toyed with the idea; but firmly and definitely his colleague Lord Fisher, First Sea Lord, took the opposite view. A political crisis was working up; the clashing of two stubborn wills in the Admiralty was really the logical result of a bad beginning, months before, founded on false strategy. The matter was clewed up in the following blunt expressions [1] which the venerable First Lord addressed to Mr. Churchill. On May 11 Lord Fisher wrote:

> I therefore feel impelled to inform you definitely and formally of my conviction that such an attack by the Fleet on the Dardanelles

---

[1] Quoted from *The World Crisis, 1915*, pp. 342 and 362, respectively.

Forts, in repetition of the operations which failed on March 18, or any attempt by the Fleet to rush by the Narrows, is doomed to failure, and, moreover, is fraught with possibilities of disaster utterly incommensurate to any advantage that could be obtained therefrom.

Five days later he followed this up with:

> You are bent on forcing the Dardanelles and nothing will turn you from it—NOTHING.

Now, luckily—as many well-informed naval officers and others still believe—the idea of staking all on one single throw did not prevail: so matters went on as usual. But for a very brief period only. Between the writing of the first expression and its confirmation on the 16th, something happened which could not help advertising the vulnerability of armoured battleships, however they might be named—*Goliath*, *Triumph*, *Majestic*, call them what you will.

It had become known (by means which will be duly mentioned) that at last enemy submarines were on their way to the Dardanelles. Long ago had this possibility been contemplated, but now the approach was said to be within days; which would somewhat complicate matters. For how could the battleships lie at anchor, supporting the soldiers, if torpedoes were threatening? The answer was to remain with torpedo-nets out; and from Tuesday May 11 this precaution came into force. Cumbersome, awkward things, regarded as obsolete, they were now to be given a new life. What they looked like, when rigged, will be seen from the accompanying illustration. Transports were now kept at Mudros within the anti-torpedo nets, and troops were carried towards the landing-beaches by means of Fleet sweepers as well as destroyers.

So we come to the night of May 12–13.

The method of working the Dardanelles destroyers was by day for one division to be patrolling off Anzac, and one off Helles. A sub-division was held at the Admiral's disposal for such duties as escort, whilst others were in Mudros coaling, resting, and provisioning; or landing troops wherever reinforcements might be needed. One division was relieved daily

MINESWEEPING UNDER FIRE
This very unusual photograph shows the enemy's shells falling close to the British destroyers whilst sweeping inside the Straits.

NET PROTECTION
This photograph shows how the battleships sought to protect themselves against enemy torpedoes.

at noon, steaming forty miles to Mudros, enjoying a night's welcome rest in harbour, and then sailing next day at 9 a.m. to relieve the other division at the Straits entrance. But always extra jobs accrued, such as landing the military Commander-in-Chief, mine-sweeping, guarding flanks, and even fetching water for the troops.

As mine-sweepers they kept the channels clear for the bigger ships, and it was no rare occurrence for ten destroyers to be sent on this mission two or three times in one day. On such occasions they would be followed by a battleship to keep down the enemy's annoying fire. Proceeding in line-abreast, with three pairs of destroyers towing kites and wire sweeps, there would be another pair astern (but in the centre) doing likewise, the battleship being one mile farther astern still. They used to perform this sweeping at 18 knots, a considerable improvement on the trawlers' speed of half that.

Just to make things awkward, the European and Asiatic batteries would put up a barrage of shells—through which the destroyers must pass—continually shifting this ahead to catch victims.

For the night routine, destroyers used to proceed up the Straits at dusk and take stations above the right flank of our troops till dawn, steaming slow ahead to maintain position against the current. On dark nights it was not easy to see the next destroyer, and the danger of collision was very present. After the French soldiers had taken over the right-flank trenches on the European shore, they used to co-operate with our destroyers by turning a searchlight on the Turkish trenches at a certain time, so that these vessels also burning searchlights would steam past and open fire, at a distance of 600 yards, with every gun enfilading the enemy, and doing great damage. Eventually the French had to discontinue their illumination, however, since it attracted such a heavy concentration of Turkish fire that many casualties were caused in the immediate neighbourhood.

On board destroyers the searchlights had to be employed with discretion, or they turned themselves into targets. The custom was therefore to train this illumination down, and not up, the Straits, else the enemy would pick up the position. During the landing at Anzac on April 25, the rising sun fell upon destroyers' searchlight mirrors and gave the Turkish snipers a good point of aim, thereby causing a number of casualties.

With that introduction, we may now carry on. The destroyer patrol on the night of May 12–13 was in a line across the Straits beginning from about a mile above Morto Bay, with the object of " strafing " Turkish reinforcements. The senior Commander (since Commander Prentis' death in *Wolverine* on April 28) was Commander H. R. Godfrey [1] in the *Beagle*. It was customary at this period for a battleship to anchor in Morto Bay as soon as it was dark, and help in repelling Turkish attacks during the dark hours, weighing and getting out of the Straits before dawn. That night it was dark and still, with also a mist, when the battleship *Goliath* arrived to take her turn in Morto Bay about 8 p.m.

A little farther down, and off Sedd-el-Bahr, lay the *Majestic*, opposite the *River Clyde*. A good deal of firing could be heard ashore, but it was noticed that the customary lights up the Narrows had not been switched on.

" I suspected that the enemy had got some little game on foot," writes the *Majestic's* Commander, " and at half-past one a signalman aroused me with the news that there was something the matter with the *Goliath*, which was covering the right wing, as we had done the night before. Getting on deck, I heard an awful noise going on, right ahead of us, where the *Goliath* had been lying off De Tott's battery. There was no doubt about what had happened : the *Goliath* had sunk, and the noise coming out of the darkness was caused by the shouting for help of her ship's company. We cleared lower deck, and I piped two of the watches to work the main derrick. We cast loose all the available woodwork, ladders, spare timber, oars, lockers, etc. The cutters were called away, and the searchlights were turned on the scene. We were the next ship

[1] Now Vice-Admiral H. R. Godfrey, C.B., D.S.O.

H.M.S. *BEAGLE* AT MALTA

One of the famous Fifth Destroyer Flotilla.

below, and the sight shown by the searchlights was one that I shall never drive from my memory.

"The sea, for an area of some half-acre, was a mass of struggling, drowning people: all drifting down towards us with the current. We thought it would probably be our own turn next. The cutters got away pretty smartly, with an officer in charge of each, and they picked up a good many survivors: to the others we threw over our woodwork. It is a curious thing, but the impression we all had was that as each man got near a bit of wood, he seemed to swim or struggle away from it. This impression, of course, was quite illusory. Only one fellow came within arm's length of the ship and, by an extraordinary coincidence, the man who grabbed him (having gone along a torpedo-boom to do so) found that he had saved his own brother-in-law!

"We were told to weigh, and scatter, which we did, as it began to get daylight; and went in search of our boats, which had been swept out to sea with the current. Eventually we hoisted them in, steamed up to our billet, and saw an eddy made by the current sweeping over the poor old *Goliath* where she lay on the bottom."

Everyone thought the culprit must have been a submarine, but actually she was the *Muavenet-i-Millet*, one of those four 30-knot destroyers purchased from Germany five years before. She was of 600 tons displacement, with a high forecastle, a couple of funnels, two guns and three 18-inch torpedo tubes. She drew 10 ft., and her commanding officer was German: Lieut.-Commander Firle, who certainly had nerve as well as pluck. Making full use of the pitch-dark night and the fog, keeping close inshore, he passed our destroyers unobserved; and, having stopped his engines, allowed his ship to drift down with the current. Of course the enemy knew well enough that a battleship would be found any night of the week in Morto Bay, and the Turkish Army would be glad to have the nuisance stopped. The job was such as would appeal to a keen destroyer officer in any service, and the conditions were perfect. One German writer claims that our recognition signals had been watched, and learnt, and practised: it is true that, after feeling her way along the land, she saw the loom of *Goliath* and came at right angles to the latter's bows, one of whose crew challenged her. The reply was made, followed by three torpedoes, which struck the *Goliath's* starboard side; and this would be easy enough, since the nets are intended for protection against attack from either side, but not from the bows.

Having perpetrated her deed, the *Muavenet* hopped off home quickly through the fog, and wirelessed to Souchon, *en clair*, a German message that she had sunk a battleship. Commander Barne tells me the *Majestic* intercepted the report that she had torpedoed a "linieschiff."[1] Admiral Godfrey says that the destroyer *Wolverine* likewise heard the message. "The wireless rating in the *Wolverine* (which, having been the Senior Officer's ship before Commander Prentis was killed, possessed more up-to-date wireless apparatus) reported strong telefunken signals." The *Muavenet* got home safely, and the Sultan thought so highly of her adventure that he presented every member of the crew with a gold watch and an embroidered purse filled with gold.[2]

The torpedoing had taken place at 1.27 a.m., and there had been time to fire only a very few rounds from a 12-pdr. at the enemy craft. But the effect was not long coming. The stricken ship heeled over to starboard, so that a medley of strange noises roared through the mist; for boats were falling out of their crutches, crockery was smashing itself to tiny particles, heavier things brought up with a rush against steel bulkheads, the guys supporting the funnels carried away and swayed about, bereft of duty: in fact, all that was not secure went charging over in a wild, hopeless scamper. The ship heeled to about twenty degrees—hesitated a few seconds—then she lurched more quickly; officers, young midshipmen but recently out of Dartmouth, seamen well past middle life and returned from civilian occupation to serve again afloat, now found themselves leaping into the current. Boats were sent

[1] Battleship. [2] Kopp, p. 229.

from the *Majestic, Cornwallis, Lord Nelson*, and others. The Commander was saved, but, as she capsized, the *Goliath* dropped her pinnace on her commanding officer, Captain T. L. Shelford, killing him. Out of a complement numbering 760, only twenty officers and 160 men were saved, some having been picked up well down the Straits.

But the *Goliath* had been too easy a mark. I am informed by more than one officer who that night were in her vicinity that she was using her searchlights: so that, with full knowledge a battleship would certainly be found in Morto Bay, the enemy would have the further advantage of steering towards what sufficed as if a lighthouse. We all know that fog does strange things—that it can be patchy here and thick there, that it contains zones of silence; to-night the noises were considerably deadened over the water, in respect of the torpedo explosions, whilst the sound of guns and rifles went on as normally.

Assuredly the enemy deserved all credit for a clever and daring plan bravely executed, but made possible only by the atmospheric conditions. These German-built Turkish destroyers were much smaller than our *Beagle* class, and it has been stated that the enemy rigged a dummy funnel so as to give the appearance of a three-funnelled *Beagle*; but among the tricks played by fog is the magnification of objects near at hand. The look-out aboard *Goliath*, knowing that our destroyers were patrolling just ahead, not unnaturally at first sight took enemy for friend.

Admiral Godfrey, who was Senior Officer on patrol, tells me he thinks *Muavenet* must have kept close in to the beach between the European shore and the left-flank destroyer. " It would in the conditions have been impossible to see her. After torpedoing *Goliath*, she instantly went up the Straits by the same route and when close to the Narrows reported her success by wireless. The *Wolverine's* Captain, on being informed by his operator of the strong telefunken signals, realised something was wrong, and steamed up towards the Narrows taking with him the destroyer *Scorpion*. He found, as he approached that defile, there was only slight mist. The enemy's shore searchlights came on, subjecting both destroyers to heavy fire. At length, presuming that these illuminations had been suddenly made to allow the enemy destroyer or submarine (for her character was unknown to our patrols till next day) to have got through, *Wolverine* and *Scorpion* steamed back to their patrol line; one sub-division simultaneously proceeding down to Morto Bay, where trawlers and boats were busy rescuing survivors. Searching about and across the Straits in rear of the patrol line, destroyers hoped to discover their foe if he were still about; yet it was all very difficult. So thick was it that very seldom any destroyer saw her neighbour during this night, and only then because they had approached very near to each other."

The reason why *Muavenet* got through is therefore quite simple. " The fog made station-keeping so hard that large gaps must have been left in the line most of the period. At dusk there was but a mist, which at the lower end of the Straits an hour later developed into a thick fog that prevailed all night until the sun dispersed it about 9 a.m. the following morning. It is of interest to note that this fog was the only one which occurred, night or day, during the destroyer patrols inside the Straits."

Now, the immediate effect of this disaster was extremely disquieting. The torpedoes had come at last, so that a fresh dilemma had been created. The Navy could not very well remain at anchor, aiding the Army by bombarding the enemy's flank, if Turkish or German torpedoes in three minutes could wipe out a 13,000-tons ship. True, the *Goliath* was fifteen years old. But the precious *Queen Elizabeth*? Lucky she had been never to have steamed over on the Asiatic side in Eren Keui Bay among the *Nusrat* mines. Amid our misfortunes we could at least be thankful for this. Torpedoes? Here came danger in a fresh guise. So forthwith the world's newest and finest battleship had to be hurried into a safe position behind the anti-torpedo boom at Mudros, and thence sent home to England. Admiral de Robeck, with his

THE STORY OF "GOLIATH" 243

considerable Staff, on May 14 transferred to the *Lord Nelson*, whence a few days later they shifted aboard the steam yacht *Triad*. The latter was one of the handsomest pleasure-vessels in existence before the War. Of 1416 tons, with a straight stem and two funnels, she looked more like a miniature liner, and had luxurious accommodation, resembling in some respects the Kaiser's well-known yacht *Hohenzollern*, which used to be seen in the Solent during Cowes week.

The removal of *Queen Elizabeth* meant the withdrawal of those valuable 15-inch guns and the lessening of our support of the Army by that amount; but a couple of the war-built monitors (which were really slow-moving floating batteries to carry 14-inch guns), together with the two battleships *Exmouth* (14,000 tons, four 12-inch guns), and *Venerable* (15,000 tons, four 12-inch guns), and the two cruisers *Cornwall* and *Chatham*, were being sent to Admiral de Robeck in addition to an increase of the French squadron. Before the end of May, the latter comprised the *Jauréguiberry*, *St. Louis*, *Henri IV*, *Latouche Treville*, *Charlemagne*, *Suffren* (after being repaired), *Kleber*, *Dupleix*, *Bruix* and *Patrie*. In the latter Vice-Admiral Nicol flew his flag, having been appointed to command a squadron already considered too big for a Rear-Admiral; but Rear-Admiral Guépratte remained as second-in-command.

On the other hand, forasmuch as Italy was to declare war on Austria from May 23 and become one of our allies, there were sent this month, under Rear-Admiral Thursby, from the Dardanelles to the Adriatic the *Queen*, *London*, *Implacable*, *Prince of Wales*, together with the four cruisers *Amethyst*, *Sapphire*, *Dublin* and *Dartmouth*.

If Lord Kitchener and the Army were annoyed at the departure of *Queen Elizabeth*, this was inevitable, and immediate events emphasised the wisdom not to risk her down here. The most our battleships could now do was to support the Army by day, lying with nets out, but this disposition led to further tragedies, which we shall now proceed to watch. Meanwhile in Whitehall was burst one of those political bombshells which create upheaval even at a time when greater explosions were being made elsewhere. For Lord Fisher, seeing the nature of the Dardanelles crisis, and being out of sympathy with his colleague, resigned his appointment of First Sea Lord on May 22, and this was followed by Mr. Churchill's departure. In their stead Admiral Sir Henry Jackson and Mr. Balfour took over Admiralty responsibilities.

CHAPTER XXII

THE SUBMARINE PHASE BEGINS

" THE Turks want a submarine, but the Austrians have refused, as being too dangerous. We have offered them a crew."

So wrote Admiral von Tirpitz [1] on March 4, 1915, and from then were sown the seeds which in less than three months were to provide a wonderful harvest for our enemy's reaping. The story has never till now been presented in all its fullness, yet it is one of extraordinary interest. Confronted by the Allied Fleet, visited successfully by *B* 11, and forced to act on the defensive, Turkey by the end of February was in dire need of under-water craft. They could have played havoc with our bombarding ships, and ruined our efforts from the earliest days. By the end of February the Turks fully realised—late in time—this possibility.

" If the Dardanelles fall," wrote Tirpitz on July 24, " then the whole of the Balkans will be let loose on us." A fortnight later he added (on August 8), " Should the Dardanelles fall, the world war has been decided against us." [2] Field-Marshal von der Goltz at the end of March visited the German G.H.Q. at Charleville at a period when the Turkish situation was looking grave. Nominally he came north to talk about military matters, and Serbia in particular; yet one cannot suppose that at these conferences he failed to back up the need for submarines.

Germany could not immediately comply with such a request, since she had just begun her Submarine Campaign with all too few; but more were being built, and she did what she could. In the autumn of 1914 Admiral Tirpitz had ordered thirty-two of the small " UB " and " UC " types, and by April Germany was able to send *UB* 1, 3, 7, 8, 14, 15, together with the four minelayers *UC* 12, 13, 14, 15, to Pola on the Adriatic for the Austrians. These ten boats were transported by rail in

---

[1] *My Memoirs*, by Grand Admiral von Tirpitz, II. p. 504.
[2] *Ibid.*, pages 537 and 549.

sections and assembled at the Pola dockyard. From them were selected *UB* 3, *UB* 7 and *UB* 8, which were to go under their own power down the Adriatic and up the Ægean into Constantinople. Of these, *UB* 3 was last heard wirelessing her report when 80 miles short of Smyrna, since when she has never been seen, though it is practically certain that on April 9 she was blown up when entering Smyrna, having fouled the Turkish mines in the Gulf. The other two got safely through into the Bosphorus, and were sent to operate in the Black Sea, where also *UB* 8, which did not reach Constantinople till June 4, was destined later to be handed over to the Bulgarians. They were quite small craft, measuring 98 feet long, drawing just under 10 feet, and of less than 9 knots speed on the surface, but 5 knots when submerged, their batteries allowing them to maintain the latter rate for only an hour. They carried but two torpedoes, and altogether were not suitable for operating in the Dardanelles current, and the Turks wisely did not employ them outside the Sea of Marmora against our Fleet. *UB* 7 survived till the autumn of 1915, when she hit a Black Sea mine. During this summer *UC* 13, 14, and 15 came to Constantinople with arms and ammunition from the Adriatic.

But to meet with her ally's request, Germany decided to send out *U* 21, which was a much abler craft. She was 210 feet long, with a surface draught of 12 feet, displacing 840 tons submerged and 650 on the surface; surface speed of 15 knots, submerged speed of 9 knots; carrying eight torpedoes, and armed with a couple of guns. She had been first commissioned in 1913, having taken two years to build. Well tried during the first months of war, she had shown herself reliable and successful. But would she be able to carry enough fuel, and would her personnel be able to endure a long voyage from Germany to the Dardanelles, calling at the Adriatic?

That was the question. Five years previously, the Swedish submarine *Hvalen* (183 tons), which had been built in Italy, at Spezia, had cruised unescorted thence up the Atlantic and English Channel to Stockholm. In 1911 certainly three

THE SUBMARINE PHASE BEGINS

British submarines (*C* 36, 37, and 38) journeyed 10,000 miles from Portsmouth to Hong Kong, which created a record; but that was in time of peace, they were towed part of the way, and moreover they called at Gibraltar, Malta, Port Said, Aden, Colombo. The Germans had no base awaiting them before the Austrian port of Cattaro, and anywhere along the route *U* 21 might be attacked. Nor could she dare to use the Dover Straits, whose barrage just then was considered unhealthy for German submarines. In short, she must go right up the North Sea, round Scotland, outside Ireland, down the Atlantic, along the Mediterranean, well up the Adriatic, making about 4000 miles. A bold undertaking, and full of every discomfort in peace time, yet thoroughly perilous when so many patrols were vigilant all round the British Isles.

Germany possessed for this difficult undertaking no abler or more experienced commanding officer than Lieut.-Commander Otto Hersing. In appearance he looked more of the Italian type, with dark eyes, a big nose, large mouth, and a somewhat sullen expression. Tall, slender, hawk-like, he did not in those days suggest the sailor, any more than he does now that he has long since retired and leads the life of a country gentleman at Rastede, happily married, afflicted with rheumatism (as a legacy of submarine work), and interested in growing potatoes.

But let there be no mistake: Hersing was one of the greatest submarine captains that any nation has so far produced, and full of pluck. This pioneer was destined to become a national hero in his own country, to turn the tide of history, and to be the saviour of Turkey. The German Admiral Michelsen has not exaggerated when calling him " Der befreier der Dardanellen." That Hersing was already a thorn in our side will be appreciated by the following brief epitome of his achievements before April 1915.

Early in the war he daringly essayed to creep up the Firth of Forth, even to the bridge. He scored the first submarine victory in history by sinking H.M.S. *Pathfinder*; was the first to take a U-boat into the Irish Sea, where he sank several steamers with the same ease with which he had caused the British S.S. *Malachite* and *Primo* to founder in the English Channel. Clearly he was just the man to try the task of reaching Constantinople and relieving the pressure on Turkey.

The date of his departure for this historic voyage is significant. He left Wilhelmshaven on April 25, the day when our troops landed on the Gallipoli peninsula. Passing up the North Sea, *U* 21 motored through the Fair Island passage and evaded the Scottish patrols, and all went well till after passing the Bay of Biscay. Her commander's initial anxiety was whether his fuel would last out the long journey, and that seemed definitely impossible. Fitted with Diesel engines, she started out with 56 tons of oil fuel, yet this had been largely expended by the time he gained the Spanish coast off Finisterre.

But the Admiralstat in Berlin had arranged, through the German Embassy in Madrid, that a small steamer should come out to meet him with oil fuel, lubricating oil, and provisions. The name of this steamer which managed to steal out was the *Marsala*, 1753 tons, owned in Hamburg.[1] We all know that a certain amount of slackness regarding internment prevailed along the Spanish coast, and she was able to make the rendezvous. Together they retired into Corcubion Bay. Hersing was glad that this supply ship had reached him, for already he had used up 31 of the 56 tons; and there are so many quiet indentations between Cape Finisterre and Vigo that it came as a relief to know how well the meeting had worked out. A small steamer against those high cliffs, and a mere dot of a low-lying submarine on the surface, are not the easiest vessels for being brought together over the Atlantic swell. He now took aboard 12 tons of oil fuel and 2 tons of lubricating oil. Secretly, using the cover of a May night, he completed his replenishment, and shoved off for the south. But now came the unfortunate truth.

---

[1] I have extracted some details from Commander Hersing's *U-21 rettet die Dardanellen*, as well as from Lowell Thomas' *Raiders of the Deep*. Other statements are from original sources.

THE SUBMARINE PHASE BEGINS

In spite of all this care, and all the typical Teutonic thoroughness, the scheming, the foresight, they had brought him the wrong oil! It was quite useless for his Diesel engines, possessing a wrong flash-point. His mechanics tried mixing it with the original lot, but that would not do at all.

What now?

He had but 25 tons for bringing him to Cattaro, and a rough reckoning indicated that his chances of holding out were remote. Should he therefore give up the effort, and return to Germany? Or take a gamble of being impotent long before reaching the Otranto Straits? Of course, being a brave officer, and appreciating how much both Germany and Turkey were relying on him, he decided to carry on. If he could avoid diving, and do most of the miles on the surface at slow speed, he might just win through. If, again, he were chased by the Gibraltar patrols, or some of the fast Mediterranean destroyers kept driving him under water, he would eventually have to come up and surrender. So, shortening the distance all he could, whilst anxious to avoid meeting with traffic, he had to make a compromise.

When 36 miles N.W. by N. of those bleak Burling Islands, some distance short of Lisbon, the submarine was sighted awash on the surface—no colours flying—by the S.S. *Teiresias*, who wondered concerning her nationality. All continued to go well, in spite of the anxiety about fuel, and she got through Gibraltar Straits unmolested, when she was sighted by the Torpedo Boat No. 92, commanded by Lieut.-Commander W. Ward Hunt, R.N.,[1] of the Gibraltar Patrol. This officer has been kind enough to give me the following particulars.

"At the end of April we received information, which we regarded as definite, that a German submarine, which was actually then on her way out, had a rendezvous at Alboran Island with a vessel who would refuel her. The Gibraltar Patrol, of which I was in command, accordingly caused this area to be closely watched, and on May 6 she was sighted by

[1] Now Captain, D.S.O.

Torpedo Boat 92 about 3 p.m., some 40 miles west of the island. A fresh easterly wind was blowing at the time and, consequently, she was steaming straight into the seas, throwing heavy spray off her bows, which made her particularly conspicuous. I estimated her to be about seven miles distant. She was the first German submarine to reach the Mediterranean, and, moreover, the first we had seen since the War began; so the moment was an exciting one.

"We at once increased to full speed, but, when about three miles separated us, the submarine appeared to recognise our hostile character and dived. After an interval of a few minutes, when I deemed we had reached the spot at which she might be, I saw her periscope come up suddenly, about 200 yards on our starboard bow. I immediately put the helm hard aport, with hopes that she would expose her hull and give us a chance to ram her. But she had evidently sighted us, for she dived, and a few seconds later, when we had passed over her hull (which was plainly visible in the clear water) she had reached a depth which brought her conning-tower well below our keel. We did, however, probably damage her periscope, since it deeply scored the bottom, as we subsequently found on docking.

"$U\,21$, in the meanwhile, had fired a torpedo at us, which we saw running away on the surface. These were the days before depth-charges, and our means of offence against a submarine were practically nil, unless she was caught on the surface. I had, however, still hopes of further encounter, as I had two other patrol vessels stationed just in sight of Alboran Island, and we in T.B. 92 followed the course she might be assumed to take for the island."

But Hersing kept on, did not meet a supply ship off the island, and sighted only one other British man-of-war. Although the torpedo-boat had not sunk Hersing, it had achieved two satisfactory results: (1) causing the enemy to consume more of his dwindling fuel, and (2) being able to report beyond all doubt that a U-boat had reached the Mediterranean. It was because of this knowledge that from May 10 anti-submarine measures were taken in the Dardanelles, and the *Queen Elizabeth* removed within Mudros away from danger just before the *Muavenet* torpedoed *Goliath*. It had been calculated that $U\,21$ would reach the Dardanelles by the night of May 11–12, and we can therefore well understand that when the *Goliath* foundered on the following night, everyone at first supposed it was through submarine action.

As a fact, Hersing had not yet got near that neighbourhood. He had sighted the second British torpedo-boat; later on he also dived when a steamer was sighted off Cartagena, and on seeing a French destroyer. He crept past the north of Malta, round the south of Sicily, and over to the eastern side of the Adriatic, finally entering Cattaro on May 13 with scarcely half a ton of oil fuel. (His own words are: " Mit knapp einer halben Tonne öl.") He had thus just managed to accomplish his wonderful nineteen-days' voyage with the smallest reserve. A fine effort indeed ! It may at once be stated that this precedent enabled other famous U-boat captains that summer to follow in his tracks. Hersing had negotiated the Gibraltar Straits " in the grey light of dawn." Captain Hunt tells me— and I have had it confirmed from a British prisoner in a German submarine—that the enemy henceforth always made their passages through this defile by night. The Spanish territorial waters extend to two-thirds of the width across to Africa, which prevented us from laying mines or other fixed defences. U-boats could always get bearings of their position from Spartel and Trafalgar lighthouses, submerge with perfect confidence in deep water, and have the benefit of a steady 4-knot current helping them through.

Cattaro was well situated as the base for future German submarines bent on attacking our Mediterranean traffic. This charming, well-sheltered bay, opening out into numerous lake-like bights, surrounded by mountains and pretty villages looking out on to an azure sea, is so shut in that the sun in winter becomes visible for only four or five hours. The Dalmatian coastline is sombre, with gaunt mountains and dark foliage, yet Cattaro is extremely healthy, strongly fortified, and its twisty channels have always been part of its protection. During three years it was a veritable haven of rest and safety for U-boats.

But *U* 21 had been damaged, as we saw, by T.B. 92, so must go up to Pola for repairs, whence already those smaller German submarines had set out with much-needed munitions for the Turks. A repair ship was subsequently established at Cattaro, but the greater facilities of Pola, together with imported German material and personnel, were a welcome boon. If the shore attractions of Cattaro were limited, Pola offered more amusement to her crew of thirty-five men. Overland by rail to Cattaro the Germans sent also a torpedo-boat to act as wireless guard, and the approaches could not readily be mined by the Allies, since deep water runs close up to the entrance.

It was encouraging to Hersing that he should now learn of what had been done on the day after he left Wilhelmshaven. One of the Adriatic submarines this April 26 had watched the French armoured cruiser *Leon Gambetta* (12,416 tons) patrolling the Otranto Straits at the slow speed of $6\frac{1}{2}$ knots, and without any destroyer screen. Moreover, it was night-time. So the submarine had no difficulty in giving her two torpedoes, and the ship carrying Admiral Sénès with 650 officers and men perished. This disaster was required to warn our Allies that deep-draught ships blockading the Austrians had best be withdrawn in favour of destroyers.

On May 20, having repaired his ship and rested his weary crew, Hersing set forth from the Adriatic, came south to the coast of Greece, through the Cerigo Straits, and up the Ægean. It is to be stressed that he had been sent from Germany not for the purpose of interfering with Mediterranean trade, but primarily to counteract our Dardanelles campaign and deliver the Turks from their attackers: therefore his attention, for the present, should be directed against men-of-war. He had not long to wait before sighting the unmistakable five-funnelled Russian cruiser *Askold*.

The attack on her failed, but if the *Queen Elizabeth* had gone away, there were still not a few targets, and he could make his selection in his own time. At 10.30 a.m. on May 22 there was the report of a submarine, and all the ships began zigzagging, with the smaller craft scooting about and making a wonderful sight. It was $U\,21$, and she showed herself more than once; whereupon Admiral de Robeck sent his battleships that Saturday afternoon into Mudros, reducing the bombarders to one pair.

Events were now about to follow each other quickly.

On Thursday, May 20, a five-horned mine came down with the current, but it was observed by the *Majestic*, who fired and sank it. On Friday this ship had relieved *Cornwallis* off Morto Bay, and had at once been fired upon, when a 6-inch shell with the first shot struck the *Majestic's* starboard cable and cut it in two, then entered the ship's side and, penetrating the chain locker lid, cut through three parts of her bower cable. On Sunday the battleship *Albion* had the misfortune to get aground off Gaba Tepe during a local fog, and this was the signal for Turkish howitzers, field-guns, as well as one of their two battleships in the Narrows to open fire. Most fortunately, $U\,21$ was not in the immediate vicinity, for the *Canopus* was trying from 4 a.m. till 10 a.m. to get her off. The *Lord Nelson's* fire was able to make the enemy battleship withdraw, and eventually *Albion* floated, though she had to be sent to Malta for docking.[1] Among other ships, the yacht *Triad* came to her rescue most gallantly, and received several hits, unarmoured as she was.

Whit Monday (24th) was terribly hot, and the Australians made an armistice with the Turks, who wished to bury the latter's dead; for the conditions had reached an unbearable stage. That night several battleships, as usual, were lying anchored with nets out supporting the Army, but everyone was on the alert for the sight of a periscope.

[1] The *Albion* was hit a hundred times. The efforts of *Canopus* resulted in the towing cables snapping, but *Albion* lightened herself by opening a terrific fire with her forward 12-inch and 6-inch guns, finally getting clear by the *Canopus'* renewed efforts.

With torpedo-nets out, the *Majestic* had been lying off Gully Beach; in the neighbourhood were also *Agamemnon*, *Triumph*, and *Swiftsure*. U 21 was cruising about for the chance of a life-time: the dream of a submarine commander was to come true. Never since the three "Cressys" went down had such a chance presented itself of so many targets. At daylight (5 a.m.) the *Vengeance* started from Mudros for Anzac beach, and on the way heard that a submarine was off Cape Helles. At 10.30 came a shout from the look-out: " Submarine on the starboard bow ! "

" Hard aport ! "

The battleship's stern swung clear, and that danger had been avoided. Transports were now ordered into Kephalos, and *Canopus* to Imbros, sighting U 21 on the way; but meanwhile the worst had happened. Let me tell the story of this May 25 as Commander Barne of the *Majestic* has been good enough to describe it.

"We weighed at about 6 a.m., having furled our nets. Just as we were heaving up, a minesweeper not far from us commenced to blow her whistle and hoisted the 'Hostile Submarine' flag. It was a fine, calm morning, and it would have been easy to see a periscope sticking out of the water. Instantly there happened a great bustle, all the small craft dashing about, hunting for the U-boat. Presently, just as we were getting under way, the *Agamemnon* fired with her 12-pdrs. at something in the water, astern of us. It was the submarine right enough. All the battleships had to weigh and spread: the submarine was indeed a fox in our hen-run. She fired two torpedoes at the *Venerable*, which was steaming full speed, and fortunately missed her. We went and anchored off Ghurkas' knoll, and were asked to fire a few rounds now and then.

" At 12.30, when we were all below having lunch, the Chief Yeoman came down and reported that the *Triumph* had been torpedoed and was sinking. She had been lying off Gaba Tepe, firing across the land towards Maidos, with her nets out. We all got up on deck in time to see her turn over, clean bottom up, and then down she went. We expected to follow her example any minute and, weighing anchor, steamed slowly back with our nets out to our anchorage off Cape Helles. Arriving there, we were joined on board by Rear-Admiral Stuart Nicholson,[1] who had come from the *Swiftsure*, bringing with him General Fuller and Ashmead-Bartlett, the War Correspondent.

"The Admiral, as he came over the side, remarked to the General, 'Now we are behind nets, we can sleep in our beds safely.' Evidently he did not know that the *Triumph* had her nets out when she was torpedoed. After dark we weighed and crossed over to Kephalos by bright moonlight, anchored and got out our nets."

Happily, I am enabled to present an even more intimate account of the *Triumph's* disaster. The following narrative has been kindly written for this chapter by one of her officers:

"*Triumph* put out her net defence, which at that time was considered to be a sure protection against torpedoes. It was necessary to remain more or less stationary, in order to concentrate bombardment on the desired points ashore. About noon on May 25 the submarine was sighted in our neighbourhood. The anti-torpedo attack armament was manned, and about half-past twelve we saw the periscope off our starboard beam, followed almost immediately by the track of a torpedo. Instead of exploding on the nets, as we expected, the torpedo passed right through them as if they were not there, striking us amidships. The *Triumph* immediately took a list of 20 degrees to starboard, making it impossible to get the boom boats out. There were a destroyer and some auxiliary craft making ineffectual attempts to locate the submarine. The appliances at our disposal then were, however, quite inadequate, unless it was possible to ram.

"Our list rapidly became worse and, after a few minutes,

---

[1] He had been flying his flag in the *Swiftsure* commanding the main squadron that covered our Army. The *Swiftsure* that morning was now sent into Mudros for protection, so at five minutes' notice he transferred his flag to the older and less valuable *Majestic*.

it was recognised that nothing could save the ship, so the order came to abandon her. A destroyer came alongside the port quarter and took off a large number of men. The remainder jumped overboard, but the net defence made things more difficult, as it was impossible to get clear on the port side, except off the forecastle and quarter-deck. I, personally, jumped in off the former, and swam well clear of the ship. Within ten minutes of the torpedo striking, she turned turtle and remained for some time on the surface, bottom up, finally disappearing slowly.

"There was one rather amusing incident I noticed. The *Triumph*, it will be remembered, had been out in China. Our Chinese ward-room steward could not swim, and refused to jump overboard, so he climbed out on one of the net booms at the port side. There he sat to await events. This Chinaman was old, and very like a monkey to look at. Stuck on the end of the boom, he looked remarkably like the proverbial monkey-on-a-stick. As the ship heeled right over, the boom got higher and higher out of the water, until it had passed the vertical; when down it fell with a crash, the Chinaman being shot off the end and turning two or three somersaults. He landed safely in the water, and was promptly picked up by a trawler.

"I continued to swim about for an hour, when I was rescued by a destroyer and there, to my astonishment, was our Chinese steward, quite unperturbed, mixing cocktails in the ward-room for the rest of the survivors.

"Between fifty and sixty officers and men were drowned when the *Triumph* sank—the majority being engine-room ratings. Luckily, the weather was fine: otherwise the loss of life would have been considerable. It was an extraordinary sight to see a ship like that (11,800 tons) turn over. Wild rumblings, as heavy weights took charge, could be distinctly heard from outside; and the ship finally sank, still growling like a wounded dog, as the things inside went adrift. Survivors were transferred to a merchant ship lying in Mudros, and we were finally sent to England in the *Carmania*."

Hersing had begun the "deliverance of Turkey" well: he had stopped that overland fire across the peninsula, and he had created a great moral effect. Combined with the loss of *Goliath*, this incident emphasised all too clearly that armoured battleships at anchor, protected by steel nets, were at the mercy of any small under-water craft. Only when under way and zigzagging could immunity be expected. Hersing began his day's work at 7.45 a.m., when he tried to get *Swiftsure*, and had closed to 300 yards, but the latter's quickfirers made him dive. Nearly three hours later came the attack on *Vengeance*, but the officer-of-the-watch had seen the torpedo's track just in time. For two hours Hersing waited off Gaba Tepe for a clear chance to get *Triumph* and, having shot his bolt, rose to the surface. Here he was given such a hot reception that he could escape only by taking a greater risk: he dived beneath the sinking battleship, scurried away, and for the next twenty-eight hours remained under water. Destroyers had made the peninsula waters too dangerous: these fast little ships seemed to cover the whole picture.

It was the trawler *Lord Wimborne* which saved no fewer than 104 people, and again it was a trawler which at 4 p.m. received a sudden, unusual job. We mentioned that in the *Swiftsure* Admiral Stuart Nicholson was flying his flag. Both he and the ward-room officers were below lunching at the time of *Triumph's* torpedoing. Mr. E. Ashmead-Bartlett [1] has left a thumb-nail sketch of the meal being suddenly interrupted "when a young signalman came to the Commander with cap in hand and said, with a most apologetic air, ' Beg pardon, sir: the *Triumph* is listing.' We rushed on deck, where every officer assembled, including Rear-Admiral Stuart Nicholson." At 3.30 the latter announced that he would transfer his flag to the *Majestic*, and this is how the rapid departure took place :

"A trawler came alongside, and all the Admiral's kit . . .

[1] *The Uncensored Dardanelles*, by E. Ashmead-Bartlett, C.B.E. London, 1928. See pp. 110 and 111.

were thrown in pell mell, without even being packed, mingled with an assortment of tinned meats, preserves, and wines."

Such was the contrast which had been begotten by the arrival of a small submersible from Wilhelmshaven, that the coming and going of an Admiral—always the opportunity for ceremony since time immemorial—now were robbed of all dignity. But the worst had yet to come, even if the oldest British battleship had been chosen now to be flagship. At 8 a.m. of Wednesday, May 26, the *Majestic*, having furled her nets for the last time, steamed out of Kephalos. The wide entrance had not yet been given an efficient boom defence, but a makeshift had been made with tunny-nets, and if Hersing had cared to force his way through, he could have again had a sitting-shot.

Zigzagging her way across to Cape Helles, this battleship anchored as close as possible into W beach, to resume her bombarding. The depth was 9 fathoms (54 feet). The nets were rigged as before, and a protecting cordon of transports was presently anchored around her. "Having a real live Admiral on board gave one a feeling of security," her Commander has told me: "no submarine would have the impertinence to molest a vessel bearing the person and flying the flag of such a potentate, attended on all sides by his retinue, whose comings and goings were accompanied by such pomp and circumstance. It was unthinkable."

This was now the one and only battleship not safely tucked away behind a boom, but the Turks, strangely enough, began to shell one of the transports, and not the man-of-war, so that the steamer soon had to clear out. This was a clever idea, since it withdrew some of the protection, but the night passed without event. Thursday the 27th dawned clear and calm, and not long afterwards came the crisis.

"I had been told," says Commander Barne, "that the Admiral would require his steam barge in the forenoon, so I had caused her to have steam raised. One watch was to stand by to get the port nets aft so as to allow her to be dropped into the water. Many of the men were already over the port side making preparations, and the time was about 6.40 a.m. I was on the after-bridge with my hand-flags, getting ready to top the boom as soon as it was cleared away. Happening to look about me, I saw some 350 yards off our port beam a whitish-coloured patch, marked also by an absence of ripple, on the surface of the water. As I looked, I saw emerging from this patch a line of bubbles extending rapidly in our direction: unmistakably the wake of a torpedo coming at us.

"There was little time to give the alarm. Doors, scuttles, and deadlights were closed. A lot of people must have seen the danger at the same time as myself. The crew of a 12-pdr. saw it, and fired two rounds at the patch where the submarine was, and one at the torpedo, in hopes of deflecting it. I was struck by the lightning manner in which the alarm spread through the ship during the short interval the torpedo was on its way. I shouted to the men over the port side to come inboard, and they needed no second bidding. I remember hearing the rush of many people over to the starboard side, and going myself towards that side of the after-bridge when the explosion came. It was terrific.

"The torpedo had struck us abreast the mainmast, and must have blown a large piece of her bilge away under the port engine-room. The whole ship seemed to lift, there was a tremendous shock, a column of water, bits of spars, net-shelf, etc., went high up in the air. I remember looking aloft, expecting the main topmast to come down on me, and saw it was waving like the top joint of a trout rod. The ship immediately began listing to port."

The Captain had been in his bunk in the upper-deck cabin, and now had reached the quarter-deck, but the Admiral could be seen nowhere.

"On going to his cabin aft, I shouted his name. It was pitch dark, all lights having gone out with the 'smack.' Not wishing to waste time on ceremony, I went to his bed and gave it such a thump with my fist as would probably have laid him out for a while. But he was not there. I made a bolt for the deck, to find the ship had listed till the water was over the quarter-deck. I was much struck with one able seaman standing on the net-shelf, under the starboard quarter. A stoker standing next to him looked up at me and said he couldn't swim. The seaman had a swimming-collar blown out, and was just about to put it round his own neck when I asked him if he could swim. He replied, ' Yes, sir,' and on my telling him to give it to the stoker, he did so without a murmur."

Meanwhile Captain H. F. G. Talbot was on the forebridge, and, with the assistance of the Chief Yeoman of Signals, was dumping over the side his box of confidential books. This done, he was able to save some men from being drowned in a dangerous place amidships, sending them all on to the forecastle. All these happenings took place quickly.

Within five minutes of being torpedoed, the poor old ship turned bottom up and sank. On the starboard side men were hanging on to the nets, which rose higher and higher out of the water. Most stood on the forecastle and quarter-deck ready for a swim.

" As she went over, we on the quarter-deck climbed down to the stern-walk, and simply walked into the water. The noise as she went over with a rush was terrific. Everything movable in the ship, from saucers to turrets, fell from their places. All the projectiles must have rolled to the tops of the shell rooms. The starboard net defence, after the booms had passed the vertical, fell in on top of her, imprisoning some few men who had not followed the majority. I have a lasting impression of the rudder within arm's length of me, bright green and bottom up. The rush of water and swirl seemed to go on a long time."

Some got sucked down and had narrow escapes as 15,000

IN HARBOUR

This shows the manner of stowing a ship's anti-torpedo nets. One of the motor-lighters (employed in landing troops) is seen alongside.

THE WRECK OF H.M.S. *MAJESTIC*

Showing the battleship's stem as it remained above water.

tons of battleship disappeared, but all sorts of craft clustered round. A French minesweeper picked up Commander Barne, who, on reaching her forecastle, saw, " to my astonishment, there, in the spot where I had first seen her, not 500 yards away, the German submarine, her periscope out of water. There was a Hotchkiss gun on the forecastle and we loaded it, and I was for having a plug at her," but there were too many boats around, picking up survivors. " I rushed to the bridge and implored the French skipper to go that way, but either he could not or was too excited to understand me. When the obstructing craft had moved on, our chance was gone: the submarine had vanished. I presently discovered our Admiral drying himself in the chart-house." And, shortly afterwards, on being taken to Mudros in the Fleet sweeper *Newmarket* with a load of the night's wounded soldiers, it was found that the total of *Majestic's* losses was only forty-two men and no officers. As to the Captain, he was found " clean, dry, shaved, in a private's khaki uniform, looking as smart as paint and donning a pair of borrowed shoulder-straps." On June 2 most of the *Majestic's* crew took passage for England aboard the Cunarder *Carmania*, which was now an armed merchant cruiser, and had distinguished herself in the famous duel with the German *Cap Trafalgar*. But for months afterwards the whole length of *Majestic's* hull could still be seen below the waves, and her stem stood erect, like a warning beacon. The British Navy's oldest capital ship ended her career, as she had begun, by flying an Admiral's flag.

Hersing's reward of two battleships in three days had come after patiently waiting for the right moment. On May 26 he had gone back to Gaba Tepe, but could see no more big warships, so went down to Cape Helles the next morning. After sinking *Majestic* he cruised about looking for more targets: but twice bitten, twice shy! For the present, at least, our bigger vessels had been withdrawn to the shelter of Imbros and Lemnos, leaving destroyers to maintain artillery support of the Army. And it was no little disappointment, alike to

s

Germans and Turks, that till the end of that period when our soldiers were on Gallipoli peninsula, *U* 21 never sank another battleship. Hersing had come a long way and begun brilliantly, yet in effect he had succeeded only in robbing the Army of some valuable help. When the approach of *U* 21 had first been heralded, Admiral de Robeck reduced the covering ships off Gaba Tepe from four to two; and from seven to four off Cape Helles. These six had been essential, owing to the Army's shortage of ammunition and the reliance which was placed on naval guns for dealing with shore batteries. After the sinking of *Majestic* only the recently arrived *Exmouth* was kept ready at Kephalos to support either flank, this battleship having extra heavy net fittings.

But on the evening of May 30, when about six miles east from the Ægean Island of Strati, off the Asia Minor coast, Hersing was surprised to see H.M.S. *Tiger* patrolling; and the sight of a crack battle-cruiser must have thrilled him. It was ten minutes past eight, and the ship could be seen zigzagging at 8 knots. *U* 21 loosed off her torpedo, which struck the ship just forward of her starboard beam, penetrating the engine-room and boiler-room, allowing an inrush of water and extinguishing the furnaces. The ship was abandoned, but the amazing sight presented itself of 13·5-inch " guns " which refused to sink. For this was not the real, but the " dummy " *Tiger*, the former S.S. *Merion*. With all his experience, Hersing was completely fooled this time. Only four men lost their lives, and the loss of this ship amounted to little; for these " dummies " had always been a nuisance and misfit.

So, after going into Smyrna Gulf for a day, he came north again, tried to torpedo the homeward-bound *Carmania*, reached the Dardanelles entrance, and got caught in a whirlpool which caused him some alarm, and again accentuates the trickiness of these currents. Finally, with no more opportunities for offence, he took *U* 21 up the Straits and (again with only $\frac{1}{2}$ ton of fuel on board) reached Constantinople by June 5. He was received with the greatest enthusiasm for having delivered the Turks from a severe threat. As for the Kaiser, he awarded every member of this submarine's crew the Iron Cross, whilst Hersing was given the decoration " Pour le Mérite," which corresponds to our Victoria Cross.

So we leave the peninsula waters for the present to the destroyers and light cruisers; soon to be joined by monitors and old cruisers with their under-water protection. Those days when ships-of-the-line could remain out at anchor and combine their artillery with the field-guns had passed. The torpedo, like the mine, had made more difficult than ever the task of bombardment. When, for example, during the last week of June, H.M.S. *Talbot*, screened by destroyers, enfiladed the enemy's trenches, it was the signal for General von Sanders to telegraph Admiral Souchon begging him to send down submarines. But of the Constantinople flotilla this summer *UB* 7 was allotted to cruise in the Black Sea, where on October 27 she torpedoed the Russian battleship *Panteleimon* off Varna, and was herself afterwards mined; *UB* 8, as we have noted, was handed over to Bulgaria; *UC* 13 was afterwards driven by Russian destroyers on to Kerphen Reef and blown up by her crew; *UC* 14 for a time remained at Constantinople, but was afterwards sent back to the Adriatic; and *UC* 15 was sent to the Black Sea. As for *U* 21, however, the entire Eastern Mediterranean was her hunting-ground.

CHAPTER XXIII

DARDANELLES DEADLOCK

THROUGHOUT the War always were being told strange stories of secret bases for submarines to replenish with oil, stores, food, or even to embark and disembark mysterious personages. Most of these narratives have no more substance of truth than is found in the outline of a novel. Nevertheless, certain unusual happenings, and some secluded bays, were to become part of the true story.

At the south-west corner of Asia Minor, lying off the coast, is the island of Kos, twenty-five miles long, with a chain of mountains parallel against its southern shore. There are terraces of vineyards exposed to the southern sunshine, and sultana raisins ripen for export into Northern Europe. The principal harbour is suitable for small craft only, but the Gulf of Kos is so pleasantly secluded, yet so near to the Ægean highway, that hither came *UC* 15 to spend a week making repairs whilst on her way to the Dardanelles. It was in this vicinity that *UB* 14 on August 13 torpedoed the S.S. *Royal Edward*, and from here that in September she sallied forth when she torpedoed also the S.S. *Southland*.

Now, the port of Budrum lies so picturesquely on the Kos Gulf that its innocence might never be questioned. Rich in ancient history, it is built on the site of that ancient Greek city Halicarnassus, whose old walls can still be traced. Under Mausolos it had once developed and prospered; after he passed way, his widow, Artemisia, erected to her husband's memory the wonderful " Mausoleum " whose ruins were excavated during the nineteenth century. This magnificent tomb, which introduced a new word for future generations through a woman's domestic devotion, was to become one of the world's seven wonders, and some of its sculptures are preserved in the British Museum.

There is no sort of doubt that Budrum was utilised by German submarines more than once, and we may anticipate sequence by saying that in the autumn of 1915 hither came

U 35 to embark a Turkish mission, together with arms for Bardia, on the north coast of Africa. She actually took from Budrum ten German and Turkish officers, at the same time towing a couple of schooners. In short, the Gulf of Kos happened to be placed so centrally, in regard alike to the Dardanelles, Adriatic, and African coast, that this Turkish territory could not fail to invite submarines: von Heimburg (commanding *UB* 14) had entered the Gulf (before sinking the *Royal Edward*) whilst on passage from Cattaro to the Bosphorus, his private hiding-place being in Orak Bay, ten miles east of Budrum.

Such details were obviously unknown to us at the time, yet even from April 1915 there were rumours that oil was being stored at Budrum against the advent of submarines: yet, again, information later seemed to negative such suspicions. For that matter, many of the Ægean islands might well be future bases to supply all and sundry who came from Cattaro. But on May 28 more definite suspicions caused the French armoured cruiser *Dupleix* (7578 tons) and the British destroyer *Kennet* to reach Budrum and examine the port. Negotiations were opened with the local Vali, who fired on our boats being sent in with armed examination parties, and the latter suffered casualties. So *Dupleix* then bombarded Budrum town for three hours, after which the *Bacchante* arrived, and with *Kennet* destroyed all shipping and added fresh ruins ashore to the ancient remains.

Similarly, along the Syrian coast the French Admiral de Fourneau on May 12 visited Castelorizo, capturing some small Turkish ships with oil, whilst a week later the *D'Estrées*, another French cruiser, set on fire an important oil depot at Alexandretta. Early that month there had been landed on the North African shores to the west of Sollum some fifty German and Turkish military officers, with sixty machine- and six field-guns, since this was the beginning of a new threat on Egypt. For the powerful Senussi Arabs, under Turco-German influence, and supplied by means of the Budrum–Sollum submarine ferry, were being roused.

Thus, aside from the direct Dardanelles endeavour, various small "side-shows" were affording work enough for our smaller craft, and creating additional anxieties for the overworked Admiral de Robeck. Of course there is always the possibility of using distant territory for attempting a feint and causing the enemy to withdraw troops from the main theatre, and on May 5 the Admiral, in sending Captain Larken to the Gulf of Smyrna, once again hoped that some relief might be made at the Dardanelles by a distant demonstration. Besides the cruiser *Doris*, Captain Larken took with him six big transport steamers, one of the dummy "Dreadnoughts," likewise being joined by the destroyers *Wear* and *Welland*, as well as the yacht *Triad*. Arrived in the Gulf, they were to suggest that a landing was about to take place near Smyrna, though really it was just a comic bit of acting. It is true one of the transports had horses, mules, and muleteers; but not one ship had any troops. From Smyrna Gulf the cavalcade steamed down to Sighajik Bay, which is just to the southward, where the comedy was staged. That is to say, the empty transports (whose load-lines would have given them away badly) were anchored not too close, and the dummy *Tiger* (to be torpedoed on May 30) was kept well out from shore. At daylight the *Doris* brought up off Sighajik harbour entrance, after which two of her cutters (manned and armed) with the two destroyers went into the bay so far as depth of water permitted.

"Not a single soul did we see," Sir Frank Larken informs me: "a gem of a place, as charming as any little harbour I've seen, with acacia trees in luxurious bloom. I've since been told that, the whole time we were inside, the enemy kept us covered by machine-guns, and any shot fired by us would have been the signal to sweep our decks. I can't think why they didn't fire: we were utterly at their mercy—especially the cutters."

But nothing happened, except that the wind freshened, transports started dragging their anchors, and the squadron got under way. By May 7 the cruise was over and the ships

One of the smaller, M-class, monitors.

H.M.S. *Raglan*, one of the big monitors. (She is seen on the left, with one mast.)

MONITORS AT THE DARDANELLES

were back in Mudros, after which *Doris* received orders to take charge of the Smyrna Blockade: nothing had been achieved by this demonstration. From June 2, however, began the Blockade of the Asiatic coast from the Dardanelles down to Samos, the aim being to stop supplies of food and other stores from reaching Constantinople. During the night of June 3 more mines were laid in the Smyrna Gulf by the British Fleet sweeper *Gazelle* and the French *Casabianca*, during which operation the latter blew up.

Otherwise, with the modification of some occasional excitement, matters in the Dardanelles region settled down to a dull negation so far as the Navy was concerned. Inside Mudros the remaining battleships and cruisers were kept ready for future developments; at Port Kephalos was based the *Euryalus*, whilst Kephalos Bay was the advanced base for such ships as were covering the Army—that is to say, one battleship and the destroyers with their mother-ship H.M.S. *Blenheim*. Between Mudros and the Gallipoli peninsula four steamers were being employed to maintain a ferry service, whilst the trawlers (like the destroyers) were maids-of-all-work: patrolling, transporting, and working anti-submarine nets. Indeed, the Army had long since got accustomed to look upon these fishermen as their very good friends, though one day a young military subaltern wearing a monocle, and rather too full of his own self-importance, was present when four of these trawlers had come across to the peninsula with ammunition. So far did he forget himself as to order the Lieutenant R.N.R. of the trawler to take the former's luggage to the beach. The R.N.R. officer properly refused, but shortly afterwards there came along the Colonel who happened to be in charge of the ammunition at the landings; whereupon the subaltern was unwise enough to report the trawler captain.

The Colonel looked at the monocled young officer and said:

" Young man, you are on a battlefield now. Take that window out of your eye, and do for yourself. You must carry your own luggage where you want it."

Large numbers of drifters had been sent out from England, and were being sent; their duty consisting in using light wire-nets shot in different parts of the Ægean so as to trap submarines, indicator-buoys being attached to the nets for the purpose of announcing when any object should get foul. Theoretically these rapid-laying nets were a sound idea for entangling the enemy, yet in practice they were no more successful at the Ægean than in Northern Europe; though a different story belongs to the Otranto Straits drifters.

Admiral Stuart Nicholson, who had been compelled to shift his flag from this ship to that with unwonted frequence, now flew it aboard the *Exmouth*. She, together with the *Swiftsure*, *Talbot*, and the two destroyers *Wolverine* and *Scorpion*, supported the Army on June 4, when a general attack was made in the southern area of the peninsula, the trawlers protecting them with the indicator nets. The recently arrived monitor *Humber* was able to begin her bombarding work off Anzac, and this revival of an old war-vessel type had been due to Lord Fisher, who intended them for use in the shallow waters off Germany.

So far back as August, 1914, the Admiralty had taken over from Messrs. Vickers three monitors which were being completed for the Brazilian Navy: these were subsequently named *Humber*, *Mersey*, and *Severn*, their armament consisting of three 6-inch, and two 4·7-inch howitzers. They were of 1260 tons displacement, with a speed of 12 knots. By mid-July Admiral de Robeck was sent also four of the later type (6150 tons) which carried two 14-inch; and six of the class which mounted each one 9·2-inch. All these monitors were of light draught—not exceeding 11 feet—the *Humber* class drawing only 4 ft. 9 in., thus being enabled to get closer to the shore and in shallow bays where a 30-ft. battleship was prohibited. This, in turn, meant that they would be less likely to be attacked by submarines.

Occasionally the *Lord Nelson* resumed her excellent indirect bombardments. At daylight on June 20, with a kite-balloon spotting for her, she shelled the ships, docks, and town of Gallipoli on the Sea of Marmora, firing 127 rounds,

THE CUNARDER *MAURETANIA*
At the Dardanelles as a troop-ship.

THE PROTECTED *EDGAR* CLASS
The middle and bottom photographs show two of the *Edgar* class at the Dardanelles after being fitted with bulge protection around the lower part of the hull.

and doing enormous damage to a port that meant much for the Turkish Army. Five days later, lying off Gaba Tepe, she shelled Chanak for fifteen minutes, setting fire to the town in several places. Again a kite-balloon spotted, but she also had a screen of destroyers, trawlers, and drifters with nets. On the last day of this month, when the Army made a strong attack against the enemy's right flank and advanced eighty yards, H.M.S. *Talbot*, with the three destroyers *Wolverine*, *Scorpion*, and *Renard*, assisted by a kite-balloon which rose from the *Manica*, were able to do valuable supporting work; even if *Manica* was attacked by enemy aeroplane.

Mudros still presented an amazing picture of crowded shipping, yet still they came. Those two crack mammoth Cunarders, *Mauretania* and *Aquitania*, arrived bringing their thousands of troops, in spite of submarines. Nevertheless, one of our supply ships was attacked off Cape Helles on June 17, and two days later either this U-boat or another was seen going up the Straits towards Chanak. There is reason to think that about this date Budrum received a visit from such a craft which left next day for the Dardanelles. She was probably that which on the 29th showed herself south-east of Mitylene at 8 p.m.

With this under-water activity, the centre of danger began to shift from the battleships (which rarely came out) to the steamers, which in bringing the new reinforcements up the Ægean had to run past islands and bays that might have been created by nature for submarine lurking-places. Thus very soon one must expect to find the enemy concentrating not only against the shipping off Gallipoli peninsula, but also against transports approaching Mudros. At the beginning of July this fresh development became all too strongly emphasised when Hersing brought *U* 21 down from Constantinople through the Straits. He had the good fortune on July 4 to find lying off Helles the 5600-tons French transport S.S. *Carthage*, which for the last three days had been landing munitions. Certainly she was a free gift to him, and such as had not presented itself since the *Majestic's* decease. He had no difficulty in torpedoing her, and thus doing the

Turkish Army a direct service. The manner of her sinking vertically, and the destroyers hunting ravenously for *U* 21, will be noticed in the accompanying photograph, which is one of the most stirring illustrations which were ever made at the Dardanelles.

On this night (July 4–5) the trawler *Lord Wimborne* experienced trials which were typical of what these fishing craft had to put up with. From 9.30 p.m. till 5.30 a.m. she was bringing troops to the *River Clyde*, and had a quite exciting time. She made no less than seven attempts to get alongside, but on each occasion was spotted by the enemy's powerful searchlight and then shelled. During the whole of this month, transport trawlers were kept so busy taking off wounded men, loading ammunition for the peninsula, towing barges, keeping the troops from starvation, that the crews got little enough time for sleep. But now thirteen 110-ft. motor-lighters arrived, which were to do such fine work at Suvla and other beaches. Back from Malta had come the French battleship *Gaulois* by the middle of June. Not merely had her injuries of April 25 been made good, but she had been given an extra hull for part of her under-water body, besides one of those bow mine-catchers that made steering so awkward.

So the hot summer days continued, the trawlers became infested with flies, which spoiled the men's food; and the steam yacht *Triad* (in which Admiral de Robeck lived) was hit by a shell from Asia, wrecking the forward cabins of this luxurious pleasure-ship. How was it all going to end? What could be the ultimate result of all this striving, these risks, this appalling expense of shells and shipping? How much longer would it be ere those in high places would perceive that which was apparent to officers and men on the spot?

There were so many things which might have happened, and just made all the difference. If only the Russians could have put pressure on Constantinople, we could have advanced through Gallipoli and the Fleet have steamed up through the Narrows. At present the Black Sea operations amounted to precious little: every phase seemed so indecisive, contri-

LOSS OF THE S.S. *CARTHAGE*

She has just been torpedoed by *U* 21, is sinking vertically, and British destroyers are hunting at high speed for the German submarine.

buting nothing to the main argument. Events were occurring, and recurring, in a vicious circle: it seemed impossible to strike away from all this indefiniteness.

Thus on May 9 *Goeben* came back from a trip in the Black Sea, having escorted three colliers, but on returning from Sunguldak one of these steamers was torpedoed by a Russian submarine. That evening, and whilst taking in fuel, there came a wireless message saying the Russian cruiser *Kagul* had anchored off Sunguldak and was landing troops. So, only an hour after getting home into Stenia Creek, off went *Goeben* to find that the *Kagul* had already departed with her landing party two hours before. Actually this was a trap to lure the Germans out; for the latter at their second home-coming in the early hours of May 10 found the Russian squadron waiting off the Bosphorus with six capital ships.

An engagement began at 6.30 a.m., and the sequel shows what can be done by an inferior force of superior speed. The *Goeben* essayed to drive the Russians towards the Bosphorus forts, the *Tri Sviatetilia* became so damaged in the fight that she got on fire and hauled out. The *Kagul* arrived and acted as observer by wireless, but *Goeben* blotted out her wave-length, so the former communicated by search-light shutter. At 7 a.m. the fighting was very hot, the range being about 15,000 yards. Then the leading ship of the Russian line, *Ivan Zlatoust*, became on fire.

But for *Goeben* the situation was more than serious. She had been hit twice, her forward turret had jambed, and she was getting desperately short of coal. She tried wirelessing Admiral Souchon aboard the *General* to send out *Breslau*, but the Russians dominated this talk as *Goeben* had negatived *Kagul's*. The faster *Goeben* travelled, the more quickly would she consume her remaining fuel, but now she must make a bold bid and risk all. So, turning away from home, and in the direction of Sebastopol, she made a feint and succeeded in drawing the Russians off. Next she swung to starboard, worked up to utmost speed, and turned back in the Bosphorus direction.

Goeben's chance was now or never, and once more in her

exciting career she must put boilers and engines to the severest strain. The pace went up, the stern settled down till her quarter-deck was flush with the water and the after-turret almost awash. Speed! And more speed! The furnaces were fed, the steam pressure rose and rose. It was a ding-dong race with the Russians, and gradually the German hauled ahead. But would the coal hold out?

Another knot was added, she was travelling faster than when running away from the British cruiser the previous August through the Ionian Sea: indeed, this May she beat all her own records, including that made during her trials as a new ship. She was now doing 30 knots over the Black Sea, and against this the Russian battleships could not compete: by 3 p.m. the latter gave up the chase, went off home to Sebastopol and only the destroyers held on. At length *Goeben* beheld the welcome picture of *Breslau* coming out with destroyers and minesweepers, and that night she steamed safely back into Stenia Creek. Victory had been won by her engineers.

During this summer both *Goeben* and *Breslau* were convoying troopships as well as colliers, encountering occasionally the Russian destroyers. Once, during July, *Breslau* hit a mine at the Bosphorus entrance, but just managed to limp into Stenia, where she entered a floating dock (that had recently been provided), and there she remained till the following month, when she got badly knocked about again. For she was escorting some laden colliers from Sunguldak towards Bosphorus. About 2 a.m. three Russian destroyers attacked her, causing damage to ship, but likewise death and wounds to her people. Three hours later she had shaken off the enemy and was inside the Bosphorus. The colliers had escaped in the darkness.

Thus nothing decisive happened on this inland sea, and every night at 11 p.m., when *Goeben's* wireless report was flashed across to Germany, it told the same old story. Deadlock at the Dardanelles end: deadlock in the Black Sea.

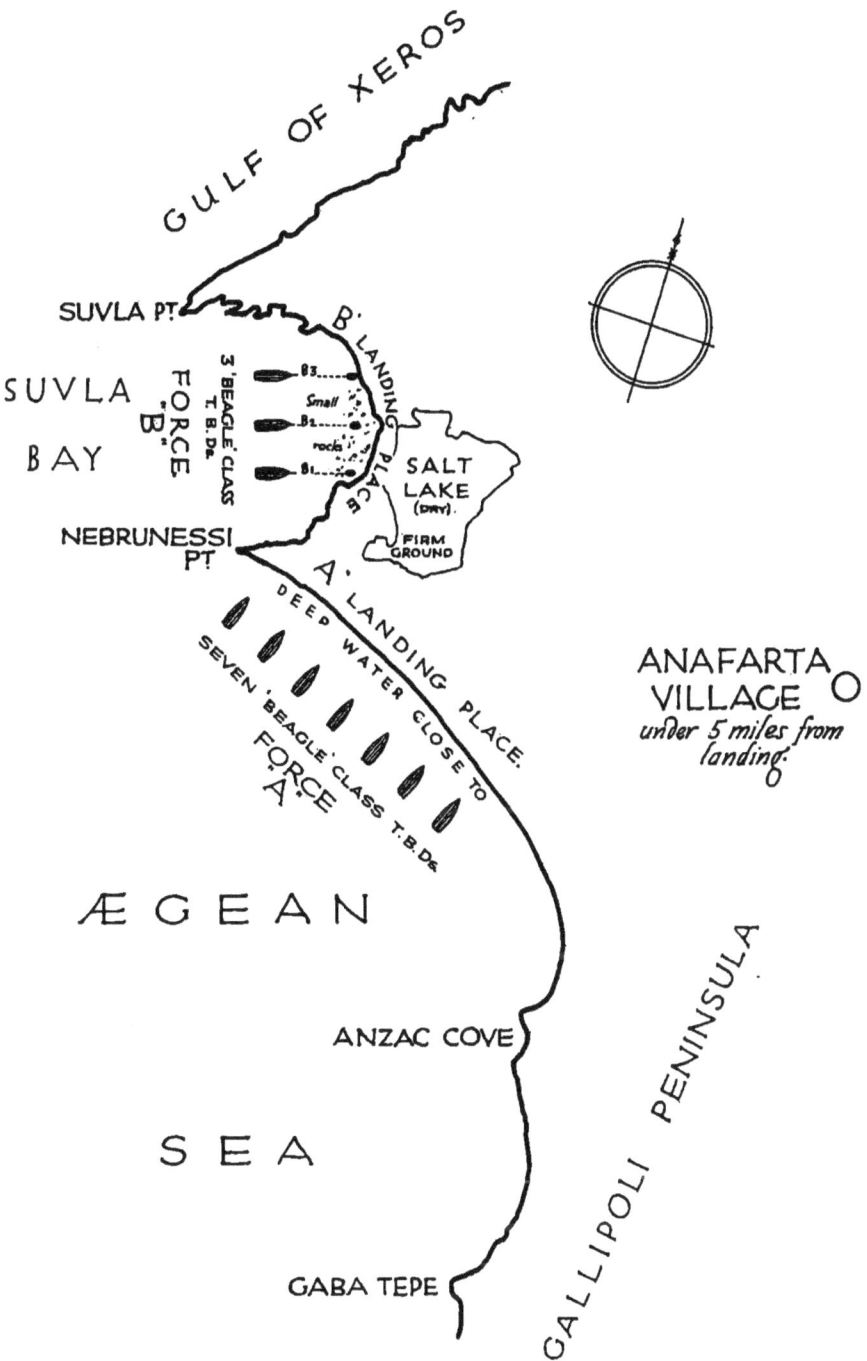

PLAN TO ILLUSTRATE THE LANDING AT SUVLA BAY, AUGUST 7, 1915

CHAPTER XXIV
THE SUVLA DILEMMA

OF all the "might-have-beens" in the history of human activities few are more sad or disappointing to contemplate than those which centre round Suvla Bay. And the pathos becomes no whit lessened when we find confirmed and emphasised in General von Sanders' own words that we failed to take advantage of ripe opportunity for gaining the goal of our entire longings.

This present volume, being concerned with the naval operations and the assistance rendered to the Army, need touch but lightly on the valour of our troops, the military tactics and strategy. The situation which had evolved by July was the logical conclusion of all the mistakes which went before, and the latter may be summed up under two headings: lack of full appreciation regarding the great undertaking, and omission to proceed with surprise. At almost every stage, whether by sea or land, we had given the enemy such warning that he was prepared to counteract our plans immediately endeavour was made to execute them. But now something happened, so well thought out, but so carefully concealed beforehand, that a universal unexpectedness amazed the enemy not less than many of our own people on the spot. As an instance of this secrecy, one officer serving aboard a principal ship who usually kept himself well informed concerning what was happening around him, says that he knew nothing till the landing had become fact. "Kept wonderfully dark," the achievement had been.

The surprise to be sprung at Suvla Bay came at the end of excellent scheming and working out of details in co-operation by the military with the naval staff. Animated by the desire to get over the deadlock and start from a fresh vantage point, high hopes were raised that at last things would begin to go ahead. But the whole success pivoted on the Navy's twofold help: landing some thousands of troops safely, and then giving them such artillery support as might be possible. For this purpose the Admiral had at his disposal such old cruisers as the *Endymion, Theseus, Edgar* and *Grafton*. These obsoletes from the " Edgar " class which over a year before were removed (on account of their inability to withstand severe northern weather) from blockade work off Scotland, had been now fitted with bulges outside the hull, which afforded complete protection against torpedo attack. Besides these units were such oldish cruisers as *Euryalus, Bacchante* and *Talbot*. The battleships, with one exception, still swung at their anchors in Mudros Bay, and were not to be risked until that hour should be heralded when they might (if events so worked) steam triumphantly past the Narrows as a compact fighting force. But additional to the cruisers, Admiral de Robeck could employ off the coast monitors (some of which had an improved form of bulge, with an air-space and water-space between outer and inner hull); one or two " Flower " class sloops (such as the *Aster* and *Jonquil*); destroyers, trawlers, drifters, and the motor lighters already mentioned. The sloops had been built since war started, and were really small, single-screw cruisers of 1250 tons, originally designed for minesweeping, but armed with a couple of 4-inch guns. In practice, most of their time was spent, whether round the British Isles or in the Mediterranean, patrolling, escorting, or doing any odd job which might come their way. One battleship—the *Exmouth*—with her specially strong nets, and the balloon-ships *Manica* and *Hector* for spotting, completed the active fleet that was to assist in the Suvla plan.

Rear-Admiral A. H. Christian was to be responsible for the actual landing at Suvla, the supporting three squadrons being commanded, respectively, by Rear-Admiral Nicholson (*Exmouth*), Captain the Hon. A. D. E. H. Boyle (*Bacchante*), and Captain Fawcet Wray (*Talbot*). The first had charge of the Helles section; the second was off Anzac; and the third off Suvla itself. The *Jonquil* carried both Admiral Christian and General the Hon. Sir Frederick Stopford, who was to command the military operation at the Bay.

So we come to the night of August 6, when 10,000 troops

LANDING THE AUSTRALIANS AT SUVLA BAY

The upper illustration shows them putting off from H.M.S. *Beagle*. In the lower picture they are seen about to land. The soldiers did the rowing; only one or two sailors were carried to bring the boat back.

were assembled at Imbros for a great venture. Here they were embarked in the following manner. Each of the ten *Beagle* class destroyers had one K-class motor-lighter secured to her, 500 troops being carried in each destroyer, and 500 in each lighter, making 10,000 in all. It was a dark, still, calm night, and moonless when the flotilla shoved off from the island; but 3000 more soldiers were borne in *Endymion, Theseus*, the sloop *Aster* and three trawlers: these last four units each towing a motor lighter containing guns and horses.

Commander (now Admiral) Godfrey, senior destroyer officer, who was in *Beagle*, has given me an interesting, first-hand, account of this memorable adventure which should be read in conjunction with the accompanying plan. Captain Unwin (who had won his V.C. at the *River Clyde* episode some months previously) was Principal Beach Master, Captain C. P. R. Coode, who was Captain (D), took charge of Force A, Commander Godfrey being in charge of Force B. The lighters were very suitable for beach work. Flat-bottomed, they could carry either 500 men or eighty horses comfortably. From the bows a large landing-stage was arranged to be let down, so that troops could run out on to landing-place " A " four abreast. Propelled by motor, giving a speed of about 6 knots, they were to come in very useful also a few months later for taking off mules, guns, supplies, and so on.

Force A consisted of seven lighters and the seven destroyers *Grasshopper, Foxhound, Racoon, Basilisk, Arno, Scourge* and *Mosquito*. Force B comprised three lighters, with the destroyers *Beagle, Bulldog*, and *Grampus*. They were to approach the shore, and not betray their presence by sound or light. All ships were darkened, perfect silence was enjoined, and precautions were taken to prevent the noise of letting go anchors; for which reason each cable was brought to the capstan, lowered to the water-line, and the enemy would not be disturbed by the rattle of so many chains. One tick on short-wave wireless was the signal for the lighters to go ahead from destroyers to beaches.

Now, landing-place " A " for the contingent of that numeral

was along the beach to the south-east of Nebrunessi Point. Imagine these seven destroyers about 10.30 p.m. quickly and noiselessly bringing up in line abreast. Here were no rocks or shoal obstructions, but a steep shelving beach, so that the destroyers had been able to get as near as 50 yards. Within a few moments the seven lighters reached the beach, landed their human cargoes, left ashore 3500 men, motored back, embarked another 3500, and the whole 7000 were speedily in occupation of the Nebrunessi beach, the total elapsed time being about 20 minutes. A more perfect bit of smooth efficiency it would be impossible to imagine.

Force B was bound for the centre of the concave formed by Nebrunessi Point on the south and Suvla Point at the north; but the conditions were more difficult. At that date our hydrographical knowledge of these waters was scanty, and, had a thorough survey been undertaken just before this operation, we should have certainly aroused the enemy's suspicions. The three destroyers anchored about 400 yards short of the beach, in line abreast, and the motor lighters slipped as before; but between this anchorage and the shore there happened to be a shoal to the north, and then a reef of numerous rocks south thereof. This series having been negotiated, the water deepened again, and finally came the beach. Not having information concerning all this, a certain amount of delay was inevitable; yet the difficulties were surmounted admirably.

The northernmost of this destroyer trio managed to land her first 500 men in about half an hour, although her lighter (drawing only $3\frac{1}{2}$ feet) got aground in the shallow water. Wading, however, the soldiers reached the beach, and back went the lighter for her second trip, depositing her load after about three-quarters of an hour. The middle, and southernmost, of the three had quite a strenuous and complicated experience owing to the unseen rocks, on which the lighters ran aground and stuck. Boats had to be sent from destroyers, motor lighters were also borrowed from Force A. All of this took time, but by 1 a.m. the task had been completed,

AT SUVLA BAY

The top photograph shows a beach party's hut just to the south of Nebrunessi Point. The middle illustration is of the artificial harbour made at the north side of Suvla Bay by means of sunken craft. A K-class lighter is alongside. The bottom picture shows a cove at the north side of Suvla Bay.

though the stranded lighters could not be refloated till morning. The 3000 men brought by *Endymion, Theseus, Aster* and trawlers were landed on Nebrunessi beach by the lighters shortly after midnight.

In such fashion did the Navy bring the XIth Division to Suvla Bay, and the sniping was so slight that landing had been quite different from what occurred at some beaches during April 25. Our troops certainly never fired at all, for they had orders to use only bayonets until daylight. It is doubtful if more than 2000 Turks were in this immediate district. To this fact, coupled with the perfect surprise, must be attributed all the success of detailed arrangements. Before landing from the destroyers, each man was given hot cocoa, and waterbottles were filled: nothing had been left to chance, no essential item omitted. The pity of it is that this covering force never reached its objective of Anafarta Ridge.

But the Navy had done its share. Half of the destroyers now went back to their patrols off Anzac, off Helles, or inside the Straits; whilst the rest landed the main force, beach parties and supplies during the following day.

It is common knowledge that the young troops of Kitchener's Army employed on this new venture, though they did very well later, were not up to the standard of veterans who might have been temporarily withdrawn from Anzac; but the initial failure, apart from fatigue and thirst, was that after the first twenty-four hours there came a lull when there should have been advance. Men were bathing in the sea when there should have been fighting: all was calm and quiet, where the sound of rifles and gun fire should have shown that the General was using opportunity and an easy landing to fullest advantage. Undue delay unquestionably threw aside all that had accrued from the surprise accompanying Suvla Bay landings.

Let us examine it from the enemy's point of view. He knew that we were massing troops, he inferred that another big landing was to be made: but where we completely fooled him was in regard to time and place. This locality (we have mentioned) was lightly held, but on August 7 von Sanders hurried reinforcements from the Asiatic side, these being ferried across to the peninsula above the Narrows and thence over the land. And whilst this was going on, we were resting instead of sweeping from success to success. Listen to what the Turks and Germans thought of our delay:

> We all had the feeling (writes General von Sanders)[1] that after the various landings beginning August 6th, the British leaders had delayed too long on the shore, instead of advancing from the landing place at any cost. ... It would have been impossible for the VIth [Turkish Army] on the evening of the 6th of August to get reinforcements to this point, the distances being too great. The British possessed the means for such an advance on their extreme flanks, in their great transport fleet protected by war vessels.

Suvla was, in fact, the key that would have unlocked to us Constantinople, but we were too tired to turn that key in the right direction. And (to drop all simile) the disappointment becomes all the more bitter when it is added that in the small hours of August 8 that old enemy battleship *Barbarossa*, steaming from Constantinople full of Turkish munitions for the peninsula Army, was exploded and sunk off Gallipoli town by Commander Nasmith in $E\ 11$, who presently torpedoed another transport of 5000 tons. We had repeated the same mistakes with which we entered upon the Dardanelles campaign—that is to say, we knocked loudly at the gate, and then waited for the irate householder to come along with his strong hand, instead of smiting fiercely at once. Thus, could it be strange if the sequel to Suvla Bay were similar to the general deadlock in the Straits and on the other sections of this peninsula? This time, however, the results were to be complicated by another new development. Bulgaria, having wavered long, but being now convinced that the Allies would never emerge victorious, mobilised her Army at the end of September and threw in her lot with our opponents, so that on October 7 the Austro-German invasion of Serbia commenced. Very shortly the railroad from Constantinople to Germany's munition factories would be opened; and, indeed, from

---

[1] *Five Years in Turkey*, p. 88.

THE TRANSPORT *SOUTHLAND*
At Mudros after being torpedoed by *UB* 14.

November the much-needed transportation of war material, artillery shells, together with other goods, was set going.

Nothing succeeds like success: but trouble often comes in large doses. And now yet another dilemma presented itself for solution. In June, British merchant vessels passing through the Mediterranean were warned to avoid the usual shipping tracks, show no lights at all—not even navigation lights except at discretion for the purpose of avoiding collision; for submarine attacks had begun against steamers that were not strictly warships.

The first British transport to be sunk in the eastern Mediterranean was the *Royal Edward* (11,117 tons). Without warning she was torpedoed on August 13, six miles west of Kandeliusa in the Ægean, with the loss of 132 men, including her Master. The wonder is that this number had been so few, for she was carrying 31 officers and 1335 men from Alexandria bound for Mudros. The culprit was Lieut.-Commander von Heimburg in *UB* 14, whilst on his way from the Adriatic to Constantinople. He was definitely working the Budrum neighbourhood of the Ægean, for on September 2 off Strati Island he torpedoed also the transport *Southland* (11,899 tons). Luckily she did not sink, and was brought into Mudros, but how narrow an escape she experienced will be realised on examining the accompanying photographs, showing a horrible big gash on her starboard side. Such incidents as these, however, were mere preliminaries of what might be expected.

Hersing's luck seemed, for the present, dead. He had come out from Germany to sink men-of-war, yet so far he had accounted only for *Triumph* and *Majestic*, though he had attacked both *Swiftsure* and *Vengeance*. The latter had now gone home, but on September 18 he again sighted *Swiftsure* at sea proceeding from Mudros to Suvla, again fired two torpedoes, and again failed. A week later he went up the Adriatic to Pola, where *U* 21 had a long refit till the end of January.

His services could now be spared, since apart from the UB's

and UC's that had come by overland route via Austria, five more of the big sea-going U-type were being sent out as $U\,21$ had voyaged; and these were to work havoc. The time for Germany happened to be singularly convenient. Ever since the torpedoing of *Lusitania* she had earned considerable unpopularity, and the diplomatic pressure exerted by the United States so perilously approached a crisis that from September 24, 1915, till March 1 of 1916 (with the exception of a short period covered by the dates December 20–28, 1915) Germany deemed it best to suspend torpedoings of merchantmen off the British Isles.

This did not prevent her from sending five of her best boats, and five of her ablest U-boat captains, to cut the Mediterranean and Ægean sea-routes; sinking transports, traders, passenger ships, and whatever came within range of attack. So on August 4 there started out from Heligoland $U\,34$ (Lieut.-Commander Rücker) and $U\,35$ (Lieut.-Commander Kophamel), both reaching Cattaro on August 23. Two days after their leaving Germany, Admiral von Tirpitz (at whose suggestion they had been sent) wrote somewhat apprehensively, " I hope all will come right if Turkey can be kept going. Our two new submarines are on the way. May the Lord protect them. I don't know whether England has got wind of them." [1]

This pair were followed by $U\,39$, which set out on August 27, and by $U\,33$ on the next day, the former being commanded by Lieut.-Commander Forstmann, and the latter by Lieut.-Commander Gansser. Like the others, these elected to go right round Scotland, and their voyages were marked by incidents. When 95 miles W. by N. of the Fastnet, Forstmann shelled the barque *William T. Lewis* but did not sink her. $U\,39$ got through Gibraltar Straits, and on September 8 at 5.30 p.m., when about 130 miles east of Cartagena, was sighted heading to the south-eastward. Between that place and Algiers she sank two French steamers, *L'Aude*, *Ville de Mostaganem*, and the British *Cornubia*, all on the 9th. Four days later she reached Cattaro. Gansser in $U\,33$ had a still

[1] *Memoirs*, p. 547.

more profitable trip. On September 1 he sank the British S.S. *Whitfield* 95 miles N. by W. of Cape Wrath (which, incidentally, gives one a good idea of his course after leaving Borkum), then came down the west coast of Ireland, and just after midnight on September 4, when twenty-nine miles west of the Fastnet, sank the S.S. *Cymbeline*. Less than half a day later she was 137 miles south-west of the Fastnet and sank the S.S. *Mimosa*, following this up at 5 p.m. by sinking the Norwegian *Storesand*. Carrying on south, she was 98 miles west of Finisterre at 3 p.m. of the 6th, when she sank the S.S. *John Hardie*, got past Gibraltar, but at noon of the 9th was about 50 miles west of Alboran Island, heading E.S.E., when she was sighted by H.M. Torpedo Boat 95, who fired on her six times. She dived and was not hit. (This incident should be compared with the similar episode between U 21 and T.B. 92 in an earlier chapter.) Finally U 33 got safely into Cattaro on the 16th. These four boats had followed in almost the same tracks as their pioneer Hersing. In November came U 38 (Lieut.-Commander Valentiner).

These five "star turns," after refitting and leaving the Adriatic, were not long in discovering the steamer tracks. They found life much more pleasant than in North European waters: better weather, better visibility—and the counter measures practically nil. They could cruise wherever they liked, sink what they wished, and (save for the Dardanelles region) be practically unmolested by patrols. Thus was commerce raiding inaugurated in the Middle Sea. One can only be thankful that these U-boats were not concentrated that autumn off Suvla Bay, where frequently a dozen or fifteen ships would be seen lying. War vessels were bombarding therefrom, nominally protected by nets; yet after the previous experiences could one be sure that enterprising submarine captains would not get their silver fish through?

Forstmann was the officer who earlier in the War had sunk H.M.S. *Niger*. Somewhat angular of appearance, and very much of the Prussian type, he contrasted with the stoutish, rather weak-mouthed Gansser. Kophamel we can visualise as a man with keen eyes and pinched-in, lean face; whilst Max Valentiner was the typical naval officer, clean-shaven, with a determined character, firm cleft chin, and fine forehead. When we call to mind that such gigantic liners as the *Olympic* and *Mauretania* during this autumn were arriving at Mudros full of troops—the famous Cunarder carrying actually 7000 in one trip—we shudder at the thought of another "might-have-been."

None the less, we had to wait a very short time before these U-boats began to produce results; for on September 4 the S.S. *Natal Transport* was sunk (not by torpedo but by gunfire) forty miles west of Crete. And, besides these, colliers, oil-tankers, transports, henceforth became the submarines' chosen targets, the favourite localities being off Cape Matapan (Southern Greece), Crete, Cerigo, Salonika; but from November onwards also off the North African coast—near Algiers—followed in December by the approaches to Egypt. In brief, all the routes between Gibraltar and Malta, Egypt and the Ægean were now so dangerous to shipping that a long list of steamers had been sent to the bottom by the end of 1915, among which was the P. & O. liner *Persia*, ruthlessly torpedoed by Valentiner, causing the loss of 334 lives. His first effort had been on November 4, between Gibraltar and Alboran Island, when he shelled the 6305-tons troopship *Mercian*. The latter put up a splendid fight by zigzagging and machine-gun fire, and finally got away with only fifty casualties. No fewer than eight more steamers after exciting moments escaped similar attentions between November 4 and 9, but many good ships succumbed, including the French transport *Calvados*, which lost 740 men. Valentiner was able to enter Cattaro with fourteen sinkings in his log, which indicated all too clearly that out of the Dardanelles dilemma had emerged another crisis. When on October 1 one of the other submarines tried to torpedo the 46,000-tons White Star liner *Olympic* (which escaped by her superior speed), some forty miles west of Cape Matapan, the future looked alarming enough.

At the beginning of December an Allied Conference met in

Paris to discuss this new problem, which resulted in a general overhaul of Mediterranean patrol strategy. One or two Q-ships, such as the *Baralong* (which had sunk two U-boats south of Ireland that summer) and the *Werribee*—both being small cargo steamers—were sent forth in an endeavour to lure the enemy along the Mediterranean; yet the area was so vast that no immediate benefits could be expected.

It needed the advent of a war to convince many senior naval officers (who were old enough to retain vivid recollections of ships under sail) that the submarine really could perform all that younger officers were claiming; and the final two years preceding hostilities had witnessed a keen rivalry between Germany and Britain in the development of under-water craft. Between the ablest submarine commanding officers in these two services there was not much to choose as to technical knowledge and daring; though there were things done at sea by certain of their opponents which no British naval officer would ever wish to perpetrate.

In negotiating the mines, the nets, the currents through the Narrows into the Sea of Marmora—not once, but time after time—British submarines contributed one of the most brilliant chapters to naval history. Some of these incidents we have already mentioned, and we must now resume our narrative from the date when Lieut.-Commander Boyle, after his wonderful cruise in *E* 14, got back to his base on May 18, and Lieut.-Commander Martin E. Nasmith the next day started off in *E* 11. One could fill a whole book with the exploits of these two and other British submarines operating in the Sea of Marmora, and only lack of space will prevent us from watching every day's exciting events. So detailed a consideration must be postponed. Each separate little voyage is a big drama in itself: each adventure a duel with death.

It was at 3 a.m. of May 19 that the quiet, cool, modest Nasmith, one of the world's pioneers of submarines, entered the Dardanelles Straits. Already in the past years, in peace and war, in the Solent and Baltic and North Sea, he had experienced some extraordinarily narrow escapes, and now in the eastern Mediterranean he was to continue this remarkable career. To-day he is a distinguished Admiral; he has been a Commander-in-Chief, and from that responsibility was appointed to be one of the Lords of the Admiralty; but it will ever be with submarines that his name must especially be associated.

Diving to 80 feet, E 11 passed under the mines, was attacked in the Narrows by destroyers who sighted her periscope, but a few days later found her at the eastern end of the Marmora Sea torpedoing a Turkish gunboat, stopping a steamer and compelling her to be abandoned. This was a troopship full of reinforcements intended for Chanak, but she never got there, and was blown up. Another steamer bound for the same destination took fright, and ran into Rodosto (on the northern Marmora shore), where she lay alongside the pier; but a torpedo from E 11 settled her fate. Next a paddle-steamer bringing bales of barbed wire became panic-stricken, and ran herself ashore to evade being torpedoed.

On his seventh day out, Nasmith at noon entered Constantinople, and torpedoed a transport lying alongside an arsenal. It was indeed a notable and spectacular achievement, and the moral effect was to create panic in the city. Next day near Marmora Island he sighted that battleship *Barbarossa* which had so often shelled our ships across the land. What a fine thing if she could now be sunk, and her guns sent to the bottom! But this was not so easy, and one of her escorting destroyers nearly succeeded in ramming E 11. Perhaps another chance would come later?

On the 26th a large cargo steamer, although escorted, was torpedoed, and five days later in Panderma Roads a large transport received similar treatment, though some tugs saved her by towing her ashore; but on June 2 an ammunition ship was sent to the bottom. E 11 got home safely after the first week of June, having sunk one gunboat, two ammunition ships, two troopships, two storeships, driven a transport ashore, and generally struck terror along the Sea of Marmora. He had vitally hindered the enemy

E-CLASS SUBMARINE IN HARBOUR

RETURN OF THE VICTOR
H.M. Submarine *E* 11 arriving back after sinking the *Barbarossa*.

H.M. SUBMARINE *E* 14
Crew on deck answering cheers of shipping on her return from Sea of Marmora.

THE SUVLA DILEMMA

from getting those troops and munitions so badly needed, and our Army at Suvla or elsewhere on the peninsula could wish for no sounder help. To keep on at this game would be to bleed the enemy of his very life.

Next went Boyle up the Narrows on June 10 for his second trip, and remained out for over three weeks, during which he sank one large steamer and thirteen sailing craft; for the enemy had been compelled to spread his risks over many, rather than concentrate in a few. Moreover, the number of his steamers was limited. Outside the Dardanelles, to the southward, watching the approaches of Smyrna, were stationed a couple of our B-class submarines, hoping to catch one of the enemy that might come in for supplies or repairs. Merely to relate these exploits is not enough. One has to imagine the discomforts on board, the heat, the whirring of motors, the continuous suspense, the confined quarters, the thousand mechanical items that could go wrong, the perpetual vigilance on the part of enemy destroyers, the possibility of traps and snares. Just below Chanak E 11 had a thrilling time when she fouled the mooring of a large mine on her way back, and actually towed mine, sinker, and cable outside the Straits: the dangerous obstacle was freed only by going full speed astern. No wonder Lieut.-Commander Nasmith was awarded the Victoria Cross and received early promotion to Commander!

In June also went E 12 for her first trip into Marmora. Lieut.-Commander K. M. Bruce [1] tells me that in this voyage one of his two motors burnt out, and he had to dive for forty-five miles with the aid of one, in spite of the mines and net; yet he remarks casually, "No difficulty was experienced." But a few days later he had a very near escape of special character in the south-eastern end of Marmora. This is his compact story, which the reader may expand without effort.

Two small steamers were sighted towing sailing craft, so Bruce opened fire with his 6-pdr. gun. The steamers then parted company, whereupon E 12 proceeded to the nearest, fired across her bows and stopped her. All the Turkish crew

[1] Now Captain Bruce, D.S.O.

put up their hands, the submarine went alongside, and the First Lieutenant with two others were sent on board. Suddenly the enemy threw down a bomb, which hit E 12 forward, but (marvellous to relate) failed to explode. She also opened fire with a small gun and rifles. For this was a trap ship! A decoy! The Turks had begun copying our Q-ship notion.

Bruce therefore recalled his party, opened fire with his gun at point-blank range, and with rifles. The action lasted about four and a half minutes, after which the mystery ship sank, as did also the two sailing craft which fired at him with rifles: so victory was complete.

The incident, however, had its amusing side. " One of my officers in jumping back to get on board, overshot the mark, and went over the side. He swam back and, on getting aboard, suddenly remarked, putting his hand into his pocket, ' By Jove! I've been shot!' But instead of extracting a bullet, he brought out a sharp piece of broken glass from his smashed watch!" His cruise ended satisfactorily, and he came back to Kephalos on June 28.

Next was the Marmora invaded by Lieut.-Commander A. D. Cochrane in E 7. During her way up on the last day of June a torpedo was fired at her from Kilid Bahr on the European side of the Narrows, but it went over, and in the Sea of Marmora she set to work with splendid effect. Besides sinking brigantines, xebecs, and other sailing craft, steamers and ferries, she torpedoed the arsenal at Constantinople, shelled the Zeitunlik powder-mills, shelled the railway, blowing up ammunition trucks, and so on. Once more this was a powerful assault on the Turkish supplies.

Such expeditions, in spite of the enemy's carefully laid minefields, were to the Turks most irritating; wherefore in July they constructed a wire net with a small gate across from Nagara, and placed gunboats as sentries. This did not prevent Cochrane from coming down, or Boyle in E 14 from coming along on his third voyage. He bumped a mine, but fortunately the latter was similar to those we used to find off the British Isles laid to entrap surface ships—that is to say, the several horns were placed on the top of the dome, and not below. And to this fact E 14 owed her safety. She negotiated the anti-submarine net by its gate, reached the Sea of Marmora, again wrought havoc and upset transport arrangements, and she also dropped shells right in the centre of troops marching along the road to Gallipoli, scattering them right and left. Thus, neither by sea nor by land were the Turkish lines of communication safe.

In the last week of July the French made a further effort with one of their submarines. This time it was the *Mariotte*, but she had no better fortune than the predecessors of her own nationality; for she got caught in the wire net and fouled a mine, came to the surface, was severely shelled by the Chanak batteries, could no longer dive, so her personnel had to surrender.

Now, on August 5 Nasmith, with a 12-pdr. fitted to E 11, began the most amazing of all these enterprises. It started in the early hours of the morning, with the accompaniment of guns and searchlights in the Suandere vicinity, but he dived, bumped a mine, dived still deeper (110 ft.) to avoid the net and hit it; for the latter's depth extended to just twice that distance—220 ft. However, by sheer weight and power, she burst her way through, and off Ak Bashi torpedoed a transport, though next day she suffered the excitement of being bombed by an enemy aeroplane. The rest of her adventures read more like raw fiction, such as one might find in one of those nicely illustrated books given to boys at Christmas time: thrill after thrill, one danger overtaking another, and always the heroes coming out alive.

After meeting E 14 at a Marmora rendezvous and shelling troops on the march, Nasmith torpedoed a gunboat, and on August 8 surpassed himself by torpedoing that oft-mentioned *Barbarossa*.[1] In spite of the escorting destroyers, she was gone at last, and could never again drop her 11-inch shells over to Gaba Tepe. As a variation to this cruise, E 11 again shelled troops along the Gallipoli road, but this time the enemy replied with field-guns: he could not afford to lose

[1] Throughout these pages I have referred to her as such, and this was how the Germans were accustomed to speak of her; but her full name was *Haireddin Barbarossa*.

units before reaching the battle line. Nasmith, however, went merrily on burning a dozen small sailing-craft, torpedoing a large steamer off Constantinople (one of the very few remaining on that inland sea), bombarding Mudania railway station on the southern shore, and then came that remarkable nocturnal episode.

At the north-eastern end of the Marmora Sea lies the Gulf of Ismid, and parallel with the shore runs from the Bosphorus the Berlin–Baghdad railway. Not till the end of September 1918 was the Taurus railway tunnel completed, so not yet was there direct communication with Mesopotamia. None the less, it had already become a valuable means of transport from across Asia Minor to the capital. Its weak link was a viaduct now abreast of E 11, yet when the latter shelled this bridge the enemy replied with such determination as compelled the submarine to desist. But there are more ways than one of smashing up railway arches.

Lieut. Guy D'Oyly-Hughes, the second-in-command, thereupon volunteered to swim ashore with a charge of gun-cotton and blow up the viaduct. Having made a small raft, he shoved off at 2 a.m. on the night of August 20–21, and swam towards the cliff, pushing before him the raft which contained a revolver and bayonet for self-defence, together with the 16-lb tin of gun-cotton. Owing to the inaccessibility of the first cliffs, he had to swim along till he found a suitable spot. Carrying his heavy weight, he climbed to the top, at last found the railway, but heard the voices of a Turkish picket. Then, evading these, he stumbled through a farmyard whose poultry inhabitants cluttered loudly their protests. It was exactly the kind of alarm he wished to avoid.

He approached the viaduct, but the men were there, and at a small culvert he laid his charge, fired it, ran along the line, heard the terrible bang, and next came the sound of the three pickets pursuing him. He swerved round long enough only to fire his revolver, to which they replied with their rifles, and then off he sped like an athlete in a 100-yards sprint. The distance, actually, was about a mile: the race a contest between death and life. At length, turning off, he rushed down to the beach, plunged into the sea, blew his whistle as a signal for the submarine ... waited ... whistled again ... saw nothing ... and not without anxiety swam towards the shore.

Here he landed, rested, threw aside his weapons and his electric torch. Day was now dawning; the pickets might come upon him any moment, but where was $E\ 11$? He took to the water once more, the pickets saw him, there were Turkish shouts and the plop-plop of rifle-fire. But what had become of the submarine? D'Oyly-Hughes was getting very tired; and feeling not less disappointed. Over there, in the half light of early day, his eyes framed three curious boats. Were the Turks about to surround him?

Now, this was not the first time that the upper features of a British submarine have been taken for three vague objects: one year previously, whilst patrolling the Dover Straits at night, a D-class submarine puzzled one of her sisters in just the same manner. What D'Oyly-Hughes gazed at was $E\ 11$ coming round the point of land; wherefore he swam towards her, and was hauled aboard with most of his energy long since expended. He had added to his ship's successes by cutting an important line of communication, but during the next few days this exceptional cruise ended after sinking another ammunition sailing-craft, and then torpedoing four transports in one day. Finally she burst her way back through the Narrows at 80 feet and got back home. Was there ever such a sequence of submarine successes? To-day Captain D'Oyly-Hughes has the D.S.C., as well as D.S.O. after his name, and still serves on the active list.

This same month, $E\ 2$ (Lieut.-Commander David de Beauvoir Stocks) was operating in the same sea, when he torpedoed a two-funnelled steamer, which was thought to be a minelayer, and armed with two guns. She went down, and most of her crew were rescued by dhows. That was on August 14. Six days later, at the entrance to Artaki Gulf, $E\ 2$ was fired on by a single-funnelled steamer which mounted three or four guns. She was chased into Artaki Bay and torpedoed. A third steamer, flying the Turkish ensign, and armed, was torpedoed off Mudania, whilst loading war stores. So the good work continued, and after the War this submarine was awarded by the Prize Court the sum of £1250. Alas! by that time Commander Stocks no longer lived: he had gone down in one of the new K-class submarines during a regrettable collision one night in the Firth of Forth.

What these under-water boats achieved, time after time, was against more formidable and complicated difficulties than ever faced a U-boat: nothing is so eloquent of the discipline, the peace-time training, and the personal valour without which such apparently impossible results could not have been obtained. And they went on from month to month. Let us accompany Lieut.-Commander Bruce in *E* 12 on an unprecedented cruise of six weeks. The date is September 16, and the hour is midnight. The following diary is reproduced by Captain Bruce's courtesy and is a remarkable record :—

"*Sept. 16th.*—Midnight. Proceeded from Kephalos to entrance of Dardanelles under escort. Proceeded up Straits, dived off Suan Dere at 5 a.m. Sea calm. Rounded Kilid Bahr about 6 a.m. Passed through net at Nagara at 7 a.m. at 80 feet; had no difficulty. Net appeared to part on the knife-edge on foremost periscope standard. The boat was brought up about 10 feet.

"Fired at steamer in Burgas Bay at 9 a.m. Heard explosion, but was put down by small craft which prevented our seeing result. Torpedo was observed to be running straight. (This ship was observed to be sunk well down in the water on our passage down: tonnage about 2000–3000 tons. She had one black funnel and two masts.)

"At 2 p.m. rose to surface about 8 miles to eastward of Gallipoli; charged batteries and communicated by wireless.

"*Friday, 17th Sept.*—Strong N.E. breeze. Sighted and attacked a destroyer off Sar Keui but did not get within range.

"*Saturday, 18th Sept.*—Dived into Rodosto but found nothing there. Chased torpedo boat of the 'Antalia' type

CAPTAIN K. M. BRUCE, D.S.O., R.N.
Commanding officer of H.M. Submarine *E* 12.

off Kalolimno Island. We both opened fire about 8000 yards, T.B. turning towards us. The fourth shot appeared to hit her aft. She then turned and proceeded at high speed towards Constantinople, appearing to be on fire aft. None of the torpedo-boat's shots came closer than 2000 yards to us.

"*Sunday*, 19*th Sept.*—Proceeded into Mudania, bombarded magazine outside the town and hit it eight times: silenced the batteries which opened fire on and damaged the railway.

"Sank two sail and proceeded towards Gulf of Ismid. Put down by destroyer and torpedo-boat patrolling there.

"*Monday*, 20*th Sept.*—Dived into Gulf of Ismid at daylight, but weather was too foggy, so retired out again. Nothing seen during the day.

"*Tuesday*, 21*st Sept.*—Sank large steamer about 3000 tons off Marmora Island, laden with live stock and other provisions. Steamer refused to stop until hit, when we ceased fire while ship was abandoned.

"Chased six sail into small bay near Panderma and sank them by gun-fire. We were fired on from the shore by rifles at a range of about 1800 yards.

"*Wednesday*, 22*nd Sept.*—Weather very rough. Proceeded to Gallipoli and communicated by wireless. Nothing seen about. No steamers in Gallipoli and no movements of troops seen.

"*Thursday*, 23*rd Sept.*—Proceeded about western end of Sea of Marmora. Nothing seen except two hospital ships.

"*Friday*, 24*th Sept.*—Heavy sea running. Proceeded up European coast, chased four steamers, but found they were hospital ships. Also sighted one destroyer going to westward, close in shore.

"*Saturday*, 25*th Sept.*—Sighted and dived for two destroyers, who were apparently patrolling eastern half of Sea of Marmora. This patrol was frequently seen, but it was very difficult to get in an attack on them, as their courses and speed were so frequently varied.

"*Sunday, 26th Sept.*—Dived off Stefano Point at daylight, and remained there till dark; two destroyers sighted patrolling from Powder Factory to Prince's Islands.

"*Monday, 27th Sept.*—Rose off Stefano just before daylight, intending to bombard factory, but was put down by destroyer before fully light. Weather, N.E. wind.

"*Tuesday, 28th Sept.*—Sank three sail off entrance to Gulf of Ismid; put under by two destroyers. Weather became too foggy to proceed up Gulf.

"*Wednesday, 29th Sept.*—Sank one sail off Rodosto. Destroyer came out, but returned again on sighting us. Proceeded down to communicate. We were opened fire on from Sar Keui, which we returned, silencing their guns.

"Sank four sail three miles farther to the westward. Communicated by wireless.

"Was attacked by aeroplane about half an hour before sunset; this came very close before it was observed, and dropped two bombs, the nearest falling about 30 yards from our stern. The aeroplane appeared to have silencers on the engine, as it was not audible when climbing.

"*Thursday, 30th Sept.*—Off European coast the weather was foggy, and nothing was sighted during the day.

"*Friday, 1st October.*—Dived into Panderma at daylight. Nothing sighted. On being attacked by aeroplane we dived, but no bombs were dropped. Weather became very foggy during the afternoon.

"*Saturday, 2nd October.*—Rose off Stefano at daylight, but put under by destroyer. Remained near Makrikeul all day. Sighted patrols coming out about two hours before dark, but nothing else seen about there. Went to bottom off Makrikeul for the night.

"*Sunday, 3rd October.*—Rose before daylight. Heavy mist off land, so unable to fire at factory. Sighted small tug and destroyer patrol. Attacked T.B.D., but could not get near enough to fire.

"*Monday, 4th October.*—Dived just after daylight for destroyer patrol. After two hours got in an attack, but did not fire torpedo, as safety gear of tube failed. Thick fog came on. Met Submarine *H* 1 just before dark; reported having been ashore at Nagara Point, but had no difficulty with net coming up. Told *H* 1 to work in eastern area, and arranged rendezvous for 7th inst.

"*Tuesday, 5th October.*—Sank one small steamer and seventeen sail in Rodosto Bay. Battery at Erekli Point opened fire on us, but we were well out of range. Put down by aeroplane about half an hour before sunset; dropped bomb when boat was at 40 feet.

"*Wednesday, 6th October.*—Communicated by wireless. Proceeded to Gallipoli. Nothing seen there, and no transport or troops on the road. Aeroplane attacked us in the evening.

"*Thursday, 7th October.*—Met *H* 1 at rendezvous. Carried out some minor repairs, hands to bathe and wash clothes.

"*Friday, 8th October.*—Arrived off Stefano Point just before dark; too misty over land to fire at factory.

"*Saturday, 9th October.*—Rose off Stefano Point at daylight, but was at once put down by destroyer. Chased a T.B. in the afternoon on the surface, but unable to get within range.

"*Sunday, 10th October.*—Proceeded to Sar Keui, saw two small steamers. Dived in after them, but could not get in there before dark.

"*Monday, 11th October.*—Dived into Sar Keui at daylight; found steamers had left. Proceeded to Gallipoli. Nothing sighted.

"*Tuesday, 12th October.*—Attacked small gunboat off Gallipoli; she altered course just as I fired, and torpedo missed her.

"Proceeded to Burgas Bay. Weather became thick.

"Attacked steamer in Lampsaki Bay and fired two torpedoes, of which the second hit her. Steamer appeared to list to port, but we were unable to observe her for long, as we were put under by small craft. Communicated by wireless in the evening.

"*Wednesday, 13th October.*—Strong N.E. wind and fog. Proceeded towards Panderma. Put down by destroyer.

"*Thursday, 14th October.*—Searched northern shore, sea very rough. Sighted nothing.

"*Friday, 15th October.*—Weather bad, short steep sea running. Proceeded to Stefano and Mudania. Sighted nothing.

"*Saturday, 16th October.*—Rendezvoused with *H* 1 and proceeded in company to Gulf of Ismid. Saw T.B.D. patrols, but nothing else sighted.

"*Sunday, 17th October.*—Sighted gunboat soon after daylight coming from Constantinople; carried out spread attack with *H* 1, but were unable to get in. Rose to chase, and opened fire on her off Kalolimno; tried to drive her over *H* 1, who dived when I opened fire. We outranged her guns, and appeared to hit her several times: she nearly ran ashore on Kalolimno Point, and appeared to be out of control, then proceeded under the land.

"*H* 1 proceeded down eastern side, and we steered to drive her round the Island. *H* 1 attacked and fired torpedo, but missed; heavy rain-squalls then came up, and we lost sight of her. Discovered her about one hour later proceeding towards Panderma, into which place we chased her. The weather became foggy, and we dived in after her, but it was too thick to see with the periscope. *H* 1, who was diving about $1\frac{1}{2}$ miles off the gunboat during most of the time we were firing, reported that the firing was very accurate, and appeared to hit her several times. Remained off Panderma during night, but saw nothing.

"*Monday, 18th October.*—Saw large explosion occur off the town of Panderma just after daylight, and the guns from there open fire into the bay on an object unknown, *H* 1 being in company with us about 8 miles away. Two destroyers came out as we started to dive into Panderma Bay; they proceeded towards Constantinople. We went up to Panderma, but saw no signs of gunboat, and nothing else in the bay.

"*Tuesday, 19th October.*—Proceeded towards Constantinople diving. Rose about 5.20. Closed on surface to 8000 yards and opened fire on Powder Factory. Obtained range with third shot and got in three more rounds, apparently hits, before being put down by shore batteries and destroyer. Shore batteries opened fire on us after our first shot, straddling us with their second salvo. Appeared by the splashes to be about 6-inch guns. Just before we dived, shots were falling about 100 yards over and short. Large quantity of black smoke was observed over factory before diving.

Wednesday, 20th October.—Proceeded to Mudania. Nothing there. Fired torpedo at steamer in small bay in northern side of Gulf. Several sail were round the steamer, and torpedo appeared to hit a sail alongside her. Petty Officer L.T.O. caught his arm in the hydroplane gear, being rather seriously injured, so proceeded out again while rendering first aid. Thick mist and rain prevented further investigation of shot.

" *Thursday, 21st October.*—Strong N.E. wind. Searched European shore, but sighted nothing.

" *Friday, 22nd October.*—Met *H* 1 and *Turquoise*, who reported: ' No trouble in passage up and all correct on board.' Gave them their areas, and proceeded down towards Sar Keui.

" *Saturday, 23rd October.*—Met *E* 20 off Marmora Island, who reported he had no trouble on passage up. Torpedoed two steamers in Burgas Bay, also saw steamer sunk there which was the one we had torpedoed on passage up. Proceeded to Gallipoli and communicated by wireless. Put down by destroyer immediately afterwards.

" *Sunday, 24th October.*—Prepared boat for passage down; weather rough and misty. Communicated with *H* 1.

" *Monday, 25th October.*—Proceeded towards Gallipoli. Put down by armed tug at daylight. Passed Gallipoli 7.30 a.m.; wind dropped, surface very calm. Came up 20 feet off Karokova Burnu to get a fix, found destroyer 200 yards on our beam, who evidently saw us. Put periscope up 20 minutes later, when destroyer opened fire at once. On next putting up periscope, observed that destroyer had been joined by two tugs. Went to bottom off Moussa Bank and remained there an hour to try to shake off pursuit. Then proceeded towards net, but was observed about half a mile to the eastward of it; small guard-boat attacked my periscope, which prevented my getting an accurate fix before shaping course through the net.

"Passed through the net at 80 feet and observed that we were towing a portion of it. Two minutes later the boat suddenly commenced to sink rapidly and take up a big angle down by the bow. Foremost hydroplanes jambed about 10° to 'dive.' Speeded up to full speed to try and force bow up, and blew external main ballast tanks. The boat was brought to 7° up by the bow, and should have had about 40 tons buoyancy when we reached depth of 160 feet, but she still continued to sink until she reached 245 feet. During this time we blew external tanks singly to make sure that they were perfectly blown. The conning-tower glasses burst in and the tower filled, also boat leaked badly forward, and the fore compartment had to be closed off to prevent the water coming over the coaming of the door before battery. Other leaks not serious.

"By putting foremost hydroplanes into hand gear, we were able to move the planes through 10° each way, using three men on them. After about 10 minutes at 245 feet the boat started to rise; we managed to check her at 12 feet, but she was very difficult to control. Six patrol vessels were close round us, and they opened fire when depth gauge showed 50 feet, so possibly we were towing something which showed at that depth. Found we had made very little progress beyond Nagara; shaped course to pass Kilid Bahr.

"Boat continued to be very unmanageable, frequently taking up big inclinations, and on two occasions going down to 120 feet before she could be checked. Both diving gauges had failed, although they had been shut off at 100 feet. Gauge by periscope being the only one remaining in serviceable condition, boat had to be conned from main gyro compass, as gyro steering compass had failed, and also conning-tower compass was flooded.

"Fouled an obstruction which sounded like chain moorings just to the southward of Kilid Bahr, depth 80 feet. Speeded up to full speed and worked the helm. After about four minutes the obstruction was heard going aft, having apparently cleared the obstruction which we had been towing down from Nagara. The boat took a very steep angle up by the bow, and rose to 4 feet very quickly; flooded tanks for two minutes before boat could be submerged again. Conning-tower was showing for about one minute, and bow for nearly two minutes. Shore batteries and patrol vessels opened a considerable fire on us at a short range.

"The boat was about 150 yards off Kilid Bahr Fort. Conning-tower was hit, and casting cracked by a small shell (probably 3- or 6-pounder). Bridge was also hit several times by small shell and fragments without serious damage resulting. Observed track of torpedo fired from Kilid Bahr, which passed about 10 yards aft conning-tower and could be heard passing over the boat. Observed track of second torpedo, which passed about 50 yards astern. Proceeded to 80 feet and corrected trim, having no further difficulty in depth keeping.

"Came to 20 feet off Kephez to fix position. Observed two large explosions about 2 miles astern, and also observed a track which looked like that of a torpedo fired from Suan Dere, but was too far off to be quite certain of this. Rose off Helles Point about 5 p.m., and proceeded to Imbros under escort."

It may be added that H 1 (Lieut. W. B. Pirie) was a new, small boat of $164\frac{1}{2}$ ft. in length, able to do 13 knots on the surface and $10\frac{1}{2}$ submerged. Built in America during the War, she had crossed the Atlantic on her own bottom. In regard to E 20 and *Turquoise*, mentioned by Captain Bruce, a tragedy was about to take place. The last-mentioned was the first and only French submarine which got into the Sea of Marmora, but unfortunately she also got aground, was captured, and taken into Constantinople. Equally regrettable was the fact that among the commanding officer's papers was found a note that he would rendezvous with E 20 on November 5 off Rodosto. Now, it so chanced that UB 14 (previously mentioned) was lying at Constantinople undergoing repairs. It was now November 2, but by a very fine effort she was got ready, went into the Sea of Marmora, arrived at the rendezvous, found *E* 20 on the surface, torpedoed and sank her, and only nine men were saved. British submarine officers have severely criticised the *Turquoise's* captain for having committed to writing such a confidential note.

But disaster likewise dogged *E* 7, which on September 4, after passing Kilid Bahr, got one of her propellers foul of Nagara net. Then a mine exploded, but did no damage. Two hours later another banged off likewise. Eight hours more, and still caught by the net, a third mine went off violently, and smashed all the electric lights. Finally, with enemy craft waiting for him on the surface, Lieut.-Commander Cochrane, being unable to clear his craft, brought her to the surface. She was promptly shelled, but next all hands were taken off by motor-boats under the orders of German submarine officers. Lieut.-Commander Cochrane, however, did not leave her before a time fuse had been fired, and she subsequently blew up. The story of his captivity and his escape months afterwards is one of the finest that came out of the War, but too well known to need recapitulation. He arrived safely back in England, and after leaving the service became a Member of Parliament. Thus in life does man play many parts.

And during the first December of Cochrane's captivity Nasmith made another successful cruise that was even longer than that of Lieut-Commander Bruce, but *E* 14 (now commanded by Lieut.-Commander White) was shelled and sunk with the loss of her Captain, only a Petty Officer and a few men surviving.

The nett result of our submarines' gallantry and perseverance may be summed up in the fewest words. Altogether they destroyed a battleship, a destroyer, five gunboats, eleven transports, forty-four steamers, 148 sailing craft, brought the Turkish Army perilously near starvation as to food no less than munitions; and thereby materially assisted our soldiers.

CHAPTER XXV

EVACUATION

But still the great dilemma at the Dardanelles remained.

Long before October the truth had been apparent to many that only one solution could be found: by cutting our losses and clearing out from the peninsula. Against this drastic method there persisted at home a definite reluctance to quit: a fear lest the moral effect might cause a serious loss of British prestige. Nevertheless, during this month, which witnessed the overthrow of Serbia, the question of evacuating Gallipoli was being considered seriously. In fact, the sequence of notable changes seemed in great contrast with the old deadlock.

At the middle of October, Sir Ian Hamilton was recalled; that fine old sailor Admiral Guépratte left the Dardanelles; a blockade of Bulgaria was inaugurated to synchronise with war between that country and ourselves; and on October 21 an allied squadron bombarded Dedeagatch. The latter was the only important place along the Bulgarian Ægean coast, and here the Salonika–Adrianople railway came down to the sea. The bombardment and associated operations were carried out by H.M.S. *Doris*, *Theseus*, three monitors, the *Ben-My-Chree*, four destroyers, and six drifters; whilst the French *Kleber*, the Russian *Askold*, four destroyers and four trawlers operated against the coast positions. Commodore Keyes, still keen to go on with a Dardanelles plan, went home temporarily at the end of October to lay his views before the authorities in Whitehall. His belief survived—in spite of the past—that the Fleet could, after certain preliminaries, force the Straits; and in this opinion he found Admiral Wemyss a sympathiser.

Developments multiplied, and by November 10 Lord Kitchener had come out for the purpose of making a personal inspection. On the 12th he visited Helles, next day Anzac, and Suvla on the 14th. That week a well-defined expectation was noticeable, in such assemblies as ward-rooms, that evacuation would soon be more than an idea. Actually on the 23rd it was recommended by the War Committee in

London, and on December 6 it was decided at an Allied Military Conference that Anzac and Suvla should be the spheres of withdrawal. Admiral de Robeck, who, on November 25, after Lord Kitchener's visit, had come home for leave, delegating the naval command to Admiral Wemyss, was opposed to the plan of trying to force the Straits, and soon he was back at Mudros concerned with evacuation plans which demanded considerable application.

It was a depressing fall of the year, the time of gales and flooded trenches, the dashing of all the false hopes once centred around this peninsula. On the last day of November the Serbians had begun their long retreat through Albania to the Adriatic, where our drifters were having a strenuous and even hazardous time assisting the refugees and rescuing soldiers from mined transport. And from the night of December 18 till 5.40 a.m. of the 21st our own retreat from Gallipoli had been accomplished in respect of Suvla and Anzac. On each of the preceding two nights 10,000 men were taken off from either position, with no damage to boats and with no accidents. The monitors' fire had been invaluable; the motor-lighters running between piers and transports had again proved their utility. Captain Unwin was there to lend his experience as Beach Master, and a supporting squadron awaited only the signal in case a mighty outburst of shells were needed. But it was good fortune united with brilliant organisation and surprise—yes, surprise at last—which completely fooled the enemy and prevented his interference. The pathos is that we kept this secrecy for the end, and did not use it at the beginning of the campaign.

In the final stages of evacuating Suvla and Anzac ten trawlers were employed. They were also to help the motor-lighters in case of bad weather springing up. The arrangements enabled the following details to be put in practice, and show how efficiently everything had been thought out, down to the last oar and rowlock. Each batch of five trawlers arrived off Suvla or Anzac before sunset from Kephalos. At Suvla the troops were fetched off by ten motor-lighters, ten

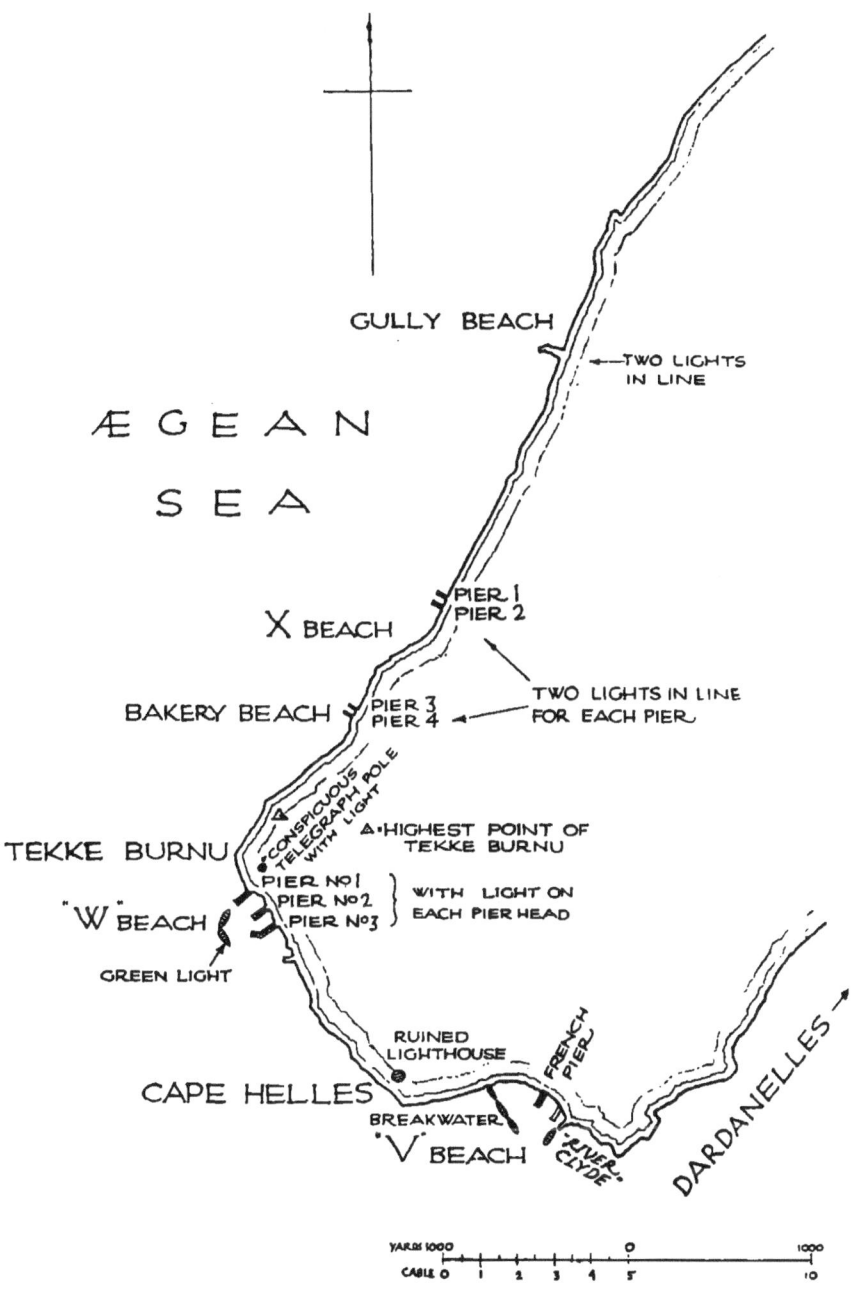

PLAN TO ILLUSTRATE THE EVACUATION FROM HELLES, JANUARY 1916.

small naval steamboats, and four pulling-boats; at Anzac by ten motor-drifters, ten steamboats, and twelve pulling-cutters. These flotillas brought them off to four ferry-steamers, two or four armed boarding-steamers, one old battleship, and one transport, at each of the two places. The battleships thus to be employed as troop-carriers (2000 men at a time) were the *Mars* and *Magnificent*.

Seldom in history has an enemy been so completely mystified.

"We, of course, knew nothing of the intended withdrawal," says General von Sanders, "and did not learn of it up to the last minute. Its possibility had been considered. . . . But the very skilful beginning and execution of the withdrawal prevented its being seen from the front line of the Turks."[1] On the night of December 18, a short spell of excellent weather succeeded hard winds. On the next night a dense land fog covered the peninsula and coast, but the firing along the fronts continued with its usual ferocity till midnight, when it became a little weaker. Shelling from different directions, our naval guns gave the Turks no reason for supposing that withdrawal was likely. Between 1 and 2 a.m. the Anzacs exploded a mine, and when the enemy advanced to seize the crater they were surprised to find no resistance. Here and there, in the fog, mines kept detonating like terrific railway-signals, but still our naval guns prevented the Turks from advancing immediately. When, however, the latter descended the steep rocky cliffs to the beach, it was to realise that our troops had departed.

So, too, at the Suvla Bay evacuation, perfect secrecy and forethought had combined. The footpaths had been marked with whitewashed sandbags to guide the soldiers down to the beach. Brief engagements had taken place at several spots, but the advancing Turks suffered great losses by land mines, and not till 4 a.m. did the startling news of our vanishing reach the German General. Our casualties were practically nil—which surprised our leaders—for two hospital lighters waiting

[1] *Five Years in Turkey*, p. 97.

at each of the two beaches had been expected to have a busy time. One naval officer tells me that 15,000 casualties had been prepared for, and there were twelve hospital ships waiting in Mudros harbour for the wounded. Well could von Sanders afford to state that our withdrawal from Anzac and Suvla " had been prepared with extraordinary care, and carried out with great skill " !

Not that it cost nothing in *materiel*. Money meant little—the War consumed millions of gold daily. Immense stores of arms, food, flour, timber, telephones, tools, medical supplies, five small steamers and sixty boats strewn along the beaches, were among the items left behind. But also we left standing those Army tents which (adds von Sanders) " probably served better than anything else to mask the withdrawal." Freshly served food was found still on the tables awaiting the hungry Turks. Thousands of British troops had disappeared as if by magnificent magic, but we still held on to Helles for the present. A week later, however, came the decision from home that this should likewise be evacuated, and at once the preliminary stage began, followed by the intermediate, which was approaching its close by January 4.

Now, the task of clearing Helles of troops and guns, ammunition, horses, mules, vehicles, was in itself a very considerable one; but to bring about such an achievement when close at hand lay an undefeated enemy, already warned by the first evacuations, seems an impossible notion in the abstract. To Captain C. M. Staveley, R.N. (commanding officer of the *Endymion*), and his Staff, belongs the credit for an historic triumph of organisation and execution. As Principal Beach Master and Naval Transport Officer, with headquarters at W beach, he was supported by naval officers as beach masters and piermasters.

The intermediate stage of evacuating Helles comprised the embarkation of as much war material and as many mules and horses as possible, together with the reduction of troops to about 17,000. The final stage would be a few days later. Three beaches, viz. V, W, and Gully, were to be used with

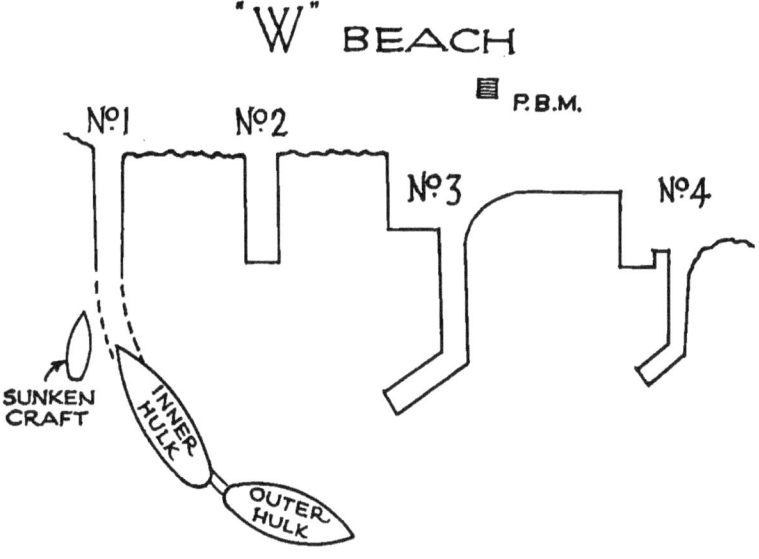

PLAN OF W BEACH
At the time of evacuation.

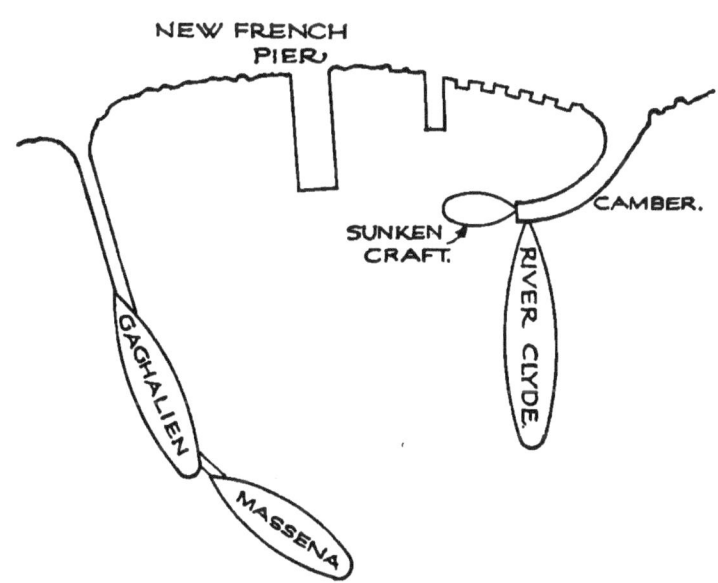

PLAN OF V BEACH
At the time of evacuation.

their limited facilities. On reference to the accompanying plan it will be seen that at V beach a little harbour had been devised with the *River Clyde* and a mole on one side, whilst two sunken ships (including the *Masséna*) extended to curve from the western end as some protection from south-west winds. The *Masséna* was an old-fashioned French battleship (11,735 tons), of the same age as our *Majestic* and *Magnificent*. Motor-lighters would be able to come alongside *River Clyde* and both sides of the new " French " pier; whilst trawlers and tugs could use the west side of *River Clyde* only.

As will be observed from the other plan, W beach had a somewhat similar shaped harbour, with four piers, of which the longest ran out from immediately below Cape Tekke; its extension being made with two hulks joined to the stone portion by means of a floating bridge. At Gully Beach the pile, stone, and concrete pier was not yet complete, and the protection afforded practically non-existent. It was planned to take off the last troops on the night of January 8. All beach craft were to have at least three days' food on board; all tugs, trawlers, and motor-lighters to have enough fuel to last seven days. These small vessels were to ferry the soldiers across to the troop-carriers from the *River Clyde* and various piers. Altogether Captain Staveley had for his disposal sixteen motor-lighters, five trawlers, four steamboats each towing four cutters. The lighters could each carry between 400 and 500, a trawler 300, a large tug 250, and a cutter 30 men, besides their crews. The old battleships *Prince George*, *Mars*, and *Magnificent*, together with some mercantile steamers, were to be the troop-carriers providing plenty of ladders for quick embarkation. Destroyers were detailed for taking off finally the naval beach-parties.

I am indebted to one of Captain Staveley's officers for the story of the last few days on Gallipoli. It begins with the evening of January 4, when he landed at W beach in several feet of water and the pouring rain to inhabit a dugout. " No lights; and roads crammed with mules." The craft off which he had just stepped was then intentionally sunk to fill in a gap at the breakwater between inner hulk and stone pier. (See plan.) Some 2000 or 3000 troops had been daily taken away, but that night it blew a north-east gale, causing a nasty sea off Cape Tekke. Some difficulty was experienced in getting away guns, and a lighter went adrift, but she was picked up later near Rabbit Island.

Morning and evening the enemy shelled W beach in great regularity from Asia, with a " Boom——(long pause)——zzzzzip——CRASH." But on the 7th there was heavy shelling all day, which aroused suspicions, and everyone began to think the Turks were not to be deceived a second time. Then a Taube aeroplane came over, and got away untouched. At last on January 8 came the final Gallipoli day, and luckily it seemed as if the weather would now be excellent. Proceedings began at 5 a.m., when the enemy's matutinal " hate " came shell-borne. Would he do his worst a little later?

The motor-lighters began arriving in force, got into position at 7.30 p.m. and the long job of the final evacuations was begun. Unfortunately, a hospital lighter rammed the floating bridge at W beach, which the Royal Engineers repaired in wonderful time. Ashore, in an improvised office, nine telephones were kept busy all the time, but things were going on well both at W beach and round the corner at V beach. Trawlers and lighters were working to schedule, loading their human freight, running out to the troop-carriers and then hurrying back for more. Very good time was being maintained, not too much shelling interfered, our guns (howitzers, 18-pdrs. and others) were being embarked in fine style, but the breeze freshened towards midnight and threatened to ruin proceedings. A nasty lop set into W beach, doing the floating bridge no benefit, and defeating the repeated efforts of the Royal Engineers to make good; but a couple of destroyers went right in alongside and did some ferrying till the damage could be repaired. Still the khaki crowd came and went; and more followed.

The hours sped on; it was now 1 a.m., when Gully beach was timed to start. Less than 700 men were waiting to embark from that unsheltered spot, but fewer than 600 could be got away owing to the heavy sea, and one of the lighters got stuck, so that about 150 officers and men had to march nearly a couple of miles round to W beach. This caused no little delay, and the sea began to get much worse. " About 2 a.m. an R.E. officer wandered into the office at W beach and informed us we must clear out, as the magazine next door had caught fire. After a few minutes, however, it died, before we had finished informing all stations of our change in address. At 3 a.m. the sea was getting very nasty, and we were still waiting for the Gully beach party."

All else had turned out splendidly, the thousands of soldiers had been taken off, and it was high time for Captain Staveley with his staff to go.

At long last arrived the Gully beach people, who were put aboard. Then came the ultimate scene of the Gallipoli drama, and the curtain was about to ring down. Suspense was over, the contest ended, the peninsula emptied of Allied warriors. " After seeing all beaches clear, we embarked in a picket-boat, helped a motor-lighter out, and lay off outside the hulks, waiting for the main magazine to touch off, having been set with a one-hour time fuse. Most of the stores had been previously fired, and now the magazine went up in a few minutes: a wonderful sight, beating any fireworks display into fits. When all was over, we ran in to see that the harbour was clear, and then embarked in the destroyer *Colne*. Beastly sea ! "

The incredible had happened. Without the enemy's cognisance we had taken our Army right away from the peninsula, and there had been but one casualty. When this magazine blew up, it scattered debris so that the above narrator received a stone on his head, about half a dozen fell in the boat, and one seaman lost his life. That was the cheap human price for saving thousands of soldiers, and even the boisterous sea had not spoiled our chance at the exciting finish.

But the enemy ? What were they doing all this while ?

During the first days of January they did notice that our land artillery grew weaker, but the ships' fire became more vehement. From the Asiatic side the Turks could notice we were removing guns, and the former were warned repeatedly to watch for any sign of our withdrawal by night. This we know from von Sanders, who gives [1] the following illuminative particulars concerning the final hours of January 8–9. " In some places there were bloody conflicts. But, all in all, the enemy here again was successful in his withdrawal, in spite of all our watchfulness." The British troops " had reached the south shores of the peninsula by the shortest routes, and were embarked at suitable points in every kind of war and transport vessels, while the last rear-guard was still maintaining a heavy fire from the advanced trenches. Fireworks had been used to give the impression of lively firing, and the artillery fire came from the ships." As previously, though the Turks reached the shores before daybreak, they were delayed on the way by our land mines; so that not one of the enemy saw our men depart. Even the tents were standing to surprise them.

We left on that peninsula not merely thousands of dead, but stores of value beyond all dreams of avarice. In the Helles region they included wagon parks, motor-car parks, mountains of arms, horses lying in rows shot dead or poisoned; food and flour, with acid poured over to make both unfit for use. " It took nearly two years to clean up the grounds," and such of this immense booty as was not pilfered came to be used for other Turkish armies. Many ship-loads of food and wood were carried up to Constantinople, whilst the " ragged and insufficiently nourished Turkish soldiers " took away large quantities. " I tried to stop plundering by a dense line of sentinels," von Sanders remarks, " but the endeavour was in vain. During the ensuing time we saw the Turkish soldiers on the peninsula in the most incredible garments, which they had made up from every kind of uniform."

It is true that, by the time our armies left Gallipoli, the enemy was already demoralised; that he had suffered 218,000

[1] *Five Years in Turkey*, p. 102.

casualties, including 66,000 dead. Nevertheless, it was expedient that the impossible struggle should be terminated by us. The Suvla Bay venture had meant nothing better than slight progress at a heavy loss; our delay had allowed the dominating heights to be occupied by the enemy, and the impossibility of any success was too blatant to be ignored. Moreover, the Central Powers had now got a railroad open to Turkey, and on November 15 the arrival of Austrian mortar batteries indicated that truck-loads of munitions for forts as well as field-guns would quickly follow.

Thus we observe the ending of one tremendous dilemma, only to be reminded that it was just a part of the whole. For the Mediterranean submarine campaign, with all its crises and excitements, had barely begun. Another campaign in the Adriatic was working up to thrilling developments; and the initial cause of this Eastern trouble still cruised at large. For the *Goeben* and *Breslau* were very much alive, and destined for over two more years to continue a serious menace. For this reason our naval forces were kept on the alert month after month—till at last these two ships sprang their surprise.

But all these events subsequent to January 9, 1916, belong to another volume.

APPENDIX

The following interesting letter, written from the Dardanelles by a Stoker Petty Officer aboard H.M.S. *Implacable* to an English journal, deserves to be given a more permanent place for its human interest. (See Chapter XIX.)

Sir,—
I have permission from the Censor to send you copies of Force Order and personal note issued by General Ian Hamilton and Major-General Aylmer Hunter-Weston, to the Army before they made their glorious landing on the morning of [April] the 25th; also a few brief notes of what has happened since. The part played by the *Implacable* in that landing was great, and drew personal praise from Admiral R. E. Wemyss and the Colonel and officers of the Royal Fusiliers, copies of which I have the honour of enclosing.

On the 23rd the troopships began to get a move on, and the send-off we gave the Australians and Fusiliers was worth coming out here to hear. The most comical part of the business was when we got under way, and passed a Russian cruiser; our band played a Scotch tune, and broke into an Irish air as we passed a French battleship. On the evening of the 24th we received a regiment of Royal Fusiliers and Naval Brigade, whom we were to land in open boats, under cover of our guns, at dawn on the morrow, and what fine fellows they were: well seasoned, in the pink of condition, for most of them had already seen service in India, Egypt and Flanders. I had twenty-four in my mess, and you can guess there wasn't much sleep for anyone.

It was interesting to walk round the ship: some asleep, any and everywhere; others writing home (the last for a good many poor fellows) and others spinning dits. Everybody was about by 3 a.m. Sunday, 25th, and fell in by 3.45; and how real to see them charge magazines before they embarked. By 4.45 all the fleet had come into line, opposite their respective positions, and the bombardment began. We ran close into our beach, and poured salvo after salvo: 12-in. shrapnel searched the cliffs, while 6-in. did ditto to the beach, and you can understand what an 850-lb. shell will do at 1000 yards range.

Under cover of our fire, our boats made for the beach,

and I am happy to say did not lose a single man in landing, but naturally suffered heavily in storming and clearing the cliffs. No pen can describe or artist can paint the scene; it was Hades with the lid off on that peninsula. The splendid manner in which our Captain handled his ship makes one feel about 10 feet higher to serve under him. The landing of the troops on the next beach to ours was also splendidly carried out under very heavy fire from the Turks and Co., and a perfect hail of bullets greeted the boats as they came within range (one wonders how anything could survive the shell-fire from the fleet). I saw hundreds of shots splashing like rain round the boats, and it was glorious to see the boys leap out and wade ashore. I will take off my cap to every soldier I pass, for everyone deserves a medal as big as my fat head.

It was something to watch our boys get a footing and dig themselves in. One particular charge was most brilliant. Two shells pitched among a group of Turks, and over the ridge came our boys, and we could see the Turks being driven pell-mell down the slope, and we cheered for all we were worth, and they answered us back as they went with the bayonet. What was left of the Turks soon held their hands above their heads, and were made prisoners.

Every inch of ground gained since that never-to-be-forgotten Sunday morning has been contested bravely, and finally won by magnificent work, and one wonders how we managed it at all.

Up to date the dear old ship has come through splendid. Am sorry to say our Fleet Surgeon has been killed. We bitterly mourn his loss, and the Navy loses one of its brightest officers and one of the finest gentlemen that ever stood in a pair of boots.

Yours etc.,
CHAS. R. COOK,
Stoker Petty Officer.

H.M.S. *Implacable*, Dardanelles.
May 1915.

(From the *Cambridge Weekly News*, June 4, 1915.)

INDEX

INDEX

A

Acheson, Lieut.-Commander Hon. Patrick, 144
AE 2, 102, 225–8
Agamemnon, H.M.S., 73, 79, 83, 84, 105, 120, 122, 132, 138, 162, 178, 217, 254
Agincourt, H.M.S., 9
Albion, H.M.S., 73, 79, 83, 84, 90, 91 *et seq.*, 111, 119, 126, 133, 139, 207, 224, 253
Amethyst, H.M.S., 83, 112, 119, 126, 128–9, 207, 243
Anne Rickmers, the, 152, 155, 156
Aquitania, S.S., 269
Arno, H.M.S., 275
Ashmead-Bartlett, E., 255, 257
Askold, the, 57, 114, 152, 173, 218, 252, 297
Aster, H.M.S., 274, 277

B

B 6, 190
B 9, 25, 51
B 10, 25, 51
B 11, 25, 51, 55–6, 74, 129, 184, 190, 225, 245
Bacchante, H.M.S., 179, 201, 221, 265, 274
Balfour, Mr., afterwards Earl of, 244
Barbarossa, the, 13, 118, 189, 222, 223, 225, 228, 278, 284, 287
Barcelona, S.S., 17, 25
Barne, Commander, later Captain M., 93, 108, 139, 184–5, 202, 240, 254, 258, 261
Barralong, S.S., 283
Basilisk, H.M.S., 77, 96, 217, 275
Bayford, Sub.-Lieut., 185
Beagle, H.M.S., 201, 238, 275
Ben-My-Chree, the, 299

Bernouille, the, 230
Bey, Colonel Djavid, 43
Birdwood, General, 81, 114, 170
Black Prince, H.M.S., 15, 29
Blaker, Lieut. A. W., 132, 136, 143, 144
Blenheim, H.M.S., 50, 267
Bouvet, the, 73, 120, 133, 140, 162
Boyle, Captain the Hon. A. D. E., 274
Boyle, Lieut.-Commander E. C., 184, 228, 229–30, 283–5, 286–7
Braemar Castle, S.S., 102, 105, 121, 207
Breslau, the, 2, 5, 15 *et seq.*, 39 *et seq.*, 49, 55, 65, 75, 83, 155, 163, 172–3, 231, 233, 271–2, 307
Britannia, S.S., 229
Brodie, Lieut.-Commander C. G., 189
Brounger, Commander K., 57
Bruce, Lieut.-Commander, later Captain K. M., 285–6, 290–7
Bruix, the, 243
Buckingham, Mr., acting Bo'sun, H.M.S. *Majestic*, 185
Bulldog, H.M.S., 201, 275
Bulwark, H.M.S., 178

C

C 3, 99
C 36, 247
C 37, 247
C 38, 247
Canopus, H.M.S., 102, 116, 124, 126, 133, 147, 175, 219, 220, 224, 232, 253, 254
Cap Trafalgar, the, 261
Carden, Rear-Admiral S. H., 38, 45, 50, 54, 65, 73, 74, 76, 81, 83, 91, 102, 105, 114, 124, 126, 130, 131, 151, 168
Carmania, S.S., 256, 261, 262

313

Carthage, S.S., 269
Casabianca, the, 267
Charlemagne, the, 73, 83, 85 *et seq.*, 120, 133
Chatham, H.M.S., 15, 243
Chelmer, H.M.S., 146, 201
Christian, Rear-Admiral A. H., 274
Churchill, Winston S., 54, 235, 244
Cochrane, Lieut.-Commander A. D., 286, 298
Colne, H.M.S., 146, 201, 305
Coode, Captain C. P. R., 275
Cook, Stoker Petty Officer, 308-9
Corcovado, S.S., 33
Cornubia, S.S., 280
Cornwall, H.M.S., 243
Cornwallis, H.M.S., 68, 73, 77, 78, 83, 85, 96, 105, 116, 124, 125, 133, 178, 206, 216, 241, 253
Cox, A. B. Seaman, 186
Curzon-Howe, Lieut. Leicester, 137
Cymbeline, S.S., 281
Czar, the, 64

D

d'Amade, General, 164, 218
D'Arcy, Captain Judge, 219
Dartmouth, H.M.S., 219, 220, 232, 243
Davidson, Captain A. P., 68, 217
Defence, H.M.S., 15, 29, 50
Demir-Hissar, the, 14, 155, 158, 199
Dent, Captain F. L., 145
Derfflinger, S.S., 50
D'Estrées, the, 265
Djemal Pasha, Turkish Minister of Marine, 12, 33
Dodgson, Lieut.-Commander W. L., 109
Doris, H.M.S., 57-60, 151, 180, 219, 232, 266, 299
D'Oyly-Hughes, Lieut. Guy, 288-9
Drewry, Midshipman G. L., 214
Dublin, H.M.S., 15, 38, 50, 84, 92, 96, 105, 207, 243

Duckworth, Admiral Sir John, *cited*, 2, 114, 170
Duke of Edinburgh, H.M.S., 15, 29
" Dummy Battleships," 104
Dumsday, Petty Officer, 186
Dupleix, the, 243, 265

E

E 2, 289-90
E 5, 184, 189-98
E 7, 286, 298
E 11, 230, 278, 283-5, 287-9
E 12, 285-6, 290-7
E 14, 184, 228, 229-30, 283-5, 286-7, 298
E 20, 295, 297-8
Eberhard, Admiral, 172, 173
Edgar, H.M.S., 274
Edinburgh, H.M.S., 177
Edwards, Coxswain of the *Implacable*, 212-13
Eggar, Captain P. A., 25
Emden, the, 37, 115
Endymion, H.M.S., 274, 277, 302
Enver, Turkish Minister of War, 76, 164, 165
Erin, H.M.S., 9
Escallonia, of Grimsby, 126
Essen, Admiral von, 64
Essex Regiment, the, 215
Euryalus, H.M.S., 151, 154, 157, 179, 200, 207, 211, 267, 274
Evstafi, the, 55, 64
Exmouth, H.M.S., 243, 262, 268, 274

F

Fearless, H.M.S., 176-8
Ferdinand, Archduke, 16
Fiennes, Colonel the Hon. E., 219
Fircks, Lieut.-Commander von, 155-6
Firle, Lieut.-Commander, 239
Fisher, Admiral Lord, 62, 74, 124, 235, 244, 268
Fitzgerald, Lieut., 190

INDEX

Forts:
No. 1 (Helles), 83 *et seq.*, 100
No. 3 (Sedd-el-Bahr), 83 *et seq.*, 99, 100
No. 4 (Orkanieh), 83 *et seq.*, 91
No. 6 (Kum Kale), 83 *et seq.*, 101
No. 7 (Messudieh), 101, 129
No. 8 (Dardanos), 92 *et seq.*, 101, 119, 134
No. 9 (Yildiz), 133 *et seq.*
No. 13 (Rumili Medjidieh), 115, 119, 120, 122, 124, 133 *et seq.*
No. 16 (Hamidieh II), 102, 117
No. 17 (Namazieh), 115, 117, 122, 133 *et seq.*
No. 19 (Hamidieh I), 102, 117, 122, 133 *et seq.*, 145, 160, 163
No. 20 (Chemenlek), 117, 133 *et seq.*
No. 22 (Derma Burnu), 227
No. 24 (Anadolu Medjidieh), 226
Formidable, H.M.S., 69
Forrester, Fleet-Surgeon A. A., 210
Forstmann, Lieut.-Commander, 280–1
Fourneau, Admiral de, 151, 265
Foxhound, H.M.S., 201, 275
Fuller, General J. C. F., 255

G

Gansser, Lieut.-Commander, 280
Gaulois, the, 73, 78, 84, 120, 133, 134, 148, 163, 270
Gazelle, the, 267
Geehl, Colonel, 121–2
General, S.S., 17, 25, 33, 40, 149, 160, 271
Georgi Pobiedonosetz, the, 64
Germanic, S.S. See *Gul Djemal*
Giffard, Lieut.-Commander Frederick, 106
Gloucester, H.M.S., 15, 28 *et seq.*, 35, 50
Gneisenau, the, 212
Godfrey, Captain, later Vice-Admiral H. R., 238, 240, 275

Godwin, Lieut. Claude H., 194–8
Goeben, the, 2, 5, 7, 10, 15 *et seq.*, 39 *et seq.*, 49, 55, 56, 64, 65, 75, 83, 115, 148, 149, 155, 159, 160–1, 163, 170, 172–3, 224, 225, 231, 233, 235, 271–2, 307
Goliath, H.M.S., 178, 207, 238–42, 251, 257
Goltz, Field-Marshal Baron von der, 55, 56, 74, 159, 245
Grafton, H.M.S., 274
Grampus, H.M.S., 190, 275
Grant, Captain Heathcoat S., 219, 232
Grasshopper, H.M.S., 91, 217, 275
Gravener, Lieut. S. M. G., 51
Guépratte, Admiral, 51, 85, 102, 119, 133, 243, 299
Gul Djemal, the, 229

H

H 1, 293, 294, 295, 297
Haireddin Barbarossa. See *Barbarossa*
Haldane, Midshipman, 221
Hall-Thompson, Captain later Admiral P. H., 60
Hamilton, General Sir Ian, 129, 131, 164, 168, 170, 171, 172, 180, 201, 218, 299, 308
Hamidieh, the, 13, 44, 65, 173
Hampshire, H.M.S., 7
Hans, Admiral, 26
Hayes-Sadler, Captain A., 146
Hector, H.M.S., 274
Heineburg, Lieut.-Commander von, 265, 279
Henri IV, the 169, 179, 218, 243
Heriot, Major G. M., 96 *et seq.*
Hersing, Lieut.-Commander Otto, 247–57, 259–67, 269, 279
Holbrook, Lieut. Norman D., 51, 55–6, 73, 129, 184, 190, 225
Hood, H.M.S., 177

Humber, H.M.S., 268
Hunt, Lieut.-Commander, later Captain W. Ward, 249, 251
Hunter-Weston, Major-General, 206, 210, 308
Hvalen, the, 246

I

Implacable, H.M.S., 169, 178, 206, 208–11, 215, 221, 243, 308
Indefatigable, H.M.S., 15, 18, 24, 35, 50, 54, 73n.
Indomitable, H.M.S., 15, 18, 23, 24, 35, 50, 54
Inflexible, H.M.S., 15, 18, 35, 70, 73, 77, 78, 83, 115, 132 *et seq.*, 142–5, 147–8, 162, 163, 175, 200, 216
Invincible, H.M.S., 18
Irresistible, H.M.S., 69, 73, 83, 84, 91, 96, 99–101, 105, 111, 116, 124, 126, 133, 139 *et seq.*, 142, 145–7, 163
Ivan Zlatoust, the, 64, 271

J

Jackson, Admiral Sir Henry, 244
Janvrin, Lieut. R. B., 200, 216
Jauréguiberry, the, 179, 218, 243
Jean Bart, the, 69
Jeanne d'Arc, the, 218
Jed, H.M.S., 146
Jellicoe, Admiral, 131
Jerram, Admiral, 115
John Hardie, S.S., 281
Jonquil, H.M.S., 274
Joule, the, 230

K

Kagul, the, 64, 65, 115, 271
Kaiser, the, 6, 39, 263
Kelly, Captain Howard, 29

Kennedy, Captain, later Admiral F. W., 19 *et seq.*
Kennet, the, 265
Kerr, Admiral Mark, *cited*, 52
Kettemturm, S.S., 17, 25
Keyes, Commodore, later Admiral Sir Roger, 91, 179, 299
Kitchener, Lord, 81, 129, 168, 243, 299
Kleber, the, 243, 299
Kophamel, Lieut.-Commander, 280, 281

L

Lancashire Fusiliers, the, 208, 211
Lapéyrère, Admiral Boué de, 17, 20, 38, 49
Larken, Captain, later Admiral Sir Frank, 57–60, 151, 219, 266
Latouche Treville, the, 243
L'Aude, S.S., 280
Leon Gambetta, the, 252
Limpus, Admiral, 11, 33, 41, 50, 72
Lockyer, Captain Hughes Campbell, 176–8, 208–11, 215
London, H.M.S., 169, 178, 201, 202, 243
Lord Nelson, H.M.S., 70, 102, 105, 108n., 109, 120, 122, 132, 136–7, 139, 142, 146, 178
Lord Wimborne, the, 257, 270
Loxley, Captain A. H., 71n.
Lusitania, S.S., 280

M

M 21, 198
Magnificent, H.M.S., 301, 303
Mahon, Admiral, *cited*, 47
Majestic, H.M.S., 62, 69, 90, 91 *et seq.*, 105, 106–7, 110, 111, 119, 133, 139 *et seq.*, 169, 175, 178, 184, 198, 201, 202, 206, 222, 223, 224, 238, 240, 253, 254, 257, 258–61

Malachite, S.S., 248
Malleson, Midshipman W. St. A., 214
Manica, H.M.S., 201, 224, 269, 274
Manipur, ex S.S., 104
Manitou, S.S., 199-200
Manx Hero, of Grimsby, 127
Mariotte, the, 287
Mars, H.M.S., 301, 303
Marsala, S.S., 248
Marshall, General, 215
Masséna, the, 303
Matthews, Lieut.-Colonel Godfrey E., 109
Mauretania, S.S., 269, 282
Mauvenet-i-Millet, the, 14, 239-42
Medjidieh, the, 13, 173
Mercian, S.S., 282
Merion, ex S.S., 104, 262, 266
Mersey, H.M.S., 268
Messudieh, the, 13, 55, 225
Meux, Admiral Sir Hedworth, 210
Michelsen, Admiral, 247
Michigan, S.S., 104
Midilli, the. See *Breslau*
Milne, Admiral Sir A. Berkeley, 15, 19, 24, 35, 38
Mimosa, S.S., 281
Minerva, H.M.S., 207
Monmouth, H.M.S., 212
Morgenthau, Herr, 74, 93, 163
Mosquito, H.M.S., 68, 126, 275

N

Nasmith, Lieut.-Commander Martin E., 230, 278, 283-5, 287-8, 298
Natal Transport, S.S., 282
Newmarket, the, 261
Nicholson, Rear-Admiral Stuart, 255, 257, 268, 274
Nicol, Vice-Admiral, 243
Niger, H.M.S., 281

Nikolaievich, Grand-Duke Nikolai, 64
Norcock, Captain L., 215
Nusrat, S.S., 14, 120, 126, 130, 155, 184

O

Ocean, H.M.S., 102, 105, 111, 133, 139 *et seq.*, 145-7
Odessa, S.S., 60
Okino, S.S., 153
Olga, S.S., 45
Olympic, S.S., 282
Oruba, S.S., 104
Ottawa, S.S. See *Gul Djemal*

P

Palmer, Major Harry, 108
Pamiat Merkurya, the, 64, 65, 172
Panteleimon, the, 64, 263
Panton, Captain H. B. N., 99
Pathfinder, H.M.S., 247
Patrician, ex. S.S., 104
Patrie, the, 243
Patterson, Engine-Room Artificer, 186
Peirse, Admiral R. H., 57, 151 *et seq.*, 157, 179
Persia, S.S., 282
Phillimore, Captain, later Admiral Sir R. F., 71, 138, 143-4, 200, 212
Philomel, H.M.S., 60
Pirie, Lieut. W. B., 297
Prentis, Captain O. J., 222
Price, Lieut. Edward J., 190
Primo, S.S., 248
Prince George, H.M.S., 102, 116, 119, 126, 133, 207, 235, 303
Prince of Wales, H.M.S., 169, 178, 180, 201, 243
Proesch, Captain F. W., 50
Proserpine, H.M.S., 60
Pruth, the, 44

Q

Queen, H.M.S., 169, 201, 224, 243
Queen Elizabeth, H.M.S., 73, 76, 77, 80, 83, 84, 103, 105, 115 *et seq.*, 121, 123 *et seq.*, 132 *et seq.*, 145, 166, 171, 178, 179, 189, 202, 222, 227, 242, 243, 251, 253

R

Racoon, H.M.S., 275
Reshadieh, the, 9
Reynard, H.M.S., 269
Ribble, H.M.S., 201
River Clyde, S.S., 213 *et seq.*, 225, 238, 270, 303
Robinson, Lieut.-Commander E. G., 96–7, 105, 193–8
Robinson, Seaman Arthur, 136
Roebeck, Admiral de, 2, 66, 68, 80, 87, 91, 109, 131, 138, 168, 169, 170, 173, 174, 179, 190, 219, 225, 227, 233, 242, 253, 262, 266, 268, 270, 274, 300
Roper, Brigadier-General, 213
Rostislav, the, 55, 64
Royal Dublin Fusiliers, 216
Royal Edward, S.S., 264, 279
Royal Fusiliers, 208, 308
Royal Naval Division, 219
Rücker, Lieut.-Commander, 280

S

Samson, Commander, 174, 184, 189
Sanders, General Liman von, 11, 33, 42, 55, 75, 76, 110, 162, 164, 167, 169, 204, 219, 231, 233, 263, 273, 278, 301, 302, 306
Sandford, Lieut. F. H., 99
Sandford, Lieut. R. D., 99
Scorpion, H.M.S., 51, 110, 190, 241, 268, 269
Scott, Lieut.-Commander J. W., 209
Scourge, H.M.S., 201, 275
Sénès, Admiral, 252
Severn, H.M.S., 268
Shelford, Captain T. L., 241
Smith, Captain Bertram H., 68, 78, 93*n.*
Souchon, Admiral, 7, 8, 11, 16 *et seq.*, 39 *et seq.*, 49, 53, 160, 165, 240, 263
Soudan, S.S., 144
Southland, S.S., 207, 264, 279
South Wales Borderers, 216
Staveley, Captain C. M., 302 *et seq.*
St. John, Lieut.-Commander, 186
St. Louis, the, 243
Stocks, Lieut.-Commander David de Beauvoir, 289–90
Stoker, Lieut.-Commander H. H. G. D., 225–8
Stopford, General the Hon. Sir Frederick, 274
Storesand, S.S., 281
Sturdee, Admiral Sir Doveton, 62
Submarines:
  $AE\ 2$, 102, 225–8
  $B\ 6$, 190
  $B\ 9$, 25, 51
  $B\ 10$, 25, 51
  $B\ 11$, 25, 55–6, 74, 129, 184, 190, 225, 245
  Bernouilli, the, 230
  $C\ 3$, 99
  $C\ 36$, 247
  $C\ 37$, 247
  $C\ 38$, 247
  $E\ 2$, 289–90
  $E\ 5$, 184, 189, 198
  $E\ 7$, 286, 298
  $E\ 11$, 230, 278, 283–5, 287–9
  $E\ 12$, 285–6, 290–7
  $E\ 14$, 184, 228, 229–30, 283–5, 286–7, 298
  $E\ 20$, 295, 297–8
  $H\ 1$, 293, 294, 295, 297
  Joule, the, 230

Submarines:
  Turquoise, the, 295, 297–8
  U 21, 246–57, 259–63, 269, 279, 281
  U 33, 280–1
  U 34, 280
  U 35, 265
  U 38, 281
  U 39, 280
  UB 1, 245–6
  UB 3, 158, 245–6
  UB 7, 245–6, 263
  UB 8, 245–6, 263
  UB 14, 245–6, 265, 279, 297–8
  UB 15, 245–6
  UC 12, 245
  UC 13, 245, 263
  UC 14, 245, 263
  UC 15, 245, 263, 264
Suffren, the, 51, 54, 73, 78, 83, 85 et seq., 119, 120, 133, 148, 163, 175, 243
Sultan Hissar, the, 228
Swiftsure, H.M.S., 102, 133, 139, 151 et seq., 157, 178, 206, 254, 255n., 257, 268, 279

T

Talaat, Grand Vizier of Turkey, 75
Talbot, H.M.S., 147, 207, 263, 268, 269, 274
Talbot, Captain H. F. G., 185, 260
Teiresias, S.S., 249
Theseus, H.M.S., 274, 275, 277, 299
Thorogood, Gunner Walter, 110
Thursby, Rear-Admiral C. F., 180, 201, 243
Tirpitz, Admiral von, 245, 280
Torgut Reis, the, 13, 222, 225
Torpedo Boat 92, H.M., 249–50, 281
Torpedo Boat 95, H.M., 281
Triad, Steam Yacht, 243, 253, 266, 270
Tri Sviatetelia, the, 64, 271
Triumph, H.M.S., 68, 73, 78, 80, 83, 87, 89, 90, 111, 133, 140, 151 et seq., 155, 156, 157, 169, 175, 178, 184, 201, 204, 223, 254–6, 257
Trotman, General, 109
Troubridge, Rear-Admiral, 19, 38, 49
Tryon, Admiral Sir George, 177–8
Turnbull, Sergeant, 98
Turquoise, the, 295, 297–8

U

U 21, 246–57, 259–63, 269, 279, 281
U 35, 265
U 34, 280
U 39, 280
U 33, 280–1
U 38, 281
UB 1, 245–6
UB 3, 158, 245–6
UB 7, 245–6, 263
UB 8, 245–6, 263
UB 14, 245–6, 265, 279, 297–8
UB 15, 245–6
UC 12, 245
UC 13, 245, 263
UC 14, 245, 263
UC 15, 245, 263, 264
Umbria, S.S., 17, 25
Underhill, Captain, later Admiral, 8
Unwin, Commander, later Captain E., 213–15, 275, 300
Usedom, Admiral von, 55, 233
Usk, H.M.S., 201

V

Valentiner, Lieut.-Commander, 281, 282
Vali of Smyrna, the, 153, 157
Venerable, H.M.S., 243, 254
Vengeance, H.M.S., 68, 73, 78 et seq., 83, 85 et seq., 89, 91 et seq., 96 et seq., 117, 119, 124, 125, 133, 139 et seq., 147, 169, 175, 193, 207, 225, 254, 257, 279

Vérité, the, 51, 54
Verner, Lieut.-Commander R. H. C., 37, 132, 136–8, 142, 144
Victoria, H.M.S., 177n.
Ville de Mostaganem, S.S., 280

W

Wangenheim, Baron von, 6, 10, 32, 39, 45, 74, 165
Warburton, Lieut. Geoffrey, 51
Warrior, H.M.S., 15, 29, 50
Wear, H.M.S., 145, 266
Welland, H.M.S., 266
Wemyss, Admiral Rosslyn, 103, 179, 200, 201, 206, 299, 300, 308
Werribee, S.S., 283
Weymouth, H.M.S., 7, 15, 35, 39
White, Lieut.-Commander, 298
Whitfield, S.S., 281

Wigram, Commander Ernest, 137, 144
William T. Lewis, S.S., 280
Wilster, S.S., 25
Winn, Lieut. S. T., 56
Wolverine, H.M.S., 51, 188, 222, 240, 268, 269,
Woolley, Midshipman John B., 96, 195-8
Worcesters, the, 215
World Crisis, The, quoted, 54, 222, 240, 268, 269
Wray, Captain Fawcet, 274

Y

Yavuz Sultan Selim, the, 41

Z

Zenta, the, 49

www.ingramcontent.com/pod-product-compliance
Lightning Source LLC
Chambersburg PA
CBHW061248230426
43663CB00022B/2945